The Developer's Guide to the Force.com Platform

By Rick Greenwald

With contributions by
Glen Martin
Andrew Fawcett
Phil Choi

The Developer's Guide to the Force.com Platform

ISBN: 978-0-9789639-5-8 0-9789639-5-4

With special thanks to Stefanie Andersen, Grant Anderson, Steven Anderson, Eric Bezar, Bulent Cinarkaya, Peter Dapkus, Susan Kimberlin, Andrea Leszek, Jesse Lorenz, Taggart Matthiesen, Rasmus Mencke, Jon Mountjoy, Vahn Phan, Jon Plax, Varadarajan Rajaram, Mary Scotton, Andrew Smith, Markus Spohn, Adam Torman, Andrew Waite.

Table of Contents

Chapter 1

Welcome to the Force Platform

Building and running business applications with traditional software has always been too complex, slow, and expensive. A new model, called cloud computing, has emerged over the last decade to address this problem. Applications that run in the cloud are delivered as a service so companies no longer have to buy and maintain hardware and software to run them.

Salesforce.com pioneered this model with our applications business over the last decade. More recently, we've opened up our infrastructure and made it available for anyone building any business application and running it on our servers using our platform—the Force Platform.

The Force Platform allows you to store structured data, implement business logic with workflow rules, approval processes and custom code, support Web browsers and mobile devices, integrate with other applications, do reporting and analytics and scale up or down—all with subsecond response time, high availability, and security you need to run your mission critical business apps.

Companies and ISVs are using the Force Platform to build everything from supply chain management to, billing, audit, tax calculation, event management, compliance tracking, brand management, pricing, accounts receivable, accounts payable, billing, HR, payment processing, employee on-boarding, claims processing, and many others.

The Force Platform is the fastest path to building complex enterprise apps. What used to take months can now be done in days or weeks. Unlike a stack of separately designed hardware and software products, the Force Platform speeds innovation through a powerful yet easy-to-use development and deployment model. Users easily assemble applications then instantly deploy them to the salesforce.com infrastructure.

The book you are reading is intended to be a rich introduction to the breadth and depth of the Force Platform. As a developer, you can use this book to provide a solid framework for achieving your goals on the platform.

This first chapter serves as an introduction—to cloud computing, the Force Platform, the application you will build through the course of this book, and the process used to maximize your learning effort.

What is Cloud Computing?

Information systems are essential to virtually every organization in the world; however, the traditional model of creating and running business applications has grown into a cumbersome process. There are too many moving parts to buy, install, configure, and maintain, including hardware and software. The entire infrastructure must be able to work together, and this type of seamless interaction requires the oil of constant maintenance to run smoothly.

This overhead burden creates barriers to productivity in creating and deploying applications. The complex computing environment means that every little change can trigger repercussions throughout the entire organization. The overall responsiveness of the IT function seems to be significantly reduced, hampering the ability of a company to address constantly changing business needs. The end result is that business managers don't get the applications they need to run their business—ending up with a welter of unintegrated, homegrown applications on spreadsheets, personal databases, or other unsupported platforms.

Enter cloud computing. Cloud computing is easy to understand—all applications are developed and run within a Web browser. With an Internet connection, your developers and users have access to your entire collection of applications—eliminating the complexity and overhead of maintaining a computing environment.

Moving to cloud computing immediately delivers enormous benefits. You no longer have to spend money to acquire and support hardware and software infrastructure, eliminating acquisition costs for your users and developers.

Even more important is the impact of cloud computing on the responsiveness of your IT systems. You can instantly add users and developers to your cloud computing environment. You can deploy applications to the cloud very rapidly, leading to greatly reduced cycle time for responding to user requests and new business opportunities. When you remove the overhead and complexity of your internal systems, your organization can dramatically speed up your entire IT process.

What is the Force Platform?

Cloud computing, based on the amount of recent coverage, may seem like a brand new development, but salesforce.com has been delivering applications from the cloud for almost a decade. The Force Platform supports almost 50,000 customers, containin more than 1 million individual subscribers, running enterprise applications offered by salesforce.com, its associated independent software vendors (ISVs) and in-house and independent developers. There are more than 70,000 custom applications running on the Force Platform at the time of this writing in 2008, and the platform supports more than 150 million transactions a day.

| Application Services | | Mobile |
| Analytics |
| Dashboard & Reporting |
| Internationalization |

The Force Platform is different from more traditional platforms, as shown in the diagram above. A traditional platform supplies only the core services of database access and containers for logic and presentation. You have to use other software to create your entire application, as well as the additional components to run the data center which supports the platform. Of course, additional components means additional expenditure, for acquisition, maintenance and integration.

With the Force Platform, you get a complete stack, including a complete user interface to your data, full reporting and analytic capabilities, a flexible security and sharing model, and other services not displayed in the diagram, such as workflow and approvals, fully available and integrated from the outset. You can even leverage extended features such as built-in internationalization, full support for mobile devices, and integration with existing systems, all of which are beyond the scope of this book.

You access the Force Platform through a Web browser, as shown in the figure below.

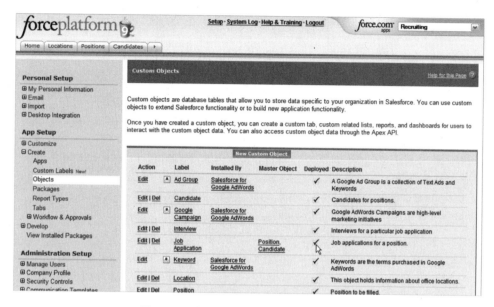

Figure 2: The Force Platform in a browser

The page shown above is not only a standard Force Platform page, but also the interface to one method of developing on the Force Platform, since you both develop from and deploy to the cloud. The platform itself provides everything you need to create robust applications through a combination of clicks, components and code. This phrase provides the key to understanding the productivity benefits of the Force Platform, with functionality coming from simple declarations of attributes, through the use of pre-built functionality and extending to a fully flexible development environment, when necessary.

The platform includes a rich depth of functionality that you can include in your applications with a few simple clicks to use the capabilities of the platform. You can define your data structures and their relationships, expose user interfaces to interact with this data, extend the internal data with logical representations of data and define workflow actions, and approval processes, all through shaping the built-in capabilities of the platform through setting the values of attributes.

The entire Force Platform reporting and analytics system is an automatic part of all your applications, giving you the ability to extract value from your data store through integrated functionality.

Metadata – the key to the Force Platform

As a developer, you may be feeling a bit cynical about all these fantastic claims for the Force Platform cloud computing platform. The description almost sounds too good to be true—how can you get all of this functionality without any code at all?

The answer lies in a single word —metadata. When you shape the built-in functionality of the platform, you are actually creating metadata, which is used by the Force Platform to dictate the runtime operations of your organization. Just as a database schema imposes certain rules on the data that can be stored in a database table, Force Platform metadata guides the execution of any and all Force Platform applications.

Because the Force Platform uses metadata to create and control your applications, you can also see the effects of your development efforts immediately. When you change the metadata for an application, your have actually changed the application's runtime behavior, so you can immediately access the application to see the effects of your changes.

The default capabilities of the Force Platform are truly deep and rich, but you get even more with the platform. The Force Platform includes a language, Apex, which gives you the ability to transparently supplement the functionality of the platform, as well as Visualforce technology, which implements a model-view-controller interface to the platform providing complete flexibility in defining user interfaces and data access. You can create reusable logical components with Apex classes, as well as user interface components with Visualforce – both of which can be used to increase your developer productivity even more through reuse of those components.

Throughout the remainder of this book, you will use the different aspects of the Force Platform to develop an application, during which you will come to profoundly understand the power presented by the Force Platform.

How Do You Work With the Force Platform?

The Force Platform is built on a foundation of multi-tenancy, which means that multiple companies share the same cloud resources, just as multiple offices exist within the same office building.

Each individual company has their own environment on the Force Platform, which is referred to as an *organization*, or sometimes as an *org* for short. An organization is your own virtual environment. Only those users and developers who are authorized can access the data and applications within your organization.

The easiest way for you to get started working with the Force Platform is to sign up for your own Developer Edition organization, which is free. A Developer Edition organization provides you full use of all the capabilities of the platform, but with limits on the number of users who can access your organization and the amount of data you can store within that organization.

The Code Share project for this book, described in more detail in the last section of this chapter, will have complete instructions for acquiring your own Developer Edition organization, which you will need to complete the hands-on examples in the rest of this book.

What Application Will You Build?

With a highly productive platform like the Force Platform, the easiest way to learn about its features and capabilities is to build an application. This book will act as a guide to creating an application used to recruit new employees for a company known as Universal Containers.

This recruiting application gives users a way to post positions, enter candidates for those positions and track the status of the positions through the life of the posting, from initial submission for approval through the end of the hiring process. The application also manages supporting tasks during that lifecycle, including proactively informing stakeholders as to the progress of the hiring process and automatically assigning interviewers for selected candidates.

The recruiting application used in this book is similar to the recruiting application used as the basis of the *Force Platform Fundamentals* book, although the goals of this book require some slight variations in the implementation details. In a similar fashion, the *Force Platform Cookbook* uses a recruiting application as the basis for some of the recipes in that book.

Another version of this recruiting application, with more depth and detail, is used in the course offered by Salesforce.com Training & Certification. Some of the exercises used in that course provided the foundation for some of the exercises in this book, but the course provides a more rigorous examination of the overall capabilities of the Force Platform. Please see `www.salesforce.com/training` for more information on these courses.

What will your application do?

You will be building this application in a very condensed span of time, but that does not mean that the application will not include a full and complete set of functionality.

You will start your development process by creating an application and the data objects used by that application. Once you define a data object, the Force Platform automatically generates a user interface for the object, as shown in the figure below.

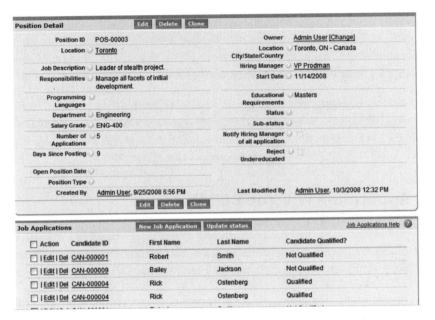

Figure 3: Force Platform default user interface

This interface provides complete access to the underlying data object, for inserting new data, viewing the details of a particular position record, and modifying or deleting the record. The Force Platform automatically integrates an automatically generated detailed view of a record in other user interface pages, so whenever a user sees a reference to a record, such as the location shown above, they can simply click the link to go to a detailed view of the record.

You can also easily modify the design of the default user interface, or create different user interfaces for different views of the same record. You will use this capability, known as a record type, in the application you develop.

The linkage between two records mentioned earlier is implemented through a relationship between the two records. You define relationships between objects, and the Force Platform automatically provides the appropriate user interface to both sides of the lookup, whether the user wants to identify the parent in a relationship or add a child to a parent record – shown in the list of job applications in the figure above.

The following diagram shows the basic objects and fields used in the recruiting application, along with their relationship to each other.

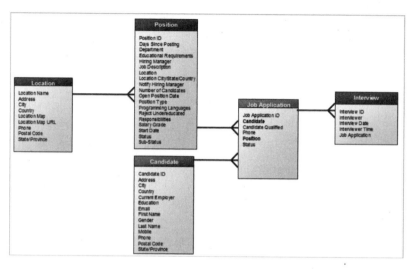

Figure 4: Objects used in the sample application

Your recruiting application will focus on more than just the data fields defined for the underlying objects. You will also expose data that is created from other data fields, through methods ranging from concatenation to calculation. The Force Platform even includes the ability to define summary fields, where values from child records are automatically rolled up into their parent record. This capability is yet another way that your Force Platform application leverages the power defined for related records.

The Force Platform also includes a complete system for creating reports and dashboards, based on aggregations of data. The figure below displays an example of a Force Platform dashboard that you will create without a single line of code.

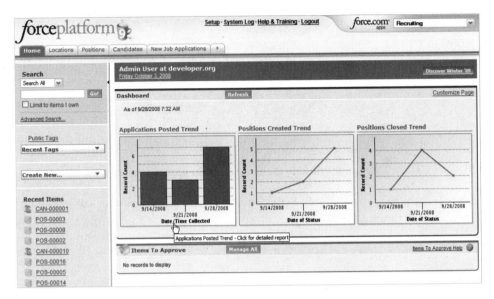

Figure 5: A Force Platform dashboard

Reports and analytic displays, like the one shown above, maximize the value users can extract through established collections of data. The Force Platform also includes the ability to perform flexible searches across your stored data for ad hoc access to collections of information. You can even give your users the ability to tag records to identify groups of information, even records from different objects. You will use some of this functionality in your recruiting application.

But there is more to the application you will build than just a user interface. You will add a series of automatic workflows actions, triggered by changes in your data. Workflow simultaneously reduces the burden on users to perform related actions and increases the reliability of those supplemental actions by spawning them automatically, with no possibility of user error.

The Force Platform allows you to define approval processes, business processes that involve human interaction. A Force Platform approval process not only automates the routing of the process, but tracks the process, providing real-time status and a history of the process, as shown in the figure below.

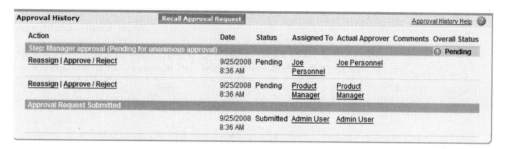

Figure 6: Tracking the progress of an approval process

You will create an approval process with a series of clicks and declarations, and learn how flexible these processes can be.

As a developer, you no doubt are already experienced in creating applications based on user requirements. As an experienced developer, you may be a bit skeptical of the ability of a completely declarative environment to be able to handle the intricacies that some customer needs present. In the later chapters of this book, you will learn how to use Apex code to extend the logical functionality of your application, and Visualforce to extend your user interfaces and the way they interact with the underlying Force Platform data objects. You will happily discover that Visualforce lets you take advantage of the dynamic Web 2.0 AJAX features, such as dynamically refreshing an existing page, with simple attribute declarations for HTML-like tags.

Finally, your recruiting application will open up the world of your Force Platform application to the outside world through email, for standardized access, and by exposing some of your application to users outside of the Force Platform environment.

Through it all, the recruiting application will benefit from the enterprise features that come standard with the Force Platform, including easy access to your organization from any browser, rapid and consistent responsiveness, and multiple levels of security to protect your data and to limit access based on user identity.

Within the remainder of this book, you will also learn how to use development environments, including the Eclipse-based Force Platform IDE, to create your applications, and a variety of techniques to deploy your applications.

It sounds like a lot to cover in a single book, but do not fear—the power of the Force Platform makes it all possible.

How will you build this application?

This book is aimed at you, the developer. As a developer, you are already familiar with most standard development tasks, such as defining data objects and modifying user interfaces. However, you may not be familiar with how to accomplish these tasks on the Force Platform, so this book covers all aspects of development and deployment on the platform.

The recruiting application was chosen as the vehicle for your learning experience because it offers use cases that exercise all the capabilities offered on the Force Platform. But to create these use cases, you would have to perform many tasks to simply create the environment to address these use cases. For instance, the application uses seven data objects, as shown in the figure above. You will not have to define seven data objects to learn how to define a data object—you will probably figure it out after one or two. So how can this sample application serve the twin masters of providing a somewhat realistic application while not requiring you to perform repetitive tasks that do not add to your knowledge of how to use the Force Platform?

Fortunately, the metadata foundation of Force Platform applications provide a way to address these conflicting requirements. Throughout the course of this book, you will only perform a development task as many times as you need to learn the task. Additional components will be created by loading metadata and, where appropriate, data itself into your Force Platform organization.

There is a Code Share project associated with this book, which you can locate by going to the Code Share home page, `http://developer.force.com/codeshare`, and searching for the name of this book. This project contains instructions on how to load the metatdata and data into your organization, when necessary.

Typically, you will be requested to perform a load at the start of a chapter. This process will add the components that are be required for the exercises in the chapter that have not been defined by the previous exercises in the book.

This book takes advantage of metadata in another way. There are two problems that are always associated with any publication that includes hands-on exercises, such as this book. The first problem stems from the relentless curiosity of developers. This book may proscribe a fixed set of steps within a particular chapter, but many developers will go beyond these steps to explore additional capabilities. Sometimes, these explorations change the environment in a way that causes problems for subsequent exercises.

Another problem stems from the focused nature of developers. Although the authors of this book believe that you should read it from beginning to end, you may make the decision to start in the middle, since you are only interested in one particular area, or you feel that you already know the subject matter covered in skipped chapters. Since the application is created in an iterative fashion, you would not normally be able to take this approach and still do the hands-on exercises.

But you can take that approach with this book. The Code Share project also includes metadata and data scripts that create the exact organization you need to perform the tasks of any one chapter. So if you decide you want to start your learning experience with *Chapter 9: Visualforce Pages*, you can simply take the required steps to bring your organization to the point where you can begin the exercises in that chapter.

This nice capability comes with a caution. The process of bringing your organization to the point required at the start of a chapter is a potentially destructive process. If the process must create an object called Position__c, the process will have to remove any existing object that happens to have the same name.

The Code Share project includes a process that will check to see if running these scripts could have an impact on any existing components in your organization, so you should never have to suffer an unexpected loss of information in your development organization. But if you have any doubts about the effect of these metadata and data loads might have on your environment, please see the instructions in the Code Share project for details on how to avoid this situation.

 Voice of the Developer: Throughout this book, you will see sections like this titled "Voice of the Developer". The main purpose of this book is to guide you to a comprehensive understanding of the Force Platform through a series of hands-on exercises. But, of course, there are plenty of considerations that you will understand after having worked with the platform for a while. Andrew Fawcett, chief architect of CODA, one of the largest Force Platform ISVs, has been through this learning curve, and he offers his council in these notes, so you can benefit from the experience of an enterprise developer who came to this platform a fairly short time ago.

Additional Resources

A variety of resources are available to supplement this book.

Documentation

This book is intended to be a productive starting point for developers new to the Force Platform. There are two additional books in the Force Platform library -

- *Force Platform Fundamentals: An Introduction to Custom Application Development in the Cloud*, available on the Developer Force website at `http://wiki.apexdevnet.com/index.php/Force_Platform_Fundamentals`, intended as a more general introduction to the Force Platform and

- *The Force Platform Cookbook*, available at
  `wiki.apexdevnet.com/index.php/Force_Platform_Cookbook`, a series of recipes
  with more detailed techniques and code samples

In addition, documentation for the Force platform is available both on-line within the platform
and in additional documents:

- Access the Help & Training window by clicking **Help** or **Help & Training** in the
  upper-right corner of any Force Platform page. Alternatively, access a context-sensitive
  view of the Help & Training window by clicking **Help for this Page** on the right side of
  any page title bar, or the help link on the right side of any related list.
- Review white papers, multimedia presentations, and other documentation at the Developer
  Force site, the home for Force Platform developers, at `force.developer.com`.

Visualforce:

- Read the *Visualforce Developer's Guide*, available at
  `http://www.salesforce.com/us/developer/docs/pages/index.htm`.
- Review white papers, multimedia presentations, and other documentation in the Visualforce
  section of the Developer Force website at
  `http://wiki.apexdevnet.com/index.php/Visualforce`.

Apex:

- Read the *Apex Developer's Guide*, available at
  `www.salesforce.com/us/developer/docs/apexcode/index.htm`.
- Review white papers, multimedia presentations, and other documentation in the Apex
  section of the Developer Force website at
  `http://wiki.apexdevnet.com/index.php/Apex_and_Visualforce`.

Force Platform Web Services API:

- Read the *Force Platform Web Services API Developer's Guide*, available at
  `www.salesforce.com/apidoc`.
- Review whitepapers, multimedia presentations, and other documentation in the Web
  Services API section of the Developer Force website at
  `wiki.apexdevnet.com/index.php/Web_Services_API`.

- Review white papers, multimedia presentations, and other documentation in the Web
  Services API section of the Developer Force website at
  `wiki.apexdevnet.com/index.php/Web_Services_API`.

- Read the *Force Platform Metadata API Developer's Guide*, available at
  http://www.salesforce.com/us/developer/docs/api_meta/index.htm.

Summary

This brief chapter provides a high level tour of cloud computing, the Force Platform and its capabilities, the application you will be creating with the hands-on exercises in this book, and the processes used to create a robust development environment. The rest of this book gives you plenty of hands-on experience with the power of the Force Platform for creating applications.

Chapter 2

Starting Your Force Platform Application

In this chapter ...

- Laying the Groundwork
- Building Blocks of a Force Platform Application
- Creating a Force Platform Application
- Creating an Object
- Creating a Tab
- Adding Fields to Your Object
- Entering Data
- Modifying Page Layout
- Filling Your Object With Data
- Using Data Loader
- Summary

Data is the foundation of all information systems. Decades ago, the area in which we work was referred to by the name of 'data processing', pointing back to the primacy of data in the overall scheme of things. The term 'information systems' points to the value of the information extracted from that data and the larger systems used to work with that data. Even though the growth of information systems is explosive, these systems are simply the tip of the iceberg, floating over large seas of data.

This chapter introduces you to the ways in which data is stored and accessed by applications on the Force platform, and how the platform uses your data to automatically build functionality for your applications.

Laying the Groundwork

Before jumping directly into the development tasks ahead of you, you need to learn about the data orientation of the Force Platform, the application you will be developing, and the data underling that application.

Welcome to the Force Platform

The designers of the Force platform are well aware of the importance of data to all systems. The Force Platform is all about data, and, as mentioned in the previous chapter, metadata. Part of the power and productivity of the Force Platform derive from this data-based approach to development and deployment.

The Force Platform delivers a lot of functionality that stems directly from your data design and specification. Good development practices call for you to carefully consider your data and its design to produce flexible and efficient applications. The Force Platform pays you back for this best practice with productivity, using the characteristics of your data design to build your applications.

The Sample Application

The application you will be building is an application designed to support and track the recruitment of employees for Universal Containers. Universal Containers is experiencing an explosive amount of growth, so finding and hiring new employees is crucial to their corporate health. This application will manage the interaction between positions and candidates, while also tracking the process of interviewing and evaluating those candidates.

This application will both manage information collected during the recruitment process and also contribute to that process by proactive intervention, helping to make the recruiting process more efficient.

This recruiting application was chosen as the core example for this book for a couple of reasons. Even though you may not be supporting an organization or department whose primary purpose is recruitment, you have no doubt been a part of that process, as an applicant or a hiring company. In addition, the recruiting process includes natural use cases that can take advantage of most of the features of the Force Platform.

There are a wide variety of applications you can develop and deploy on the Force Platform; for example, recruiting applications, project tracking applications, inventory systems and complete financial systems, as illustrated by some of the offerings on the salesforce.com

AppExchange. With the knowledge you will gain in this book, you will be well equipped to tackle almost any development task ahead of you on the Force Platform.

The Data

As mentioned above, the Force Platform database provides more than just simple data storage. Every Force Platform application provides automatic functionality based upon the design of your data structures.

The following figure lays out the basic data structures and relationships that you will be creating and using to build the recruiting application.

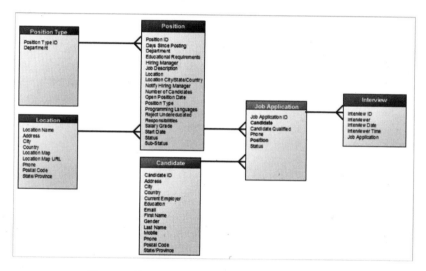

Figure 7: Data entities for the sample application

The complete data schema will be built up over the course of this book, with some sections emerging from your work in this chapter, and others entering the database in later chapters. For the purposes of this learning experience, it makes sense to only create data objects as you need them. For your own applications, of course, you should design and create robust data structures as a key initial step in your development effort. The better the data design, the more productive your development efforts over the lifetime of the application

Building Blocks of a Force Platform Application

The Force Platform consists of a few core components. These core components define the outline of all applications you will build on the platform.

The figure below shows the way that these core pieces relate to each other.

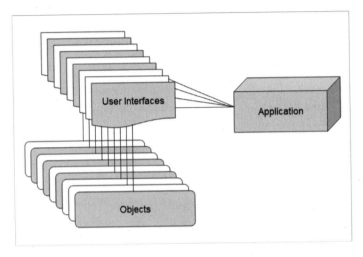

Figure 8: Application, tabs and objects

The foundation for all Force Platform applications is the *object*. In practical terms, an object is roughly equivalent to a table in a relational database. As with a table, an object is a collection of fields that can be accessed and modified together.

You may hear veterans talk about custom objects and standard objects. A standard object is used in one of the standard applications sold by salesforce.com. This book, and your work as a developer, occasionally uses some of these standard objects in an application, but your focus is on custom objects, which are created specifically for use in your applications.

 Note: The remainder of this book will use the term objects to refer to custom objects only by default.

In the Force Platform world, defining an object also generates the user interfaces to viewing and editing the data in that object. These default interfaces are accessed in the application through a tab on an HTML page, or as the target of links produced for the record in related objects or reports. The standard Force Platform application uses a tabbed interface, where the user can select a particular tab to display in a page in the application. When you create a tab for an object, the home page for that tab acquires several different features, such as showing a list of recently accessed records for that object on the tab as the default initial view, and automatically including fields from the object on the tab. If an object evolves over time, with additional fields, the user interfaces can automatically include the new components, as ou will see in this book. This automatic generation of a user interface increases your development productivity and shortens the time required for successive iterations of a tab and object.

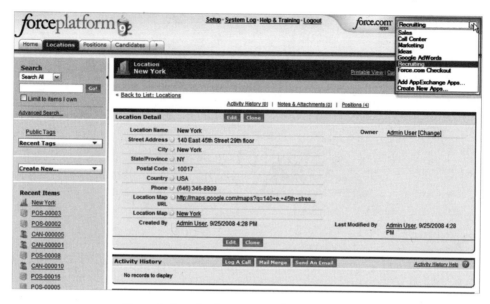

Figure 9: Standard Force Platform user interface

The figure above displays a Force Platform application. An *application* is a collection of tabs presented to the user. You define the tabs that are displayed in an application, and the user selects a particular application through the picklist in the upper right corner of the page, which is highlighted in the figure.

With these basic definitions out of the way, you are ready to create your first application and objects.

Creating a Force Platform Application

Your first hands-on task is creating the application you will construct throughout the course of this book.

1. Log into your Force Platform account. Your account resides in a Force Platform organization, or org, as described in the first chapter of this book. Your account opens onto the home page for the default application, as shown in below.

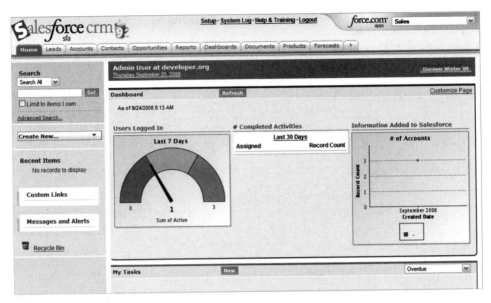

Figure 10: Home page for the Force Platform application

2. A set of links displays at the top, right-hand side of the page. Click the **Setup** link to enter the Setup menu, shown in the figure below.

   The Setup menu has a set of menu choices on the left, grouped into three categories:

   - **Personal Setup** - allows you to customize the interface and environment for the current user
   - **App Setup** - contains the choices you use for most of your development work
   - **Administration Setup** - provides a number of options for managing your Force Platform org

    Tip: Although all users have a **Setup** link in a standard Force Platform application, standard Force Platform users are only able to access the **Personal Setup** options. As a developer and administrator, you will have access to all setup options.

   You are now ready to create an application.

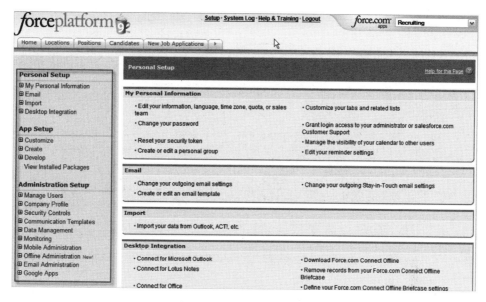

Figure 11: The Setup menu

3. Click the plus sign (**+**) to the left of the **Create** option in the App Setup section to expand your set of choices.

4. Click **Apps** to begin creation of your application. A list of currently installed applications displays. The list has two buttons at the top, giving you the ability to specify the order for the existing applications in the application picklist, as well as the ability to create a new application.

5. Click **New** to bring up the page shown below.

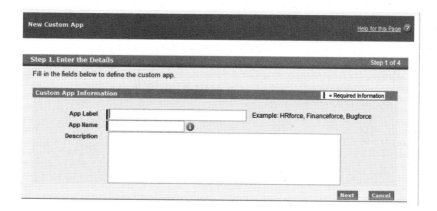

Figure 12: Creating an application

6. Assign an `App Label` of `Recruiting` for your new application. The `Label` field is preceded by a red line, indicating that a value is required. Required fields in your application display the same indicator.

7. Tab through the `App Name` field to set the value to the `App Label`.

8. Give your new application a description, such as `The sample Recruiting application.`

Before leaving this page, note your position in the overall definition process, indicated by the label in the upper right corner of the header page, as shown below.

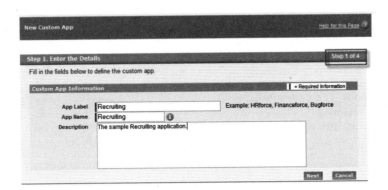

Figure 13: Your progress through the definition process

9. Click **Next**

10. The next page allows you to assign a logo for your application. The logo must be stored in a Force Platform document, conforming to the size and layout restrictions listed on the page. For this application, you can simply click **Next**.

11. You can now indicate any existing tabs you want to use in this application, as well as specifying which of these tabs is the landing tab for the application. Since you will be creating this application from scratch, you do not need to add any of these tabs, although you can always come back and add tabs to your application with the same interface. Click **Next** to bring up the page shown below.

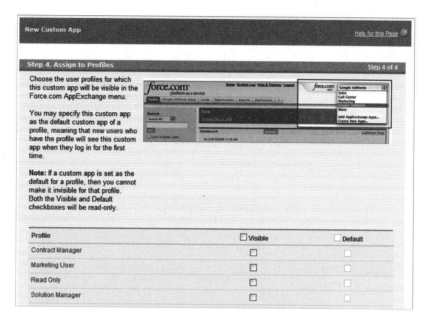

Figure 14: Defining security for an application

12. This final step in creating an application is extremely important. Access to your application, as well as many other entities on the Force Platform, are controlled through the use of profiles. Every user is assigned a profile, which typically represents a group of users. This page, which assigns access to this application based on profiles, is repeated for most of the interface components you create. Profiles, and how they are used in the Force Platform security scheme, is covered in detail in *Chapter 7: Protecting Your Data*. For now, you can simply make your application visible to all user profiles by clicking the checkbox at the top of the **Visible** column.

You should also make your new application the default app for all of the profiles with the checkboxes in the second column if you are using an organization specifically for the use of the exercises in this book.

13. Click **Save** to complete your work

That's right, complete your work. You have just defined an application, and you can prove it immediately.

14. Go to the `Application` picklist and select the `Recruiting` application to bring up the page shown in the figure below.

You have just had your first experience of the power of on-demand development. When you were defining your application, you were actually specifying the metadata attributes that are used by the Force Platform to present the application. Once you completed the definition process, the application was listed as one of the values in the Application picklist. When you selected an application, the Force Platform constructed the application from the metadata for the application.

This immediacy is a core part of the Force Platform environment. As soon as you define a Force Platform entity, the entity is available to those with the proper access rights. You will be experiencing this power repeatedly as you create applications on the platform.

The application you have created is not much more than a shell at this early stage. You can see that there is only a Home tab, required for all applications, and no others, since you did not include other tabs when you defined the application. But the tabs that you did not select for the application are still available through the right arrow tab.

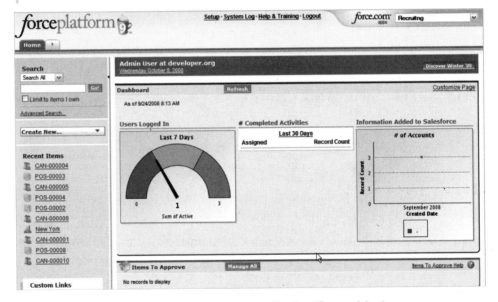

Figure 15: Your Recruiting application (first revision)

15. Click the **right arrow** tab to bring up the page shown below.

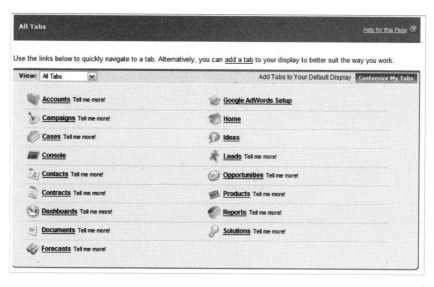

Figure 16: Available tabs

This page includes all the tabs that the current user is allowed to see, based on access privileges. Assigning tabs to an application adds the tab to the user interface for the application, while the underlying security controls access to tabs.

Your next step is to create a custom object and its tab to add to your application.

Creating an Object

As described earlier in this chapter, an object is the Force Platform equivalent of a database table, a structure used to store data on the platform. Creating an object using the Setup menu is another simple, wizard-driven task that creates immediate results.

1. Return to the Setup menu menu by clicking **Setup**.
2. Expand the **Create** choice of the App Setup menu and click **Objects**. The list view for Objects includes the objects that came with your development environment.
3. Click the **New Custom Object** button to bring up the page shown, in part, below..

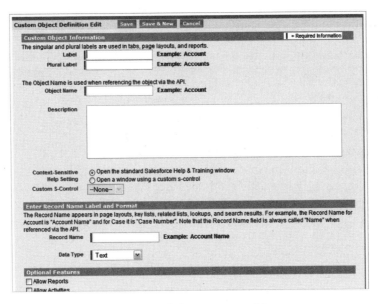

Figure 17: Defining a custom object

This page has a number of sections which allow you to specify key attributes of your new object. Each of these sections is discussed below.

Custom Object Definition

In this section, you give your object an identity. You are required to enter the following:

- `Label` - the name used to identify the object
- `Plural Label` - the label shown on the tab for the object and in some other places in the Force Platform environment
- `Object Name` - defaults to the string specified for the name, with spaces replaced by underscores. The object name is used to reference the object in Apex code, as well as when you are accessing the object through the Force Platform Web Services API, described briefly in *Chapter 8: The Force Platform IDE*. The name used in both of these languages is the string specified in this field, with two underscores and the letter 'c' (`__c`) appended to the object name. For instance, the name of this object is `Location`, while the object name used in Apex code is `Location__c`.
- `Description` - an optional string that gives more detail about the purpose of the object for internal documentation

You can also specify that context-sensitive help will either call up the standard Force Platform help for an object, or custom help in a component called an s-Control, which is outside the scope of this book.

 Voice of the Developer: S-Controls are an older part of Force Platform that are being replaced with Visualforce, which you will learn about later in this book. S-controls are, in essence, HTML fragments, as such should be used with care, as the dependencies hardcoded within them lead to lower productivity in creation and, even more so, ongoing maintenance. When it comes to customizing your Force Platform application pages beyond the limitations of built-in pages, Visualforce should always be your first choice, due to its integration with the Force Platform, its increased performance by reducing communications with the cloud, and the ability for greater productivity and manageability; however, due to their history with the Force Platform presence, s-Controls are still required in some areas of the platform, such as defining your own help topics for custom objects. Over time, these requirements will be met by Visualforce.

Give the new object the `Label` of `Location` and a `Plural Label` of `Locations`. Enter `This object holds information about office locations.` as the description.

Record Name

The `Record Name` of an object is a required field that has a special place in the life of the object. The record name attribute is intended as a human-readable identifier for a record. It's not required to be a unique identifier, but it is supposed to be the primary way users distinguish one record from another. The value for the `Record Name` is always displayed as a link to the record itself, in its own detail page. This automatic connection between records reduces the work you would have to do to integrate different objects in your Force Platform application.

A record name can be one of two types: a text string or an auto-number field. For an auto-number field, you must specify the format for the field and the starting number. Auto number fields increment by one each time a record is created.

A text `Record Name` does not have to be unique, although you may want to create procedures to automatically generate a unique record name. You will learn about these types of procedures, called triggers, later in this book.

For this application, leave `Location Name` as the `Record Name` and `Text` as the `Data Type`.

Real versus artificial keys The differentiation between text and auto number `Record Names` may sound a little bit like the difference between a real key value, or one which represents some real world aspects of a record or row, and an artificial key, which is arbitrarily assigned and has no direct relationship to the content of the record. Well, not exactly. All Force Platform records are uniquely identified by an internal field called ID. This ID field comes in two forms – a 15-character case sensitive form, which is used for links within Force Platform applications and other places, and an 18-character case insensitive form, returned from Force Platform Web Services API calls. The `Record Name` is used in many different guises, as you will see throughout this chapter and the book, but the value of the `ID` field is used directly within a Force Platform application for identification purposes.

The comparison is appropriate in one way – a text `Record Name` is likely to be more meaningful than an autonumber value, but a text `Record Name` will not necessarily be unique, while an autonumber value will be.

Optional Features

The three checkboxes in this section open up vast areas of functionality with just a simple mouse click:

- `Allow Reports` indicates that this object will be available to the Force Platform reporting tools. Selecting this option automatically adds report types for the object to the Force Platform reporting system, which is described in detail in *Chapter 6: Reaping Value Through Reports.*
- `Allow Activities` indicates whether a user will be able to attach Activities, which represent tasks and calendar event that are associated with a record. When you allow activities for an object, a user will be able to log a call or send an email from a record in that object with the click of a button, and have that activity be associated with the record.
- `Track Field History` is the most power feature of these three. When this box is checked, the Force Platform automatically keeps track of changes made to a record in the object. As you will see shortly, you can also track changes to individual fields within a record. These history records can be used with the Force Platform analytic tools to create usage and audit reports.

Click all three boxes in the `Optional Features` section.

Although this sample application will not need to use the `Activities` option for this record, you can remove it later to learn how to modify page layouts.

Deployment Status

With this group of radio buttons, you indicate whether you want this object to be visible to all users in your organization or only to developers. Best practices for the Force Platform call for development activities to take place in a Developer Edition organization, which you are probably using for these exercises, or a sandbox, which you will learn about later in this book. When you work in these alternative organizations, you can deploy your objects immediately, since they will not affect your production environment.

Leave the default `Deployment Status` of `Deployed` selected.

Object Creation Options

The last two checkboxes on the page apply to different types of activities. The first checkbox lets you specify a section for `Notes and Attachments` on the page layout used by the tab for this object. This built-in capability of the Force Platform lets your users add notes and attachments to individual records through the standard user interface. As with Activities, you may want to check this box even if you do not have any immediate plans to include this functionality for this object. You can always remove this section from the display of the page later. The last checkbox indicates that you want to start up the `Custom Tab Wizard` immediately after saving this object. You use the `Custom Tab Wizard` to define the basic attributes of the tab which, by default, exposes this object within an application.

Click both of the boxes in this section and click **Save**.

Creating a Tab

As described earlier in this chapter, Force Platform apps use tabs as the primary way for users to access the main objects in the application. Since you asked for the Custom Tab Wizard to be spawned once the object is created, you are presented with a page that looks like the figure below.

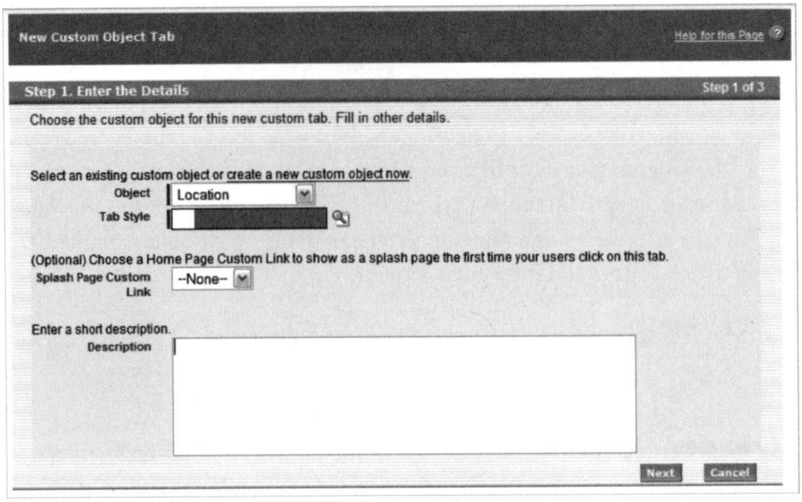

Figure 18: Creating a tab

Creating a tab adds a user interface for an object which can be added to your application, but this action also adds two more important pieces of functionality to your Force Platform application. When you add a tab for an object, you give the user the ability to add a new record to the object through the `Create New` list in the left hand panel, as well as adding records for this object to the list of the most recently accessed records in the same panel.

On the Tab definition page, you link an object with a `Tab Style`. A `Tab Style` is an icon and color scheme that appear on the tab for the object, as well as in the Recent Items list in the left-hand panel of the default Force Platform interface, to identify the type of a listed object.

1. Click the search icon to the right of the `Tab Style` field and select the `Building` style. You should also give a description of the tab, such as `Interfaces with the Location object`.

2. Click **Next** to bring up the page shown in below.

   This page requests you to specify which profiles will be allowed to access this tab

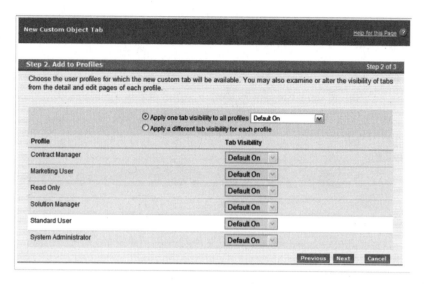

Figure 19: Assigning security to a tab

3. Leave the default choice of `Default On` and click **Next**. Remember, users will be able to change their individual display, if they wish to eliminate the display of this tab.

4. Click **Next** to bring up the page shown in the figure below.

This page lets you specify the applications that will include the new tab by default.

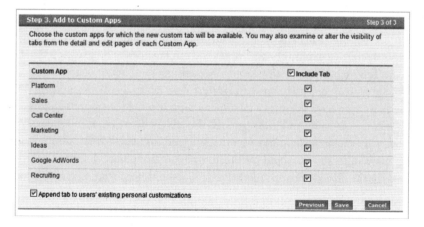

Figure 20: Including a tab in existing applications

5. Click the **Include Tab** checkbox to deselect all the applications, and then click the **Recruiting** checkbox to include the new tab for only this application.

Once again, witness the power of on-demand development. Your new tab is instantly available within the application.

6. Click **Save**.

7. Click the tab to show the page below.

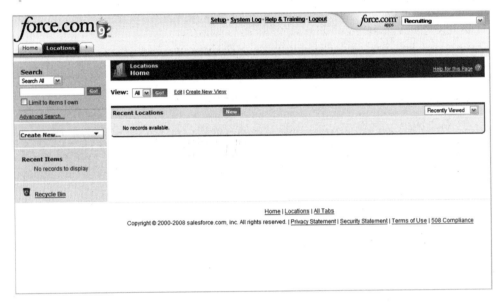

Figure 21: Your new tab

You can see that not only is your tab present, but also all the contents of the Sidebar on the left. Although you chose to create a tab for an object immediately after creating the object, you do not have to create a tab at the same time. You can create tabs by selecting the **Tab** menu choice. The **Tab** menu choice can take you through the same set of pages you just used for a tab associated with an object, or you can create a Web tab to display a standard Web page for a tab. You don't even have to create a tab for an object if you do not want to allow direct access to the data in the object by end users through the tabbed interface. For instance, you might decide that you only wanted Interviews to be assigned for a Job Application through an automatic procedure, so you would not create a tab for that object. Users could still get access to the data for the objects through reports or lookup links, for instance, but not through a tab.

Voice of the Developer: Tabs in Force Platform come in three types, including the Custom Object tab used in this chapter, which relates to a single custom object. You can create a Web tab, which can be used to link to anything that can be referenced by a URL or an s-Control. You can also create a tab that is related to a number of objects or even starts a wizard by creating a tab that links to a Visualforce page. You will learn about Visualforce later in *Chapter 9: Visualforce Pages*, and *Chapter 12: Extended Visualforce Components and Controllers*.

Adding Fields to Your Object

The page shown in the figure above looks pretty bare, as there are no records within this object. Even if you click **New**, you only bring up the page shown in the following figure, where there admittedly is not much going on.

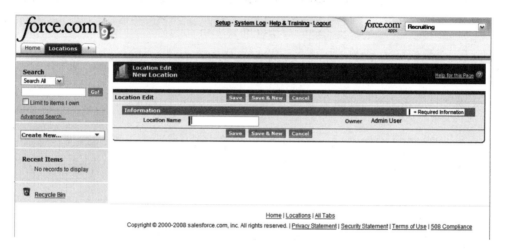

Figure 22: Adding a new location (first version)

You have to add some fields to the object to make the object more useful.

1. Click **Setup ➤ Create ➤ Objects** to display the Location object in the object list.

   There are three ways you can get to the Location object from this page. The **Edit** link takes you to a page to edit the values you entered in the last section, except for the inclusion of the Notes and Attachments option. You can still add the Notes and Attachments section to a tab page after creation, but you have to do it through the **Page Layout**, as you will see shortly.

   The **Del** link deletes the object, after confirmation from you. When you delete an object, you also delete the associated data. By default, deleted objects and their data are kept for 45 days, during which time you can either restore them or erase them permanently from the Force Platform. The link for the name of the object takes you to a page where you can specify most of the attributes for the object, as you will see in the next step.

Clicking on the name of the object takes you to the page you will use most often in your development efforts.

 Voice of the Developer:

When editing custom objects, there are two types of pages you will need to access. The first page provides access to top level attributes that define the name and description of the object, and also control use of platform behavior such as Workflow and Reports. The second page is the one you will most likely be visiting more often, as it provides a means to add and edit new fields and layouts.

Clicking on the name of the object takes you to the second page, while the second first is accessible through the **Edit** link. You should train yourself to use this object name link to improve your development productivity and avoid the cursing that accompanies repeated frustration at the appearance of the first page.

2. Click the **Location** link to display the page shown below.

This page includes a large number of attributes for your object. You will learn about all of them over the course of the next few chapters, but for right now, only the first three require descriptions:

- Custom Object Definition Detail – includes all the information you entered when you defined the object. You can edit that information by clicking **Edit**.
- Standard Fields – lists the fields that are included by default for this object. The fields are used to track the owner of the record, as well as information about the creation of the record and last modification of the record. The Record Name is the only one of the standard fields that you can edit.
- Custom Fields & Relationships – the focus of the rest of this section

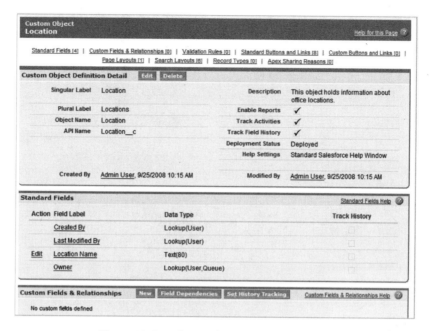

Figure 23: Detail page for the Location object

3. Click **New** in the Custom Fields & Relationships section to display the page whose upper section is shown in the following figure.

This first page of the field definition process is used to select the data type for your new field. The page is divided up into three basic sections:

- Read only data types - where the Force Platform system automatically generates the value. These data types include the `Auto Number` type you already encountered on the object definition page, a `Formula` field for displaying information derived from other sources, and a `Roll-Up Summary Field`, which is currently not enabled since the Location object does not include the prerequisites for the use of a `Roll-Up Summary Field`. You will define a `Roll-Up Summary Field` in the next chapter, and several formula fields in *Chapter 4: Expanding data options*. All of these data types produce a read-only field on the detail page for the object.

- Relationship data types - defines two different types of relationships between the current object and another object. These data types establish the same type of relationship you define with a foreign key in a relational database. Relationships are the main focus of *Chapter 3: Relationships*.

- Standard datatypes - used for the fields you will define in this section.

These data types both control the type of data allowed in the field, and, in some cases, the formatting of the user interface for the field in a tab. You have already created the Location Name field for this object as part of the object definition process. The first additional field you will define is the Address field.

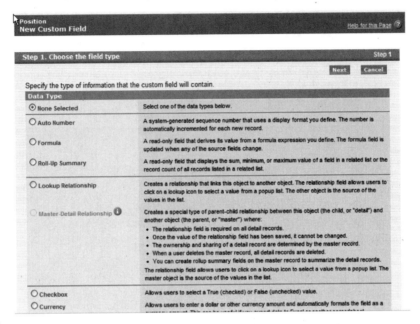

Figure 24: Defining a custom field's data type

4. Select `Text Area (Long)` and click **Next** to bring up the page shown below .

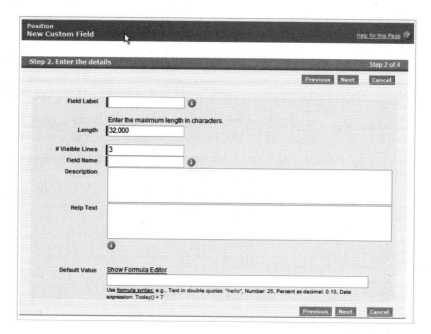

Figure 25: Defining a custom field's attributes

5. Enter `Street Address` for the `Field Label`, limit the `Length` of the field to `2,000` characters, and set the number of visible lines as `4`.

You can see that when you enter a Field Label, the Field Name is automatically defaulted to the label, with underscores in the place of spaces. As you will see, the actual name of the field, like the name of the object, is the name listed on this page followed by two underscores and the letter 'c' (__c).

Voice of the Developer: When adding fields, the `Field Name` is defaults to the `Field Label` by replacing spaces with underscore characters. Since the `Field Name` is the identifier you will later use in your Apex code it is worth considering your coding conventions at this point. If you have a Java or .Net background, you might prefer to see and use mixed case identifiers, such as `newCandidate.CurrentEmployer__c` vs `newCandidate,Current_Employer__c` in your Apex code. You can achieve this result, but only by changing the default `Field Name`.

6. Enter a description for the field and some help text for this field.
7. Click **Next**.

The next page gives you the ability to impose field level security restrictions on your new field. You will learn about security in *Chapter 7: Protecting Your Data* of this book, so you can accept the defaults on this page.

8. Click **Next** to bring up the page shown below.

This page provides a recap of the most important attributes you have defined for your new field, as well as the ability to include this field in a **Page Layout** for its object.

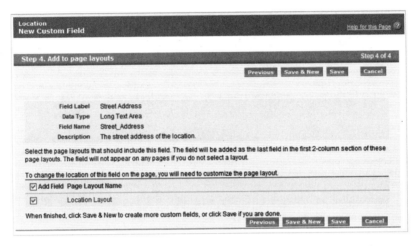

Figure 26: Custom field attributes and inclusion on page layouts

9. You will modify the Page Layout later in this chapter, so for now you can click **Save and New** to accept the default of adding the field to the page layout and complete the creation of this field and define another field.

This action takes you back to the Data Type page for your next field.

10. Define the rest of the fields for the Location object with the attributes specified in the table below, accepting the default security and page layout options for each.

Table 1: Additional data fields for Location custom objects

Data Type	Field Label	Length	Required
Text	City	50	Yes
Text	State/Province	3	Yes
Text	Postal Code	11	No
Text	Country	20	Yes
Phone	Phone	N/A	No
URL	Location Map	N/A	No

As you define these additional fields, you will see that the detail options differ based on the data type you have specified for each field. For example, there are three checkboxes available for the `Text` fields you define, which allow you to specify that the value for the field is required, or that the value must be unique. These two attributes would not really make sense for a `Text Area`, which is typically used to hold optional data. Similarly, you are not prompted to enter a length for a field with a data type of `Phone`. This special data type automatically formats phone numbers entered by the user. The checkbox for an `External ID` will become more meaningful when you learn about relationships in *Chapter 3: Relationships*.

11. When you have completed defining the last field, click **Save** to return you to the object page for the Location Object, as shown below.

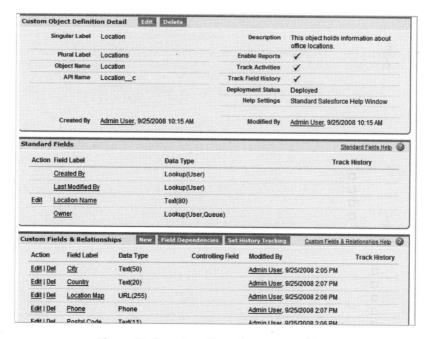

Figure 27: Completed Location custom object

The fields you have just entered are listed in the Custom Fields and Relationships section of the Location object detail page in alphabetical order.

Entering Data

Although you have been simply defining fields that will be part of the Location object, the page layouts associated with that object have also been changing. The best way to see the results of those changes is to simply access the tab.

1. Click the Locations tab at the top of the page, and then click **New** to bring up the page shown in below. You could also use the **Create New** picklist in the left hand panel and click the Location object in that list.

    Since you did not uncheck the option to add the fields to the page layout, the fields you have added to your object are automatically added to its associated layouts. Although you might want to modify how these fields are laid out on the page (and will shortly), you might as well enter a location record while you are on this page.

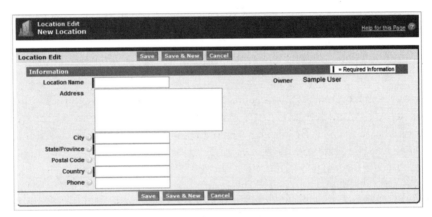

Figure 28: Entering data for the Location object

2. Enter values for the `Location Name`, `Address`, `City`, `State/Province`, `Postal Code` and `Country`.
3. Enter 10 digits for the `Phone` field and tab to the next field. .

    Notice how the Force Platform automatically formatted the Phone data type field for you. In a similar manner, do not enter the http:// for the URL field, since the data type automatically places that prefix on the URL.

4. Enter a URL, such as `www.salesforce.com`, and click **Save** to display the detail page for the record you just entered, as shown below

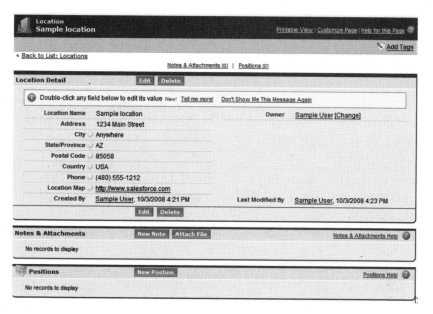

Figure 29: A complete Location record, in its detail page

When you click **Save**, an entry with a link for the record you just created is also placed in the Recent Items list in the left hand panel, along with the icon you assigned for the related tab to identify the object type. By keeping a list of the most recent records of all object types with tabs defined, the Recent Items list makes it easy to switch rapidly between records of different types.

This may seem like a little thing, but this combination of object records in a single list points back, yet again, to the metadata driven nature of the Force Platform. Every record in every object in the Force Platform database has a unique identifier. This identifier points to an individual record, whose metadata includes the object which holds the record. When a user requests that record, the Force Platform knows the record belongs to that object, and uses metadata to create the user interface.

You can see that some of the items listed in the detail page are shown as links. The link for the Location Map leads to the URL you entered for that field, while the Created By, Owner, and Last Modified By fields link to related records in the standard User objects. Clicking the link for any of these last three fields brings up the detail page for the listed user.

The automatic creation and deployment of these page layouts is a great productivity feature, especially since you can easily modify the layout of the fields on that tab.

Modifying Page Layout

The appearance of the fields in a page layout is controlled by the Page Layout option for the object.

1. Click **Setup** to return to the Setup menu, and then **Create ➤ Objects** to bring up a list of objects.

2. Click the **Location** link to bring up the attributes for the object.

   The **Edit** link for the Location object lets you edit the attributes for the object itself.

   At the top of the page you can see links for different attribute sections.

3. Let your mouse hover on the **Page Layouts** link to bring up the Page Layout section at the top of the page, and then click the **Edit** link for the page layout to bring up the page shown in figure that follows.

> **Page Layouts**
>
> A default page layout includes a number of sections, including a section for detail page buttons, a section for related lists, which you will learn about in the next chapter, and a section for system information, as well as a section with two columns for fields in the object.
>
> One page layout represents the detail page and edit page of an object, but that some elements only appear in one context. For example, related lists, custom links, and formula fields only show up on detail pages, not edit pages.

The Edit Page Layout page allows you to change the layout of the View, Edit and Detail pages for an object. You can see that there are different sections of the page shown, including the Button Section, the main section, labeled Information, and later sections to hold system information, custom links and related lists. You can add more sections to the page with the **Create New Section** button, but you will only need to move fields, buttons, and lists around on the current page layout.

You can also see that some of the basic attributes of the fields, such as whether they are required or read-only, are indicated on the fields by icons that are described in the legend to the right of the page layout.

Your first task is to rearrange the fields in the main Information section.

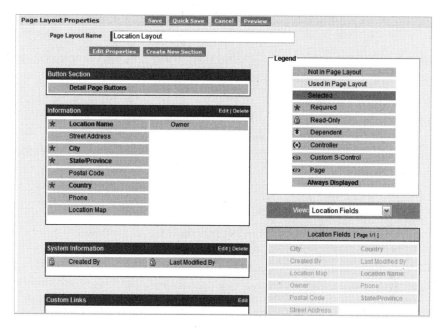

Figure 30: A page layout

4. Grab the `Location Map URL` field by clicking the field and holding down the left mouse button. Drag the field to the right-hand column and release the mouse button, causing the field to appear just below the `Owner` field, the only field in the right column.

5. Drag the `State/Province` field to the right column, next to the `City` field, and drag the `Postal Code` field to the right of the `Country` field.

   You've improved the look of the main section, but you will probably want to take out some of the related lists that don't make a lot of sense for this page, `Open Activities` and `Activity History`.

6. Grab the `Open Activities` related list and drag it to the box just below the icon legend on the right as shown in the figure below. Release the mouse to place the list in this box.

   The box that just received the related list allows you to view any fields, related lists or s-controls that are associated with this object. If you want to place any of these onto the page, grab them from this box and drag them to the desired section of the form.

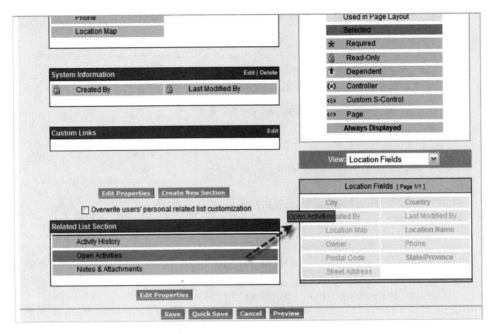

Figure 31: Dragging a field in a page layout

7. Drag the `Activity History` related list to the lower box.

Your final beautification task is to eliminate some of the pushbuttons on the standard page. You may have noticed when you looked at the detail record that there was a button showing that was probably were not necessary – the Clone button, which makes a copy of the current Location record.

The Force Platform development environment automatically puts a standard set of buttons to implement built-in functionality on every new page. You can eliminate this and other buttons if you do not need the functionality they deliver.

8. In the page layout editor, double click on the Detail Page Buttons section to bring up the page shown below.

This page shows the default buttons used for a standard detail page. You can eliminate the display of any of the buttons by deselecting the checkbox for the button.

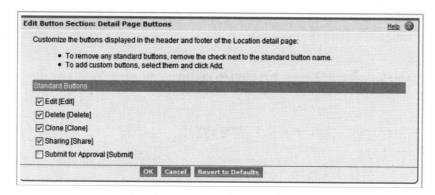

Figure 32: Detail Page Button assignment

9. Deselect the checkbox for the `Delete` and `Sharing` buttons.

   Since you will only be using a small set of locations that will not change very often, and you do not want a location to disappear by accident, eliminate the display of the Delete button.

   Additionally, you will want to share the records in the Location object with all users, so there is no need to have the Share button visible. The Share button is only visible if the security settings for the record allow it to be shared, as you will learn in *Chapter 7: Protecting Your Data.*

10. Click **OK** in the Detail Page Buttons page, and **OK** in the reminder dialog.
11. Click the **Edit** link for the Information section. In the dialog that appears, change the `Tab Order` from `Top-Down` to `Left-Right`.
12. Click **OK** to return to the Page Layout editor.
13. Once you return to the Page Layout editor, click **Save** to save the new page layout.
14. Click the Locations tab and then the Location record you just created to display your new page, as shown in the following figure.

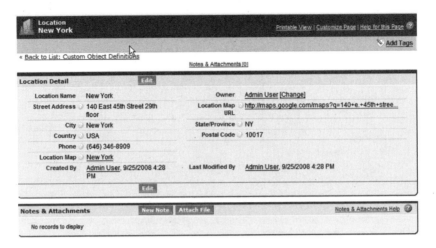

Figure 33: The new page layout for the Location record

This new page is more appropriate for the purposes of this application, so you can leave it just as it is.

Filling Your Object With Data

You have your data object defined, and the Force Platform-generated pages to interact with that data. But this application, like most, models a process that already exists in the real world. Universal Containers already has locations defined, so it is more efficient and accurate to load data from an existing source rather than have to reenter it all.

The Force Platform environment has two different tools that you can use to load (and unload) data: Import Wizard and Data Loader.

Using Import Wizard

To load data into the Locations object, you can use the Import Wizard, a utility built into the Force Platform Setup menu.

1. Return to the Setup menu and click **Data Management ➤ Import Custom Objects**.
2. After reviewing the information in the splash page for the Wizard, click on the link for the Import Wizard.
3. Select the Location object and click **Next**.
4. In the next page, leave the selection for inserting all records. If you choose to prevent duplicate records from being inserted into the custom object, you have the option

of specifying that you want to either simply refrain from inserting duplicates, or that you want to update values in the existing record from the record being loaded.

5. Change the value for the owner of the record to `None` and click **Next**.

   Every record in the Force Platform database has an owner specified. This page allows you to either use the internal Force Platform ID for a User record to identify the owner, or the Name of the user. If you do not specify an owner, the user performing the import (in this case, you) are the owner, which is the result you want.

6. Browse for the file that contains the records for the Location object. This file is available from the Code Share project for this book and has the name of `Location.csv`. Select that file and click **Next**.

7. The next page gives you a list of the fields in the Location object and a picklist that contains the fields in the designated comma-separated variable file. Map the following fields to their like-named fields in the .csv file. The fields with identical names are automatically mapped for you.

Table 2: Field name mapping for Location Import Wizard

Force Platform Field Name	File Name
Location Name	Location: Location Name
Street Address	Address
City	City
State/Province	State/Province
Postal Code	Post Code
Country	Country
Phone	Phone
Location Map URL	Location Map

8. Click **Next**, which will prompt you for the fields you have not assigned. Since these fields have values assigned by the system, click **OK**.

9. Click **Import Now** to import the 4 Location records.

Regardless of the text on the button, clicking **Import Now** does not mean that the actual import of your records occurs immediately. Instead, the next page informs you that your import job is placed in a queue, and you will be notified at the email address for the organization once the import job is completed. In a multi-tenant environment, there may be many other orgs importing data at the same time, and some import jobs could be quite large, so using a queue is the fair way to handle imports.

The Data Loader, described in the next section, will allow you more control over when the actual import of your records occurs.

Using Data Loader

As a developer, you may have found the previous process a bit tedious, with all that clicking. In addition, if you are going to perform the same load task repeatedly, with different data, you won't want to have to go through the Import Wizard every time. The Force Platform includes the Data Loader tool for not only importing data, but also for exporting data and deleting existing records.

You can download Data Loader from the same Data Management menu you used to access the Import Wizard. Data Loader is a desktop application that uses the Force Platform API to access objects on the platform. The Data Loader application includes a user interface that walks you through the same set of tasks as the Import Wizard, in a slightly different manner. But for you, the developer, Data Loader also includes a command line interface, which means you can simply use a command file to run any Data Loader job.

The script to use, and detailed instructions on how to use it, can be found in the Code Share project for this book, as described in *Chapter 1: Welcome to the Force Platform.* You use Data Loader to load the users for the book into your organization.

Throughout the rest of this book, you will be using Data Loader and command line files to add data to the objects that will be a part of your application.

Summary

You have taken the first step towards creating the recruiting application, and defining and populating your first data structure. More importantly, you have gotten familiar with the basics of the Force Platform Setup menu environment.

In the next chapter, you will learn about one of the most powerful aspects of your Force platform data, the relationship, as well as the functionality relationships provide for your applications.

Chapter 3

Relationships

In the last chapter, you laid the groundwork for your recruiting application and got familiar with some of the basics of Force Platform development through the Force Platform Setup menu. You are ready to start using one of the most powerful aspects of the Force Platform environment: relationships.

Early in the history of computing, scientists and designers realized that they could optimize the flexibility and performance of their database systems by breaking the stored data up into separate objects. This approach, known as normalization, allowed users to access smaller amounts of data in a table or an object.

Normalization worked well for data designers and developers, but users frequently required a broader view of their data than those fields that were contained in a single object. Relational databases offered a structure known as a foreign key, where a value in a child record pointed to the primary key of the parent, to make joining data from separate tables easier and to provide better performance. The Force Platform accomplishes this same goal through the use of relationship fields, as well as quite a bit more in the way of implementation.

Important: If you have been following the examples in the previous chapter, your Force Platform organization should be ready for the exercises in this chapter. If you have not done the exercises, or want to start with a fresh version of the sample Recruiting application, please refer to the instructions in the Code Share project for this book. You can find information on how to access that project in *Chapter 1: Welcome to the Force Platform.*

Types of Relationships

The Force Platform supports two variations of parent-child relationships between objects: lookup relationships and master-detail relationships.

Both types of relationships work like foreign key relationships in a relational database, and produce some of the same effect on the pages for the objects in the relationship.

When you define the relationship between two objects, the Force Platform does a number of things:

- Creates a field in the child object with an icon that allows users to look up valid values from the parent object. When a user views the child record in a detail page, the `Record Name` of the parent is shown for the field as a link that takes the user directly to the detail page for the parent record.
- Creates a list of related child objects, which you can include as part of the page for the parent object
- Creates a report type, described in more detail in *Chapter 6: Reaping Value Through Reports*, and that provides a way for users to make reports with data from both objects

You will see all of these features in action in your first hands-on example.

A lookup relationship generates all of the above features. A master-detail relationship adds some functionality and restrictions to these common features:

- When a user deletes the master record in a master-detail relationship, all associated detail records are also deleted
- The child records always have the same security specification and owner as their parent record in a master-detail relationship; in fact, the `Owner` field of the child record is not available
- All child records in a master-detail relationship must have a parent record specified
- The relationship field is required on the page layout of the child
- You can use Roll-up Summary Fields with master-detail relationships, a field type used to store values aggregated from the child records in the relationship. This option is discussed later in this chapter in the section Roll-up Summary Fields.

A Force Platform object cannot be the master in one relationship and the detail in another relationship. An object can be the master in more than one relationship, but Force Platform relationships cannot be used to implement multiple levels of detail.

Tip: You cannot create a master-detail relationship for an object that contains data, since master-detail relationship fields are required; however, you can convert a lookup relationship to a master-detail relationship. If you want to add a master-detail relationship to an object with data, you can create a lookup relationship to the master, add a value for the relationship for all child records, and then convert that relationship to a master-detail relationship.

As with so much of the Force Platform , the easiest way to understand relationships is to simply create some to see how they work.

Creating a Relationship

At this point, you only have one object defined, so you will have to create another object to implement any relationships. The Position object is used to hold information about positions at Universal Containers, such as a description of the job.

1. Return to the Setup menu and click **Setup ➤ Create ➤ Objects ➤ New Custom Object**.
2. Give the new object a `Label` of `Position`, a `Plural Label` of `Positions`, and a `Description` of `Position to be filled`.
3. Set the `Record Name` to `Position ID`, the `Data Type` as `Auto Number`, the display format to `POS-{00000}`, and the `Starting Number` to `1`.
4. Allow reports, activities, and field history tracking for the Position object, allow `Notes and Attachments`, and choose to launch the `Custom Tab Wizard` after creation.
5. Click **Save**, which will launch the Tab Wizard. Select an appropriate `Tab Style`, such as the `Treasure Chest`, and click **Next**.
6. Leave the default visibility of the tab as `Default On` and click **Next**.
7. Since you will only want to display this tab as part of the Recruiting application, click `Include Tab` to deselect all the custom apps and then the Recruiting app checkbox to include this tab as part of your new app. Click **Save** to add the tab to your application. The main page for the Position Object displays.

You can create a relationship in the same way that you created fields for the Location object.

Voice of the Developer: When setting up master-detail relationships, you should keep in mind that the relationship between the master object and the detail object is expressed by adding a field to the detail object and not, as you might expect, the master object.

1. Click **New** in the Custom Fields & Relationships section.

2. Select `Lookup Relationship` as the data type for the field and click **Next**. The next page prompts you to select the parent object for this relationship.

3. Select the Location object and click **Next**.

4. Give the relationship a `Field Label` of `Location`, and a description and help text of `The location of the position`. Click **Next**.

5. In the next page, accept all the default field-level security settings and click **Next**.

6. The next page asks you if you want to include the new field as part of the page layout for the Position object. Accept the default and click **Next**.

   The next page, shown in the figure below, is new to you.

   This page asks if you want to include the related list in the page layouts for the parent object. Even if you don't add the related list to the page on this page, you could always go back to the page layout and add it.

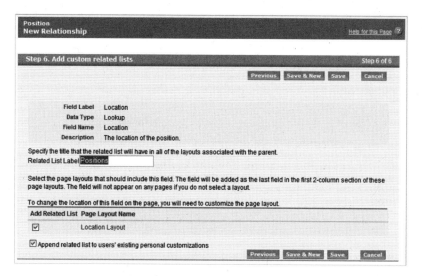

Figure 34: Adding related lists to page layouts

7. Click **Save and New** to save this relationship and start to define another one.

   The lookup relationship to the Location object provides a simple user interface allowing your users to only select a valid location for a position. The next relationship you add associates each position with a hiring manager. The potential hiring managers are already defined in the User object, which contains all current users of your organization, so you can leverage an existing standard object to implement this relationship.

8. Select the `Lookup Relationship` data type again and click **Next**.

9. This time, select the `User` object as the related object and click **Next**.

10. Give the new relationship a `Field Label` of `Hiring Manager`, and a description and help text of `The hiring manager for the position`. Click **Next**.

11. Accept the default field level security and placement on both the Position and User pages. Click **Save** to finish the creation of the new relationship.

Once again, you can quickly see the result of your most recent work.

12. Click the Positions tab to bring up the view on the initial page and click **New** to display the page shown below.

As expected, the two lookup fields, with their search buttons, are on the page.

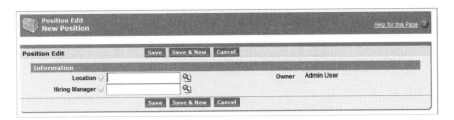

Figure 35: Lookup fields in a page

13. Enter values for the location and a hiring manager for the position, using the lookup search capability, and save the record.

14. Click the link for the Location list to see the related list of Positions on that record detail, as shown in the following figure.

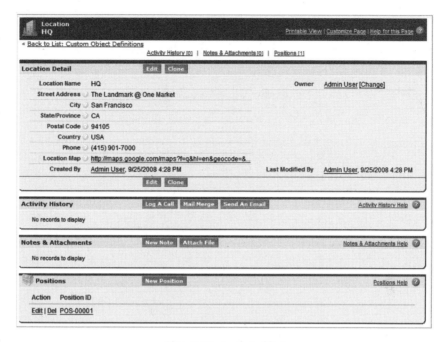

Figure 36: A related list

Adding relationships with a few mouse clicks results in quite a bit of functionality in your application. For any type of real-world application, you need to add more fields to the Position object.

Adding Fields

Once again, you can quickly add a few more fields to the Position object.

1. Return to the Setup menu for the Position object by clicking **Setup ➤ Create ➤ Objects ➤ Position**.
2. Add the fields described in the table below to the Position object, clicking **Save and New** each time.

Table 3: Additional Fields for Position object

Data Type	Field Label	Length	Required
Text Area (long)	Job Description	2,000 - Visible Lines - 5	N/A

Data Type	Field Label	Length	Required
Text Area (long)	Responsibilities	2,000 - Visible Lines - 5	N/A
Date	Start Date	N/A	Yes

The fields in the previous table give you a bit of practice using the Setup menu to add fields. In your every day development tasks, you can use either the Setup menu or the Force Platform IDE, which you will learn about in *Chapter 8: The Force Platform IDE*, to define objects.

The Force Platform includes a Metadata API, which also allows you to use a script for creating Force Platform components. You will use scripts to create almost all of the remaining objects and fields you use for examples in the rest of this book.

You have one more field to add to the Position object at this time, a field which unlocks some key flexibility in moving data from external sources into the Force Platform database.

3. Add a Text field and give it a `Field Label` of `Legacy ID`, a `Length` of `10` and an appropriate description and help text.

4. Select the `Unique` and `External ID` checkboxes.

The `External ID` provides an important piece of flexibility for the Force Platform database. Like many organizations, Universal Containers is creating a Force Platform application to replace and improve an existing application with an on-demand system. In the existing application, each Position has a unique ID.

As mentioned earlier, every record in the Force Platform database has an internal ID uniquely identifying the record. This ID is used to implement relationships between objects, among other things. As you load data into your Force Platform objects, the ID is assigned when the records are inserted into the database.

This simple fact creates a problem for records that are children in a relationship. The actual value stored in the relationship field is the ID of the parent. How can a child record know that ID in advance so the relationship can be established as part of the data load?

The `External ID` is the solution. When you define an `External ID`, you can specify that the value in that field be used to establish relationships. The Force

Platform identifies the parent record with that value for the `External ID` and automatically copies the ID of the record into the relationship field of the child.

With this identification established through the `External ID`, you can complete the definition of the Position object.

 Tip: You can also use an External ID to update records which already have values, which the scripts you use to update your organization at the start of some chapters will have to do. For this reason, most of your objects will have an External ID field added to them as part of those scripts.

5. Click **Next** to save the information, and **Next** again to accept the default security settings.
6. On the final page, uncheck the `Add Field` box, since there is no need to see this Legacy ID on the user interface page. Click **Save**.

   Once the object is created, click the Positions tab to see the new layout. The Recent Items view displays, which currently only shows the Position ID. This view can be much more informative, a situation addressed in the next section.

7. Select the Position record you entered before to bring up the new detail page and then **Edit** to show the page below. Enter values for the fields displayed and click **Save**.

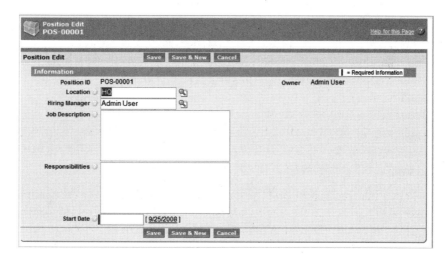

Figure 37: The new Position entry page

Note: You will learn much more about searching for records in a variety of ways in *Chapter 6: Reaping Value Through Reports*.

When you return to the detail page, you can see that the long text areas are displaying correctly. But you will still like to fix that initial view, and you can add some additional user interface functionality at the same time. You will, indeed, improve the appearance of the view, but first you should load more data into the Position object.

Loading Your Data

Universal Containers has been in business for a while, so they have some open positions already. Once again, you import data from an existing source to populate the Position object using the Import Wizard.

This is the last time you use the Import Wizard in this book, to take advantage of the ability of that tool to link to values in the Record Name. In your normal operations, you will probably use Data Loader most of the time, utilizing an External ID when appropriate to establish relationships while loading.

1. Click **Setup ➤ Data Management ➤ Import Custom Objects**.
2. Click the **Import Wizard** link and select the Position object. Click **Next**.
3. Leave the default choice for duplicates and click **Next**.
4. Select None as the field used to designate the owner of the record.
5. Select both Location and Hiring Manager as lookup fields that are included in the import file and click **Next**.
6. Leave the default mappings for the lookup fields selected on the next page and click **Next**.
7. Select the file Postitions.csv to load. Refer to the directions in the Code Share project for this book, as described in *Chapter 1: Welcome to the Force Platform*, to obtain the file. Click **Next**.
8. Match the fields in the csv file with like-named fields in the Positions object and click **Next**.
9. Click **Import Now!** to load the records into the Positions object.

You have just integrated your existing data into your Force Platform database. Now you will polish up some aspects of the user interface.

Refining the User Interface

You can tweak the appearance of the default view to include more relevant information in the user interface.

1. Click **Setup ➤ Create ➤ Objects ➤ Position** to return to the main page for the object.
2. Scroll down the page to the Search Layouts section. This section contains layouts for the different ways that users can access this object, other than the home page for the object.
3. Click **Edit** for the Positions Tab to bring up the page shown in the following figure.

   This page allows you to select other fields for display on the home page for the Position object tab.

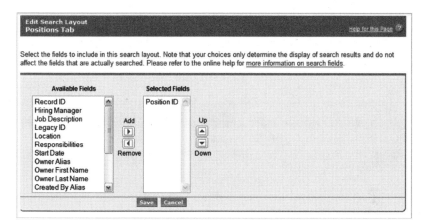

Figure 38: Selecting fields for a home tab

4. Move `Job Description` and `Start Date` to the Selected Fields box and click **Save**.

   Before leaving the development environment, you can enable a few more features to make the Force Platform user interface more useful and flexible.

   This modification changes the appearance of the default view for the tab. You can create additional views for the tab by selecting **Create New View** on the Home page for the object, or edit existing views by clicking the **Edit** link for a selected view. The interface to create and change views is like the interface you just used.

5. Click **Objects ➤ Location** and then the link for the default page layout in the Page Layouts section of the object.

6. At the top of the page, click **Mini Page Layout**. The Mini Page Layout is used to show some of the fields for the object in a reduced window.

7. Make sure that the `City`, `State/Province` and `Country` fields are in the Selected box and click **Save**.

   One of the places this Mini Page Layout is used is when a user 'hovers' over a link to a Location record.

   In order to allow organizations to add this new feature into their environment at their own pace, the hovering feature was not enabled by default. Turning it on, along with another two features, is simply a matter of configuration.

8. Click **Customize ➤ User Interface** in the App Setup section of the left hand panel to bring up the page shown below.

   You can see a number of interesting features available to your environment by just checking a box.

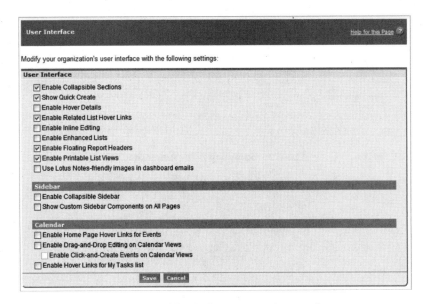

Figure 39: Modifying the User Interface settings

9. Check the `Enable Hover Details` and `Enable Inline Editing` checkboxes in the top section, and the `Enable Collapsible Sidebar` checkbox in the Sidebar section, and click **Save**. As their names imply, the two additional features you enabled

allow users to edit values in a detail page without having to explicitly go to an Edit page and 'collapse' the sidebar, giving the main page more screen real estate.

10. Click the Positions tab. The sidebar should be collapsed, as shown in the figure below. If not, grab the right edge of the sidebar and drag it to the left to see the fruits of your labor.

You are already getting used to the instantaneous effects of your efforts in the runtime application. In the page shown below, the sidebar starts out collapsed, with little arrows that allow the user to bring it back into the picture when they want to see it.

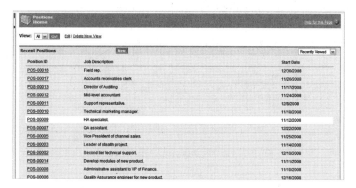

Figure 40: The sidebar hidden

1. Bring the sidebar back by dragging the edge to the right.
2. Click a Position record and double click on a field to see the inline editing capability you enabled for the fields. Click on **Cancel** to return to the page.
3. Leave your mouse over the Location field on the page to bring up the Mini Page Layout, as shown in the figure below.

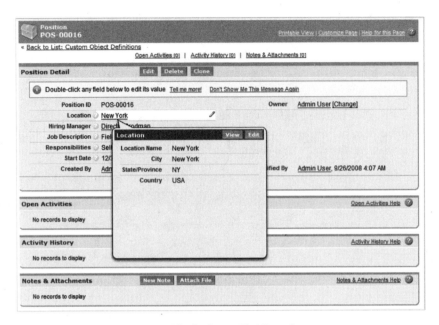

Figure 41: Displaying a Mini-Page Layout

You have changed the way your application displays and the information readily available to users in a significant way, with only a few configuration changes. Your next step enlarges the logical capabilities of your application by adding more objects and relationships to the Force Platform.

Many to Many Relationships

So far, you have defined a couple of Force Platform objects and created a productive link between them. The power of relationships drives data design on the Force Platform, and good development practices suggest that you spend time designing your objects to leverage the full productivity of these relationships. In this section, you will learn about a different tyype of relationships you can easily create in your Force Platform database.

The relationship you created in the previous section is known as a one-to-many relationship. Each Position record is associated with one Location record, and a Location record can be associated with many Position records.

But what about situations that call for a many-to-many relationship? In this type of relationship, a record on each side of the relationship can be associated with many records on the other side.

The Recruiting application you are building contains a good example of this type of relationship. Each Position record can be associated with many different Candidates, an object you will create shortly. And each different Candidate can apply for many different Positions.

Creating a Junction Object

In order to implement this type of relationship, you need to create an intermediate object, referred to as a junction object. This object has a relationship to the objects on both sides of the many-to-many relationship, with a single instance of this junction object for each relationship between an individual Candidate and an individual Position.

1. Follow to the instructions in the Code Share project for this book, described in *Chapter 1: Welcome to the Force Platform*, to create the Candidate object and its fields.
2. Follow the instructions in the Code Share project for this book to create the Job Application object.

The Job Application object is used to create a junction between a Candidate record and a Position record. You are now ready to implement a many-to-many relationship.

Implementing a Many-to-Many Relationship

Your objects are in place, so you can now link the Position and Candidate objects through the Job Application object. As mentioned above, each Candidate can apply for more than one Position, and each Postion can have many different Candidates. The Job Application record links together a single Candidate for a single Position, as well as including other information.

1. Click **Setup ➤ Create ➤ Objects ➤ Job Application** to modify the junction object the script just created.
2. Add a new master-detail relationship field to this object, linking the Job Application object to the Position object.
3. Accept the default `Field Label` and `Field Name`, and give the field an appropriate description and help text. Note that the field is automatically set to required.

   You can limit access to this detail record based on the shared setting for the master record. You can either require users to have read and write access to the master record in order to create, edit, and delete this detail record, or you can only require read access to the master record. In this scenario, you probably want to require the more limited access.

Note: You will learn all about the Force Platform security model in *Chapter 7: Protecting Your Data*.

4. Select the second `Sharing Setting`, requiring Read/Write access of the master record, and click **Next**.

5. Accept the default security and page layout choices on the next two pages, clicking **Save and New** on the final page of the wizard.

 You want to have a master-detail relationship between the Job Application object and the Position object to be able to use Roll-up Summary Fields to aggregate information about the applications for the jobs.

6. Add a master-detail relationship from this object to the Candidate object, again including an appropriate description and help text, the more limited `Sharing Setting` as with the Positions relationship, and accepting the default security and page layout choices. Click **Save**.

Although you will not have an immediate need to use Roll-up Summary Fields from the Job Application object to the Candidate object, the master-detail relationship is still appropriate here because of the way you want the Candidate and Job Application records to interact. For the purposes of this system, you will want to delete all individual Job Application records once either the Candidate record is deleted or the Position is deleted. The Job Application record is not meaningful if either side of the many-to-many relationship is no long available.

The order in which you define the two master-detail relationships has an effect on the representation of this object in the Force Platform environment. When displaying links to a record in the Job Application object, the icon used is the icon associated with the tab of the first master-detail relationship defined for this object.

With these two steps, you have implemented a many-to-many relationship. You can add more information to this object, such as status indicators that apply to individual Job Applications, rather than an Candidate or Position – an action you will take in the next chapter.

At this time, there is no need to define a tab for Job Application since you will be able to create new Job Application records directly from either the Position or Candidate pages.

Many-to-Many Relationships at Work

Your recruiting application now has the ability to define and use many-to-many relationships. You did not load any data into the Job Application object you defined, so you can see how this object works behind the scenes to implement the relationship.

1. Click the Positions tab and select a position from the home view. Notice that the Job Applications are now shown as a related list.

2. Click **New Job Application** in the Job Applications section to bring up the page shown the following figure to add a new Job Application from the Position.

   This page is as you would have expected. No need to add an ID for the Job Application, since that is an Auto Number field, and the Position relationship is automatically included for the new application, since the page was called from a position record.

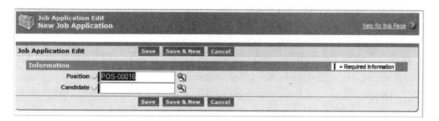

Figure 42: Adding a new Job Application junction object

3. Use the lookup button to select a Candidate for the Job Application.

   Tip: You can add fields to the lookup dialogs in the same way you modified the fields shown on the Home page by modifying the Lookup Dialogs in the Search Layouts section of an object.

4. Click **Save** to save the new Job Application record and return to the detail page for the Position record.

   Since the Job Application implements a many-to-many link between Positions and Candidates, you can also create a Job Application from a Candidate record.

5. Click the Candidates tab and select a candidate.

6. Click **New** in the Job Applications related list and associate this candidate with a particular position.

   You can add multiple positions for a candidate, or multiple candidates for a position, by using **Save and New** for the Job Applications page.

Relationships, and the functionality they provide, are one of the core pieces powering the productivity of the Force Platform. Understanding the relationships inherent in your overall data scheme helps you create more flexible applications with cleaner implementations.

Best Practices for Data Design

You have already noticed that a good data design can have a pretty significant impact on your development effort on the Force Platform. You can maximize your developer productivity for both initial implementation and ongoing maintenance work by adhering to a few best practices:

- Normalize your data into objects, just as you would for tables in a relational database. Since related objects are automatically connected in your Force Platform applications, designing your objects to keep the number of fields limited to those that are directly related to the main purpose of the object is a great approach. Just because you can add more and more fields to an object does not mean that you should. At best, you end up with large pages that present a cumbersome user interface.

- Avoid duplicating values in many records in an object. Related objects make this easy to implement, so one location, in this sample application, is represented by one, and only one, name and record. By storing a the name of the location in a single Location record, and having multiple Position records access that record, you not only reduce your storage needs, but you make it easier to both maintain data integrity for the name and to change the name, if necessary, down the road.

- Avoid copying data from one object to another. For instance, it would not make sense to have a Location field in a Position record, copying the value from the Location table. What happens when the value for that location changes in the parent record, or one or more child records, or both at once? Copying data starts out as a bad idea and gets worse, so use relationships to unique parent records to express repeated values.

- Help your users avoid duplicating data. As the previous two points highlight, duplicate values present problems. Your users may be entering duplicate records unknowingly. The autocomplete feature of search lookups can help them identify the proper related value, but you might want to consider adding logic to your applications to prevent users from accidently duplicating values.

Of course, none of these recommendations should be seen as hard and fast rules. You should use these best practices as your defaults, and take a different approach only when your particular development task requires it.

Roll-up Summary Fields

In the previous discussion on master-detail relationship, there was a rather tempting mention of a feature called Roll-up Summary Fields.

Roll-up Summary Fields, sometimes referred to as RSFs, perform different types of calculations, based on the child records in a master-detail relationship. A Roll-up Summary Field is available just like any other field, in pages, related list views and reports.

You can use Roll-up Summary Fields to obtain the following aggregates:

- COUNT - holds the number of child records in the master-detail relationship
- SUM - holds the sum of the values of the child record field indicated
- MAX - holds the maximum value of the child record field indicated
- MIN - holds the minimum value of the child record field indicated

You can also add criteria to limit the aggregation to a subset of all child records. For the first Roll-up Summary Field in your recruiting application, you only need to count the number of applicants for a particular position.

1. Select **Setup ➤ Objects ➤ Position**, and then click **New** in the Custom Fields & Relationships section to add a new field to the object.
2. Select Roll-up Summary Field as the data type and click **Next**. Remember that this data type was not enabled when you were initially adding fields for the Position record. The Force Platform Setup menu only enables this choice if the object is a parent in a master-detail relationship, a requirement for Roll-up Summary Fields.

   Also notice that the Master-Detail Relationship data type is no longer available. Since Position is a master to Job Applications, the object cannot be a child in another master-detail relationship.

3. Give the new field a Field Label of Number of Applications, and an appropriate description and help text, then click **Next** to bring up the page shown below.

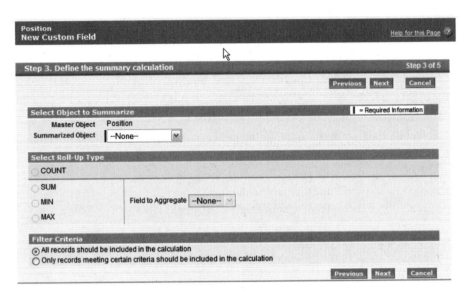

Figure 43: Defining a Roll-up Summary Field

4. Select Job Applications as the Summarized Object, the only choice available. Select COUNT as the Roll-Up Type, which does not require you to select a field to aggregate, since you are counting records. You do not need to define a filter, so click **Next**.

5. Accept the default field-level security choices and click **Next**.

6. Complete your work by clicking **Save** on the final page of the wizard.

If you go immediately to the Positions tab and select a record, you see a small hour glass next to the new Roll-up Summary Field. This indicator means that the Force Platform database is still calculating the value for the new summary – a process that takes very little time for small numbers of objects, as you have in this example, but could take a while if you add a summary field to a master with many detail records.

Even if the initial calculation takes a bit of time, keep in mind that this initial aggregation only occurs once. Subsequent modifications to child records appear with virtually no delay in the display of a Roll-up Summary Field.

The use of a Roll-up Summary Field in this particular scenario has been very simple, but through the use of selection conditions and other aggregations, you can derive quite a bit of information from your data. You will see the use of Roll-up Summary Fields to aggregate data further in subsequent chapters of this book, but for now, your initial introduction to data objects and relationships is complete.

Summary

In this chapter, you learned about one of the most powerful data-driven features of the Force Platform platform—relationships. Although you have probably been using related data objects in your development work for quite a while, the Force Platform automatically adds powerful functionality to your applications based on these relationships.

You can choose to define either lookup relationships or master-detail relationships, as well as implementing one-to-many, or many-to-many relationships.

Finally, you saw how Roll-up Summary fields can blend in aggregate information from children to the master in a master-detail relationship, all through the simple act of definition.

In the next chapter, you will learn how to use features of the Force Platform to extend the data available to users, and to insure the all-important integrity of that data.

Chapter 4

Expanding data options

In the last two chapters, you got a whirlwind introduction to the basics of creating and using data and data relationships on the Force Platform.

The Force Platform automatically handles all the basic, and some not so basic, functions required for your applications. All you had to do was to define an object, and the Force Platform platform generated a set of user interface objects, including pages for data entry, retrieval, and search, as well as links between related objects.

In this chapter, you enhance and refine these standard interfaces to help users avoid entering incorrect data values, or to derive and display relevant data from other sources. All of these refinements move your application towards the goal of greater data integrity, insuring that the data in your Force.com database is meaningful and correct.

The relationships you defined in the last chapter already began this process. A user cannot, for instance, add a job application while associating that application with an existing candidate and position, or enter a position for a location that does not exist.

You will now learn about picklists, formulas and validations, giving you a variety of strategies to help users maintain the integrity of your shared data.

 Important: If you have been following the examples in the previous chapter, your Force Platform organization should be ready for the exercises in this chapter. If you have not done the exercises, or want to start with a fresh version of the sample Recruiting application, please refer to the instructions in the Code Share project for this book. You can find information on how to access that project in *Chapter 1: Welcome to the Force Platform.*

Picklists

You have no doubt seen a picklist in action—one of those drop-down lists that provide a selection of valid values. The Force.com platform picklist data type allows you to specify the values for the picklist and displays the object in the appropriate user interface.

Picklist Usage

There are several places in your application that cry out for picklists to guide your users to correct data values.

In the Position object, these fields require only a limited set of values:

- Department - departments in Universal Containers
- Education - levels of educational attainment
- Status - progress of the position towards being filled

The Candidate object also has an opportunity for a picklist

- Education -specifies the maximum level of education for this candidate

In addition to these basic picklists, which will limit the user selection to a single value from a list of values, the Position object also contains a different type of picklist, one that limits the selection of values for a user, but allows the user to select more than one value. You can use this type of functionality for a picklist that lists all the programming languages required for a particular technical position.

Adding Picklists

As you might have noticed when defining fields in the previous chapters, the picklist option is available as a data type for fields.

1. Go to the Builder area for the Position object by clicking **Setup ➤ Create ➤ Objects ➤ Position**.
2. Click **New** in the Custom Fields & Relationships section.
3. Select `Picklist` as the data type and click **Next** to bring up the page shown, in a completed state, below.

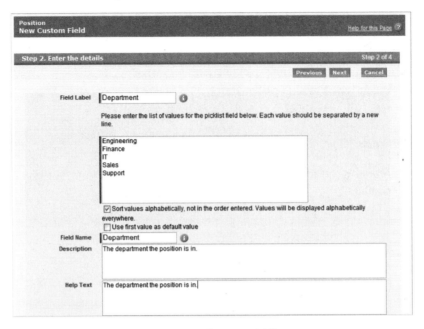

Figure 44: Defining a picklist

4. Set the `Field Label` to `Department` and add the following values in the text area, each on a separate line:

- `Engineering`
- `Finance`
- `IT`
- `Sales`
- `Support`

> **Voice of the Developer:** The values you are adding are the labels that will be displayed in your picklist. You can change these labels without affecting the stored value for individual records. For instance, if you want to change the name of the Support department to Customer Support, you simply change the value for the picklist, and the values displayed for every record also change.

5. After entering the values for the picklist in the text box, specify whether the values are displayed in alphabetical order and whether the first value is the default for the field. Select the checkbox to sort values alphabetically, since that will probably make it easier for the user to find the right department. If you do not choose to specify a default value, the field does not have a value. Later in this chapter, you learn how to create a validation to require a value for this picklist.

6. Accept the default **Field Name** of Department, give the field an appropriate description and help text, and click **Next**.
7. Accept the default field level security and click **Next**.
8. Accept the default placement in the Position Layout and click **Save & New**, since you want to add more picklists for this object.
9. Add two more picklists for the Position object with the following attributes:

Name/Label	Values	Alphabetical	Default
Educational Requirements	High school College Masters PhD Post-doc	No	No
Status	New Open Closed	No	Yes

10. After adding the picklists, click the Positions tab, and click **New** to see the newly revised appearance, as shown below.

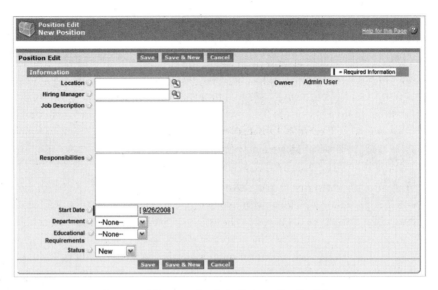

Figure 45: Your revised entry page for Position

The picklists look just as you had hoped. The Candidate object could use a picklist, but since you already understand how to use the Field Creation Wizard to make picklists, you can just follow the instructions in the Code Share project for this book to add the Education picklist to the Candidate object, since you will need that picklist to define a formula field later in this chapter. The Education picklist has the same values as the Educational Requirements picklist for the Position object.

Voice of the Developer:

You can edit picklists while the field is in production, but you should be aware of the potential implications of this action.

If you delete a picklist value, existing records with fields containing this value will be unaffected. The platform does not invalidate the data entries so that you can later decide what value should take its place in these records. You can replace the value with the **Replace** link next to a given picklist field.

If you choose to edit a pick list value, the platform will update existing records with the new value for you; however, if you have written Apex code (covered in Chapters 10 and 11) that references this value, the code will not be modified, which, depending on the implementation, can potentially cause run-time errors. For this reason, best practices suggest careful consideration of picklist values before releasing any applications into the wild.

Multi-select Picklists

There is still one more basic picklist to add to the Positions object, one that allows the user to select one or more defined values from a list. This picklist is called a multi-select picklist, and the interface for this picklist presents two columns to the user for selection of values.

1. Click **Setup ➤ Create ➤ Objects ➤ Position** and then **New** in the Custom Fields section of the page to create a new field.
2. Select `Picklist (Multi-select)` and click **Next**.
3. You can see that the first step of defining a multi-select picklist includes all the fields you used to define a picklist, with one additional field where you can indicate how many lines should be displayed in the selection list box. If you enter more values than visible lines, the list box includes a scroll bar. Enter the following values for the new picklist, along with an appropriate description and help text:

Name/Label	Values	Alphabetical	Default	# Visible Lines
Programming Languages	COBOL	No	No	9
	FORTRAN			
	.Net			
	Java			
	PHP			
	Perl			
	Python			
	Apex			

You specified nine visible lines since each of the columns used to implement this picklist also has a title.

4. Click **Next** on this page and the next, and then **Save** to add the new picklist to your page layout.
5. Select the Position tab and click **New** to show the page below.

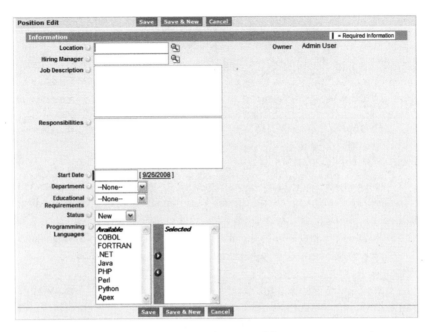

Figure 46: Next version of your Position entry page

The new picklist displays more of the built-in functionality of the Force Platform. A multi-select picklist includes two list boxes for value selection and arrow buttons to move the selections between the boxes. When a user selects more than one value, multiple values are stored in the field.

The Force Platform gives you one more choice for default picklist functionality.

Dependent Picklists

The final bit of picklist productivity is ideal for one category of use cases. Limiting value selection is a good way to guide users to proper data entry, but there are times when you might want to have one set of valid values for one situation, and a different set for another situation. The Force Platform offers dependent picklists for these scenarios.

Dependent picklists work in pairs, with the value selected in the parent picklist controlling the values shown in the child picklist. For the recruiting application's Position object, there are two places where dependent picklists work perfectly: status and salary range.

For the Status picklist, you are allowed three values: New, Open and Closed. There are a number of different reasons why a position might be closed, such the position being filled, canceled, rejected by management or pending a response on an offer. If the position is not closed, you do not want to allow the user to enter a value for this sub-status.

For the Salary picklist, each of the different departments at Universal Containers has their own set of salary levels, as well as a custom range. You want to limit the display of salary ranges to those appropriate for the position's department.

Using Dependent Picklists

With the on-demand immediacy of the Force Platform, you can quickly define these two dependent picklists.

1. Jump back to the development environment for the Position object by clicking **Setup ➤ Create ➤ Objects ➤ Position**, and then **New** to create a new field.
2. Create a new picklist with a label and name of `Sub-status` and values of `Filled`, `Canceled`, `Rejected`, and `Pending`. Include an appropriate description and help text, accept the default security and page layout placements, and click **Save & New** to create another picklist.
3. Create a picklist with a label and name of `Salary Grade`, with values of `Custom` and salary grades for each department, numbered from `100` to `400`. For instance, add salary levels of `ENG-100`, `ENG-200`, `ENG-300` and `ENG-400` for the engineering department, using the prefixes of `FIN`, `IT`, `SAL` and `SUP`. Accept the default field level security and page placement, and click **Save** to return to the main page for the Position object.

    You have your parent and child picklists—now to combine them together in a dependent relationship.

4. Click **Field Dependencies** in the Custom Fields & Relationships section.
5. Click **New** to create a new dependent picklist pair.
6. On the next page, select `Status` as the `Controlling Field`, `Sub-status` as the `Dependent Field`, and click **Continue** to bring up the next page, shown below.

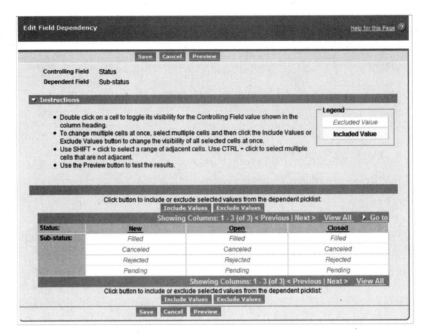

Figure 47: Defining dependent values

7. You can see that this page lists the values in the controlling picklist as column headings and the values in the dependent picklist repeated in each column. To associate values in the dependent picklist with a value in the controlling picklist, select the four values in the Closed column by dragging your mouse over them while holding down the left mouse button, and click **Include Values**.

    Selecting values for inclusion highlights their cell and changes the text from italic to bold.

8. To see how the dependent picklist works, click **Preview** to bring up the small window shown in the following figure.

    The dependent picklist remains disabled until you select the `Closed` value in the Status picklist, at which time the lower picklist enables with the selected values included.

Figure 48: Preview of dependent picklist

9. Click **Save**. You are reminded that two of the values in the controlling picklist have no dependent values specified.

10. Click **New** to define the second set of picklists. Set `Department` as the controlling picklist, `Salary Grade` as the dependent picklist, and click **Continue**. The page shows up this time with a much longer list of values, with an additional listing of the controlling values for ease of selection.

11. Pick out the four department-specific salary grade values to include for each of the values in the Department picklist. Add the Custom entry for each department to give that additional flexibility sometimes needed to hire the best people.

12. Click **Preview** to demonstrate the action for this new set of dependencies, and then **Save** to add the dependent picklist specification to your application.

 Tip: The metadata that you load at the start of the next chapter changes the page layout for Positions and Candidates to a more attractive arrangement.

The new version of the Position entry page looks like the figure below.

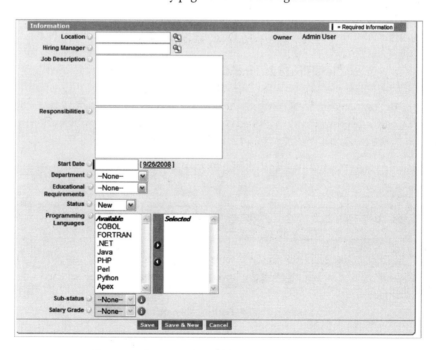

Figure 49: Next version of the Position entry page

Dependent picklists add a whole new level of utility to the standard picklist. In the next section, you will learn how you can modify the presentation of your pages based on individual records in an object.

Record Types

Dependent picklists give you a way to add flexibility to your use of picklists. You can limit the entries in one picklist based on the entry in another picklist. The Force Platform also includes a way to limit the display of picklist values based on a different criterion. This functionality, and more, is delivered through the concept of record types.

Record types allow you to define multiple user interfaces for data stored in the same object. Users are grouped in profiles, which is discussed in *Chapter 7: Protecting Your Data*, and record types are assigned to one or more profiles.

Every object in your Force Platform data store can have more than one record type. Each record type has two areas of presentation options—the ability to define a record type's page layout and to limit the values available for a picklist for that record type.

As with most Force Platform features, the best way to understand how record types are used is to simply create some. You want to use record types with the Position object—one record type with a particular page layout and picklist values for technical positions, and another for non-technical positions. Before you can create the record types, you have to create an alternative version of the existing page layout to use for non-technical positions.

1. Select **Setup ➤ Create ➤ Objects ➤ Position**.
2. Scroll down to the Page Layout section and click **New**.
3. In the next page, shown completed below, select the `Position Layout` as the `Existing Page Layout`, and give the new page layout the name of `Non-Technical Position Layout`.

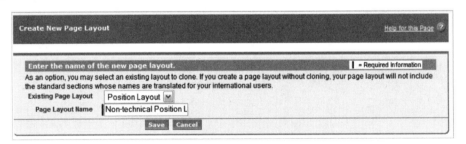

Figure 50: Non-Technical Position Layout

4. Click **Save**, which will bring up the new page layout. Click **Edit** to edit the layout and drag the field for Programming Languages from the Information section to the Position Fields box in the lower right.
5. Click on **Save** to create your new page layout and return to the page for the Position object. You are now ready to create two record types for this object.

6. Go to the Record Types section and click on **New** to bring up the page shown below.

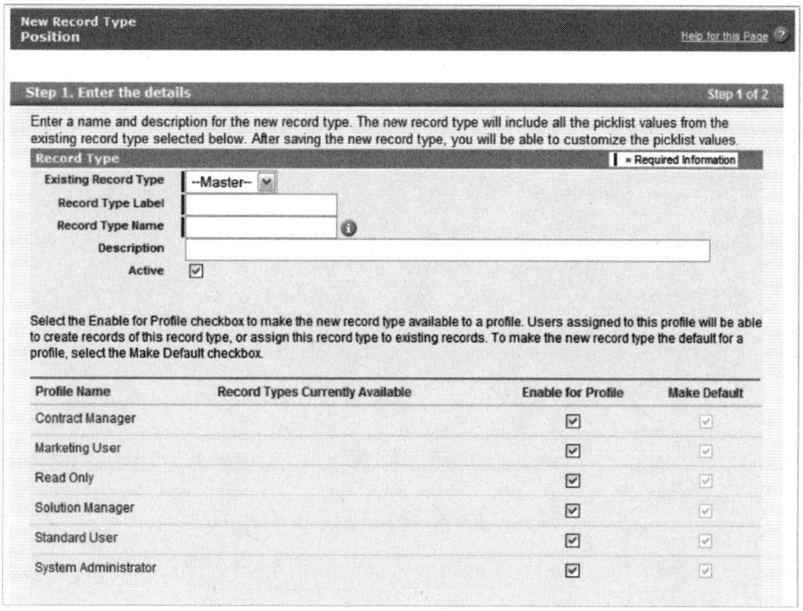

Figure 51: Defining a new record type

7. Leave the `-Master-` record type as the `Existing Record Type` and enter `Technical Position` as the `Record Type Name`, with an appropriate description. Make sure to check the `Active` checkbox.

8. Leave the `Enable for Profile` checkbox checked for each of the profiles listed. Once you enable a record type for a profile, you can designate the record type as the default record type for the profile. Although you may want to do this in your own application, you should not use this option before you see how users can choose record types later in this section. Click **Next** to bring up the page shown below.

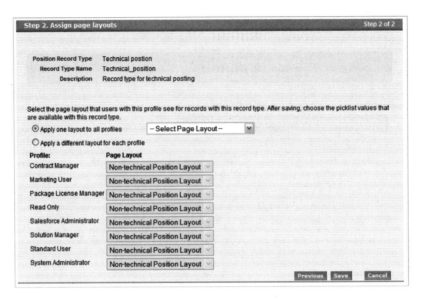

Figure 52: Assigning record types

9. Leave the `Apply one layout to all profiles` option selected, and choose the `Position Layout` as the layout. You can create a separate page layout for this record type, but the Position Layout includes all the fields that you want to include for technical positions.

10. Click **Save**.

11. Click the **Edit** link for the Department picklist to bring up the page shown in the following figure.

This page allows you to prevent certain picklist values from appearing for Position records of this record type. Technical positions will only be posted for the Engineering, IT, and Support departments, so you will want to remove the other departments from this picklist.

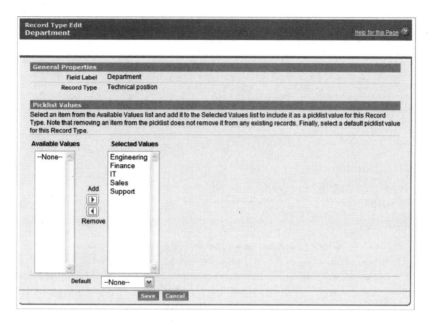

Figure 53: Defining picklist values for record type

12. Select the `Finance` and `Sales` values in the right-hand picklist and move the to the `Available Values` list box on the left.

13. Select `Engineering` as the Default in the picklist at the bottom and click **Save**.

14. Return to the Position object with the link at the top of the page and click **New** in the Record Types section to create another record type.

15. Give the new record type the name of `Non Technical Position`, an appropriate `Description`, and make the profile `Active`.

16. Enable the record type for all the profiles and click **Next**. Of course, in your own application, you may not want to make all record types available for all profiles.

17. Assign the Non-Technical Page Layout to the new record type and click **Save**.

18. Edit the Department picklist and remove the `Engineering`, `IT`, and `Support` choices from the Available Values list. Click **Save**.

Your record types are defined for your users. Time to see them in action.

19. Click on the Positions tab in your application.

20. Click on **New**, which will bring up the page shown below.

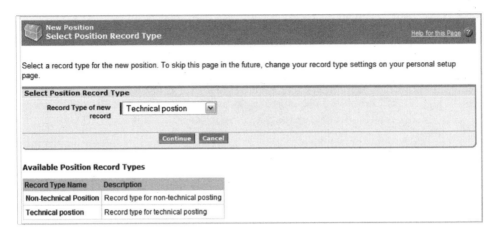

Figure 54: Selecting a record type for a new record

21. Select the `Non-Technical Position` record type and click **Continue**.

Your new page layout displays as shown below, complete with the reduced set of picklist options for the department. Since the Department picklist is the parent for the Salary Grade picklist, your record type has essentially prevented the non-relevant entries for salary from appearing for this type of Position.

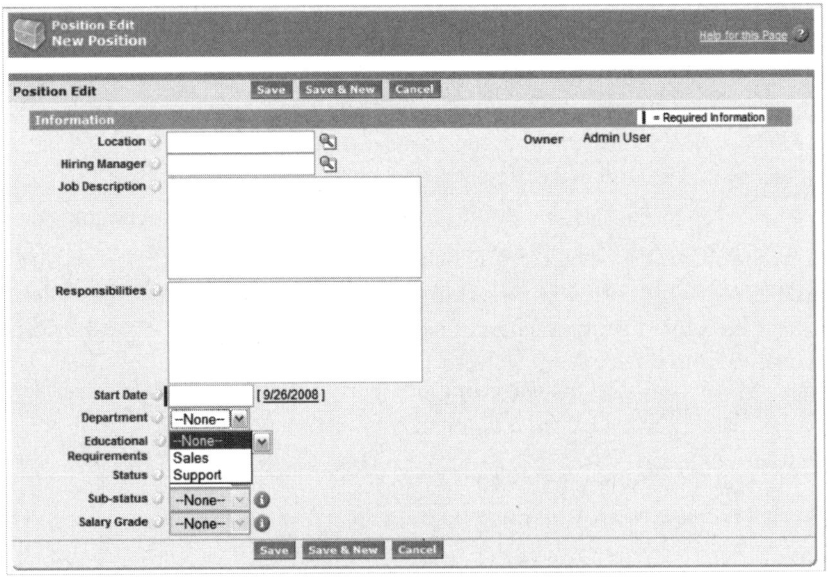

Figure 55: Record type at work

Record types provide a lot of flexibility for your Force Platform application, but some of your users might not need this flexibility since they are only creating one Position record type. You can eliminate this step by assigning a default record type for an object. The user then chooses to use the default record type at all times in the Record Type Selection option in their Personal Setup menu.

Record types and records

Keep in mind how record types actually interact with your Force Platform applications and data. When creating an object containing record types, the user can only select record types allowed for their profile. The selected record type used to create the record is then associated with that record, and used to determine the display of the detail page for the record.

However, users can view all records without concern for record types. A user can see records with a record type that they will not be allowed to assign. The user can even change the record type of a record to any available record type. The record type limitation imposed by profiles is only enforced when a record is created.

Record types and picklists can expand the interface possibilities for your objects, but always keep in mind that you are only limiting the user interface—not the actual data stored in your Force Platform object. *Chapter 7: Protecting Your Data* focuses on Force Platform security, which you use to actually define the access to data within an object.

Formula Fields

As you probably noticed when creating fields for the Location and Position objects, another data type available for Force Platform fields is the formula. A formula field is a field that is calculated from other data, frequently using Force Platform functions to massage that data.

A formula field is available on a page and for reports like any other fields; however, since the value is calculated, a formula field is automatically read-only and never appears on an insert or update page.

Formula fields provide a wide range of flexibility and functionality for your Force Platform applications. This section walks you through four uses of formula fields in your recruiting application.

Formula Fields for Calculation

Your first use of formula fields tracks the age of a Position posting with a simple calculation.

1. Return to the main page for the Position object and click **New** in the Custom Fields & Relationships section.

2. Select Formula as the data type and click **Next** to bring up the page shown below.

   You define the basic attributes of the formula field on this page.

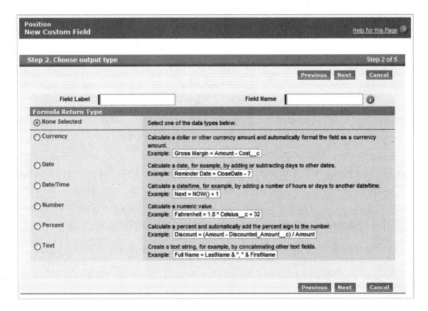

Figure 56: Defining a formula

3. Enter Days Since Posting in the Field Label field and select Number as the return type for the formula since this formula returns the number of days since the position was posted. Set the number of Decimal Places to 0 and click **Next**.

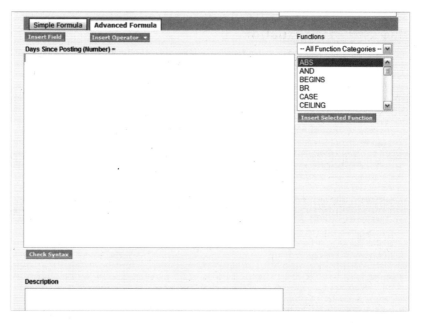

Figure 57: Advanced formula editor

4. Click the Advanced Formula tab to show the page above.

There are four buttons and pick lists that can help you build formulas: `Insert Field Type`, `Insert Operator`, `Functions` and `Insert Selected Function`. The `Insert Field Type` picklist contains all the objects whose fields you can use in this formula. The objects whose name is preceded by a dollar sign ($) are system objects, while the other objects are related to the current object.

Your selection in this first picklist controls the selections shown in the `Insert Field` picklist. When you select a field in the rightmost picklist, the Formula Editor automatically places the name of that field into the Formula text area.

`Insert Operator` lets you insert a logical operator into the Formula text area in the same way.

The `Functions` picklists give you access to all native Force Platform functions. The top picklist allows you to display only a certain type of function in the lower picklist. Once you select a function in the lower picklist, the syntax for the function appears below the picklist, as well as a link to the section of the on-line help, which gives more help for the function. Once you find the right function, the `Insert Selected Function` does exactly what it says.

5. Select the TODAY() function in the function list box and click Insert Selected Function.

6. Click Insert Operation to insert the subtraction operation (-) after the TODAY() function.

7. Insert the DATEVALUE() function, needed to convert the CreatedDate field from a datetime field to a date field, to perform the calculation.

8. Highlight the text expression in the DATEVALUE(expression) string and use the Insert Field picklist to insert the CreatedDate field into the formula.

9. Click **Check Syntax** to verify that you have not made any syntax errors, add an appropriate description and help text, and click **Next**.

10. Accept the default field level security settings and notice that the Read-Only checkbox is automatically selected for a formula field.

11. Click **Next** and accept the placement on the Position page by clicking **Save**.

12. Click the Positions tab and select an existing position to display the results of your work, as shown below.

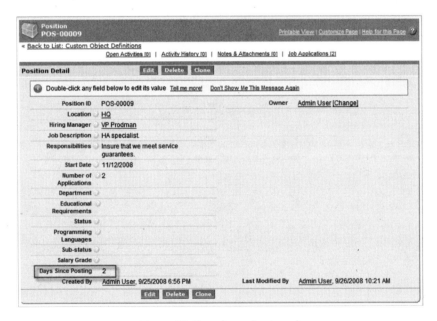

Figure 58: Your formula at work

You can easily imagine the usefulness of this formula in future reports. You can even think of a potential problem here. A more useful time span is the number of days since a job was actually opened for applications—a modification you make possible using workflow in the next chapter.

Formula Fields for Related Object Display

Another common use for formula fields is the ability to access fields in related objects for display on a page. The next formula field is an example of this type of use.

1. Return to the main development page for the Position object and click **New** to create another new field.
2. Select `Formula` as the `Field Type` and click **Next**.
3. Set the `Field Label` to `Location City/State/Country` with a return type of `Text`. Click **Next**.
4. Select `Location>` (to bring up another picklist with fields in the Location object) in the `Select Field Type` picklist and `City` in the `Insert Field` picklist. The right arrow indicates that an entry is for a related object, and selecting that entry will bring up another picklist to the right of the current list. Notice that the related field is inserted with the object name acting as a qualifier for the field.
5. Click `Insert Operator` and insert the `&` operator for concatenation.
6. Type a comma and a space in single quotes (`', '`) into the text area, and insert a concatenation operator again.
7. Insert the `State/Province` field into the formula, then a concatenation operator, followed by a space, a dash, a space in single quotes (`' - '`) and another concatenation operator.
8. Insert the `Country` field from the Location object into the formula and click **Next**.

   Although you didn't check the syntax, the formula editor prevents you from moving to the next field if your formula does have a syntax error.

9. Give the formula field an appropriate description and help text, accept the default field level security and layout placement, and click **Save**. Notice that the default layout placement puts the new field on the page layouts for both record types.
10. You probably want to show this information next to the relationship field for Location, which is where the new formula has been placed on the edited page layout shown below.

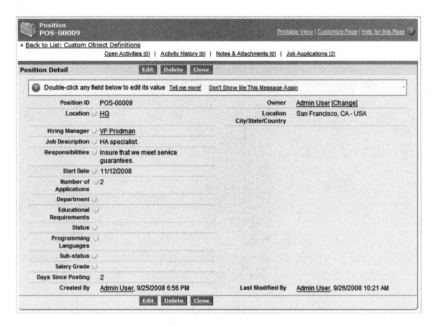

Figure 59: Formula for concatenated values

Formula Fields for Integration

As you saw in the previous example, formula fields can be used for more than just calculation. Some of the formula functions are ideal for making information from other Web sources easily available from a Force Platform page.

1. Return to the development environment and go to the Location object this time.
2. Create a new formula field for the object. Enter `Location Map` for the `Field Label` with a `Return Type` of `Text`. Click **Next**.
3. Select the `HYPERLINK()` formula. Highlight the `URL parameter` and replace it with `'http://'`, the concatenation operator `&`, and then the `Location Map URL` field from the Location object. Remember, the URL field does not store the `http://` prefix, although it displays the value with that prefix on the detail page.
4. Highlight the `friendly_name` parameter and replace it with the `Location Name` field, which shows as the `Name` field. Delete the optional final parameter.
5. Enter an appropriate description and help text, and click **Next**. Accept the default security and layout placement on the next two pages and click **Save**.
6. Click the Location tab and select a location. Click the `Location Map` link to open a Google Map in another tab or window, as shown below.

Figure 60: Google Maps in your Force Platform app

You can also add the new formula field to the Mini-Page Layout to make the Google Map available from a Position detail field, a related list or the recent items list in the left hand panel.

You can use other formula field functions to integrate other types of data. For instance, use a URL to call a Google Chart, passing the data from the chart in the URL, and display the returned image by using the IMAGE function instead of the URL function.

Formula Fields for Data Realization

The last use of a formula field utilizes a number of functions to introduce a new piece of data to an object. As you know, there is both a picklist for educational requirements on each Position record and a picklist for educational attainment on each Candidate record. It is useful to understand how a Candidate's education matched up with the requirements for a Position as part of the Job Application record.

This formula field uses a few different functions. You can enter the formula for the field with the help of the Formula Editor or just load the new field with the script file Candidate_Qualified.txt, available in the Code Share project for this book. The name of the field in the Job Application object is Candidate Qualified, with a question mark following as part of the label.

The completed formula for the field is as follows:

```
IF
  (CASE( Position__r.Educational_Requirements__c  , "High School", 1,

    "College", 2, "Masters", 3,
    "PhD", 4, "Post-doc", 5, 0)>
  CASE( Candidate__r.Education__c , "High School", 1,
    "College",2, "Masters, 3,
    "PhD", 4, "Post-doc", 5, 0)),
  "Not Qualified", "Qualified")
```

The formula includes two Force Platform functions: CASE and IF. The CASE function translates the education picklist into a number for the Candidate and the Position. The CASE function starts with an expression, in this case a field, to evaluate, and follows that with a list of value pairs for possible choices, ending with a default value.

The IF function starts with a logical test that evaluates to either TRUE or FALSE – in this formula, whether the Candidate has the appropriate academic qualifications. The logical test is followed by a value to return if the test is true (Not Qualified), and then a value to return if the test is false (Qualified).

Once the field is added to the Job Application record, you can immediately see it in action, as shown below.

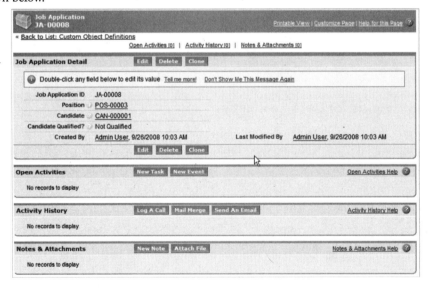

Figure 61: Formula field result from CASE statement

Caution: If you ran the upgrade script that added the Education picklist to the Candidate record earlier in this chapter, you can define this formula, although the results will not be very interesting, since there are no values for either this picklist or the Educational Requirements picklist in the Position object. You can get everything you need by performing the required upgrade process at the start of the next chapter, which will add this formula as well as a modified page layout for the Position and Candidate objects. This initialization process also adds values for the new fields you created in this chapter, which makes the results of this comparison function more meaningful

This brief overview of formulas has introduced you to formulas and some of the built-in functions of the Force Platform. You can also use these functions when you define validation rules on incoming data.

Validation Rules

In this chapter, you have learned about ways to insure the integrity of your all-important data. You can achieve this goal by limiting the values available for entry by a user, either with picklists or relationships, or by eliminating the need for users to enter data by creating the data with a formula field. This last section gives you one more tool for enforcement: validation rules.

Validation rules are defined in much the same way as formulas, with access to the same helpers and functions. But a validation rule works in a more specific way:

- Uses an `Error Condition Formula` that evaluates to either TRUE or FALSE
- Prevents the user data action that spawned the validation if the formula evaluates to FALSE
- Displays a custom error message for the user, either at the top of the page or next to a specified field, in the case of a false condition

Validation rules are pretty straightforward, so defining one teaches you enough to define many more. The following validation rule makes sure that a Position record always has a value for the Education Requirements picklist.

1. Go to the development page for the Position record. Click **New** in the Validation rules section to bring up the page shown below.

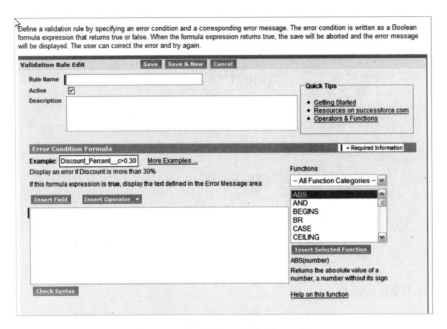

Define a validation rule by specifying an error condition and a corresponding error message. The error condition is written as a Boolean formula expression that returns true or false. When the formula expression returns true, the save will be aborted and the error message will be displayed. The user can correct the error and try again.

Figure 62: Defining validation rules

2. Enter `Required education specification` for the `Rule Name` and give the rule an informative description.

3. Select the `ISPICKVAL` function, which compares the value in a picklist with a literal, and click **Insert Selected Function**.

4. Highlight the `picklist_field` in the function and click **Insert Field** to bring up the dialog box to select a field.

5. Select the `Educational Requirements` field and click **Insert**. Enter "" for the literal text.

6. Enter `You must specify an educational requirement for this position` as the error message, select the `Field` choice for error location, and `Educational Requirements` as the `Field`. Click **Save**.

7. Go to the Positions page, edit a record to change any value and attempt to save the record. Since the values for the Educational Requirements picklist have not been populated, you will see your validation in immediate action, as shown below.

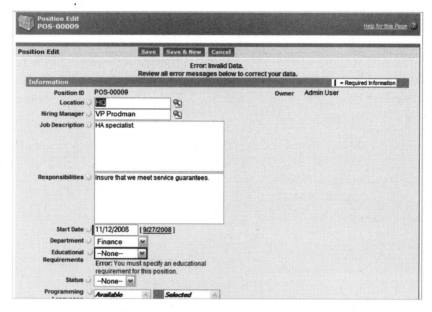

Figure 63: Your validation rule in action

Note that the validation is executed whenever a user attempts to insert or change a record. Existing records are not checked to see if they pass any new validation checks. This implementation presents a caution as well as some flexibility. If you have a validation that you absolutely require for all data, take care to implement it before data is added to the object. Conversely, if you do not want to force validation for some records, you can always make a validation rule inactive on the detail page for the validation rule.

An attempted save of a record can result in more than one validation error, in which case all errors display.

Summary

The information you extract from your data is only as good as the quality of that data. Picklists limit the values a user can enter for a particular field to prevent invalid data entry.

Formula fields can be used to calculate values from existing data, removing the possibility of user error. Formula fields can also be used to display fields from related objects and to integrate information from other sources.

Validation rules, when active, guarantee that data entered adheres to specified guidelines.

These three options give you the ability to quickly and productively maintain data integrity for all users. In the next chapter, you learn about one of the greatest productivity features on the Force Platform—the ability to define and use workflows and approval processes.

Chapter 5

Workflow and Approvals

In this chapter ...

- Workflows
- Approvals
- Summary

As you have already seen, the Force Platform development environment can really boost your productivity by automatically implementing functionality you need in your applications. One of the strongest examples of this type of productivity benefit is provided by workflows and approvals.

Workflows allow you to implement automated actions, based on changes in your Force Platform data. You can specify a number of different actions, and limit the execution of those actions on conditions defined by the workflow.

In the real world, many business processes follow a standard set of steps. Based on the business conditions associated with an event, Force Platform workflow gives you the ability to define specific actions to be executed in response to changes in data under specific conditions, eliminating the need for additional actions by users, as well as the possibility of errors caused by incorrect or missing actions.

In order for the entire process to execute efficiently, these processes need a 'minder'—someone or something to perform an action once a step is complete, and to trigger the next step.

Force Platform approvals are used to implement business processes involving human interaction on the Force Platform.. With Force Platform approvals, you can easily define a whole series of steps and actions to be taken at each step. Each step is triggered by the successful completion of the previous step. Each participant in the approval process can eithergrant the approval, moving the process to the next step, or reject the approval, which typically prevents the approval from continuing to the next step. You can also define actions to automatically occur once an approval process is completed, with either an overall approval or rejection.

In addition to implementing the rules and actions that make up the approval process, the Force Platform automatically monitors the process and proactively informs participants of their pending role in the process.

Workflows can significantly reduce the overall work of developing an application by simply adding standard actions to built-in data operations. Approvals can be used to create virtually complete applications, or to dramatically improve the efficiency of a business process. By the end of this chapter, you will understand the power of workflows and approvals, and probably be thinking of ways these capabilities can be used in your organization.

Important:

If you have been following the examples in the previous chapter, your Force Platform organization should be ready for the exercises in this chapter. If you have not done the exercises, or want to start with a fresh version of the sample Recruiting application, please refer to the instructions in the Code Share project for this book. You can find information on how to access that project in *Chapter 1: Welcome to the Force Platform*. In addition, the project contains instructions on how to update your organization with changes required for this chapter. For this chapter, those changes will include modifying the appearance of the Candidate and Position page layouts. The remainder of this book will use these enhanced page layouts in subsequent illustrations.

Workflows

On the Force Platform platform, workflows are associated with particular Force Platform objects. The diagram below presents the anatomy of a workflow.

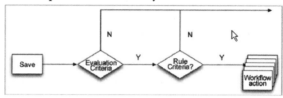

Figure 64: Steps in a workflow

Workflow processing is triggered by a user saving a record with a workflow action assigned to it. The Force Platform workflow engine evaluates whether this particular data change should trigger the workflow action. If the save action is appropriate, the workflow engine checks to make sure that this particular record meets the criteria described for the workflow rule. If the record meets the criteria established for the workflow, one or more actions are performed.

There are four types of workflow actions available:

- Task - an action assigned to a user or a role. Every task has a subject, a due date, which can be a specific date or a relative date, a status and a priority. You can also include comments on the task record.
- Email alert - sends an email message, based on a template, to a specified email address. The email can include data from the record spawning the email.
- Field update - updates another field on a Force Platform record. Field updates are part of the same transaction as the Save action spawning them.
- Outbound message - sends data to an external endpoint. Outbound messages are handled by a separate Force Platform service. If delivery of an outbound message fails, the service continues to retry the delivery for 24 hours. Outbound messaging is a powerful feature used to coordinate data updates of Force Platform data with external data stores.

As with the other Force Platform capabilities you have seen in this book, the best way to learn about workflows is to create some.

A Simple Workflow for Alerts

The first basic workflow you create familiarizes you with the process. This workflow sends an email message to the hiring manager for a position whenever anyone applies for that position.

1. Begin the definition of a workflow by clicking **Setup ➤ Create ➤ Workflow & Approvals ➤ Workflow Rules**. Click **Continue** to proceed beyond the introductory page, and then click **New Rule** to begin the definition process.

2. Select the Position object and click **Next**, which will bring up the page shown, in its completed form, in the figure below.

   You want to have an email alert sent whenever a new Job Application comes in, so why are you entering the workflow rule on the Position object? The reason you want to use the Position object is so you can direct the email to the Hiring Manager, who is identified on a field in the Position record.

   Remember, the Number of Applicants field is a Rollup Summary Field on the Positions record, and this field is updated each time a Job Application record is added or deleted for a position. These changes can trigger a workflow on the Position record.

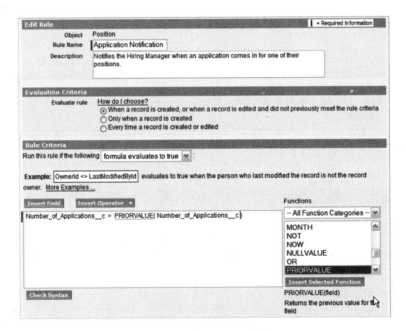

Figure 65: Defining a workflow

3. Enter `Application Notification` for the **Rule Name,** and give the rule a description of `Notifies the Hiring Manager when an application comes in for one of their positions`.

4. Set the **Evaluation Criteria** to `Every time a record is created or edited`.

You can set the `Rule Criteria` to limit when a workflow is fired. Remember that the Number of Applications Rollup Summary Field is updated every time a Job Application record is added or deleted. You do not want to send an email alert when a Job Application is deleted, so you can use the formula option to specify a Rule Criteria to handle this scenario.

5. Change the **Rule Criteria** to `formula evaluates to true`. Enter the following formula into the text area by clicking **Insert Field, Insert Operator, Insert Selected Function** and then highlighting the argument for the `PRIORVALUE()` function and **Insert Field** again to produce the following code:

```
Number_of_Applications__c >
PRIORVALUE(Number_of_Applications__c)
```

This function checks to make sure the Rollup Summary Field is incrementing, indicating a new application, rather than decrementing from an application being deleted. The formula also prevents the workflow from being triggered by changes to any other field in the Position record.

6. Click **Save and Next** to save the workflow rule and bring up the page shown below.

You have defined a workflow rule, indicated when the rule is evaluated, and specified criteria that limit when the workflow actions associated with the rule are taken.

Your next task is to define the workflow actions to be taken when the workflow is triggered.

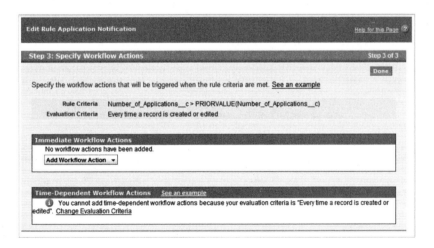

Figure 66: A workflow defined

7. Click **New Email** to bring up the email alert definition page shown in the following figure.

The list of available workflow actions includes creation of a new task, email, field update or outbound message, and the option to assign an existing action to the workflow.

 Voice of the Developer: Workflow actions exists separately from use in any workflow, so you can execute the same action from multiple workflows. This reuse can help to standardize your actions as well as reduce ongoing maintenance overhead, should you want to change a particular action that is used in more than one workflow.

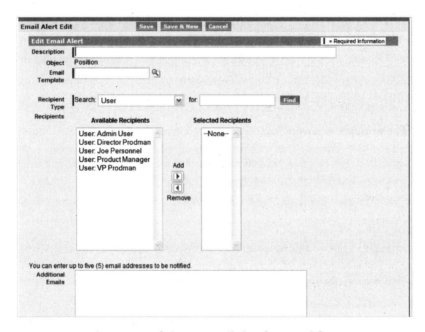

Figure 67: Defining an email alert for a workflow

8. Give the new alert a description of `Notifies Hiring Manager of job application`.

9. Select an email template of `Application Notification`. This email template was loaded into your organization at the start of this chapter. The email includes data from the Position record.

10. Select `Related User` for the **Recipient Type**, causing Hiring Manager and Last Modified By options to appear in the Available Recipients picklist. Add the `Hiring Manager` to the Selected Recipients picklist.

You have quite a bit of flexibility in terms of the recipient of this email alert. You can specify that the email goes to the owner of the record, the people in a particular role or public group (security designations you will learn about in *Chapter 7: Protecting Your Data*), or an email field on the record. You can choose multiple email addresses from as many of these categories as you like, or even include up to five specific email addresses entered in the text box at the bottom of the page.

11. Click **Save** to return to the Workflow Actions page. Click **Done** to go to the detail page for the workflow rule, which contains a summary of the workflow.
12. Click **Activate** to activate this workflow.

    Forgetting to click `Activate` is one of the most common errors in creating and using workflows. The ability to activate and de-activate workflows allows you to turn off a workflow if you do not need or want the workflow actions to execute, such as when you are doing a bulk data load.

     Note: There may be some bulk actions which will not cause workflow rules to be fired. Check the online documentation for the latest list of these exception cases.

    The workflow is now in operation.

13. Click the Positions tab and select a position. Add a new Job Application for a position.
14. Check the email assigned to the owner of the Position record to see the results of the workflow rule.

Implementing this type of automatic notification is pretty easy on the Force Platform platform. But your initial pass at this functionality may not be appropriate for all position owners. In the next section, you modify the new workflow to adapt to the preferences of your user community.

Modifying the Simple Workflow

The good news is that the Hiring Manager for a position now gets an email every time someone applies for one of their open positions. The bad news is that some of these owners actually don't want to be bothered every single time one person applies for what may be a very popular position.

You can accommodate these owners with a simple change to the Position record, coupled with a modification of the Evaluation Conditions for the workflow.

1. Return to the Position object by clicking **Setup ➤ Create ➤ Objects** and then the **Edit** link on the Position object.

2. Add a new **Checkbox** field. Give the field a **Field Label** of Notify Hiring Manager of application, a default value of Checked and a **Field Name** of Notification, rather than the default field name as usual, as well as an appropriate description and help text.

3. On the next page, accept the default security and click **Save**, accept the default layout option on the next page and click **Save**.

   Finally, modify the formula, taking this new option into account. Why modify the formula? For a workflow, you can have either multiple criteria or a single formula. As you will see, though, you can create a formula that checks for multiple criteria.

4. Go to edit the workflow you just created by clicking **Workflows & Approvals ➤ Workflow Rules** and the **Edit** link for the workflow rule. Modify the formula to the following code:

```
( Number_of_Applications__c >
PRIORVALUE(Number_of_Applications__c)
    && Notification__c
```

   The && is used to link together required conditions, similar to using AND in other languages.

5. Click **Save** to save your changes.

6. Go to the Positions tab and select a Position.

7. Check the notifications checkbox and add a new application. Check the email for the Hiring Manager.

8. Uncheck the notifications checkbox and add a new application. Check the email to make sure that no notification is sent.

9. Recheck the notifications checkbox and delete an application. Check the email to make sure no notification is sent.

The changes you made in your Force Platform object and your workflow provide an example of one of the great virtues of the Force Platform environment. Since changes you make to your applications can be instantly available to your users, you can make these two small modifications in near real time. This velocity has the effect of allowing you to make development a truly interactive and iterative process, involving users to get their signoff as you shape and hone their applications.

Workflow Field Updates

The previous workflow example caused an email alert to be sent in response to a data action. Another option for Force Platform workflows is the ability to actually make changes to data in Force Platform objects.

The previous workflow also gave hiring managers the option to be notified when anyone applied for a position. Frequently, though, managers are looking to hire someone when there is too much work for existing staff to complete, so they don't want to be bothered with a lot of superfluous emails.

They also don't want to be bothered with an overlong process of screening too many applicants, so senior management at Universal Containers has decided that as soon as a position receives 20 applications, the posting will be closed to prevent spending too much time culling out applicants.

1. Go to the **Workflow & Approvals** section of the left hand panel, click **Workflow Rules** and then **New Rule** to begin defining this workflow.
2. Select the Position object as the source of the workflow action and click **Next**.
3. Give the new rule a **Name** of `Close position` and an appropriate description. Leave the default **Evaluation Criteria**. Set the **Rule Criteria** to `Number of Applicants equals 20`.

    Tip: Of course, you can add another field to the Position record to accept the number of applications allowed for that position and compare the Rollup Summary Field to that value, making the process more dynamic.

   As soon as the number of applicants reaches 20, the position is closed and no longer open for new applicants.

4. Click **Save and Next** to define workflow actions.
5. Add a new **Email Workflow Action** with a description of `Position Closed alert`, an **Email Template** of `Position Closed`, and the Related User of Hiring Manager as the recipient. Click **Save**.
6. Click **New Field Update** to begin adding another workflow action for this workflow rule.
7. On the next page, give the Field Update a **Name** of `Close out position`, an appropriate description, and select the `Status` field, changing the page to look like the page below when you select the Closed value.

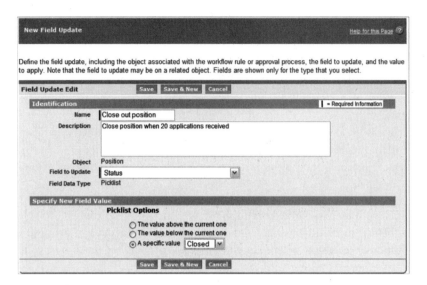

Figure 68: Defining a field update for a workflow

8. Click **Save** to complete the workflow action definition.
9. Click **Done** and then **Activate** to finish off the workflow rule definition.

You can add a number of job applications for a particular position to see this workflow at work.

Adding this workflow has shown you that workflows can take multiple different actions in response to the same workflow rule. Before leaving this extremely brief overview of workflows, you will learn about the use of a time-based workflow to address some specific use cases.

Timed Workflows

When you were creating workflow actions for the previous workflows, you probably noticed that the action entry page, as shown in the earlier figure, allows for two types of workflow actions – immediate workflow actions, which you have been using up until now, and time-dependent workflow actions.

Time-dependent workflow actions give you the ability to set up a workflow action to occur at some specific point in the future. You can quickly imagine some good user scenarios for this type of action—checking on customer follow-up actions, automatically sending reminder notices or, in this case, alerting a hiring manager that their position was posted two weeks ago and is still open.

You implement this last scenario in the final workflow example in this chapter. The specific workflow notifies the hiring manager for the position two weeks after the position is posted.

1. Return to the **Workflow Rules** page and click **New Rule**.
2. Select the Position object and click **Next**.
3. Give the new rule a **Rule Name** of 14 Days Later since posting and an appropriate description. Leave the initial choice for when to evaluate criteria.
4. Add a **Rule Criteria** to the rule, requiring Status equals Open, and click **Save and Next**.

   This rule makes sense—you want the workflow action to only take place two weeks after a Position is posted and its status is changed from New to Open, not after it is first added as a record.

5. Click **Add Time Trigger** in the lower section of the **Edit Workflow Rule** page to bring up the page shown below.

   You have the option of setting a time value in either days or hours, before or after an event, and choosing either the date the rule was triggered or any standard date fields on the object. On the Position object, you can see the standard date fields of Created Date and Last Modified Date, as well as the custom Start Date field. You can use any Date field on the object to trigger the rule as a potential starting point for the time measurement.

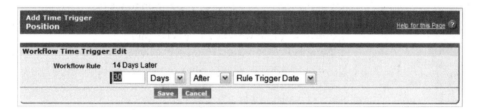

Figure 69: Defining a time-based workflow

6. Enter 14 for the number of days, and leave the default choices of After and Rule Trigger Date. Click **Save** to return to the Edit Workflow page.

   You can now add workflow actions to the time-based workflow rule.

7. Click **Add Email**. Give the new Workflow Alert a description of Two-week notice and use the Two-week notice email template. Send the email to the **Related User** of Hiring Manager and click **Save**.
8. Click **Done** to save the action.
9. Click **Activate** to put the rule into play.

   This time you are prompted to assign a default user for the workflow rule. You have to do this in case the user who is normally the 'owner' of the workflow process is no longer around when the workflow action is actually taken.

10. Assign the Admin User user as the default user and click **Save**.

11. Add a new Position and set the Status to Open. Click **Save** to save the record.

There you go—you fired off a time-based workflow. But how do you know the workflow fired and, more importantly, how can you monitor scheduled time-based workflows?

The answer to both of these questions lies in the Administration Setup area of the **Setup** menu, specifically the **Time-Based Workflow** choice under the **Monitoring** area. You can enter limiting criteria, if you wish, on this page, and then click **Search** to display results, as shown in below.

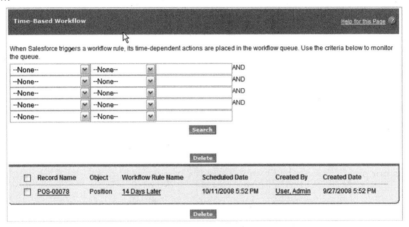

Figure 70: Monitoring workflow results

 Tip: If you didn't set the Status for the new Position to Open, the timed workflow would not have been scheduled, since the record did not pass the evaluation criteria.

Time-based workflows are quite sophisticated in their evaluation and scheduling. If any values in a record associated with a time-based workflow change, that workflow entry rule and criteria are re-evaluated to insure that the time-based workflow should still be evaluated. For instance, in this scenario, an email alert is scheduled for two weeks from the date of posting. If the status of that position is changed to Closed before those two weeks have elapsed, the workflow is automatically deleted from the workflow queue.

If a timed workflow is based on a date field, and the value of that date field changes, the timed workflow is rescheduled for the correct time. If the new date is in the past, the workflow action is immediately placed in the workflow queue.

If you deactivate a time-based workflow, pending actions are not deleted; however, workflow entry rules are evaluated when any pending workflow actions are scheduled to be initiated. If you deactivate a time-based workflow rule, you disable the evaluation of any conditions associated with that rule, meaning pending actions are automatically executed, regardless of the state of the triggering object at the time of execution. You can use the timed workflow monitoring tool to clean up any pending alerts when you deactivate the rule.

Approvals

Force Platform's approval process gives you the ability to implement a chain of actions to createa single business process, with each step of the overall process performed by different people. All Force Platform approvals can include the following automatic features:

- Automatic tracking of the progress of the approval
- Predefined approval and rejection actions for each option at each step of the process
- Flexible routing paths allowing you to implement an incredibly wide range of processes

Approvals deliver a very high level of built-in functionality while still providing configurable flexibility to address your own business needs. These two aspects of approvals suggest that you spend some time thinking about your approval process. It is much easier to design and implement an approval properly the first time than to go back and try to fix up an approval that was not properly thought through from the beginning.

Designing Your First Approval

For every approval process, you have to initially plan out the steps of the process and its accompanying actions. Before you can begin your first design process, you have to understand a few things about how an approval works:

- You must designate a standard email template for proactively informing all parties involved in the approval process. The template is used to notify every person involved in the process to approve or reject the request.
- Each step in the process gives you the option of assigning workflow actions for the approval or rejection of each step in the process
- The progress of an approval is tracked in a separate section of the detail page for the record being approved. But like all sections in a detail page, you can modify the page layout to prevent its display.

Your first approval process is used to handle approval of posted positions. Universal Containers allows managers to add positions, but these positions have to be approved by management before they can be officially posted. This business process can be more efficient and better managed through implementation as a Force Platform approval process.

Implementing Your First Approval

The process of creating an approval shares some steps with the process of creating a workflow, but the more flexible approval process requires additional configuration.

1. Start the process by clicking **Setup ➤ Workflow & Approvals ➤ Approval Processes**. This action brings up the page as shown below.

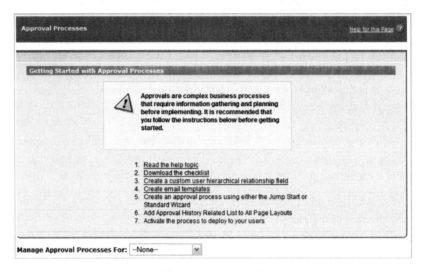

Figure 71: Defining an approval - first page

2. Select the `Position` object, click **Create New Approval Process** and select `Use Standard Setup Wizard`.

   The Jump Start Wizard reduces the amount of information you have to enter to create an approval process, but defaults are used in many places. As a developer, the task of creating a basc approval process, like this one, is not very difficult. Opt for a few more parameters to enter to gain greater control and understanding of the eventual approval process.

3. Set the `Process Name` to `Approve position posting` and give the approval an appropriate description. Click **Next**.

   The next page looks familiar from the workflow wizard, where you are allowed to set an entry condition for the workflow step. You can either use one or more conditions, or create a single formula to combine multiple steps. For this particular entry condition, you can simply use a filter on the Hiring Manager field, use the `not equal to` operator, and leave the right side of the condition blank to insure that a Hiring Manager has been defined for the Position.

4. Click **Next** to bring up the page shown in the following figure.

This page only requests two pieces of information, but this data is crucial to understanding how approvals work.

The first section asks for an automated approver designation. You can automatically assign the approver for each step in the approval based on a hierarchical relationship between users. There is a standard hierarchical field, Manager, on the User record, which you can set as the default. You could also add a custom field on the User record to denote an alternate hierarchy and use that as the default. For instance, if the current approver is the Hiring Manager, the default approver of the next step in this process is the Manager of the Hiring Manager. You can override this default as you define each step and you do not have to accept either of these defaults. If a field on the User record can act as an intelligent default for multiple steps, you can improve your productivity by designating it here.

For this first approval, you will designate a specific related user as the recipient of the approval step, which will override this Manager designation, but the automatic approver designation will come in handy in the next section.

The second option illuminates one aspect of how approvals work. You do not want any changes in the record being approved while an approval is being processed. To enforce this restriction, the Force Platform platform automatically locks the record from the beginning of the approval until the process ends with either an approval or rejection.

The second option allows you to specify whether the record is locked to everyone but an administrator, or whether the current approver can also edit the record. When you finish defining the approval, you see how the locking process is implemented.

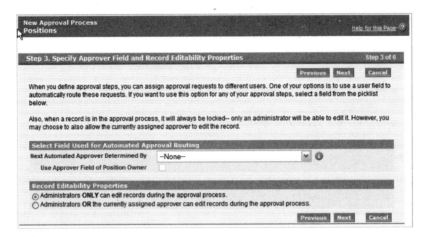

Figure 72: Defining default approver and locking

5. Leave the default of – None – field for the **Automated Approver** and accept the second default of Administrator ONLY. Click **Next**.

6. On the next page, select the Position approval waiting email template. This email template is sent to each approver when the approval is sent on to them. Click **Next** to bring up the page shown below.

   This page lets you modify the information that an approver sees on the actual page they use to approve or reject an approval.

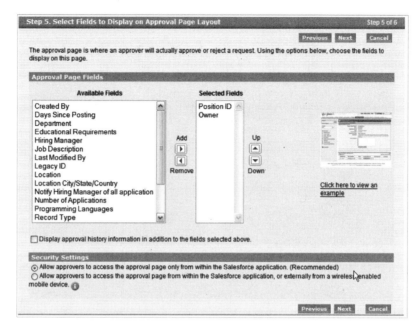

Figure 73: Adding fields to the approver page

7. Add `Job Description` and `Responsibilities` to the Selected Fields picklist.

   You can show the approval history on the approval page. This option is handy since approvers can add comments when they grant the approval, and the comments can be relevant to subsequent approvers.

8. Check the box below the picklists to display the approval history on the approval page.

   The bottom section of the page gives you the option of allowing approvals and rejections from a mobile device as well as a standard approval page in the Force Platform environment.

9. Use the default of not allowing mobile approvals and click **Next**.

   The final page lets you specify who can submit an approval. The default of the Record Owner works for your first approval, but keep in mind that you can select any other users, public groups or roles for this capability.

   There are two useful checkboxes towards the bottom section of this page. The first allows you to include a related list tracking the progress of the approval to all Position page layouts. The second specifies that the approval submitter has the option to recall an approval, an option that can remove the consequences of an accidental submission.

10. Check both of the checkboxes towards the bottom of the page.

11. Click **Save** to complete the definition of your first approval. Select the middle choice on the next page, `No, I'll do this later, take me to the approval process detail page . .`, and click **Go** to see the results of your work shown partially in the figure below.

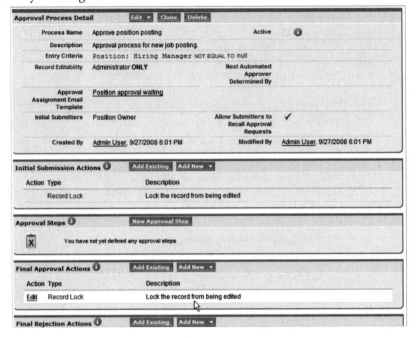

Figure 74: Approval summary

This page presents a summary of the approval process you just defined. Notice there are five areas where you can add to the approval process – initial submission actions, an area to add new approval steps, final approval and final rejection actions, and a section to add actions taken if the approval is recalled..

The action sections have default actions indicated. The approval process locks the record being approved at the start of the approval process. If the record is approved, the lock, by default, remains in place since you typically do not want to change the data in a record once that record has been approved with certain values. If the approval is rejected, the record is unlocked. Although you cannot remove any of these locking actions, you can change the final actions from setting a lock to unlocking a record. You can also add additional actions in any of these sections to supplement the operation of the approval process.

Now that the approval process is set up, you can add steps to the overall process.

1. Click **New Approval Step** in the Approval Steps section of the page.
2. Give this approval step a **Name** of Manager Approval and an appropriate description. Click **Next**.
3. On the next page, leave the default of All records should enter this step. Click **Next**.

On the next page, you can specify how the approver for this step is set. You can automatically assign the step to the user field you selected for the entire approval process, in this case the Manager field, automatically assign the step to another User, Queue or Role, or let the user designate the next approver.

 Tip: You can assign approval steps to a queue, which can be consumed by different users who have access to the queue.

4. Chose Automatically assign to approver(s) and then select Related User and Hiring Manager for the user. Click **Save**.

Dynamic approval routing

In the previous step, you assigned the approval to a related user indicated by the Hiring Manager field. In this case, the value for the Hiring Manager field was assigned by the person who created the record for the position. But the ability to use a field value to identify an approver opens the door to dynamic routing of approvals.

As an example, say you wanted to assign three interviews as three approval steps. You can add three fields to the Position object that are lookups to the User table, such as Interview1, Interview2, and Interview3. You will, in fact, assign interviewers for a job application automatically in *Chapter 11: Apex and Data*, logic which could easily be extended to set the values of these fields.

With these selections, you have directed the first step of the approval process to the manager of the Hiring Manager.

The next page lets you either return to the detail listing of the approval or create an action for this approval step. You can define two types of actions: actions taken when the approver approves or rejects this step.

You can also define a final approval and rejection action for the entire process. Since this approval only has one step, approval and rejection actions for that step can be the same as overall approval and rejection actions. And since you are adding more steps to the overall process later in this chapter, simply create final approval and rejection steps.

5. Select the option to not define any steps at this time, and click **Go!**

6. On the Summary page, select **Add New Email** under **Final Approval Actions**. The resulting page is the workflow alert definition page you used earlier in the chapter. Give the alert a description of `Position approved` and use the Email Template with the same name. Make the recipient the related user Hiring Manager since you want to send a proactive email to the Hiring Manager to let them know the position has been approved.

7. Click **Save** to return to the detail page for the approval process.

8. Under Final Rejection Actions, click **Add New Email**.

9. Give this workflow alert a description of `Position Rejected` and use the Email Template with the same name. Once again, make the Hiring Manager for the position a recipient of the alert, but also add the Role of `SVP Human Resources` since HR wants to be aware of rejected positions.

10. Click **Save** to complete the definition of this alert.

Later in this chapter, you will add two field updates to close the position if it is rejected or to set the status to `Open` if it is approved. You can use the Field Update you already created for your workflow action to set the Status field to `Closed` for the rejection action. In this way, a single workflow action can be used many times in the different workflows and approvals.

11. Your final step in creating the approval is to click **Activate**. A dialog box informs you that you cannot edit an approval process once it is activated. There are many internal dependencies used within an approval process, so locking down the process makes sense.

In the next section, you will modify this approval process, but before modifying the approval, you will see exactly how Force Platform approvals work.

Your Approval in Action

Creating an approval process has added functionality into your existing Force Platform tabs to enable the use of the approval process. As usual, the best way to understand how the approval process works is to simply execute the process.

As you saw when you defined the approval, approvals revolve around specific users taking specific actions. To best understand how the approval process operates, imitate one of your users posting and approving the position.

1. Log out of your Force Platform organization and log in as prodman@developer.org, with the standard password.

    Caution: If you don't see the tabs you were expecting for this user, perhaps you forgot to assign the Recruiting application as the default app for this user's profile. If so, you can simply pick the Recruiting application from the picklist in the upper right corner of the page.

2. Create a new Position and set the Hiring Manager to the Director Prodman user. Only the Record Owner of a Position can begin the approval process as it is defined.

3. After saving the Position, scroll to the bottom of the page to see the new section for Approval History with the **Submit for Approval** button, as shown below.

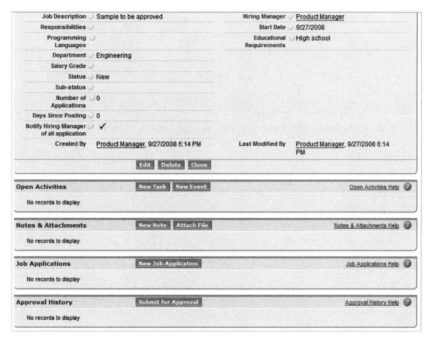

Figure 75: Submit for approval button

4. Click **Submit for Approval**. You are warned that the approval process can lock the record, and that the process might not be able to be recalled. Click **OK** to bring up the page shown below.

   As soon as you submit a record for approval, the entry criteria for the approval process is checked. If the position did not have a Hiring Manager indicated, or if the user submitting the approval was not authorized to begin the process, or if the approval process was not active, you receive a message informing you that your approval submission is not accepted because the approval failed to meet the entry criteria.

The Approval History section of the page has changed. There is now a listing for the initial submission of the approval, as well as the first approval step, which is shown with a status of **Pending**. There is also a button for recalling the approval request since you allowed this button in the definition of the approval process.

Approval History		Recall Approval Request			
Action	Date	Status	Assigned To	Actual Approver	Cor
Step: Manager approval (Pending for first approval)					
	9/27/2008 6:20 PM	Pending	Director Prodman	Director Prodman	
Approval Request Submitted					
	9/27/2008 6:20 PM	Submitted	Product Manager	Product Manager	

Figure 76: Approval in process

5. Check the email account for the Director Prodman user. You see an email generated from the Position approval template.

6. To move the approval process along, log out from the Force Platform platform and log back in as dpm@developer.org, with the standard password.

7. Select the Position that was just submitted for the Director's approval. Scroll to the bottom of the page to see the approval waiting for the Director

 Tip: You can also include a section on the home page of an application to display approver requests, as discussed in the next chapter.

8. You can see that the pending approval step has two links next to it, one to assign the approval to a different user and the other to process the approval. Click the **Approve/Reject** link to display the page shown below.

The Approve/Reject Approval Request page gives the user the choice of approving or rejecting the approval request, as well as adding comments for the step, which are displayed in the Approval History section.

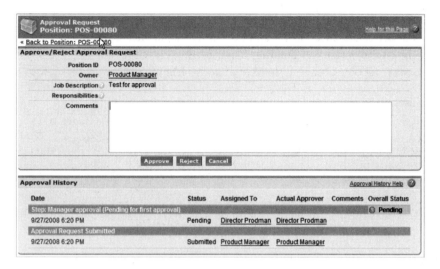

Figure 77: Approve/Reject Approval Request page

9. Enter a relevant message in the Comments section and click on **Approve**.

Returning to the Position record, you see that the status of the step has changed to **Approved** and the comment you entered is visible. In addition, the section has **Approved** in the bar at the top of the Manager Approval portion of the section.

If you check the email for the Product Manager, you see that you received an email generated from the Position Approved email template and sent from the final approver, the Director of Product Management.

You can see how even this most simple approval process does quite a few things—allows for an approval process that locks down the record subject to approval, sends out emails to the participants in the process, informing them of the initiation and completion of the process, provides a page for approval, rejection and comments, and tracks the history of the approval.

In the next section, you modify this simple process to add another step and more flexibility to the process.

Modifying Your Approval

The approval you created in the previous section is useful, but most approval processes are a little more involved than that simple example.

In this section, you expand the approval process to include the manager of the manager in the approval process. This second-level manager is only included in the approval process if the position is offered with a custom salary range indicated for the position.

1. Log out of the Force Platform environment and log back in with the developer/admin user name.

2. Go back to the main page for approvals by clicking **Setup ➤ Create ➤ Workflow & Approvals ➤ Approval Processes**. Select the approval process you created in the last section.

   Notice that there is no button available to add another step to the approval process. As you were warned in the last section, once you activate an approval process, you can no longer edit some parts of the process. You can address this issue by simply cloning the approval and adding another step to the resulting approval.

3. Click **Deactivate** for this approval process, and then click **Clone**.

4. Give the new approval process the name of `Flexible Position Approval` and a description of `Approval routing for new position with an optional step`. Click **Save**. You are alerted that the approval process needs to be activated.

5. Click **Edit** and then select the `Approver Field and Record Editability` choice. On this page, change the **Next Automated Approval Determined By** field to `Manager` and click **Save**, since you will want to use this hierarchy in this approval process.

6. Click **New Approval Step**. Give the new approval step the name of `2nd Level Approval` and a description of `Approval by second level manager`. Leave the default **Step Number**. Click **Next**.

7. This is a conditional step so on the next page, select `Formula Evaluates To True` for the **Step Criteria**.

8. You will want to obtain the approval of a second level manager if the `Custom` salary grade is selected. Add the following formula in the formula text area:

```
ISPICKVAL( Salary_Grade__c ,"Custom") && $UserRole.Name <>
"CEO"
```

   This formula allows only this approval step to be entered if the salary grade for the position is set to `Custom`. In addition, the formula checks to see if the current approver has a profile for the CEO. The CEO does not have a 2nd level manager so there is no need to perform this step if the hiring manager is the CEO.

9. Click **Next** to bring up the next page.

10. On this page, you are again asked for the approver of this step, and this time you want to leave the default of the `Manager` for the manager of the current approver.

11. In the bottom section of the page you have the choice of sending the approval back to the previous approver in the event of a rejection. Leave the default choice of combining the final rejection actions with any rejection actions for this step.

12. Click **Save** to save this step and go to add actions for the approval.

13. On the next page, select the last option to define approval actions later. You do not need to define any actions for this approval step since the final approval and rejection steps take care of the outcome of this last step in the approval process.

You need to add an approval action to mark the Position as Open once it has been approved, as well as setting the Position Open date, and a new rejection action to set the Status and Sub-status fields.

14. In the Final Approval Actions section, click **Add New** to add a new Field Update.

15. Give the Field Update a **Name** of Open Position and an appropriate description. Select the Status field as the **Field to Update**, and set the **Picklist Option** to Open. Click **Save and New** to add another approval action.

16. Give this Field Update a **Name** of Set Open Position Date and an appropriate description. Select the Open Position Date as the field, select the choice to use a formula, and use the TODAY() formula to set the date.

 Note: This Open Position Date was added by the initialization process you ran to prepare your organization for this chapter. The formula you created in the previous chapter, comparing today's date with the CreatedDate of the Position, was also modified to now use the Open Position Date to display the more meaningful calculation.

17. Click **Save** to save the workflow action.

18. In the Final Rejection Actions section, click **Add Existing** to reuse the Field Update that set the Status to Closed.

19. On the next page, choose the Action Type of Field Update and select the Close out position choice. Click **Save** to return to the main page for the approval process.

20. Select Add New and Field Update to add another approval action to the Final Approval. Give this Field Update a **Name** of Set Substatus and an appropriate description. Select the Sub-status field as the Field to Update and set the Picklist Option to Rejected. Click **Save** to save the workflow action.

21. Now that you have finished modifying and expanding the approval process, click **Activate**.

Time to see how these changes have expanded the range of your approval process.

1. Go to the Positions tab and enter a new Position with a Salary Grade of `Custom` and a Hiring Manager of the `Product Manager` user. Save the record.

2. Submit the Position you just created for approval.

 Tip: You can also submit approvals automatically with Apex code, which will be discussed later in this book.

3. As an administrator, you can act on all levels of the approval process for the Position record. Approve the record as if you were the Hiring Manager.

4. See the record enter the next approval step, as it should with the Salary Grade set to a salary of `Custom`. Approve the record and see the approval enter the second step of the process.

5. Approve the record as the second level manager and observe how the Status and Position Open Date are properly set.

6. Perform this same process again for a Position with a Salary Grade of `Custom`, but have the second approver reject the position to see the Status and Sub-status fields set properly.

7. Finally, add another Position that does not have the Salary Grade set to `Custom` to see how the final approval step is skipped when the entry condition is not met. The final approval actions are still taken correctly.

The modifications you made to this approval process start to give you an idea of the possibilities within these approvals. You can see that you might not even need to give users edit access to the Status field since the approval process sets the value for this field automatically and correctly.

Before leaving the land of approvals, there are a couple more areas of extended approval functionality to discover.

Email Approvals

In the approval process described above, each approver needed to log into the Force Platform application in order to approve or reject a particular step in the approval process. There might be times when an approver can learn of a pending approval via email, but not be able to easily or quickly log into their Force Platform environment.

You can enable email approvals to address these issues. With email approvals, an approver can simply respond to the email approval request with either APPROVE or REJECT as the first line of the response.

Allowing email approval responses is configured by going to **Setup ➤ Create ➤ Workflow & Approvals ➤ Settings** to show the page displayed below.

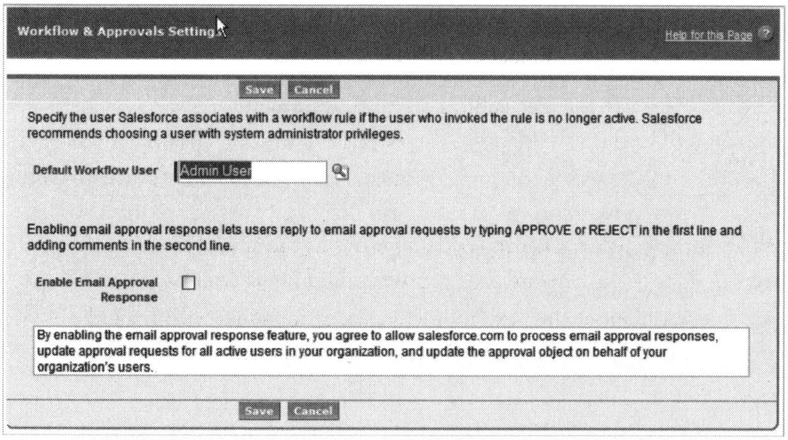

Figure 78: Configuring email approvals

Checking the lower box in on the page allows email approvals for all approval processes in this Force Platform environment.

Parallel Approval Steps

The approval process you created is fairly simple, but still offers a fair amount of flexibility in modeling real world business processes.

In the often consensus-driven world we live in, there may be times to specify an approval step that flows to multiple users, with the step being successfully completed when either one of or all of the group approves.

You can create a parallel approval step that uses this type of logic within the context of the approval you have already created.

Up to this point, the process of creating a position and having that position approved for posting has been a linear process within the particular reporting structure: the person entering the position asks their manager, who may ask the second level manager, if the position is going to have a custom salary range.

But in many organizations, the Human Resources department also likes to have a voice in whether a position gets officially posted. You can, of course, add in another step to the approval process to include an HR representative, but this additional step prolongs the approval process.

Instead, you can modify your existing approval to allow for a parallel approval step. A parallel approval step sends the approval to more than one approver. You can specify whether the step has to be approved by all parallel approvers, or simply one of the parallel approvers, before moving on to the next step in the process.

For this particular scenario, direct all new positions to the Hiring Manager for the position and an HR person.

1. Return to the approval you just created. Click the **Edit** link for the first approval step submitted for approval to the Hiring Manager for the position.

2. Click **Next** to pass by the first two pages whose values remain the same.

3. Go to the **Automatically assign to approver(s)** link as you did when you initially defined this step.

4. Click **Add Row**.

5. Select the User named `Joe Personnel` for the second user.

6. Select the second option in the radio buttons below labeled `Requires UNANIMOUS approval from all selected approvers`.

7. Click **Save** to return to the approval summary page, which is shown below.

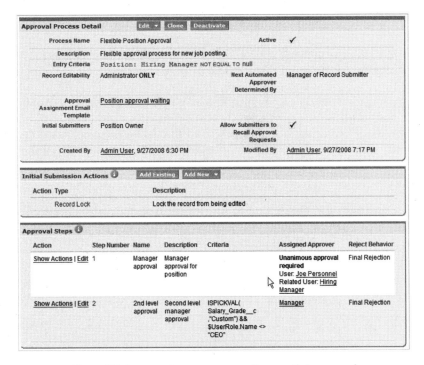

Figure 79: Approval summary page for parallel approval

You can now see that there are two assigned approvers and that the approvals require unanimous approval to proceed to the next step.

You can check out the operation of your new and improved approval process by creating a new position and submitting it for approval. You see that two approvers appear in the first step of the Approval History and that the status of that step is set to `Pending`, even after one of the users approves the position.

Once the second user approves the position, the approval process moves on to the next step in the process.

Enhancing the approval

You can make this approval process more appropriate and flexible by adding a little more data to the Position object. Instead of directing the approval to the VP of Human Resources, add a lookup relationship to the User record to designate the appropriate HR rep for the department. The approval step can then be directed to the User represented in that lookup relationship.

Approvals and Beyond

This last example has pointed the way to the expanded role that Force Platform approvals can play in your organization. Typically, the word 'approval' brings up an image of routing paperwork through an organization, such as submitting an expense report.

But, in fact, a Force Platform approval can be used to manage and monitor any business process. For instance, you can create an approval process to manage interviewing a candidate, with a parallel approval process requiring unanimous consent on the suitability of a candidate before an offer can be extended. This type of approval effectively tracks the overall interview process, provides proactive notification of tasks to accomplish, monitors the overall results and spawns another action, such as when the interview process successfully completes. An approval like this increases the efficiency of the process, as well as collecting data on how interviews are conducted for future analysis.

Once you start to understand approvals in this light, you can start to find many places where you can use the power of the Force Platform to optimize and track business processes across your entire organization.

Summary

This chapter has introduced you to one of the most powerful declarative features of the Force Platform—workflow and approvals.

A workflow is a way to automatically implement actions in your organization, such as sending emails or setting the values of fields. You can add conditions to determine when a workflow is executed.

Approvals give you the ability to implement complete business process flows, all through a wizard-based interface. You can have multiple steps, optional steps, parallel approvers or even dynamic approval routing. At each step in an approval process, you can implement multiple workflow actions, based on the response of the current approver.

With the automation provided by workflows and approvals, you can simultaneously make your users more productive and your business processes more reliable.

Chapter 6

Reaping Value Through Reports

Up until now, this book has been focusing on the parts of the Force Platform that deal with individual pieces of data. The user interfaces you have created and the functionality behind them has been centered on entering and updating data, or retrieving individual data records.

Being able to work with individual records is a necessary precursor to any use of larger amounts of data, but users can extract more valuable information from working with groups of records. Typically, people think of reports when they think about groups of records, but the Force Platform offers you several approaches to working with aggregation, including search results, tags, reports and dashboards.

This chapter covers different options available to you, as a developer, and to your users, for collecting larger groups of data, and for extracting information from the aggregation of data records and values.

Important: If you have been following the examples in the previous chapter, your Force Platform organization should be ready for the exercises in this chapter. If you have not done the exercises, or want to start with a fresh version of the sample Recruiting application, please refer to the instructions in the Code Share project for this book. You can find information on how to access that project in *Chapter 1: Welcome to the Force Platform*. In addition, the project contains instructions on how to update your organization with changes required for this chapter.

Searching

The first method of aggregating data is built into the Force Platform: the ability to collect groups of records through searching. Users can search one or more objects for records that contain a particular value.

The results of a search return as a list of records, with the `Record Name` of each record acting as a link to the actual detail page for the record. This automatic linking is a feature of all the techniques of data collection covered in this chapter. Each technique includes this easy and automatic drill-down capability for accessing the base record. In this way, Force Platform data collection methods and tools are different from standalone reporting tools that normally need additional modification in order to deliver this essential feature.

As with most other default Force Platform features, the best way to learn about the capabilities of the built-in search feature is to simply use it. In order to use search, you need to make it available as part of the user interface, helping you to understand some of the configuration options for the standard user environment.

Adding Search to the Sidebar

You have already seen some of the features of the Sidebar at work, such as the ability to create new objects directly from a button and the list of links to recent items. You have also configured the user interface to allow users to collapse the Sidebar if they want more screen area for the main area for tabs.

You can configure the components available in the Sidebar in a similar manner. The Sidebar is one of the core components of the Force Platform environment, so the contents of the Sidebar are part of the page layout for the Home page of the organization.

1. Click **Setup ➤ Customize ➤ Home ➤ Home Page Layouts** to display the existing home page layouts for the organization.

   The Customize section of the App Setup covers areas of the Force Platform that exist in all organizations, such as standard objects, user interface specifications, home page components and layouts.

2. Click the **Edit** link for the home page layout to bring up the page shown in the Home Page layout below.

   This page allows you to include different components in the "wide" section of the home page, on the right, and the "narrow" section of the home page, which echoes through all the pages as the sidebar.

The default choices for the main portion of the Home page are to display tasks, a calendar and a dashboard snapshot. You will create dashboard snapshots later in this chapter.

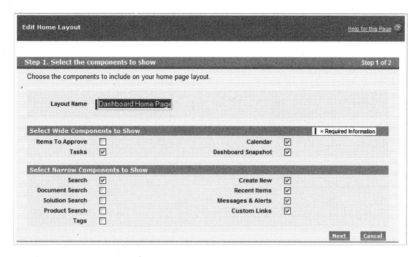

Figure 80: The Home Page layout

3. Deselect the `Calendar` and `Tasks` components and make sure the `Items To Approve` component is selected in the Select Wide Components to Show section of the page.

   Since your recruiting application uses approvals, adding items that need approval to the home page is useful to your user community. Right now, you do not really have a need to display tasks or the calendar component, so you do not have to show them in the main portion of the Home page.

   The default options selected for the Sidebar are Search, Create New button, Messages & Alerts and Custom Links. You can edit both the Messages & Alerts and the Custom Links through the Home Page Components menu choice.

4. Make sure that the Search checkbox in the Select Narrow Components to Show section of the page is checked and click **Next**.

5. Leave the Search component at the top of the Narrow (Left) Column picklist and click **Save**.

   You can see that there is also a button marked **Save & Assign**. Every organization can have more than one Home Page Layout, and you can assign different layouts to different groups of users. Home Page Layouts are assigned to specific user profiles, discussed in detail in *Chapter 7: Protecting Your Data* on security.

The results of a search are shown in the search layout for the particular object. The Objects attribute page includes a section labeled Search Layouts, where you can modify the page layouts for the results of different types of searches. For the purposes of this book, the Search Results layout has been modified to display more columns than the default of Position ID.

You can add further customizations to the built-in search capabilities of the Force Platform with the **Setup ➤ Customize ➤ Search** page, shown below.

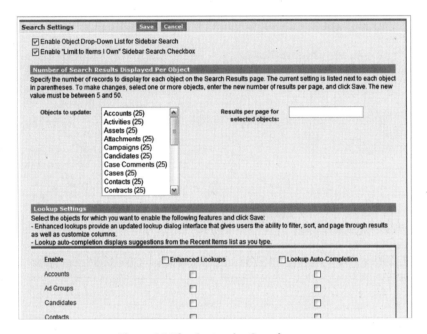

Figure 81: The Customize Search page

Using Search

Adding search to the home page layout adds a search capability to the Sidebar that is displayed with all tabs.

1. Click the Home tab to show the new version of the Home Page, as shown below.

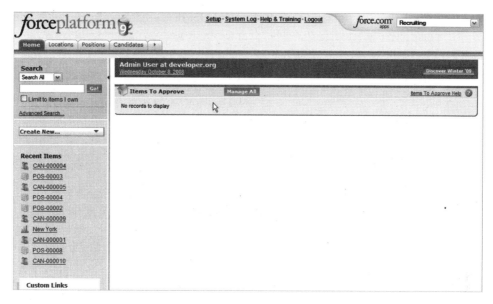

Figure 82: New version of Home Page

The Sidebar for all your applications now contains a search entry box and a link to advanced search. Force Platform search offers the following options:

- By default, Search looks in all objects, notes and reports. Advanced search also searches in descriptions and comments. You select an individual object in the Sidebar search, if you enable this option through the **Customize ➤ Search** page, or multiple objects in the advanced search page.
- The Sidebar search uses the characters entered as the initial characters in a text string, as if a wild card were appended. In advanced search, you use the * wildcard, following the initial string, to indicate any number of characters, or the ? wildcard, following the initial string, to indicate a single character.
- Search only looks in text fields.

Advanced search offers a little more flexibility, as shown in the figure below.

Figure 83: Advanced Search page

The search text box in the Advanced Search page also accepts logical syntax, such as AND, OR and NOT AND, as well as allowing exact search matches for multiple words by surrounding the words with quotation marks.

There are other search capabilities in different areas of your Force Platform application, such as the search dialogs that look for related records. Searching for lookup values includes a couple of features that can make the search more useful and user friendly. As soon as the user enters more than three characters in the search box at the top of the page, the Force Platform attempts to automatically complete the search term by looking at the most recently used items for a match. This feature, turned on by default after the Spring 08 release, can help guide users to the best choice for a lookup value. In addition, users can customize the columns that appear in the search lookup themselves.

Once a set of records has been returned from a search, a user can specify filters to further limit the records in the set.

Voice of the Developer: This section has focused on how users can find records through the Search feature. There are several ways in a Force Platform standard application that allow users to view lists or records, as well as filter those lists. Users can also use views to display objects from a particular object. When users click on a custom object tab they are taken to the view of that object. All objects have a default view, but you can also create custom views, which allow a user to specify selection criteria and what fields are displayed in the view. You can also create a Visualforce page with similar features, which is described in *Chapter 9: Visualforce Pages*.

Filters

Filters give users a way to further limit the results returned from an initial search. There is a page layout for Search Filter Fields in the Search Layouts for an object. To enable the use of search filters for an object, you have to add some fields to this layout, which has been done for the Position object in your current application.

In the search results page, there is a link to show filters if a search filter layout with fields exists for the object. You can click on the link to show the filters, as illustrated below.

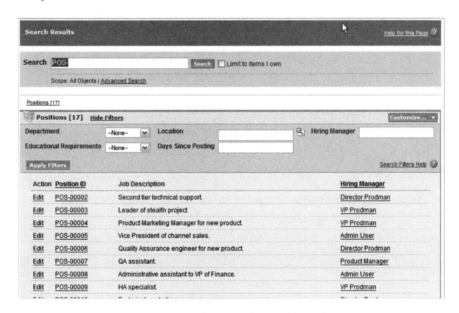

Figure 84: Filters in Advanced Search

Users can enter one or more values in each search filter fields, separating the values with commas or, for numeric fields, with the OR operator. If a user enters more than one value in a filter field, the filter limits the display to records that match any of the values. Values entered for dates, numbers or record IDs are compared with an = (equals) operator, while all other fields compare with the contains operator.

Conditions listed in different search fields are combined with an AND operator, which means that listed records must match a value in all of the specified filter fields.

The Force Platform supports a number of special date filter criteria, which allow users to indicate values relative to the current date. For more information on these filters, please refer to the on-line help.

Although you do not really have to do much to enable search capabilities for all your Force Platform applications, knowing about what the built-in search can do for your users helps you plan how to use these capabilities to enhance your application and design your data structures.

Tagging

The search capabilities discussed above give users the ability to find a group of records in an ad hoc fashion, but there is no permanence to the results. Tagging gives users the opportunity to identify records in an ad hoc fashion by associating tag values with individual records. You use these tags to find groups of records with one or more tags.

Tagging is a familiar process on Web 2.0 sites. A tag adds another value to the metadata for a record that can be used to retrieve records with the same value.

Tagging functionality is built into the Force Platform, but is not enabled by default. As with search, you add tags to your application through the Customize menu.

1. Click **Setup ➤ Customize ➤ Tags ➤ Tag Settings** and select the **Enable Public Tags** checkbox to display the page shown in the figure below.

    As you can see, there are two types of tags available: personal tags, which are only visible and useable by an individual user, and public tags, which are available to all users. Both tagging options work in the same way, but both sets of tags are separate; you cannot search on personal and public tags at the same time.

    You now have the option of adding tag sections to notes, documents, reports, and individual page layouts. If you enable personal tags, you have the same option for those tags.

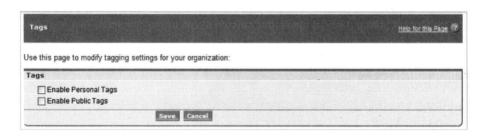

Figure 85: Tag Settings

2. Click **Enable Public Tags** and make sure all of your custom object layouts are in the `Selected Page Layouts` list on the right. Click **Save**.

3. Go to the Home Page Layout page and check to make sure that Tags are included in the narrow section of the Home page.

4. Go to the **User Interface** menu under **Customize** and select `Show Custom Sidebar Components on All Pages`, as the Tags component is considered a custom component. If you did not select this option, the interface to tag searching only appears in the Sidebar of the Home Page. Click **Save**.

5. Click the Candidate tab and select a candidate. The **Add Tags** link displays in the upper right. Click the link to bring up the tag interface, as shown in the figure below.

You can add one or more personal or private tags through this interface, separated by commas.

 Note: The initialization process for this chapter described how to get these tags attached to your existing records.

One of the potential problems from ad hoc labeling, such as tags, is the use of similar tags to denote the same quality. This can lead to incorrect data or reduced relevance of results, a common data problem discussed in *Chapter 2: Starting Your Force Platform Application*. Although the Force Platform implementation of tags cannot eliminate this possibility, both public and private tags use an autocomplete function, which gives suggestions for the use of existing tags as soon as the user enters a letter for the tag.

For this example, the records loaded into the Candidate object already have tags associated with them. Users have created tags to indicate whether a candidate is recommended, the office closest to a candidate, and whether a candidate is available for remote work. You can use multiple tags to find those candidates that fit multiple criteria by using the Tags interface.

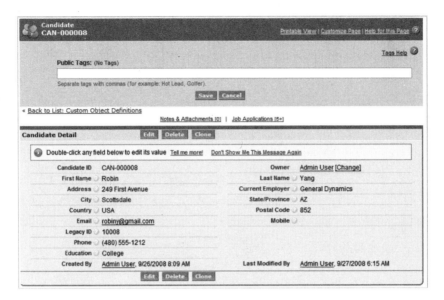

Figure 86: Tag interface

6. Go to the Home tab to see the Tags link and the Recent Tags list button. Click the Tags link to bring up the page shown, in completed form, in the figure below.

   With the Tags page, users locate specific tags alphabetically or enter tags directly into the search box. In the alphabetical listing, select a tag to be used as a filter by clicking the tag.

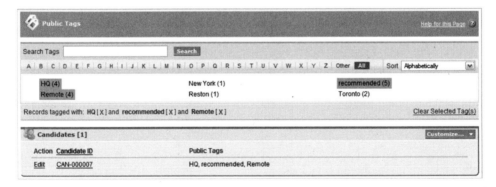

Figure 87: Tags page

7. Click on the HQ tags.
8. Add in the recommend tag.
9. Add in the remote tag.

Notice two things in this three step process: a tag can be associated with more than one object, and that the filtering effect of adding more tags is cumulative. When you added the `remote` tag to the filter set, you limited the number of records selected.

10. Delete the HQ tag from the filter by clicking on the red **X** next to the tag.

Since the records returned from a tag search include a link to the specific records that satisfy the tag filters, tags give your users the ability to combine records into many different groups, and to use those groups to identify specific records for investigation.

Giving users ad hoc capabilities helps them to add some additional data to any object without having to modify the fields in that object. Tags provide almost unlimited flexibility in identifying and filtering records.

But for standard business functions, you need to provide something more than an ad hoc approach. The remainder of this chapter discusses the reporting and analytic capabilities of the Force Platform.

Reporting

Reporting is arguably the most important part of the entire information environment since reporting extracts business value from the data entered into your data stores. The Force Platform includes a complete system for creating and running reports.

Force Platform reports are tightly coupled with the Force Platform database and the individual records stored in the objects in that database. Whenever you create a report with the Force Platform reporting system, users have instant access to the detailed records included in the report. In this way, Force Platform reports are ways to create collections of records, as well as aggregate information from these collections.

Force Platform Reporting Concepts

The Force Platform reports system takes a layered approach to creating standard and analytic reports, as shown in the diagram below.

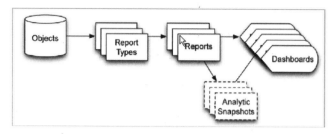

Figure 88: Force Platform Reporting Architecture

At the base of all reporting are the Force Platform objects. These objects not only contain data in the Force Platform system, but also form an extended mesh of data by means of relationships defined between objects.

The Force Platform reporting system includes a layer between the actual data objects and reports called report types. A *report type* is the foundation for all reporting activities higher in the stack. The report type provides access to fields in one or more related objects. The Force Platform provides a set of standard report types used in this first section, as well as giving you the opportunity to create your own custom report types. Custom report types can include fields from up to 20 related objects and can specify the fields that are available for report activities, either through user selection or by default.

A user creates standard reports based on report types. Typically, many reports are based on an individual report type since there are many ways to look at the same set of data. A report can be created on the fly or saved for reuse. Reports, by default, have selection criteria specified at runtime, so the same report can be used to get many different sets of data.

Including the Name field of a record in the row of a report allows that field to act as a link to the underlying detail record. This tight integration is a distinct advantage for Force Platform reports. In this way, you can see Force Platform reports as not only an aggregation of data, but also as a kind of switchboard directing you to the core data on which the report is built.

Force Platform reports are, in turn, the building blocks for dashboards, explained later in this chapter, which present a higher level of aggregation for display on home pages. Dashboards can be charts or graphs for a more intuitive presentation of combined information, and dashboards can also drill down into other dashboards or the reports that provide the data for the dashboards. You can also use Analytic Snapshots, explained later in this chapter, to collect data for specific periods or uses, and base your dashboards on those snapshots.

With this understanding of how different components in the Force Platform reporting system interact, you can jump right in to building some reports.

Creating a Standard Report

As with most things in the on-demand world of the Force Platform, the easiest way to learn about reports is to create some.

You are already familiar with the Force Platform objects in your organization, so you can use that data as the place to start your explorations.

You can get access to the Force Platform reporting system through the Reports tab.

1. In the runtime environment, click the arrow to the right of the tabs for the Recruiting application to bring up a list of additional tabs. Select the Reports tab to bring up the figure below.

    You can prevent users from accessing this tab, or limiting other interactions with reports, through their profile permissions, discussed in *Chapter 7: Protecting Your Data* on security.

    On this page, you see a list of reports, separated into categories. You can search for reports through the search box at the top of the page and you can also use tags to identify groups of reports.

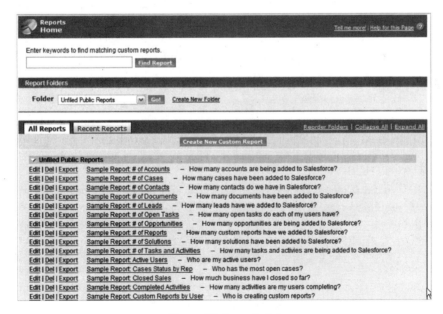

Figure 89: Reports tab

2. Click **Create New Custom Report** to bring up the next page.

3. Select the report type to use as the foundation of the report. The top picklist has categories of report types to limit the choices shown in the lower picklist. Later in this chapter, you learn about custom report types that can be stored in any category, but standard report types for custom objects are listed in the Other Reports category.

4. Select `Other Reports` in the top picklist to bring up the list of report types for custom objects, shown in the figure below.

   You see that there are four basic categories of report types that are automatically created for the Force Platform report system:

   - Report types based on a single custom object
   - Report types based on two related objects
   - Report types based on three objects used to define a many-to-many relationship, such as `Positions`, `Job Applications`, and `Candidates`
   - Report types based on history records for objects that have history tracking enabled.

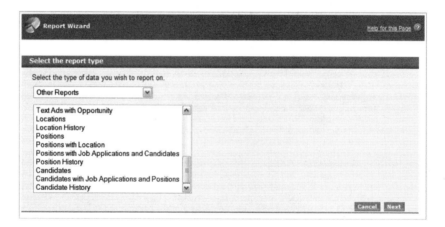

Figure 90: Other Report Types

5. For your first report, choose the `Positions with Job Applications and Candidates` report type and click **Next** to bring up the page shown in the figure below.

   The next page presents you with the most important decision you need to make to define a report—the type of report to create. You can start with the most basic type of report.

   There are four buttons in the bottom left corner of the main area. These buttons, repeated on every page of the wizard, allow you to do the following:

- Run the report
- Export the detail rows of the report to an Excel format file or a comma-separated variable file
- See the report in a printable view, stripping out the artifacts of the Force Platform environment in preparation for printing
- Save the report, which saves the report definition

You can perform any of these choices at any stage of the report definition wizard. All the steps in the wizard include defaults that are used if you do not modify any particular options.

You can also modify a part of the report through the picklist in the upper right corner of the report wizard pages.

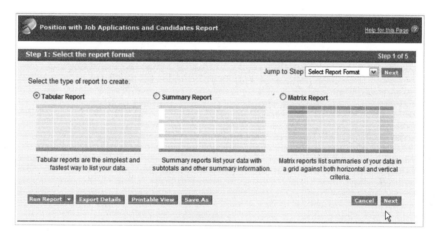

Figure 91: Report format selection page

6. Leave the default selection of `Tabular Report` and click **Next**. You can now choose the fields to include in the report. Some of the fields have been preselected, but you can simply unselect them if you do not want them in this particular report.

7. Select the following fields for the report: in the `Position` object, the `Position ID` (which should already be selected), `Days Since Posting`, `Department`, `Hiring Manager`, `Job Description`, and `Number of Applications`; in the `Candidate` object, the `Candidate ID` (which should already be checked), `First Name`, `Last Name`, and `Education`. Deselect the `Job Application ID` field in the `Job Application` object since this report does not need any information from that object.

8. Click **Next** to bring up the page shown below.

This page allows you to add standard summary fields to this tabular report. Since you do not have a way to group the records in the report, these summaries are only listed for the entire report. You can have summary values on any numeric or checkbox fields, a sum, average, largest or smallest value for each of these fields, as well as a record count for the records in the report.

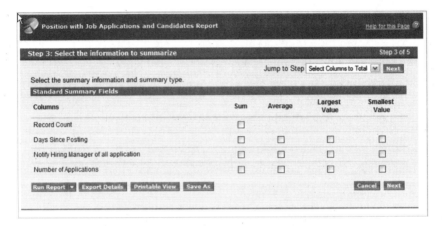

Figure 92: Standard Report Summary Fields

9. Select the `Record Count` option and click **Next**. The next page allows you to adjust the order in which fields appear in the report.

10. Change the fields to display in the following order:

    - `Department, Position ID, Hiring Manager, Job Description, Days Since Posting, Number of Applications`
    - `Candidate ID, First Name, Last Name, Education`

11. Click **Next** to bring up the page shown below.

    On this page you specify selection criteria for the report. The top section lets you limit the report based on ownership of the records or a date range for any date fields in any of the records in the record type.

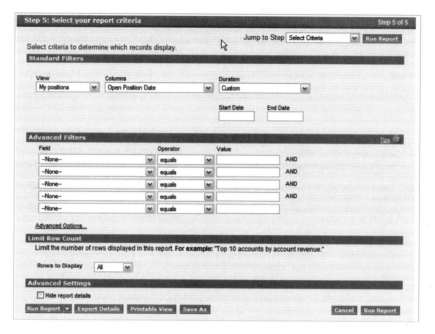

Figure 93: Select Report Criteria page

12. Change the `Standard Filter for View` to `All positions`, which shows you all records, regardless of owner.

The Advanced Filters let you limit the records returned based on field values, or a combination of field values, as illustrated when you click the Advanced Filters link.

The third section of this page lets you limit the report to the 'top' rows in the report. If you select a number of rows to display—either 10, 25 or any number up to 99— you are prompted for the field on which you want to sort the data, and whether you want to sort in ascending or descending order.

The final section gives you the ability to hide the detail rows for the report, an option you also see available in the actual report.

13. Leave all other options with their default values, as they do not impose any selection conditions, and go directly to the report.

14. Click **Run Report** to bring up the page shown in the figure below.

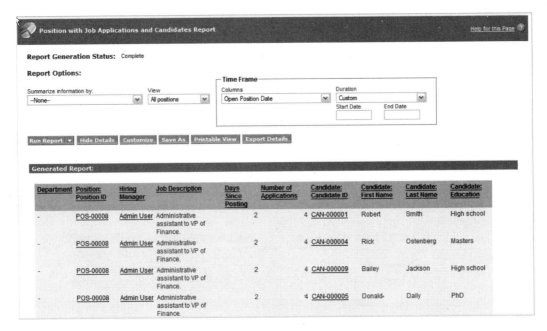

Figure 94: Your first report

Here it is—your first report. On one hand, it may not be the most beautiful report you have ever seen, but even this simple report packs a load of functionality.

First of all, each of the columns in the report is either a lookup to another object or the name field in an object shown as a link.

You can sort the report by the values in any of the columns by clicking on the column headers.

Report users have a number of options for modifying the report results on this page. They can specify a time frame for the records shown in the report through the same options you had available to you when you designed the report.

You can also see the same four buttons which were present on each of the pages of the report wizard, along with two others: Hide Details, which hides all of the detail rows of the report, and Customize, which takes you back to the wizard pages to change the values.

Saving Your Report

Your last step is to save the results of your work.

1. Before leaving this report, save the report to see your options in this area. Click **Save As**.

2. Set the report name to `First report`, enter an appropriate description and save the report in the `Unfiled Public Reports` folder.

You can also save the report as a personal report, which would only be visible to you.

This action saves the report definition, not the report. You can give access to this report to groups of other users, based on their profiles, which will be explained in the next chapter.

You can save the report in a printable format through the Printable View button. This button saves the report as an Excel spreadsheet formatted for printing. In this way, you can keep the results of your report in a format that can then be made available to a wider audience.

You can also distribute reports on a scheduled basis, which is discussed later in this chapter after the discussion of Analytic Snapshots.

Limiting access to reports

When you save a report, you are prompted for a folder. Folders, like other objects in the Force Platform environment, have a set of permissions you can use to limit access by users with different security profiles. Administrators can create a report folder with the `Create New Folder` link in the top section of the Reports tab, and limit access to that folder when you define it using roles, described in the next chapter.

Just as you can limit what reports a user can see, you can limit the amount of customization a user can apply to a report. One of the privileges assigned to security profiles is the ability to create and customize reports. Users whose profile does not have this privilege are not allowed to change any of the onscreen parameters or customize any reports. These users can only run reports available as public reports.

Creating a Summary Report

With the basics of creating a report behind you, you can create a summary report. This report has three levels of grouping: `Department`, `Hiring Manager`, and `Status`.

The report allows management to see how the hiring process has been coming along, highlighting any differences between different departments and managers within those departments. This valuable information helps the company determine not only how well their hiring process is proceeding, but also provides a tool to determine if there is a need to focus on training to improve the hiring process for any particular department or hiring manager.

1. Return to the Reports tab in the runtime environment.

2. Click **Create New Custom Report** to select the report type. Select `Other Reports` and then the same report type you selected in the previous example, `Positions with Job Applications and Candidates`. Click **Next**.

3. Select `Summary Report` and click **Next**.

The next page looks familiar since it is the same page you encountered while creating a standard report. Since a summary report focuses on, well, summaries, it makes sense that this page is in the preeminent position in the wizard.

There is one additional option in this page; you can create custom summary fields. A custom summary field uses formulas to create new values out of standard report summaries. For instance, you can create a custom summary field to multiply the Average summary by the Record Count for a particular report. You can use formulas to extend the range of the summaries available to your reports.

 Tip: You can specify the format and title for a custom summary formula. Later in this chapter, reports and charts use the title of a formula to identify the values in the axis of the chart. There are times when you might use a custom summary formula to duplicate the effect of a built-in formula, simply to change the axis titles on a dashboard, discussed later in this chapter, or report.

You do not need to use any custom summary formulas for this report.

4. Select the `Record Count` standard summary field, and the `Average`, `Largest Value` and `Smallest Value` for the `Days Since Posting` field. When you specify an aggregate, the value is shown in each summary level, as well as a grand total for the entire report.

5. Click on **Next** to bring up the page shown below.

This new page lets you specify up to three levels of groups for your report. Each group has a group heading and the summaries you defined in the previous page, with each subsequent heading having a slightly larger indentation. You can group a report on a field value that is included in the report, or not included. If the field is included in a grouping definition, the value displays in the group heading, whether the field is included in the report or not. You see this type of display when you view the summary report you are currently working on – the `Department`, `Hiring Manager`, and `Status` fields show up in their headings.

If you use a date field for any of the groupings, you can select different ways to group the dates, from grouping them by individual days to calendar weeks, months, quarters or years, to fiscal quarters or years.

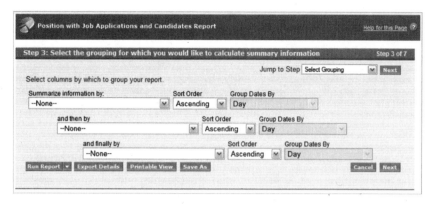

Figure 95: Summary Report grouping

6. Select `Department` for the top level grouping, `Hiring Manager` for the second level grouping, and `Status` for the lowest level grouping. Click **Next**.

7. On the next page, select the same fields you used for the previous report: in the Position object, the `Position ID`, `Days Since Posting`, `Department`, `Hiring Manager`, `Job Description`, and `Number of Applications`; in the Candidate object, the `Candidate ID`, `First Name`, `Last Name`, and `Education`. Deselect the `Job Application ID` field in the `Job Application` object since this report does not need any information from that object. Click **Next**.

8. Order the fields as you did for the previous report:

   - `Department Position ID`, `Hiring Manager`, `Job Description`, `Days Since Posting`, `Number of Applications`
   - `Candidate ID`, `First Name`, `Last Name`, `Education`

9. Click **Next**. This page is very similar to the page from the standard report, although the option to include a limited set of records based on sort order is not available on this page. Add an Advanced Filter that limits records selected to those where `Status` is not equal to `New`. You want this report to display information and calculations about all open and closed positions, so you must eliminate those positions still in the midst of the approval process.

10. Change the **Standard Filter for View** to `All positions` to show you all records, regardless of owner.

11. The final step in defining a summary report gives you the option of creating a chart out of this report. Later in this chapter, you will learn about creating graphical displays in dashboard, but you will not need to create a chart in this abbreviated reporting overview. Click **Run Report** to produce your first summary report.

    The report is similar in appearance to the standard report, with the exception of the three levels of grouping.

Although this report does not include that much data, you can see a more typical use of summary reports by hiding the detail data, producing the page shown below.

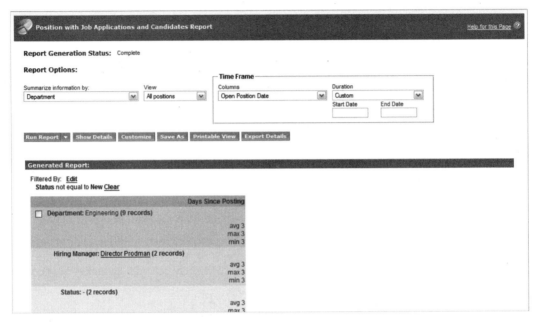

Figure 96: Your first summary report, details hidden

12. Click **Hide Details**. This action focuses the report on the crucial aggregate data for each level of grouping, highlighting any differences between the groups. You can still get to the detail data for the report by clicking **Show Details** or by selecting some groups and drilling down on the details for those groups. You can also save the detail data for either of these options with another click of a button.

13. Save this report as `First summary report` in the `Unfiled Public Reports` report folder.

You can use the results of a summary report as the starting point for further exploration of a subset of data in the report. Next to each top level sort value is a check box. You can select the groups of data you want to use as the basis for the next iteration of the report by checking this box. Once you select the desired groups, you can choose another top level sort value in the picklist at the bottom of the page and click `Drill Down` to reorder the selected data. Summary reports add another level of information to your reports without interfering with the ability to drill down through groups to the individual data records. In this way, a summary report not only provides you with highly useful aggregations of data, but an easy way to explore the reasons behind variations in these aggregations, making Force Platform summary reports a great tool for investigating business conditions.

This ability to dynamically slice and dice report data turns Force Platform summary reports into powerful analytic tools.

Creating a Matrix Report

The matrix report is the final report option in the Force Platform reporting system. A matrix report uses two dimensions to present data—a vertical dimension and a horizontal dimension. You can have up to two groupings of data along each dimension and, of course, all the functionality inherent in summary reports carries over to this new option.

The matrix report for our example tracks the posted positions and some information about the time the positions have been posted in one dimension. In addition, this report dimension lists the number of applicants for a position, as well as some data about those applicants.

The other dimension of the report sorts this data based on the location of the position posted. With this dimension, management sees if any particular location is having more trouble attracting qualified candidates, which will help them determine the areas most suitable for an expanded workforce.

1. Go to the Reports tab and start a new report. Select the same report type, based on `Positions`, `Job Applications` and `Candidates`, as you did for the two previous reports, and click **Next**.

2. This time, select the `Matrix Report` option and click **Next** to bring up the page shown below.

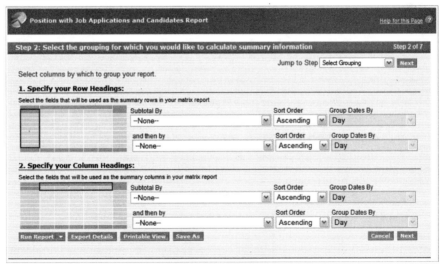

Figure 97: Grouping for matrix reports

This page looks similar to the page used to identify groups in a summary report, with two differences: You have the option to specify groups for rows or columns and you can only specify two groupings per dimension. The fields used to define the groups are exactly the same as in the other grouping page.

3. For the Row Headings, select `Department` and `Hiring Manager`. For the Column Headings, select the `Location City/State/Country` formula field.

   You could use the `Location` field for this heading, which only shows the name of the location, but automatically provides a link to the detail record for the location. You do not need the link in this report and the formula field provides a little more information for the row column headings.

4. Click **Next** to go to the summary page. Select the `Sum` checkbox for `Record Count`, and the `Average`, `Largest Value` and `Smallest Value` for the `Days Since Posting`. Click **Next**.

5. On the next page, select the same fields you used for the previous report: in the Position object, the `Position ID`, `Days Since Posting`, `Department`, `Hiring Manager`, `Job Description`, and `Number of Applications`; in the Candidate object, the `Candidate ID`, `First Name`, `Last Name`, and `Education`. Deselect the `Job Application ID` field in the `Job Application` object since this report does not need any information from that object. Click **Next**.

6. Order the fields as you did for the previous report, with the exception of not having to include the Department field:

   • `Position ID`, `Hiring Manager`, `Job Description`, `Days Since Posting`, `Number of Applications`
   • `Candidate ID`, `First Name`, `Last Name`, `Education`

7. Click **Next**.

8. On the penultimate page of the wizard, select the view for `All Positions` and add the Advanced Filter to eliminate records with a **Status** of `New`. Click **Run Report** to bring up the report shown below.

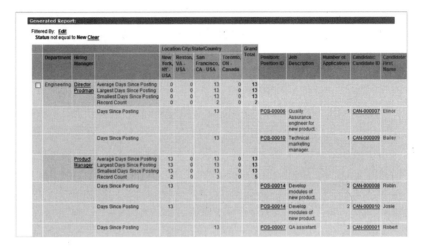

Figure 98: First matrix report

The matrix report looks a bit different from the reports you have seen before. The matrix displays on the left side of the report with a cell for the intersection of each set of group values, such as a hiring manager for Engineering, and each location where that hiring manager has a position posted. The detail rows display in the right side of the report.

9. Click **Hide Details** to display the matrix report in a different form, as shown in the figure below.

Department	Hiring Manager		Location City/State/Country				Grand Total
---	---	---	New York, NY - USA	Reston, VA - USA	San Francisco, CA - USA	Toronto, ON - Canada	
☐ Engineering	Director Prodman	Average Days Since Posting	0	0	3	0	3
		Largest Days Since Posting	0	0	3	0	3
		Smallest Days Since Posting	0	0	3	0	3
		Record Count	0	0	2	0	2
	Product Manager	Average Days Since Posting	3	0	3	0	3
		Largest Days Since Posting	3	0	3	0	3
		Smallest Days Since Posting	3	0	3	0	3
		Record Count	2	0	3	0	5
	VP Prodman	Average Days Since Posting	0	0	0	3	3
		Largest Days Since Posting	0	0	0	3	3
		Smallest Days Since Posting	0	0	0	3	3
		Record Count	0	0	0	2	2
	Sub Total	Average Days Since Posting	3	0	3	3	3
		Largest Days Since Posting	3	0	3	3	3
		Smallest Days Since Posting	3	0	3	3	3
		Record Count	2	0	5	2	9
☐ Finance	Admin User	Average Days Since Posting	0	0	3	0	3
		Largest Days Since Posting	0	0	3	0	3
		Smallest Days Since Posting	0	0	3	0	3
		Record Count	0	0	4	0	4
	Director Prodman	Average Days Since Posting	3	3	0	0	3
		Largest Days Since Posting	3	3	0	0	3
		Smallest Days Since Posting	3	3	0	0	3
		Record Count	2	2	0	0	4
	Product Manager	Average Days Since Posting	3	0	0	0	3
		Largest Days Since Posting	3	0	0	0	3
		Smallest Days Since Posting	3	0	0	0	3
		Record Count	2	0	0	0	2
	Sub Total	Average Days Since Posting	3	3	3	0	3

Figure 99: Matrix report with hidden details

10. Save the report under the name `My first matrix report`

This report might be the most useful report yet. The report is loaded with aggregate information that provides facts necessary to evaluate the performance of your hiring process, as well as crucial guidance for business decisions, such as where to post positions to garner the greatest number of applicants.

With details hidden, extended columns for each level of detail record are no longer needed; therefore, the matrix report shown without details is actually narrower than the matrix report with the details displayed. Of course, you still have the option of isolating certain groups to drill down on detail data, as you did with the other types of reports.

The ability to show data in two dimensions makes it significantly easier to analyze data and the option to drill down on details or selected groups of details turns this type of report into a cause analysis tool.

But you can be forgiven for feeling that you still want more flexibility in creating reports. In particular, the limitation to only use two levels of related records, or three in the case of many-to-many relationships, is a limiting factor. In the next section you overcome that limitation, as well as opening up your reports to a new method of collecting data for the reports.

Custom Report Types

You have already been introduced to the concept of report types. You have used default Force Platform report types with the reports you created in the previous section. You can also create your own custom report types. These custom report types connect more than a pair of related objects. Custom report types can include data normally not included. You can enlarge the scope of your Force Platform reports without sacrificing any of the power and functionality that you have already discovered.

A Custom Report Type links up to four levels of an object hierarchy. In addition, each level in the custom report type includes fields from up to a total of 20 related objects across all the levels of the Custom Report Type.

So far, you have used objects with a fairly simple set of relationships, reducing the complexity of the model while still learning some of the basics of the Force Platform. To understand more about Custom Report Types, you need to add a more complex object to your Force Platform database.

The recruiting application you have been building has left out a critical component of the recruiting process—the interview. The script file you were directed to run at the start of this chapter created and populated a new object in your application for connecting interviewers and job applications, the Interview object. The Intervier object has a lookup relationship to both the Job Application object and the User object. The Custom Report Object combines the Job Application object with the Interview object, bringing in fields from objects that are related to these objects.

Defining a Custom Report Type

You can create a Custom Report Type that incorporates the Job Application, the Interview object, and a couple of related objects.

1. To create a Custom Report Type, click **Setup ➤ Create ➤ Report Types**. A page with a basic explanation of how Custom Report Types work displays. Click **Continue** to go to a list view for Custom Report Types, and **New Custom Report Type** to bring up the page shown in below.

    This page prompts you for the Primary Object for the Custom Report Type. The primary object is the object at the top of the Custom Report Type hierarchy, the object that drives the entire record type.

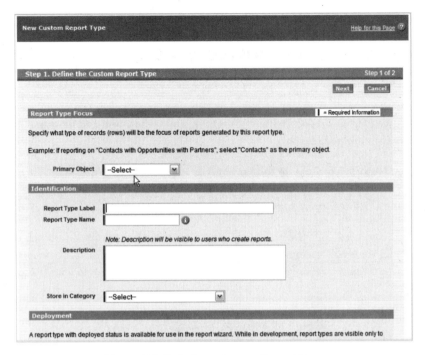

Figure 100: Defining a Custom Report Type

2. Select the `Positions` object as the `Primary Object`. Note that the object is referred to here by its plural name. The Positions object is the parent in a lookup relationship with Job Applications, which is, in turn, the parent of Interviews, making it the primary object for this Custom Report Type.

3. Give the Custom Report Type a `Report Type Label` of `Interviews, Positions and Candidates`, and accept the default for the Report Type Name. Add a description that explains the purpose of the Custom Report Type and select the `Other Reports` category for storage.

4. Mark the Custom Report Type as `Deployed` to allow the Custom Report Type to be used for reports by standard users. If you leave the default of `In Development`, the Custom Report Type only displays to administrators and their delegates.

5. Click **Next** to bring up the page shown, in its completed state, in the following figure.

   This page begins with the primary object, a diagram to the right of the object indicating that all of the records in the object are used, and a box below the object you can click to bring up a list of related objects.

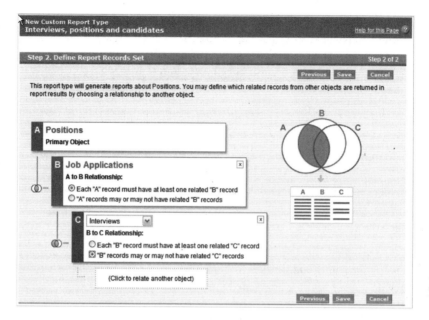

Figure 101: Objects in a Custom Report Type

6. Click the box to bring up a list of related objects and a choice as to how to combine the objects.

7. Select the `Job Applications` object. This action changes the diagram in the center of the page to show the records for the Custom Report Type as the intersection between the Job Applications object and the Positions.

   The diagram is more than just a pretty picture. The current state of the diagram represents the standard use of related objects by the Force Platform report system. In order for a Position record to be included in the record set of the Custom Report Type, there must be at least one Interviewer record associated with it. In relational terms, this linkage is called an inner join.

   This type of selection is appropriate for this relationship since you do not want to see any positions that do not have at least one application. But the story is a little bit different for the next object in the Custom Report Type.

8. Click the box below Job Applications to bring up a list of related objects.

9. Select `Interviews`, which was added to your organization as part of the initialization process described at the start of this chapter.

   Assigning interviews is one of the later steps in the recruiting process, so there may be positions with a lot of applications, but no interview scheduled yet. If you used the standard inner join, this report type will not include any job applications that do not have associated interviews, and also rejecting the associated positions. This is not what you want.

In relational terms, you want to use an outer join to link Job Applications and Interviews, which will include Job Applications in the report whether they have associated Interviews or not.

10. To retrieve all Job Application records, click the lower choice in the B to C relationship radio group labeled "B" records may or may not have related "C" records.. A Job Application record may or may not have related "C" records (the Interviewer records, in this case). Notice that clicking on this lower choice changes the diagram to increase the section shaded.

11. Click **Save** to save the Custom Report Type.

You have defined the basic Custom Report Type, combining Positions with Job Applications with Interviews, while allowing Job Applications to be listed even if they do not yet have any associated interviews.

The final step in creating your new Custom Report Type is to make fields from related objects—in this case the Candidate object, which is related to the Job Application object—available to report designers.

12. Click **Edit Layout** in the section at the bottom of the page. This familiar looking page lets you adjust the page layout shown to users of the Custom Report Type when they are building reports. Start by getting rid of the fields that your users do not need in the reports this report type supports.

13. Drag and drop the Created By, Created Date, Last Activity... and the two Last Modified... fields from all three objects to the box in the lower right, removing them from their respective sections. Select multiple objects to move with the Control-Click keyboard combination.

14. Remove the Owner field from the Interviews section in the same way.

15. Double click the checked field in the Job Applications section to bring up the properties for that field. Uncheck the checkbox to prevent this field from being checked for inclusion in the report by default, and click **OK**.

You can also change the label displayed for a field in a report through the same method. As with custom summary fields above, you might sometimes create a custom report type to duplicate standard report types to change the labels for the fields.

The reports you want to base on this Custom Report Type might also require include data from the Candidate object related to the Job Application object. For ease of understanding, create another section in this page to hold the Candidate fields.

16. Click **Create New Section** to create a new section with the name of Candidates. Drag the section to reside between the Positions and the Job Applications section.

17. Use the box that received the fields you removed from the existing page sections to add fields to the Candidates section. In the box on the lower right, select the Job Applications object, and click the **Add fields related via lookup link** below the picklist to bring up a dialog with a list of objects related to Job Applications. Select the `Candidates` object.

18. In the list of Candidate fields, select the `Candidate ID`, `Email`, `First Name`, `Last Name`, `Mobile`, and `Phone` fields. Click **OK**. These fields will automatically be added to the Job Applications section of the layout—you will recognize them by the magnifying glass lookup icon.

 Tip: The reports for this Custom Report Type might not require all of these fields, but the report type is used for additional reports that might want access to some of these fields in the future.

You can also define a field as 'checked' for inclusion in a report by default, saving users the time of checking frequently used report fields. Set this attribute by double-clicking on a field in the field layout and selecting `Checked by Default`.

19. Select the fields just added from the Candidate object and drag them to the Candidates section.

20. Click **Save** to save the new page layout and return to the detail page for the report type.

You have successfully created your first custom report type that you can use immediately to create a new report.

Using a Custom Report Type

You can use the newly created Custom Report Type as the basis of a matrix report.

1. Return to the reporting tab of the Force Platform environment. Create a new matrix report based on the Custom Report Type you just created by clicking **Create New Custom Report ➤ Other Reports ➤ Interviews, positions and candidates ➤ Matrix report ➤ Next**.

2. Set the Row Headings to `Job Description` and `Candidate: Candidate ID` and the Column Heading to `Interviewer: Full Name` and click **Next**.

3. Since the number of records is automatically included in the cells and totals of the matrix report, you do not need to select any summary fields. Click **Next**.

4. Deselect `Position ID` and `Interviewer ID` in the report columns page. Select `Candidate: First Name`, `Candidate: Last Name`, `Candidate: Phone`, and `Candidate: Email` for the report columns. You do not need to select the `Job Description`, `Candidate ID` or the `Full Name` of the Interviewer object since these are already included in the headings. Click **Next**.

5. Leave the ordering of the columns as is and click **Next**.

6. Change the View selection to `All positions` and remove the Start Data and End Date values to allow for all records to be displayed. Add a selection condition to only include Positions with a `Status` of `Open`. Uncheck the `Show report details` checkbox at the bottom of the page to initially display only the summary information. Click **Run Report** to display the report shown in the figure below[

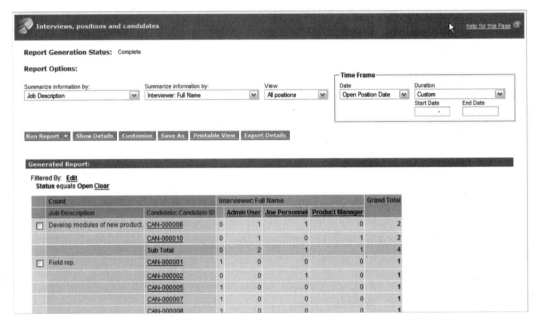

Figure 102: Report created from a Custom Report Type

This report provides a nice concise display, highlighting the open jobs with applications pending. If someone wants to get a detailed look at the candidate, they click the `Candidate ID` link. To simply see the basic information about the candidate, the user chooses **Show Details** to reveal the candidate's name and contact information.

This section has introduced you to the concepts behind an implementation of custom report types. Custom report types can give you and your users a vastly more robust foundation for your Force Platform reports.

Since the introduction of the Force Platform reporting system with your first standard report, you have seen how the same system can support increasingly flexible and sophisticated reports. But one of the nicest things about Force Platform reports is that the development and user interface remains pretty much the same, even with this greatly enlarged scope of functionality and coverage. You still define reports with a simple wizard, you still modify reports at runtime or save them in a specific format, and all reports still include the ability to both isolate key groups of data, and to drill down to the detail level of individual records.

The next section broadens the footprint of Force Platform reports by giving you the ability to create objects with built-in analytical calculations, to enlarge the range of how you can manipulate data and increase the performance of reports.

Analytic Snapshots

Reports, by their nature, are a representation of the state of your data at a certain point in time, including data values taken from underlying data objects at that time. If the data changes, a second, minute or day after the report, the existing report does not reflect those changes.

The data in a report is static by its very nature–there is no getting around it. Typically, report users understand this inherent limitation. Data in a report is old, but there is such a thing as data that is too old and therefore invalid.

Individuals can, of course, run a report whenever they want to see the latest data. This approach has some virtues, but also some downsides. Running a report over and over again not only increases resource requirements for the report and its consumers, but there is no guarantee that these multiple reports contain the same data, leading to potential problems of data integrity.

The Force Platform includes a way to address these problems—the *analytic snapshot*. An analytic snapshot is a way to direct the output from a report into a custom object. This custom object can then be used as the basis for report types and a wide range of reports, based on a static set of data.

You can schedule an analytic snapshot to run at certain times, controlling its refresh rate. By setting up a regular refresh of analytic snapshots, you create the data groundwork for spotting and understanding overall trends in your systems. You also use analytic snapshots to emulate the functionality provided by 'batch' reports run on a daily or weekly schedule.

Creating an Analytic Snapshot

Creating an analytic snapshot involves three steps:

1. Create a custom object that receives the data produced.
2. Create a report that generates the data directed to the custom object.
3. Link the report to the object and schedule the execution of the collection.

These analytic snapshots can also be used as the basis for dashboards, discussed in the final section of this chapter. They focus on the overall progress of the recruiting process, displaying trends in the number of applications received each week, the number of positions posted each week and the number of positions closed each week.

Creating the Custom Object

The data for the first trend is captured in the custom object you create in this section.

1. 1. Go to **Setup ➤ Create ➤ Objects** to start the creation of a new object. Click **New Custom Object**.
2. Create a new custom object with the `Object Name` of `Recruiting Tracker`, a plural name of `Recruiting Tracker Records`, an appropriate description, a `Record Name` of `Recruiting Tracker ID` with a `Data Type` of `Auto Number`, and a `Display Format` of `TRACK-{00000}`. Allow reports for this object, but there is no need to allow activities or track field history. Click **Save**.
3. Add the fields listed in the table below.

Table 6: Field for an analytic snapshot

Data Type	Name	Size
Lookup	Job Application	
Lookup	Candidate	
Text	First Name	30
Text	Last Name	30
Lookup	Position	
Application Created Date	Date	
Date/Time Collected	Date/Time	

 Note: Why did you include more information in this custom object than just the summary information? You will see, in the next section, that the reports you create from the analytic snapshot can also be used for a more detailed view of the data.

The other components required to receive the analytic snapshot data were created by following the instructions for this chapter in the Code Share project for the book, called out at the beginning of this chapter, and explained in *Chapter 1: Welcome to the Force Platform*.

Creating a Report

The report you create to feed data to the analytic snapshot is pretty simple since the purpose of this snapshot is only to collect basic data on a weekly basis.

1. Go to the Report tab and create a new report, based on the report type in Other Reports named `Positions with Job Applications and Candidates`.
2. Accept the default of a tabular report and click **Next**.
3. Select the following fields for the report:

   - `Position: ID`
   - `Job Application: ID`
   - `Job Application: Created Date`
   - `Candidate: Candidate ID`
   - `Candidate: First Name`
   - `Candidate: Last Name`

   These report columns match up with the fields in the custom object you just created. Make sure to uncheck the `Job Application: Job Application ID`, `Candidate: Candidate ID`, and `Postion: Postion ID` fields.

4. You do not need to add any summary information or order the columns, so jump to the Select Criteria page. Change the `View` to `All positions`, the next `Columns` field to `Job Application: Created Date` and the `Duration` to `Last 7 Days` under the `Day` heading in the picklist.
5. You can run the report now and then save it, or simply save it as an unfiled public report named `Applications Posted`.

Now that you have created the destination and collection reports for the analytic snapshot, you can put them into action.

Creating an Analytic Snapshot

Once you have a custom object as a destination and a report to feed data to that destination, you can define an analytic snapshot.

1. Go to **Setup ➤ Data Management ➤ Analytic Snapshot** to see a splash page with an overview of analytic snapshots. Bypass the splash page and click **New Analytic Snapshot** to bring up the page shown in below.

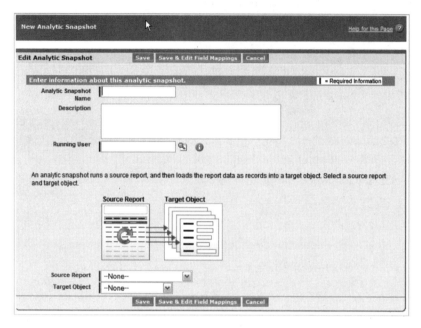

Figure 103: New Analytic Snapshot definition page

2. Name the new analytic snapshot `Recruiting Snapshot` and enter an appropriate description.
3. Set the running user to the administrator so that the snapshot picks up all the job applications.
4. Select the report and custom object you just created for the `Source Report` and the `Target Object`. Click **Save** to bring up the page shown in the following figure.

    You can see the basic information in the top section and three additional sections. The second section, Field Mappings, must be completed before scheduling an analytic snapshot.

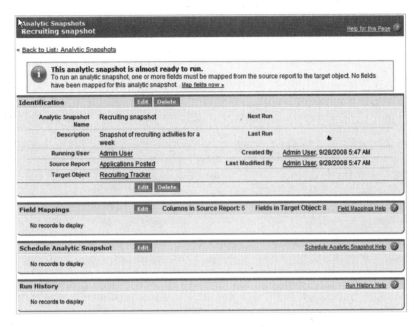

Figure 104: Analytic Snapshot configuration page

5. Click **Edit** in the Field mapping section to map the fields in the report to the fields in the custom object on the page shown below.

The picklists on the left contain all the fields in the report that are appropriate to match with the fields in the target object. For the Job Application, Candidate, and Position lookup fields, there is only one field available for matching. The picklists for the text fields contain all the fields in the report and the picklists for the date fields contain only date fields from the report.

Text and data field picklists also contain three fields that are related to the analytic snapshot itself: Analytic Snapshot Name, Analytic Snapshot Running User and Execution time. Use these fields to identify rows in the target table based on attributes of the scheduled run of the analytic snapshot.

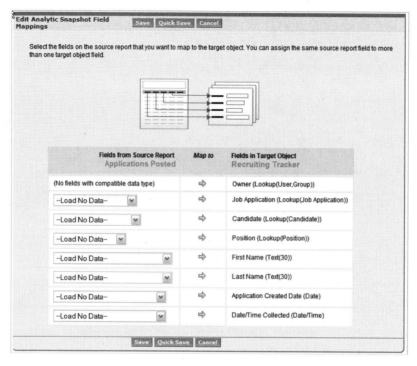

Figure 105: Mapping fields for an Analytic Snapshot

6. Select the following fields from the source report to match up with their corresponding fields in the target object:

Table 7: Mapping report fields to object fields for analytic snapshot

Source Report Fields	Target Object Fields
Owner	Unassigned - user who runs snapshot is assigned
Job Application: ID	Job Application
Candidate: Record ID	Candidate
Position: ID	Position
Candidate: First Name	First Name
Candidate: Last Name	Last Name
Job Application: Created Date	Application Created Date
Execution Time	Execution Time

Source Report Fields	Target Object Fields
Position: ID	Position

7. Click **Save** to save the field mappings and return to the detail page for the analytic snapshot. When you return to the detail page, you see that the warning message about your analytic snapshot is gone since you have defined your field mappings. You can now schedule your analytic snapshot to run.

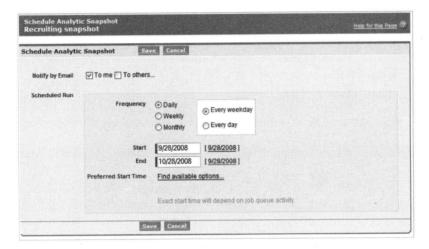

Figure 106: Scheduling Analytic Snapshot

8. Click **Edit** in the Schedule Analytic Snapshot section to bring up the page shown above.

In this page, you can specify who receives an email notice that contains information on the outcome of a scheduled run. Typically you leave the default selection of To Me checked, although you can also specify any individual user or public group, described in the next chapter.

In the lower section, you assign the times you want the analytic snapshot to run. You can choose from daily runs, either every day or only on weekdays, weekly or monthly and set the range of dates to use this schedule.

If you click the Preferred Start Time, you receive one or more options for the start time of the analytic snapshot run. The number of choices depends on the specifics of the your Force Platform edition. The choices are determined by the geographic region supported by your organization's Force Platform instance, with three random start times chosen from off-peak hours for that node. To avoid overloading the Force Platform servers, a randomized start time is assigned for each snapshot run, somewhere within 30 minutes of the selected start time.

Your particular edition of the Force Platform has limits on the number of snapshots you can run over a certain period of time. Analytic snapshots also have a limit on the number of rows they can contain. If the report feeding the snapshot produces more than the designated limit, additional records are not inserted into the object, and are reported as failed inserts.

9. Select `Weekly` as the `Frequency` and `Sunday` as the selected date. Leave the default start and end times, which allocate a month of runs, and select a preferred start time.

10. Click **Save** to save the schedule and return to the detail page for the snapshot. When you get to the detail page, you see your new schedule listed in the Schedule Analytic Snapshot section.

When the snapshot runs, you receive an email listing the results, including a link to a detail page for the report run. The report run is also listed on the detail page for the analytic snapshot.

An analytic snapshot run can have several results. A run can result in some row failures, such as if a row was not inserted due to a missing value for a required field, or a failed validation, or a run can completely fail to run, such as if the user designated to run the snapshot is not active at the scheduled time.

 Caution: Triggers and workflows on a target object are not executed as a result of an analytic snapshot run. In fact, you are not allowed to use an object with a trigger as the target of a snapshot, and adding a trigger to a target object results in the run failing.

You have now learned how to create and use analytic snapshots. The final section in this chapter covers dashboards that require a few more analytic snapshots, as well as historical data, to work properly, which were loaded in the initialization task for the chapter, described in the Code Share project for this book.

Scheduled Reports

Analytic snapshots include a way to schedule a report to run at a specific time. This functionality is also available for any report in the Force Platform report system. You might have already noticed the interface to this scheduling capability. The **Run Report** button on report pages actually has a dropdown arrow on the right hand side of the button with a choice for running or scheduling the report. Choosing to schedule a report brings up the same scheduling page that you used with your analytic snapshot.

When a scheduled report runs, the content of the report is delivered in the email message specified on the scheduling page. This approach is different from analytic snapshots that save the data from the report in a custom object for later examination and use. In a scheduled report, the data is not persisted in the Force Platform database. There is also no record of the success or failure of a scheduled report run outside of the email messages sent on its completion.

Dashboards

Throughout this chapter, you have been moving to higher levels of collection and aggregation: from collections of individual records identified through search and tagging, to standard report, to summary and matrix reports, and to collection of data for trend analysis with analytic snapshots. The greater the aggregation of data, the more far-reaching and potentially valuable the information you can extract.

But you cannot keep increasing the complexity or size of your reports as you increase the amount of data used for the report, as the key points in the report will be obscured by its complexity. To solve the problem of making data understandable, without sacrificing either the aggregation or the ability to easily drill down to determine the sources of the aggregations, the Force Platform gives you dashboards.

You have already seen an example of a default dashboard on the home page of the intial application, which was certainly not meaningful to the purposes of your recruiting application. In this last exploration of the Force Platform reporting system, you create a dashboard to provide a quick overview of the overall progress of Universal Containers' recruiting effort. This page area contains charts to illustrate the trends for the number of applications posted for all jobs, the number of positions created and the number of positions closed, all on a weekly basis. In addition, the dashboard indicates the number of currently open positions. All of these components automatically link to reports that provide more detail for further exploration of the data represented.

Creating a Dashboard

The first step to adding dashboards to your application is to create the dashboard itself.

1. Go to the listing of additional tabs and select Dashboards to bring up the Dashboard tab, and then the **Go to Dashboard list** link.
2. The Dashboard list view contains the default dashboards for your organization. Click **New Dashboard** to begin creating your specific dashboard with the page shown below.

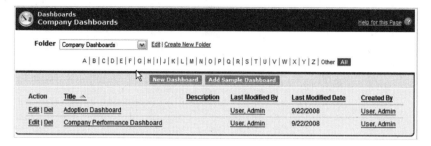

Figure 107: Defining a Dashboard

3. Give the new dashboard a `Title` of `Recruiting Overview Dashboard` and an appropriate description. Leave the default `Dashboard Layout Style` of `Three columns`.

4. Assign the administrative user as the `Running User`, and leave the default folder of Company Dashboards selected.

   As with report folders mentioned above, the folders used for storing dashboards are the way that you can control access to a dashboard. You grant access to dashboard folders, allowing or preventing users from being able to use the dashboards in those folders.

    Tip: You can also limit user access to dashboards through the Home Page Layout you used earlier in this chapter. You can create multiple page layouts for the Home page, some with the dashboard component visible and others without. If you assign a Home Page Layout without dashboard components to a user, that user will not be able to display any dashboards on their home page.

   The dashboard is created from a report that is executed with the privileges of the Running User. This feature allows you to create dashboards that give a higher level view of data to an individual user who might not normally have access to that data, such as a component that shows aggregate information from all positions, rather than positions owned by a user or the user's group.

5. In the bottom section, change the `Title Size` to `14 pt`, leave the `Background Fade Direction` as `Diagonal` and change the `Ending Color` to a light shade. This bottom section allows you to assign a common look and feel to all the graphical components that are in this particular dashboard.

6. Click **Save** to take you to the page shown below.

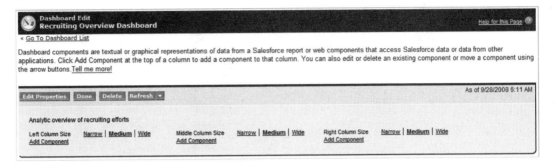

Figure 108: Starting to define a dashboard

On this page, you add components to the newly created dashboard.

Creating a Dashboard Component

A dashboard component is created from an existing report. The first dashboard component you create compares the number of applications submitted per week over time.

You have already created an analytic snapshot for collecting the data that exposes this trend, so you have to create a simple report based on that snapshot.

1. Go to the Reports tab and click **Create New Custom Report ➤ Other Reports** and the custom object that was the target of the analytic snapshot you created linked to the Candidate object, `Recruiting Tracker Records with Candidate`.

2. Select `Summary Report` and click **Next**. Jump to the Select Grouping page and select `Date/Time Collected` as the top level group.

3. Jump to the Select Criteria page. Change the `View` to `All recruiting tracker records`, the `Columns` to `Date/Time Collected`, and the `Duration` to `Last 90 Days`. Click **Run Report** to insure that the data being displayed is appropriate and save the report as `Applications Posted Trend`.

4. Return to the Dashboards tab to take you to the empty dashboard you just created. Click **Edit** to take you back to the page where you can define dashboard components.

5. Click **Add Component** in the left column to bring up the page shown below.

   On this page, you define the attributes for a dashboard component.

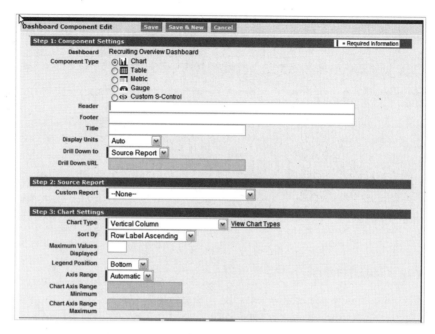

Figure 109: Defining a dashboard component

6. Leave the `Component Type` as a `Chart`, and add a `Header` of `Applications Posted Trends`. Select the `Applications Posted Trends` report as the source and leave all the other values as defaults.

7. Click on **Save** to see your new component, which will look something like the following figure.

Your new dashboard component looks pretty good. The use of a chart makes it easy to see how the number of applications submitted has changed on a weekly basis. You can use links at the top of the component to edit the properties of the component or delete the component entirely. You can also add more components to this column of the dashboard and size the column to one of three sizes.

Now that you understand how easy it is to create a component, you (and your users) no doubt want to add more components to the dashboard. Use the reports that were loaded as part of the initialization process for this chapter.

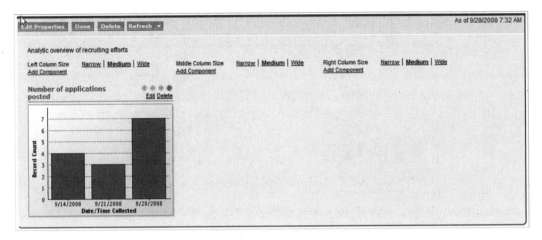

Figure 110: Your first dashboard component

8. Click the **Add Component** link in the middle column of the dashboard. Give this new component a `Header` of `Positions Created Trend`, use the `Positions Created Trend` report for the component, and choose a `Line report` as the chart type. Click **Save** to return to the dashboard layout page.

9. Create the third component in the column on the right. Set the `Header` to `Positions Closed Trend`, use the `Positions Closed Trend` report, and select `Line` as the chart type. Click **Save** to return to the layout page for the dashboard.

 Note: The analytic snapshot underlying these two reports, Positions Tracker, was loaded as part of the initialization process for this chapter. In practice, you would enabling field history for the Status field in the Position record and collect the records for the snapshot by running reports against that history.

Just like that, you have created your first dashboard. The Force Platform report system builds in a lot of functionality based on defaults taken from the underlying reports, such as the proper axis labels and metrics for the axes.

Your Dashboard at Work

The Force Platform allows you to see your dashboard at work in your application immediately.

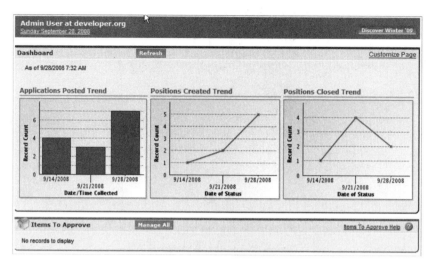

Figure 111: Your dashboard at work

1. Click the Home tab of your application. You can see your new dashboard already in place, as shown in the figure above.

    You can start with the **Refresh** button at the top of the page. By default, dashboards are not rebuilt every time the dashboard is retrieved. This approach makes sense since a dashboard can be assembled from a large amount of data, and since dashboards are typically used for an overview, rather than a real-time display. A single dashboard can also be used by many different users with similar requirements, so reusing a single dashboard makes sense.

    All dashboards have a status message at the top of the dashboard that indicates when the dashboard was last created. A user can click on the **Refresh** button to recreate the dashboards for the current state of data.

    Keep in mind that the Refresh button does not really have an effect on these particular reports since they are all based on an analytic snapshot that is only refreshed on a weekly basis. Later in this section, you add another component that accesses real-time data.

Dashboards and data refresh The Force Platform keeps a single copy of a dashboard for all uses of that dashboard. When any user refreshes a dashboard, the single copy of the dashboard is refreshed, which means that any subsequent use of the dashboard by any user displays the new version, noted with the time of the refresh.

You can schedule periodic refreshes of a dashboard through the **Run Dashboard** button. If you are using dashboard components based on an analytical snapshot, as these dashboard components are, schedule an automatic refresh for the dashboard just after the snapshots are refreshed.

The other aspect of this page is the **Customize Page** link in the upper right corner of the dashboard section. This link gives your users the option to select another dashboard snapshot for their home page. By default, the last dashboard viewed by a user is displayed on their Home Page. Selecting a specific dashboard snapshot through the customize page link sets the selected dashboard as the default for that user.

Notice too that component for the Home page is referred to as a Dashboard Snapshot, not a Dashboard. The reason for this different name is that a dashboard can have many components in each column, but the Dashboard Snapshot only shows the first row of components.

Dashboards give a high level view of data and trends, but all dashboards also include the built-in ability for a user to get to the source data for that dashboard.

2. Click the **Applications Posted Trends** dashboard component in the left column to bring up the report on which the dashboard was based.

All dashboard components include this drill down mechanism. This report presented is run on real-time production data. This difference means that the detailed report shown when a user drills down from the dashboard component might actually show different data than the component itself since the data in the report is current and the dashboard might not be. Of course, the current usage does not have this potential issue since the report is based on an analytic snapshot.

In the components you created so far, you accepted the default target for the drill down action, the underlying report. But you can also designate a specific URL as the drill down target, which could be any page—including another dashboard to give users three levels of detail.

Multiple Levels of Dashboards

For the previous dashboard, you created components that displayed trends based on data collected into an analytic snapshot. Although trend analysis is a powerful analytic process, your users probably also want a way to quickly look at some aggregate information about currently open positions.

You can implement this by creating a dashboard with some components to analyze this information in real time, and a way to get to this dashboard from the dashboard you just created.

1. Return to the Dashboards tab. Click **Edit**. Select the **Add Component** link in the left hand column.

2. Select `Metric` as the `Component` type and use the `Open Positions` report as the source report. Set the `Metric Label` to `Currently Open Positions`.

3. Add some `Indicator Colors` to display the metric in different colors. Choose 5 as the `Breakpoint #1` value and 10 as the `Breakpoint #2` value. The breakpoints work in conjunction with the different range colors. If the value displayed is lower than `Breakpoint #1`, the value is shown in the `Low Range Color`. If the value is between `Breakpoint #1` and `Breakpoint #2`, the `Middle Range Color` is used, while the `High Range Color` is used if the value is greater than `Breakpoint #2`.

4. Change the `Low Range Color` to green and the `High Range Color` to red.

5. Click **Save** to return to the dashboard, as shown below.

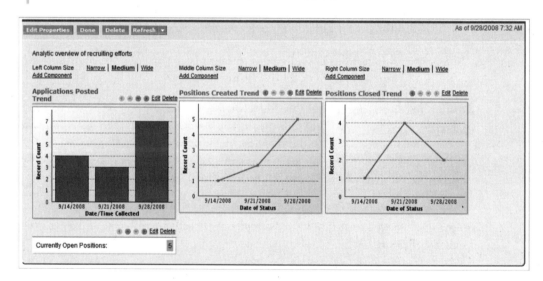

Figure 112: Modified dashboard

6. The new metric looks fine, but you need to display it at the top of the rightmost column. Click the little up arrow above the metric you just created to move the component to the top of the left column.

Dashboard snapshots and dashboards

If you return to the Home tab for your application, the components displayed look like the figure below.

What happened to the second component in the left column? Remember, the Home Page Component is a dashboard snapshot, not a complete dashboard, which means only the first line of components in a dashboard is displayed. You can give users access to the complete dashboard with a Custom Link in the left hand panel that you can configure through the **Customize** option for the Home Page. You can also change the design of your top level dashboard to have only two components, one that drills down to an additional dashboard on open positions and another that drilled down to the analytic components.

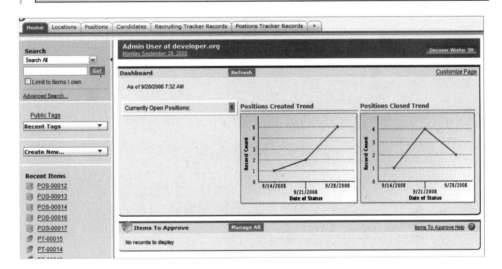

Figure 113: Dashboard snapshot

When you created this new component, you left the default drill-down destination of the source report. But once a user sees the number of open positions, they very well might want to get some analytical information about those open positions. You can provide this by creating another dashboard and linking the component to that new dashboard.

1. Click the **Go to Dashboard List** link and click **New Dashboard**.

2. Give the new dashboard a `Title` of `Open Positions` and an appropriate description. Change the `Dashboard Layout Style` to Two Columns. Set the `Running User` to the administrative user, as you did for the previous dashboard. Click **Save**.

3. Add a component to the left-hand column. The component must be a Chart with a `Header` of `Open Positions by Department`. Set the `Custom Report` to `Open positions by department` and the `Chart Type` to `Pie`. Click **Save**.

4. Click **Add Component** in the right-hand column. Set the `Component Type` to `Chart`, the `Header` to `Open Positions by Days Since Posted`, the `Custom Report` to `Open positions by days since posted` and the `Chart Type` as `Line`. Click **Save**.

The new dashboard is shown in the figure below, and it looks good.

The last step in creating multiple levels of dashboards is to make this dashboard the target of the metric you just created, rather than the source report. As mentioned above, you can direct the user to any URL when they click on a dashboard component.

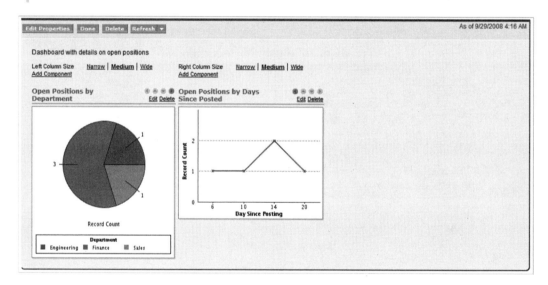

Figure 114: Open Positions dashboard

5. Copy the URL from the navigation bar in your browser and return to the Dashboards tab. Select the overview dashboard you previously created and click **Edit**.

6. Click **Edit** for the metric component you created. Change the `Drill Down to Picklist` value to `Other URL` and paste the URL you copied into the `Drill Down URL` field. Edit the URL so that all that remains is a forward slash and the record ID, such as `/01Z0000000000aB4`. The Force Platform adds the appropriate server for the current org.

7. Click **Save** to return to the dashboard itself. Click the metric component to take you to the dashboard you just created.

Your users can drill down to this additional level of graphical display and then click to the base reports for each of these components for even more detail. The simplicity of dashboard creation and linkage make it easy for you to give your users powerful analytic tools, which not only adds to the value created by your Force Platform systems but also makes you a hero to your user community.

As mentioned earlier, you can also limit access to dashboards. The Force Platform includes a complete security system that allows you to grant access to most Force Platform components, as well as limiting the data that users can access within Force Platform objects. The Force Platform security system is the subject of the next chapter.

Summary

You have covered a lot of ground in this lengthy chapter. Using your collected data to present higher levels of information through aggregation is one of the keys to unlocking the value stored in your data repository.

In this chapter, you learned about ad hoc data aggregation, through search, and semi-structured aggregation using tags. You now understand the reporting hierarchy built into the Force Platform, from simple to matrix reports, all the way to dashboards. And you can see the ways you can created snapshots of data for trend analysis.

Of course, as with all the areas covered in this book, there is still a lot more to learn about Force Platform data aggregation, but you now have the foundation to conduct your own explorations and investigations. In the next chapter, you will move from unlocking value in your data to protecting your data from unwanted examination.

Chapter 7

Protecting Your Data

Data is the core of your information stack, and, more importantly, the repository of the business value of all of your systems. The value provided by your data justifies the very existence of your company's entire IT investment—including you!

You have to be sure that your data is safe and sound, protected from unauthorized access from outside your company, as well as safeguarded from inappropriate usage by your user community.

The Force Platform is built with security as the foundation for the entire platform. This foundation includes both protection for your data and applications, and the ability to implement your own security scheme, which must be able to flexibly reflect the structure and needs of your organization. The security features of the Force Platform provide both strength and flexibility.

In this chapter, you will learn how the platform itself is protected with built-in security guards and controls. More importantly for your task as a developer, you will come to understand how you can implement access limitations for your own data and applications to meet the specific requirements of your organization.

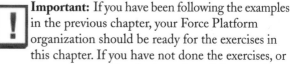 **Important:** If you have been following the examples in the previous chapter, your Force Platform organization should be ready for the exercises in this chapter. If you have not done the exercises, or want to start with a fresh version of the sample

Recruiting application, please refer to the instructions in the Code Share project for this book. You can find information on how to access that project in *Chapter 1: Welcome to the Force Platform.*

Force Platform Security

Justifiably or not, a multi-tenant, on-demand platform is the subject of more doubt in the area of security than an in-house platform. To guarantee the security of your own organization, the Force Platform includes a range of security defenses that are automatically used to guard your data resources.

Organization Security

One of the core features of a multi-tenant platform is the use of a single pool of computing resources to service the needs of many different customers. The Force Platform protects your organization from all other customer organizations by using a unique organization identifier that is associated with your Force Platform session.

Once you log into your Force Platform organization, your subsequent requests are associated with your organization, and only your organization, using this identifier. With this safeguard, all access to your organization is protected by the user authentication.

User Security

Users are identified to the Force Platform by their user name and password. You can specify the password policies through the **Setup ➤ Security Controls ➤ Password Policies** as shown below.

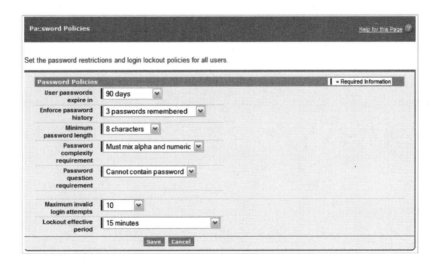

Figure 115: Password Policies

This page gives you the ability to set policies involving how frequently passwords must be changed, whether a user can re-use a recent password, password complexity requirements and how the platform treats invalid login attempts. These password domain settings are usually handled by administrators, but you can rest assured that your deployment environment can be secured with these settings.

Security settings and API access

The focus of this book is on applications running on the Force Platform, rather than applications accessing the platform through the Force Platform API. But you should be aware that some of the standard security features discussed in this section work somewhat differently for API access. For instance, if a user logs into an application running on the Force Platform and their password has expired, they are prompted to change the password. An expired password prevents access through the API, but applications that access the platform through the API have to detect this problem procedurally.

The session timeout discussed later in this section is sensitive to any user interaction through the standard Force Platform user interface, but the time limit on a session is enforced on an entire API session, regardless of user interaction. In addition, there is no warning given before an API session is terminated. Because of this, access through the Force Platform API should not assume the existence of an active session.

Administrators can force the expiration of passwords for one or more users through the **Setup ➤ Manager Users ➤ Users** page, or force the expiration of all passwords for all users with the Expire All Passwords option in the Security Control area of the Administrative Setup section of the Setup menu.

All users are assigned to a user profile, which is examined in more detail in the section on user-based permissions below.

User Authentication

The Force Platform has its own system of user authentication, but some companies would like to use an existing single sign-on capability to simplify and standardize their user security.

You have two options to implement single sign-on with the Force Platform: delegated authentication and Security Assertion Markup Language (SAML).

- **Delegated Authentication** - With this approach, a user logs into the Force Platform as usual, but the platform uses a web service callout to submit the user name and password to an external authorization authority. Once that authority approves the logon, the approval is passed back to the Force Platform and the user can proceed. If you want to use delegated authentication, you will have to contact Salesforce.com to enable this feature for your organization and then create a Web Service callout to the authentication authority.

- **SAML** - Using SAML, your request goes to the SAML authority that validates your identity and returns a token. The token is passed to the Force Platform that verifies the user with the authority. This approach is typically used when your users are accessing your Force Platform applications through a portal, which would handle the initial authentication and avoid the need to log into the Force Platform environment again. You can configure SAML for your organization through the **Setup ➤ Security Controls ➤ Single Sign-On Page**.

Both of these single sign-on options are described in much more detail in the online documentation and in articles available at the developer.force.com site.

Network-based Security

To provide a level of network-based security, the Force Platform includes the ability to limit access to your organization based on the IP address of your client in two different ways.

You can use a whitelist to indicate the IP address ranges that are allowed to access an organization by default. You can define a whitelist for an entire organization clicking**Setup ➤ Security Controls ➤ Network Access ➤ New**, as shown in the following figure.

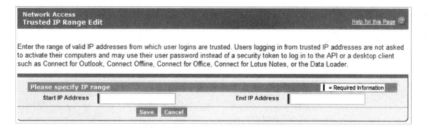

Figure 116: Network Access

You can define multiple IP ranges for your organization. You cannot use this feature to whitelist all IP addresses since there is a limit on the number of IP addresses that can be defined in a range; however, the limit is generous enough to allow for a broad range of specified IP addresses.

If you define a set of allowable IP addresses for your organization, all login attempts from those IP addresses are accepted by default. If a user tries to log in from an IP address that is not specified for the org, they are challenged by the Force Platform, which then sends them an email. The user must click on a link in the email to allow access from the new IP address. Once this reply is sent, the user can log in from the current IP address in the future.

If no IP addresses are defined for the organization, a user must respond to this challenge the first time they log in from an IP address.

This challenge mechanism is fine if a user is actually attempting to log into the platform, but does not work if a user or application is trying to access the organization through the Web Services API, described in the next chapter. In this situation, a login request must include a security token appended to the password for the user. The user generates a security token through the **Setup ➤ My Personal Information ➤ Reset My Security Token** option that sends an email to the user with the security token. Some utilities, such as Data Loader, use the Web Services API to access the Force Platform, so use of these utilities from an unfamiliar IP address requires the use of a security token.

Profiles can also be used to define a range of acceptable IP addresses, although the IP addresses defined for a profile are restrictive, rather than acceptable defaults. If a profile has IP addresses defined, any user with that profile cannot log into the Force Platform from any other IP address.

Profiles are also used to restrict the hours that a user can log into the platform. You can set either of these restrictions for a particular profile from the bottom of the Profiles page under **Administrative Setup ➤ Manage Users**.

The limitations imposed on IP addresses are used to help protect against phishing attacks. A malicious attack cannot be triggered from outside your range of IP addresses, even if the attacker has a correct user name and password.

Session Security

The final area of security for the Force Platform revolves around an individual Force Platform session. The **Setup ➤ Security Controls ➤ Session Settings** page, shown below, allows you to require secure connections to the platform or to lock a session to the originating IP address.

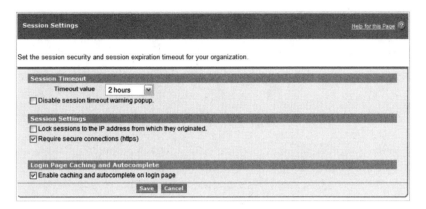

Figure 117: Session Settings

You can also set the time limit for an individual session to between 15 minutes and 8 hours. Once a user's session is inactive for this length of time, the user has to respond to a warning popup. If the user does not respond, the session ends and the user has to log back into the Force Platform. You can also suppress the use of the warning popup.

The session timeout provides some protection from unauthorized access caused by leaving your computer while still logged into the Force Platform.

Auditing

Auditing features do not secure your Force Platform environment by themselves, but these features provide information about client usage of the platform that can be critical in diagnosing potential or real security issues. All objects include fields to store the name of the users who created the record and who last modified the record, providing some basic auditing information, but the Force Platform has features to extend the auditing capabilities of your application and data.

The **Setup ➤ Manage Users ➤ Login History** page displays the last 20 logins to your organization, as well as giving you the ability to download 6 months worth of logins in a comma separated variable file. This file includes session-specific attributes, such as IP address and browser type, which are not available in record and field auditing.

As mentioned earlier, you can turn on auditing for objects with a single click. Object-level auditing tracks changes in the overall object records, such as record creation. You can also enable auditing for individual fields, automatically tracking any changes in the values of selected fields. Although auditing is available for all custom objects, many standard objects do not allow auditing.

Under **Setup ➤ Security Controls**, administrators can use **View Setup Audit Trail** to monitor when meta-data definitions for objects have changed. With this feature, you can track the evolution of your application over time.

Force Platform Security Framework

The previous section of this chapter covered the built-in mechanisms used by the Force Platform to insure that your individual organization is protected from external access. The platform also has a framework you can use to offer different access permissions to authenticated users within your organization.

There are three tiers to the Force Platform security framework:

- Administrative permissions that grant overall security permissions to users or profiles
- Component-based permissions that control access to a range of components, including applications and objects
- Record-based sharing that limits access to individual records

The remainder of this chapter covers the use of each of these areas of the Force Platform personalized security scheme.

Administrative Security

The Force Platform includes a wide range of built-in capabilities. You usually do not want to give all the power of the complete platform to all users in the environment. Administrative permissions are used to grant or deny access to some areas of Force Platform functionality for particular users.

Profiles

Profiles are a way you can group users together for easier administration. A user can belong to one and only one profile, although administrators can change profile membership for a user.

You have already used profiles in previous chapters of this book – to assign access to objects, default record layouts and record types. Profiles are the basis for allowing administrative and component permissions.

Profiles are defined and edited through the **Setup ➤ Manage Users ➤ Profiles** page, which gives you access to detail pages for a profile by clicking on the profile name, as partially shown in the figure below.

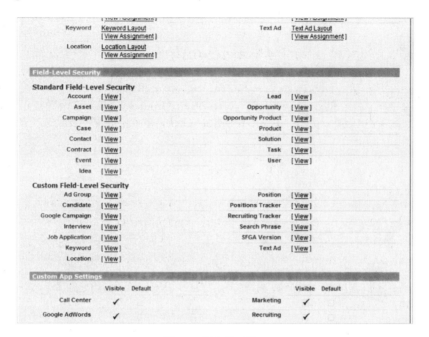

Figure 118: Profiles

This page allows you to assign page layouts, application and tab access and record type settings. Component-based permissions, described in the next section, can also be assigned from this page, along with various administrative and user permissions.

Your Force Platform environment comes with several predefined profiles. Administrators can create custom profiles to fit the needs of their organizations.

Administrative permissions

Administrative permissions allow users to manage higher levels of their Force Platform environment. The highest administrative permissions are granted when a user is assigned to the System Administrator profile, allowing access to all of the Administrative Setup choices.

Some of the other administrative permissions revolve around the use of Salesforce platform applications. The following table provides a summary of the relevant administrative permissions for Force Platform developers.

Table 8: Administrative permissions

Permission Type	Permission	Description
Security	Manage Users	Allows creation and modification of users for the organization, and access to profiles and sharing settings. This permission allows the owner to grant all other permissions to users, so should be assigned with care.
	Password never expires	Eliminates password policy requirements to expire passwords after a designated interval.
	API-enabled	Allows access to organizations through the Force Platform API. Without this permission, users cannot access the platform from outside of native applications.
	API-Only User	Only allows access through the Force Platform API.
	View Setup and Configuration	Gives users the ability to see the organization setup information, but not make any changes to this information.
Supporting Objects	Customize application	Allows user access to the complete Setup menu for Force Platform applications.
	Edit HTML Templates, Manage Letterheads, Manage Public Templates	Allows users to edit various components used by Force Platform components, such as messages sent from workflow and approval processes.
Reports	Manage Custom Report Types, Manage Dashboards,	Allows users to modify various components used in Force Platform reporting. A user

Permission Type	Permission	Description
	Manage Public Reports, Schedule Dashboards	with the Manage Custom Reports privilege can also create new folders for reports.
	Create and Customize Reports	Gives users the ability to create new reports or modify existing reports.
	Export Reports	Allows exporting of data from a report to Excel spreadsheets.
	Run Reports	Without this permission, the Reports tab is not available to the user.
Apex	Author Apex	Allows users to create Apex triggers and classes. Only available in editions that allow access to Apex code, and requires that the user also have the Modify All Data permission.
Data	Disable Outbound Messages	Prevents the use of outbound messages as a workflow activity.
	Edit Read-Only Fields	Overrides read-only limitations set in page layouts.
	Weekly Data Export	Allows users to run a weekly data export.
	View Encrypted Data	Allows users to see data in encrypted fields as plain text data. This feature is not turned on, by default—you can request the feature through salesforce.com.

Four permissions are extremely powerful, and deserve special discussion. The most powerful permission is Manage Users. When a user has this permission, they can grant any other permission to themselves and other users. This permission makes a user into a super administrator who can grant any other permission.

The `Customize Application` permission grants a broad range of permissions that allow a user to control all aspects of an application from creating, editing, and deleting custom fields, to implementing workflow rules. Application developers need this permission, but you should be aware of the range of operations this permission grants. For a full description of these permissions, please refer to the online help.

The `View All Data` and `Modify All Data` permissions override any restrictions on data in any Force Platform objects. These privileges also circumvent the entire system of record-based sharing described later in this chapter. These permissions are granted to the System Administrator profile and can be granted to any custom profile.

Caution: `Modify All Data` grants full object-level privileges (create, read, update and delete) to a user who possesses this permission. A user with this permission also ignores sharing rules for data access. If the permission is revoked, the user will still have the full object-level privileges, but sharing rules will now be in effect.

`Modify All Data` is an extremely powerful permission. A user with this permission can not only edit all data, but also delete all data, and then empty the recycle bin to eliminate all traces of the data—certainly not something you would grant lightly. Any developer creating Apex code needs to have this permission.

Component-based Security

User-based permissions, granted to profiles, cut across the entire Force Platform environment. Profiles are also used to grant different levels of access to individual Force Platform components.

Once again, you have already seen that profiles can be used to define permissions when you create your application and custom objects. The following sections describe the different types of permissions granted to profiles for different types of components.

Application Permissions

You can grant access to an application by making the application visible, as shown in the drop-down list from the upper right corner of a Force Platform application, as shown below.

Figure 119: Application selection

If a user does not have access to an application, the name of the application does not appear in the picklist in the top right corner of the page. You can specify one application as the default application for a profile, causing the user to go to that application immediately after initially logging into the Force Platform. After the initial login, the default application becomes less important since the user's last application is retained the next time the user logs in.

Tab Permissions

Tab permissions allow you to show a tab by default with the setting of `Default On`. This setting also adds the object associated with the tab to the **Create New** picklist in the sidebar.

The `Default Off` setting suppresses the display of the tab in the tab set at the top of the page, but allows users to get to the tab with the right arrow at the right of the tab set, or to add the tab to their default display with the same **My Personal Information ➤ Change My Display ➤ Customize My Tabs** option.

If a tab is marked as Tab Hidden for a profile, users with that profile cannot access the tab. Preventing access to a tab eliminates access through the Force Platform tab set, but you must use object permissions, described later in this section, to circumscribe access to an object. Access can also be granted to a tab through the use of lookup fields and related lists that act as links to a record and its tab.

Voice of the Developer: Custom tabs are associated with an application, but restricting access to an application does not automatically restrict access to the tabs. If a user still has permission to access a tab, they can reach it through the additional tabs interface, even if the application which normally contains the tab is not available to them. This security implication flows directly from the fact that tabs are separate entities from applications. A user can add any tab they can access to any application which they can access—so security settings are likewise separate.

Record Type Permissions

You learned about record types in *Chapter 4: Expanding data options*. Record types are Force Platform features that allow you to assign different page layouts and picklist values to different profiles. If you have defined record types for an object, these types are listed in the Profile detail page.

Apex Class and Visualforce Page Permissions

In *Chapter 10: Apex* of this book, you will learn how to define Apex classes, which encapsulate procedural functionality defined with Apex code, and Visualforce pages.

You can give profiles permission to access individual Apex classes and Visualforce pages through the Profiles page.

Apex classes execute as the system user, so user permissions associated with profiles are not in effect for the execution of these classes. You can prevent users from accessing an Apex class to prevent users within a profile from using the functionality provided by that class.

Object Permissions

Object permissions are slightly more complex, since you can limit the type of action performed on an object through these permissions, rather than just allowing access or not.

You can edit object permissions for custom profiles from the detail page for a profile, as shown in Figure 7-6.

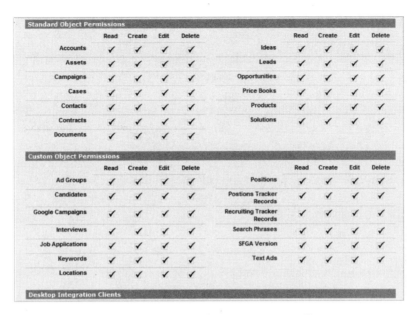

Figure 120: Object permissions in a profile

You can allow the following actions for any standard or custom object:

- `Read` allows read access, and is required for all other permissions. If this permission is removed, all other permissions are also removed
- `Create` and `Edit` permissions also grant `Read` permissions.
- `Delete` permission grants `Read` and `Edit` permissions.

If a user does not have at least Read access to an object, all associated components for that object, such as tabs and report types, are also inaccessible.

Field Level Security Permissions

You can also define permissions on individual object fields. A field can be limited to Read-Only access or hidden completely by removing the `Visible` permission.

You can access field-level security permissions from either the Profile page, to see and edit field level permissions for all fields in an object, or the Object page, to see and edit field level permissions for all profiles for a particular field.

Field-level security affects the display and access to fields through all standard Force Platform interfaces, including page layouts and reports. If a field is not visible to a user, the field display is suppressed on all page layouts for the user, and the field is not available for reports.

Record-based Sharing

The previous sections covered the standard security mechanisms that protect your Force Platform environment and the use of permissions to allow access to different pieces of Force Platform functionality, as well as the components you create. These permissions are fairly coarse—you have permission for a type of access to all the records in an object. The Force Platform gives you a way to implement different access to different data records stored in a single object. This type of security is based on individual rows of data, and implemented with a different set of tools and concepts. These tools and concepts are illustrated in the figure below, and the rest of this chapter is dedicated to explaining this chart in more detail.

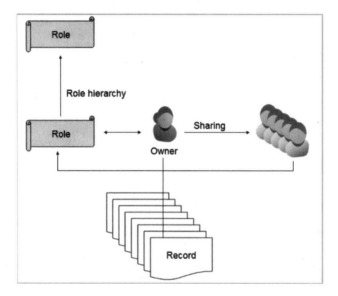

Figure 121: Record-based sharing

Object-based and record-based permissions are complementary, not alternate ways to implement access. Object-based permissions allow access to an object and all the records contained within the object. If a user has the permission to access data in an object, access permissions for individual records can be limited through the use of record-based sharing. If a user does not have access to an object, record-based sharing cannot grant access to the object.

Record Ownership

The core concept behind data-based permissions is record ownership. The owner of a record has all privileges for that record—the ability to delete the record, share the record with other users or even transfer ownership of the record.

The owner of a record created through the user interface is, by default, the user who created the record. A record owner always has read and write access to the record, as well as delete, transfer, and the ability to share the record with other users. A queue, which is a collection of users, can also be designated as the owner of a record. You can change the owner of a record, either through the standard Force Platform interface, as shown in the following figure, or with Apex code, the Force Platform procedural language that is the topic of Chapters 10 and 11.

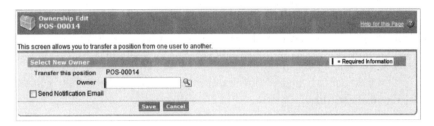

Figure 122: Changing record ownership

A record can be owned by one or more users, or groups of users. Any owner of a record can transfer ownership of the record to another user by using the Change link next to the name of the owner in the detail page for the record. In addition, any user with the `Modify All Data` permission, discussed above, has full privileges for all data in all objects.

 Tip: Later in this section you will learn about roles and the role hierarchy. The role hierarchy grants all record privileges for a user to all those who are above the user in the hierarchy, including ownership.

For the rest of this chapter, the term owner refers to anyone with ownership permissions, including users who have `Modify All Data` permission and users whose role is above the owner in the role hierarchy.

Organization-wide defaults

To properly implement record-based permissions, you have to follow a two-step process:

1. Lock down access to all records for an object based on the lowest level of permission that exists in your organization.
2. Open up access to particular records for particular users.

To lock down records, the Force Platform provides a concept known as organization-wide defaults, usually referred to as org-wide defaults. As the name implies, this specification defines the default access to all records in an object for all users.

There are three settings for org-wide defaults:

- `Public Read/Write` allows all users to read and write data to all the records in an object.

 Caution: This org-wide default does not grant delete, transfer or share permissions. These are only available to owners of a record.

- `Public Read` allows all users to read all the records in an object.
- `Private` only allows the owner of the record, and users with the appropriate permissions, such as `Edit All Data` or `View All Data`, to view or edit a record in the object.

By default, all custom objects are created with an org-wide default setting of `Public Read/Write`. You can change org-wide defaults through the page accessed by **Setup ➤ Security Controls ➤ Sharing Settings ➤ Edit**, shown below.

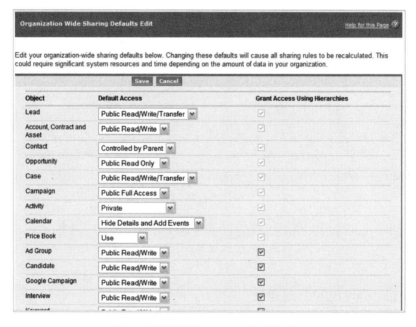

Figure 123: Editing org-wide defaults

The org-wide default you choose should be based on an analysis of the intended usage of the data. Since org-wide defaults are used to lock down data, select the setting that matches the least amount of access granted to the least privileged user of your organization.

If all users of your organization are allowed to edit all records in an object, then the `Public Read/Write` setting is appropriate for the org-wide default. If all users of your organization are able to read all records in an object, but not be allowed to edit some of the records, the

`Public Read` setting is appropriate. If any of the users of your organization are not allowed to read or write any of the records in an object, the `Private` setting is appropriate.

 Tip: Remember, the sharing settings are used to grant differential access to individual records within an object. If a user is not allowed access to any records in an object, you can simply not grant their profile any permissions on the object. Record-based permissions cannot override component permissions. For instance, if you do not want a user to be able to see any Position records, deny them access to the Position object. If the user is able to see some Position records, allow them the appropriate access at the object level but then limit their access to records through sharing.

The diagram shown below explains the decision flow for selecting an org-wide default for an object.

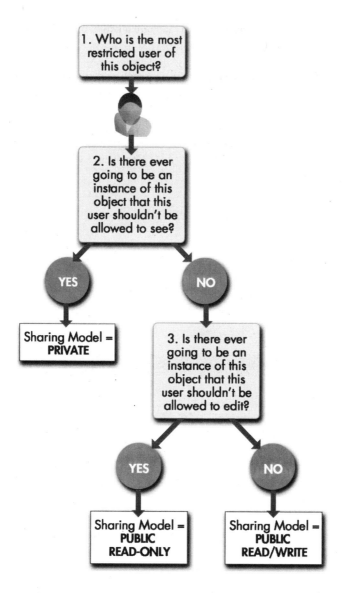

Figure 124: Decision flow for setting org-wide defaults

Sharing

You use org-wide defaults initially to lock down the data in an object, since the core goal of security is to prevent unauthorized access to critical data. You can think of org-wide defaults as adding a door to a room where your precious data is kept—a solid door that is locked (private), a door made of glass and locked (read-only) or a door that is left open (read-write access). The Force Platform gives you a way to share a key to open that door with individual users, a process known as *sharing*.

When a record is shared with a user, the sharing privilege defines the type of access to that record. There are three levels of sharing access: Private, Read Only and Read/Write.

You use sharing to assign access rights that are greater than those assigned by org-wide defaults. You can only assign Read Only, and Read/Write sharing access to records in an object with a Private org-wide default setting and Read/Write to records with a Public Read org-wide default setting.

Ways to share

There are three ways that you can share a record:

- Manual sharing – If an object has an org-wide default other than Public Read/Write, a **Sharing** button displays on the detail page for each record. Clicking **Sharing** brings up the page shown in the following figure.

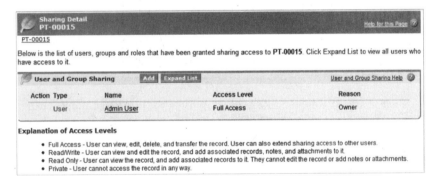

Figure 125: Sharing a record

Clicking **Add** brings up the page shown below.

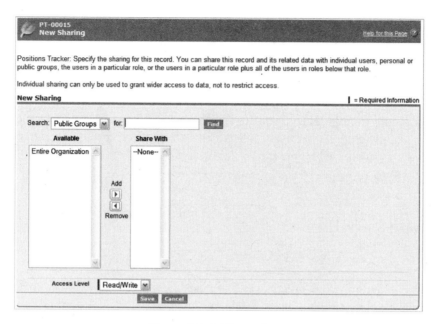

Figure 126: Adding a share

On this page, you can choose to share a record with individual users or groups of users. You are given the choice of the type of sharing you wish to grant to the selected users, although you cannot grant sharing, delete or transfer permissions that are greater than the privileges you possess for the record.

Once you add sharing for users, those users show up in the list shown above. The owner of a record, or any user with Full Access permission for the record, can drop any shares added through this manual method.

- Sharing rules – In some scenarios, you want to automatically share records owned by one group of users with those in another group. You can implement this type of sharing by using sharing rules. The Sharing Settings page of the **Security Settings** menu, partially shown in the figure below, has a section for sharing rules for each object in your Force Platform database.

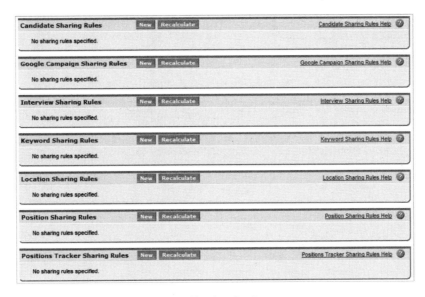

Figure 127: Sharing Settings page

These rules automatically grant a type of sharing access for records owned by one group of users to another group. For instance, you might want to assign all users in the HR group read access to all Position records owned by users in the Recruiter group.

> **Note:** The Winter '09 release of the Force Platform also supports criteria-based sharing, which allows you to define sharing rules based on logical criteria evaluated against the record. This feature is available as part of a Developer's Preview—please see developer.force.com for more information on this feature.

- Apex code - The end result of adding a sharing privilege is an entry into a sharing object. The Force Platform automatically creates a sharing object for every object in your database. Apex sharing uses Apex code to add entries into the sharing object. Apex code is a complete procedural language so you can implement sharing using virtually any type of logical and data-based conditions.

The *Apex Language Reference* contains code samples to demonstrate how to implement sharing with Apex code.

Sharing Recipients

A record share is associated with either individual users or groups of users. The Force Platform comes with two ways to group users—roles, discussed later in this chapter, and public groups.

Both entities are groups of users, but roles have some special features. You can create a public group through the following steps.

1. Go to **Setup ➤ Manage Users ➤ Public Groups**, which brings up a standard list view of existing public groups.
2. Click the **New** button to define a new group on the page shown below.

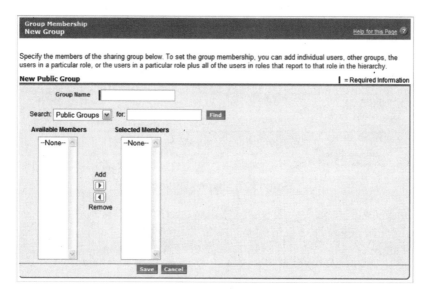

Figure 128: Defining a public group

You can add individual users, other public groups, or two different choices for roles, which are discussed later in this chapter, to a public group.

To reduce the entries in a sharing object, strive to share with groups of users, rather than grant extensive sharing entries for individual users.

Changes Which Affect Sharing

Best practices suggest that you design your sharing scheme as part of your overall application design effort; however, there may be times when you will have to make a change that affects the sharing rules for a record.

Normally, changing a sharing rule automatically recalculates the sharing privileges affected by the change. If the Force Platform determines that the change affects a large number of users, you have to manually trigger a recalculation of shares. In the Sharing Settings page shown above, you can see the **Recalculate** button for each object.

If you change the org-wide defaults for an object, Force Platform recalculates shares on the object. Any shares granted to a record are dropped if they are now redundant, in that the new org-wide default encompasses the previous permission granted by the share. For instance, if you changed the org-wide default for an object from `Private` to `Public Read Only`, any read shares granted to records for the object would not be re-applied.

If you change the owner for an object, all shares for that object are dropped. New shares, based on sharing rules, are added as appropriate.

This final possibility brings up a potential problem. You might have created fairly sophisticated shares using Apex code, and if the owner of the record goes and transfers ownership to another user, all that sharing information is lost. The next section covers Apex-managed shares that address this and other issues.

Apex-managed Sharing

As mentioned previously, you can use Apex code to add shares for a record. Normally, these shares show up in the list of shares, as shown in the figure titled "Sharing a record" above. The owner of the record has the ability to delete any of these shares, and all of these shares are lost when the owner of the record changes. How can you create shares for a record and protect them from this type of destruction?

The solution is Apex-managed shares. You begin the process of creating an Apex-managed share by adding an `Apex Sharing Reason`, accessible from the main page for an object. The page for adding an `Apex Sharing Reason` is shown in below.

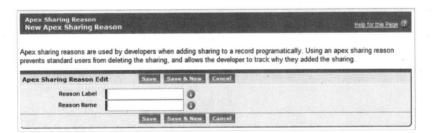

Figure 129: Apex Sharing Reason page

Once you create an `Apex Sharing Reason`, you can add shares to a record through Apex code, labeling them with the `Sharing Reason`.

Any shares that are associated with a `Sharing Reason` cannot be deleted by a user or a change of ownership. Additionally, you can use standard Apex data access statements to retrieve all the share records for a particular reason.

For more detail on Apex-managed shares, such as sample code and dealing with recalculation of these shares, see the *Apex Language Reference*. Apex-managed shares add a final bit of subtlety that can be crucial in designing sophisticated sharing schemes for your data.

Roles

You learned about using public groups to share records with more than one user earlier in this chapter. The Force Platform also includes a rich feature called a *role*. A role, like a public group, can include one or more users. But what makes a role different is the concept of a role hierarchy.

Each org has its own role hierarchy—you can see the sample hierarchy that comes with a default organization below.

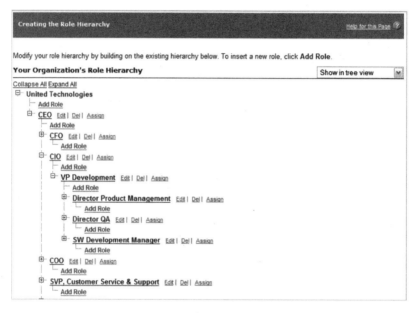

Figure 130: Role hierarchy

A role hierarchy is used to enforce a basic rule—all superior roles have all the sharing permissions granted to all roles below them in the hierarchy. In the hierarchy shown on the Roles page under Manage Users in the Force Platform environment in the figure above, anyone who is in the VP of Development role automatically has all sharing privileges assigned to anyone in the Director of Product Management role. These permissions include those of record ownership so that anyone in the VP of Development role has ownership permissions on all records owned by the Director of Product Management.

When you set org-wide defaults for a custom object, you can specify when the Force Platform should use hierarchies to grant access to users whose role is superior in the hierarchy to a specified user.

Since many organizations have a hierarchical reporting structure, using roles can help you to implement a sophisticated record-based sharing system without extensive rules or coding.

There are two main differences between roles and public groups. One is that a role hierarchy grants permissions in only one direction; your boss has all the permissions you have, but you do not have the same permissions that your boss owns.

You can have public groups that are members of other public groups, but the permission sharing is reciprocal. If Group A is a member of Group B, all members of Group A have all the permissions granted to Group B, and all members of Group B have all the permissions granted to Group A.

Secondly, a user can only belong to one role, and each Force Platform org only supports one role hierarchy, while a user can belong to many public groups. Due to these limitations on roles and role hierarchy, you might be in a situation where roles and a role hierarchy have already been defined for your org, and those definitions do not match the security scheme you would like to implement for your application. Because of this, there may be times when you have to use public groups with your sharing scheme.

Designing Security

This chapter began with a brief discussion of why security is so central to the well-being of your application. As the remainder of the chapter has demonstrated, you have an extremely flexible security model for components and data on the Force Platform.

The flexibility you have with component permissions and record sharing can deliver a sophisticated implementation scheme, but arriving at the proper definition of that scheme is, in most cases, non-trivial. You should create a robust security plan, which takes into account the eventual uses of your applications and data, as part of your design process. Although you can change the security implementation in your Force Platform org at any time, you should start to plan security as part of your initial design process. Creating a comprehensive sharing plan can help to reduce development overhead and implementation time, as well as eliminating the need for sharing recalculations.

Although this chapter has not included hands-on exercises, you can use the information from this chapter to design and implement a security scheme that is reflective of the needs and requirements of your own organization.

Summary

The Force Platform is designed to protect your data, with a host of security features built into the infrastructure of the platform.

The platform also gives you a flexible security scheme that you can use to provide differential access to your applications, data objects and other components. Additionally, you can limit access to individual records through sharing permissions.

The Force Platform provides all you need for the security of your applications and data, in its foundations and in the security tools it provides.

Chapter 8

The Force Platform IDE

In the previous chapters, you covered a good amount of ground in Force.com development, from creating an application and its associated data objects, through using workflow and analytics. You explored these capabilities with the Force.com Setup menu, which let you make these and many other customizations to your Force.com organization easily. When using the Setup menu directly in your production Force.com organization, you have a very dynamic environment capable of simple declarative changes that are immediately available to your users. And, in many cases, that process works very well.

But there are a number of reasons why you would want to use a more traditional IDE for your development efforts, as follows:

- Your development methodology is not appropriate for this approach, whether for scale of the change, scale of the development team, or the mission-critical nature of the applications in your organization.
- Some of your developers are focusing on the procedural portions of the Force Platform, such as Apex code, and are looking for a development environment designed for that area of endeavor.
- If you are part of a team, it is often easier for each team member to only interact with isolated portions of the overall development effort. The Setup menu shows you everything in your Force.com organization, while your IDE environment allows you to tailor the components of the application that are included in your project.

- Some developers or teams like to keep track of when changes are made to their application, which is usually done with a version control system such as CVS, SCCS, or Subversion.
- Your development effort may involve repetitive tasks. In cases like these, the wizard-driven approach can be more time-consuming than an alternative development environment.
- You may be familiar with a standard integrated development environment, such as Eclipse, and you want to use those skills in the Force.com environment.

In this chapter, you will learn how to use the development capabilities of the Force Platform that are delivered by the Force.com IDE and Metadata API.

Important: If you have been following the examples in the previous chapter, your Force Platform organization should be ready for the exercises in this chapter. If you have not done the exercises, or want to start with a fresh version of the sample Recruiting application, please refer to the instructions in the Code Share project for this book. You can find information on how to access that project in *Chapter 1: Welcome to the Force Platform.*

Metadata & the Metadata API

Throughout this book, you have been reading references to Force.com metadata. As you no doubt understand by now, metadata is the driving force behind all your Force.com applications. In your work with everything from objects and fields to reports and workflow, you have been simply defining metadata, which the Force Platform uses at runtime to determine the operation of your application and its components.

The Force.com Metadata API is used to access metadata in your Force.com organization. The Metadata API is comprised of a transport, a web service API that allows reading setup information out of a Force.com organization, and a payload—the organization setup information itself. The API provides two modes that control how the configuration information is conveyed—either as text files, or as programmatic objects in web service calls.

The IDE uses the text file representation of organization metadata, so the remainder of this discussion will focus on text mode operation of the Metadata API.

Files and Types

The Metadata API provides access to the same metadata that you have been defining using the Setup menu. When you request metadata for a Force.com component from the IDE, the IDE sends that request through the Metadata API to the Force.com server. The server, in response, creates an XML file from the stored metadata on the fly.

Each component in a Force.com application returns its own file, such as a file for a custom object, an application, a tab, and so on. Some components, such as custom fields, are returned as part of the XML for their parent component. If you have a number of custom fields on a standard object, there will be one file for the standard object that includes the custom fields you've defined.

The files are organized into a directory structure that makes navigation to specific files easier. For instance, the files corresponding to your schema, the custom objects and custom fields, are in a directory called 'objects', while the files containing profile information are stored in a directory called 'profiles'.

The Metadata API uses ZIP files to pass files between the Force.com IDE on your client machine and the Force.com servers, although that transport is transparent to your use of the Force.com IDE.

The contents of some of the files look like source code, such as Apex and Visualforce components, which you will learn about in the four chapters following this one. Others represent components that were defined declaratively through the Setup menu. These files are formatted as XML text files.

The XML files themselves contain pretty much what you'd expect, with values for the attributes you declare in the Setup menu. For example, in the case of a custom object, the text file contains the name, label, plural label, description, and help text. It also contains information about all the fields in the object, such as the name of the field, the data type for the field, and any field level help text.

Whether you create the custom object using the Force.com IDE or through the Setup menu, you get the same custom object in your organization. The final repository of the information created by wither of these methods is the metadata, regardless of how those values are created. You can think of the text files together as the source code for the applications in your Force.com organization.

Metadata Interaction

When working with the Force.com IDE and metadata, you should understand an important distinction between working with a platform like Force.com and a more traditional platform. This distinction underlies important differences between development-as-a-service and traditional development.

As stated above, all the information available to you in the Force.com IDE is metadata; however, the metadata in the IDE is copied from the metadata for your Force.com organization. When you create components, make changes in components, or delete components in the IDE, you are making these changes in your local copies of the metadata files.

The changes you make must be saved back to the Force.com server. By default, a save action in the Force.com IDE will flush your changes back to the server, which may require additional interaction to confirm that these changes should permanently alter the Force.com metadata.

Similarly, you can refresh your local copy of the metadata from the Force.com server. You can perform either of these actions, as well as additional actions, such as creating a new component, by right-clicking on the component, component folder, or top level src folder.

The figure below shows the context menu that appears when you right click on the objects category in the Package Explorer pane. The main menu contains a submenu labeled Force.com, which gives you the ability to save and refresh from the server. You can also deploy the metadata to another server, which is covered in *Chapter 15: Deployment*.

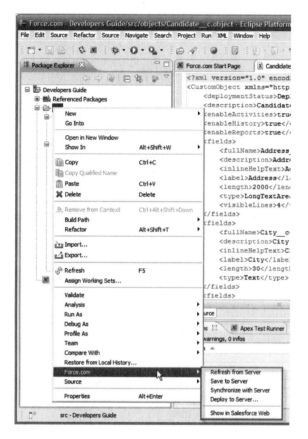

Figure 131: Object context menu in the Force.com IDE

The Force.com IDE

The Force.com IDE is available to support more flexible development of applications for the Force Platform. The Force.com IDE is a professional tool for professional developers, providing editors and version control integration, along with the ability to upload application changes into a Force.com organization for testing or deployment.

The IDE is built on Eclipse, an open source tool framework developed and released by the Eclipse Foundation.

Installing the Force.com IDE

The Force.com IDE is an important tool in the Force.com development arena. You can find the most up-to-date instructions for installing the IDE at the home page for all Force.com developers—`developer.force.com`.

1. On the home page of `developer.force.com`, select the `Tools` option in the Wiki menu on the left, as shown below.

Figure 132: The Tools link on the developer.force.com home page

2. Select the link for the Force.com IDE. You will be taken to a page with some descriptions of the latest release of the IDE, as well as a section entitled Getting Started. In this section, you will find links to installation instructions for the Force.com IDE, with a choice of using different versions of Eclipse or upgrading an existing Force.com IDE installation. This page also includes directions on installing Eclipse, if you do not have it already.

3. Click one of the installation options, which will take you to a page similar to the one below.

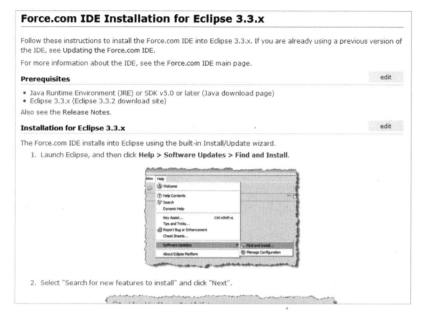

Figure 133: Installation home page for the Force.com IDE

At the top of the page, you can see links that will help you install the prerequisite software, the Java Runtime Environment, and the core version of Eclipse. The remainder of the page contains step by step instructions for installing the Force.com IDE plug-in into the Eclipse environment.

Once you complete these installation tasks, you are ready to start using the Force.com IDE.

Overview of the Force.com IDE

If you are familiar with the Eclipse environment, using the Force.com IDE will probably seem pretty natural to you. For those of you who are not familiar with this popular tool, this section will provide a high level overview of the basic look, feel, and operations of the IDE.

Note: This walkthrough is based on Eclipse 3.3. Your specific version of Eclipse may vary from this version.

1. Open Eclipse on your machine. You will be initially prompted for a workspace. Enter an appropriate name. You can also check the box in the lower part of the window to make this your default workspace, which would prevent this prompt from appearing in the future.

A workspace is a place to store development projects, and is implemented as a directory in your file system. The workspace can have any projects in it that you like, but it is sometimes helpful to use a workspace as a container for related projects

2. Select a workspace and click **Next**. When Eclipse opens, you will initially be presented with the page shown below.

Notice the box in the upper right corner of the page. This box controls the perspective, which is a general configuration for the overall environment.

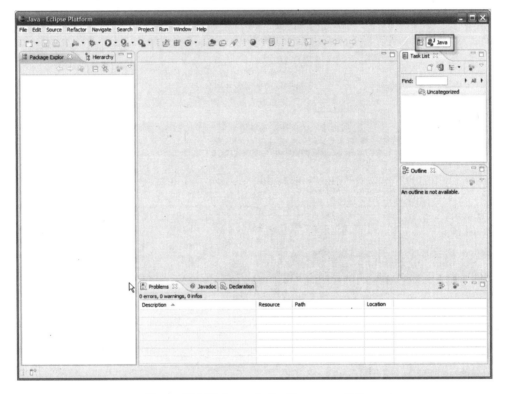

Figure 134: Welcome to the Force.com IDE

3. Click the box to the left of the perspective name and select Other, and then the Force.com perspective, which will change the appearance of your environment to the page shown below.

Figure 135: The Force.com perspective

Once you save a workspace, the perspective for the workspace will also be saved, so that the contents of the workspace will open in the appropriate perspective.

The remaining descriptions in this chapter will use the default layout of the panes within the Force.com IDE; however, the IDE is very configurable, so you can change the arrangement of the panes to match your preferences.

 Note: The Eclipse tool platform provides a very rich set of capabilities that we'll only touch on here in the briefest fashion. You can learn much more about Eclipse by starting the IDE and navigating to **Help ➤ Welcome** and selecting **Workbench Basics**.

The Force.com perspective includes the Package Explorer on the left, which is a view of the projects in the current workspace. A Force.com package is a collection of components for an application, similar to the scope of a project in the Java world. The Package Explorer is shown below on the left, as it will be for any workspace dedicated to Force.com projects. Each package provides a tree view of its contents.

Figure 136: Package Explorer in the Force.com IDE

The IDE pane that you will focus on most of the time is the central tabbed window, which displays file contents and permits editing. When you double-click a file in the Package Browser, the IDE opens that file in the central workspace using an editor appropriate to the file type.

By default, the Force.com perspective contains a number of useful views in a tabbed pane along the bottom of the IDE window. Three views you will be using when you begin to develop code in *Chapter 10: Apex* are the `Problems` view, the `Apex Test Runner` view, and the `Execute Anonymous` view. The `Problems` view captures any warnings or error messages created when you save and compile your Apex code. The `Apex Test Runner` view, as its name implies, is used to run test methods on your Apex code. The `Execute Anonymous` view can be used to try out snippets of Apex code. You can remove tabbed views by clicking the view and then the X icon on the tab, and you can bring them back by navigating to **Window ➤ Show Views** and selecting the view you want to add. Views may be moved by simply dragging their tab to a new anchor, or they can be undocked from the main IDE window by dragging them outside it.

Exploring the IDE

Now that you are familiar with the basics of the Force.com IDE, you can start to use this tool.

1. Start the Force.com IDE, if you didn't already perform this action in the previous section. The Eclipse application is typically an executable file called `eclipse.exe` in the directory where you installed the product.

2. Create a workspace, or choose a workspace that already exists.

3. If you are opening the workspace for the first time, your IDE will display with the default perspective. Change the perspective by clicking the button in the upper right corner. Select the Force.com perspective and click `OK`.

     Tip: If you can't see Force.com in the list of perspectives, the Force.com plug-in is incorrectly installed, or perhaps not installed at all. This problem will occur if you haven't completed the installation described on the page at `developer.force.com`.

4. You can play around with the views to get a feeling for how you can customize the environment. There is an outline view on the upper right side. Click its tab, then click-drag it to a different place in the IDE window.

5. Make sure that the IDE is not maximized on your machine. Drag the Outline view outside of the IDE window. This action undocks that view and gives it a window of its own directly on the desktop.

6. Finally, you can close views entirely by clicking the **X** icon in the upper right corner of the view. Click the **X** for the Synchronize window in the lower tabbed view.

7. To restore the IDE to its original view settings, click **Help ➤ Reset Perspective**. This will put all the panes and tabs back in their original positions.

You will still be able to get access to the synchronize functionality in the IDE, as well as reopen the view, with the **Windows ➤ Show Views** menu choice.

Now that you are acquainted with the Force.com IDE, you are ready to start using this tool to shape the metadata for your application.

Working with the Force.com IDE

The Force.com IDE is used for working with your Force.com metadata. In this section, you will learn how to create a project and retrieve metadata from the Force.com server, use the Schema Explorer to create data access statements and retrieve data, and actually make changes in your metadata.

Creating a Project

Your first step is to create a project in the Force.com IDE.

1. If you have not started the Force.com IDE, bring up the environment by double-clicking the desktop icon. You may be prompted to select a workspace, as explained above.
2. Change the perspective to the Force.com perspective.
3. Navigate to **File ➤ New ➤ Force.com Project**, which will bring up a dialog like below.

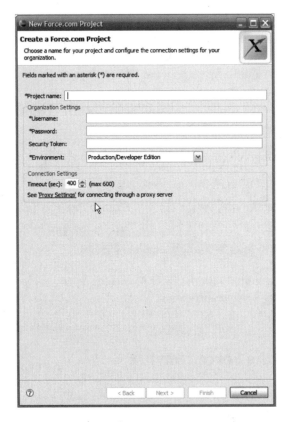

Figure 137: Defining a Force.com project

4. You will be prompted for a `Project Name`, which must be unique within the workspace, as well as a user name, password, and security token.

   Since the Force.com IDE interacts with the Force.com data through the Force.com API, you may be required to use a security token for the organization, if you are outside of the IP addresses listed for your organization, as described in *Chapter 7: Protecting Your Data*. You can get a security token by going to **Setup ➤ Reset My Security Token**, which will prompt you to click the **Reset Security Token** button to generate this token. The value of the token will be sent to the email address for the requesting user.

The next page, shown below, allows you to specify the metadata you want to retrieve. The default choice will bring down all of your Apex and Visualforce components. Typically, these code-intensive components are the most likely area you will work on with the Force.com IDE.

The second choice will bring up a list of different component types, and the actual components of those types, as shown below. You can select a subset of component types or specific components within those types. Since you do not have any Apex or Visualforce components in your organization yet, you should use this option to retrieve the metadata for some types of components.

 Tip: Be aware, though, that the IDE is typically not used for editing declarative metadata of the kind that you have created previously in this book. The most common use of the IDE is to create and edit Apex code and Visualforce components, which you will learn about in the following four chapters.

Remember that the selections you make will only specify which metadata files are downloaded to your workspace. Whenever you run your application, the application will be run from the Force.com servers and utilize all metadata for your organization.

5.

Figure 138: Specifying project contents

6. Select the second option on the page to select metadata components, and then click **Choose**.

7. In the next page, select `applications`, and `objects - custom`, and click **OK**. When you return to the previous dialog box, the components you selected will be listed in the lower text area.

8. Click **Finish** to begin retrieving metadata files. Once the retrieval process is completed, the project you just created will appear in the Package Explorer.

 Voice of the Developer: Your selection of components for a project on this page indicates the components initially included in the project. You can add other components to a project after the project has been created by using the **Properties** choice on the context menu for the project, and the selecting **Force.com ➤ Project Content ➤ OK ➤ Change**. This selection will bring up the same selection page you just used. If you choose to include all the components of a certain type, you can also subscribe to that component type. This subscription means that any new components of the specified type will be added to your project each time your refresh your project from the server.

9. Click the plus sign to the left of the project name, the plus sign to the left of the `src` (source) directory, then the plus sign to the left of the `applications` and `objects` directories, which will make your environment appear like the page shown below.

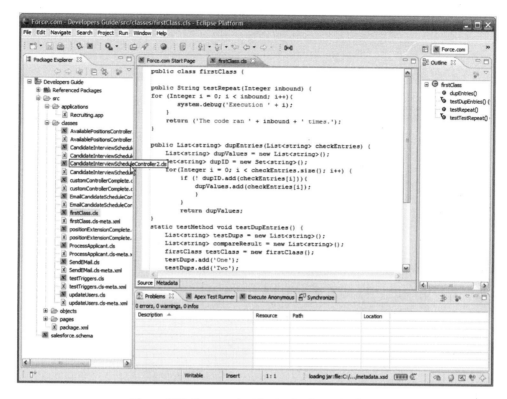

Figure 139: Your project in the Package Explorer

This view shows you the different types of components available in this particular project.

Using the Schema Explorer

At the bottom of the list is an entry for the `Salesforce.schema` file. This link brings up the Schema Explorer.

1. Double-click the `Salesforce.schema` file, which will open the Schema Explorer, as shown below.

    The Schema Explorer gives you several tools for interacting with the objects in your organization. You can see the objects, their fields, and their relationships. By selecting fields, you can build a valid query in the upper left panel to retrieve the data. This query is implemented with SOQL, which is described in *Chapter 11: Apex and Data*. Once your query is built, you can run the query to see the results. As usual, the best way to understand how all this fits together is to try it.

Figure 140: The Schema Explorer

2. In the right hand Schema panel of the Schema Explorer, scroll down to the Job_Application__c object and click the plus sign.

3. Click the plus sign for `Fields`, which will give a view of the panel as shown below.

Figure 141: Fields in the Schema Explorer

4. Select the `Name` and the `Candidate_Qualified__c` fields. Notice that a SOQL query appears in the Query Results panel.

5. Click the plus signs for `Candidate__c`, `Type Data`, `Reference To`, `Candidate__c`, and `Fields` to drill down to fields in the related Candidate object. These actions will present a view of the panel as shown below.

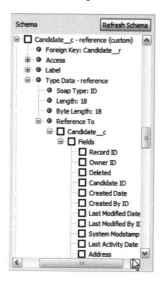

Figure 142: Accessing a field in a related object in the Schema Explorer

6. Select `First Name` and `Last Name` in the expanded area, and observe the changes in the Query Results panel.

7. Click **Run Me**, above the Query Results panel, which will send the SOQL query back to the Force.com organization and return the values into the panel below the Query results panel.

   This Schema Explorer is terrifically handy for creating and testing SOQL statements.

8. Close the Schema Explorer by clicking **X** in the tab for the Schema Explorer.

Working with Metadata Files

The final step in exploring the Force.com IDE is to perform some simple modifications of the metadata you retrieved, so you can see how the development environment interacts with the Force.com environment.

1. In the Package Explorer, expand the `src/applications` folder.

2. Double-click the `Recruiting.app` file, which will open it in an editor in the middle pane of the IDE.

There are two views of the file, selectable by a tab at the bottom of the panel. The Design view is a hierarchical representation of the XML document, while the Source view, shown for the Recruiting application below, shows you a text view of the file. You can edit values in either view, but for this exercise, you will be using the Source view.

Figure 143: The Source view of metadata in the Force.com IDE

3. Click the Source tab in the Recruiting app panel.

4. Change the value in the description attribute to `This is NOT a sample app`.

   If you don't see description tags in your XML, you did not define a description for the application.

5. Delete the Location tab from the list of tabs in the XML for the Recruiting application.

6. Click **Save** in the top toolbar. You can note the progress of the save back to the Force.com server from the status indicator in the lower right corner of the IDE.

   You have made changes to your application, but are you sure? You can find out easily.

7. Right-click the `Recruiting.app` in the Package Explorer, then `Force.com` and `Show in Salesforce Web`. This action brings up the page shown below.

   You can see that the Locations tab is no longer a part of the tabs listed in the Recruiting application, although the tab is still present at the top of the page. You did remove the tab description from the metadata for the application, but you did not force the tab to be removed from users' personal customizations.

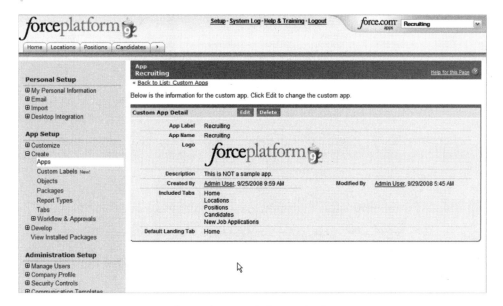

Figure 144: The application definition in the Setup menu

8. Click **Edit** for the application definition in the Setup menu, select the choice to overwrite users' personal customizations, and click **Save** to remove the Locations tab from the user view of the application.

9. Double-click the `Candidate__c.object` in the objects folder in the Package Explorer. Make sure the Source is showing, as it is in the figure below.

This file is more complicated, with definitions for many fields as well as attributes for the object itself. You can add additional fields to the object by entering the appropriate XML for a field definition.

Figure 145: Metadata for a custom object in the Force.com IDE

10. Select all the attributes for the Address__c field, including the beginning and ending `<fields>` tags.

11. Paste the copied XML after the closing `</fields>` tag.

12. Change the `fullName` to `Number_of_Interviews__c`, the `description` and `inlineHelpText` to Number of interviews for the candidate. Change the label to Number of Interviews. Change the `type` to Number and delete the `length` and `visibleLines` attributes.

The completed XML will look like the highlighted code below:

```
<fields>
    <fullName>Number_of_Interviews__c</fullName>
    <description>Number of interviews for the
candidate.</description>
    <inlineHelpText>Number of interviews for the
candidate.</inlineHelpText>
    <label>Number of Interviews</label>
    <type>Number</type>
</fields>
```

13. Click **Save**. You will see a little icon in the lower left displaying a status of Building workspace and a percentage complete indication.

This time, the XML does not successfully save. You get an error in the Problems panel at the bottom of the page, informing you that a field with a data type of Number must have a precision attribute.

14. Delete the newly added field from the XML document and save again.

This whirlwind trip through the Force.com IDE has hopefully given you some feeling for developing in this environment. If you have experience with Eclipse or related IDEs, you probably feel pretty comfortable with this development environment, and you can see why using this development environment might be more productive for some development tasks. If you have not had experience with Eclipse or a similar IDE, you will quickly learn how to use it productively as you work with your Force.com projects.

You will be using the IDE much more in the coming chapters on Apex code, to both write and test your code. You will also learn about using the IDE to deploy your code in *Chapter 15: Deployment.*

The next section will present another powerful reason to use the Force.com IDE as your development environment—coordinating the efforts of multiple developers on a team.

Team development and the Force.com IDE

So far, you have learned about tools an individual, disciplined developer might use for smaller development projects. When you are working on larger projects with longer application lifecycles, or with groups of developers in team environments, they will need the ability to manage change and track versions of their code.

While some applications can be developed by one person, many will be developed by teams. Sometimes this is because there is simply too much to do for one person, other times because different participants have different skills.

Whatever the reason for the team, team development brings challenges of change isolation and controlled synchronization. You won't be pleased with your teammates when they make changes that break your code and stop you from finishing your tasks. A developer's work should be isolated with a separate environment until it is complete enough to share, but, at that point, the separate changes should not break the other functions of the application.

Beyond team development, revision control is also very useful as the application lives through an extended lifecycle. After you deliver your application to users, they will no doubt find bugs and suggest minor enhancements that can be done quickly; however, you may also be working on larger extensions of the functionality that will take some time. You'll want to work on these two sets of changes concurrently, keeping them isolated from one another so you can deliver the quick fixes before the new application is ready, and also merge those changes together so you don't need to fix the bugs all over again in the extended application.

Tip: With the Force Platform, you can create and modify applications very rapidly, rolling changes out in near real time. But just because you can make application changes instantly available to end users does not mean that you should. Organizational issues, such as end-user training, frequently call for a more measured approach to iterative development.

In traditional software development practice, some of these needs are served by revision control systems. Revision control systems (also known as version control or source code control) are used to track sets of related changes, the completion status of those changes, and to coordinate bringing changes together into a complete version of the application for test or deployment.

The Force.com IDE is built on the Eclipse tool framework, and can take advantage of the large number of revision control systems that are either pre-integrated with Eclipse, or that are supported in Eclipse via plug-ins.

 Note: For a list of revision control plug-ins for Eclipse, see `http://eclipse-plugins.info/eclipse/plugins.jsp?category=SCM`.

Version control integration works in Eclipse through three views within the IDE:

- A repository view for connecting to, managing, and browsing projects and contents in a revision control repository, which varies by revision control system
- Team-related context menu items and status icons on files in the Project Explorer
- A Text Compare editor that allows identification and resolution of concurrent changes

Resolving Change Conflicts

Team development naturally includes the possibility of more than one person working on the same metadata. In fact, since the Force.com IDE uses a local copy of metadata, you can end up with a conflict that stems from changes that have been made by one person through the Setup menu while you are working on the same objects in the IDE.

The Force.com IDE includes capabilities to address this type of issue. You start your exploration of team development by exploring the conflict detection and resolution capabilities of the IDE.

1. Start the IDE if it isn't already running, and return to the project you created earlier in this chapter.
2. Click **src ➤ objects**.
3. Double-click the `Candidate__c` object to bring the XML file into view.

4. Right-click to bring up the context menu and select `Force.com` and `Show in Salesforce Web`. A browser window will open with the attribute page for the Job Application custom object.

5. In the browser, scroll down and edit the Description of the Address field and save the changes.

6. Return to the Force.com IDE and the XML for the `Candidate__c` object.

7. Change the description to a different value than you did through the Setup menu.

8. Use **Ctrl-S** to save. This saves the change to disk and also pushes the change into your organization.

   This Save will not be successful, due to a conflict. An error marker will appear in next to the component with the problem in the Package Explorer, and an error message will appear in the Problems panel, as shown below.

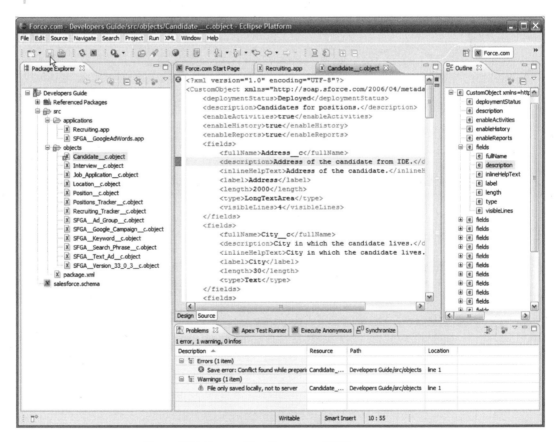

Figure 146: Error with a Force.com IDE Save

9. Right-click to bring up the context menu on `Candidate__c.object`, and select `Force.com` and `Synchronize with Server`. This action brings up a dialog box that prompts you as to whether you want to open the Synchronize view. Click **Yes** to continue.

10. In the Synchronize view on the right, double-click the project to open up the hierarchy, and then double-click the `Candidate__c` object to open up a text comparison on the right, as shown below.

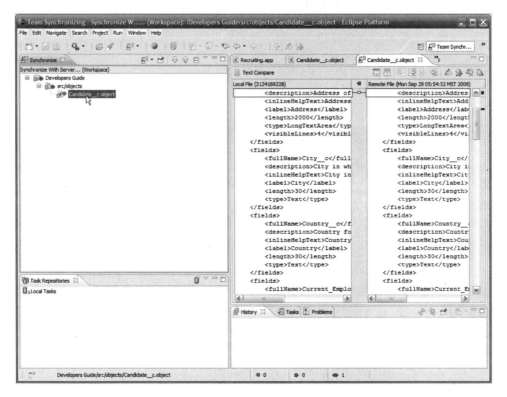

Figure 147: The Synchronize view in the Force.com IDE

11. In this case, the lines with differences between the two versions are indicated by the red line between the two versions.. The tool bar in the Text Compare editor has two buttons, which will allow you to copy the value from the right window to the left window or vice versa. Copy the changes either way that you wish.

12. Right-click the project in the Synchronize window and select `Apply project to Server`. Click **OK** to save the two files. The Synchronize navigator should display a message indicating no changes in synchronizing.

13. Return to the Force.com perspective, and then close the extra tab by clicking **X** on the tab.

This example showed you how the Force.com IDE detects conflicts between a local version of a metadata component and the version on the Force.com servers, protecting the integrity of this metadata, and how you can resolve this type of conflict. This procedure will take care of basic conflict issues that may arise in a team development scenario, but you may need to go to the next level of tracking and resolving in a larger team environment.

Behind the scenes of an IDE Save

Once you understand exactly what happens when you save a project from the Force.com IDE, you can understand some of the intricacies of the interaction between the development environment and the server metadata.

When you create a project in the IDE, the Metadata API returns an XML file that is constructed from the metadata on your Force.com server instance. When you save a project back to the server, the Metadata API first checks to see if any of the metadata in the saved project has changed since it was initially retrieved. If there is a conflict, the Save is not successful and you must take corrective action, as demonstrated in this section.

If the save is successful, the Metadata API returns an updated version of the XML file to the Force.com IDE, replacing the old version. This action may create results that can be confusing at first.

For instance, if you add a new custom field to an object, the new XML file will include the field in alphabetical order—which means the field may be returned in a different spot than when it was initially saved.

Remember that you can specify selected components for inclusion in a particular project. This flexibility has other implications on some of the actions you can accomplish with the IDE. In Force.com metadata, custom fields exist independent of the custom object that contains them, although the only way to access that metadata in the Force.com IDE is through the object.

If you delete the XML definition of a field from a custom object in the Force.com IDE, the deletion will have no effect. The Metadata API will not delete the field definition in the metadata, so when the new XML file is built to return to the IDE, the custom object metadata will be refreshed to include the custom field.

As a consequence, good practice calls for you to use the Setup menu to Force.com metadata as the ultimate authority. If you feel that something is not working in the way you expect through the API, be sure to check the results and consequences through the Setup menu.

Team development with a Revision Control System

Now that you have gone through a simple case of conflict resolution, you can move to the next step of using a revision control system. Selecting a revision control system and organizing your repository in the Force.com IDE to meet the specific versioning needs of your project are beyond the scope of this book. For the examples that follow, you will use Subversion with the Subclipse plug-in and a very simple repository structure to demonstrate some common versioning use cases.

In real life, your revision control system will no doubt run on a server located in a server room or data center, and shared between your project staff. For this example, however, you will create and use a Subversion repository on a local machine.

In order to understand the use of a version control system, you will have to perform the following high-level steps:

- Install subversion to your desktop
- Create a repository
- Install the Subclipse plug-in into the Force.com IDE
- Configure Subclipse to see the repository you created
- Save your development project into the repository
- Make some changes and save them to your development organization
- Pretend to be a second developer, create a new IDE project from the repository
- Make and commit some changes to the repository as that second developer
- Merge those changes back to the initial project and organization

Keep in mind that the setup steps are only required once—you can reap the benefits from version control forever!

Install subversion

Your first step is to install Subversion in your environment.

1. Go to the site `http://subversion.tigris.org/getting.html`, and select the `CollabNet` binary.
2. At the CollabNet site, download the CollabNet Subversion Server and Client. You will have to register on the site to receive the download.

     Note: The example in the remainder of this chapter was done with Subversion 1.2.4 for Windows and version 1.2.4 of the Subclipse plug-in for Eclipse. The most current versions of these two components may or may not fully cooperate with the steps in this example. You can generally download previous versions of both Subversion and the Subclipse plug-in from their respective sites.

3. Install Subversion, using all the defaults.

Create a Repository

With Subversion installed, you can now create a repository for your code.

1. Open a command prompt and enter the following code:

```
C:\>svnadmin create c:\svn_repos
```

2. In the same command prompt, change the directory to `c:\svn_repos\conf`, the `conf` directory under the directory you created for the repository.
3. Use Notepad, or some other editing tool, open the `passwd` file in the `conf` directory and add a user name and password to the file.
4. Save the `passwd` file and exit the command prompt.

In this example, you will access the repository in a special local mode through Subclipse, so you do not need to worry about configuring the svnserve daemon or apache to act as a subversion server. If you are allowing others to access this repository, though, you have to configure one or other of these services. Please refer to the Subversion site you originally accessed for more information on this task.

Installing the Subclipse Plug-in

The Subclipse plug-in links the Eclipse environment to your new repository.

1. Go to `http://subclipse.tigris.org` to get the latest Eclipse Update Site URL compatible with your version of Eclipse.
2. In the Force.com IDE, navigate to **Help ➤ Software Updates**, and select the Available Software tab. Click **Add Site**, and enter the URL from the previous step.
3. Select the new site and click **Finish** to fetch the latest version of the Subclipse plug-in. Select the required Subclipse plug-in from the list returned from the site.
4. Click **Next**, accept the terms, and click **Next** again.
5. Click **Finish** to begin the installation, and then **Install All** when prompted. You will be required to restart Eclipse once the installation completes.

Configuring Subclipse with a Repository

You have now linked the Force.com IDE environment to Subclipse in a general way. Your next step is to connect your repository to the environment.

1. Open the SVN Repository Exploring perspective in the IDE, which will open the SVN Repositories view.
2. Use the **Add SVN Repository** icon on the far right to configure Subclipse to access the local repository. The URL to access your repository locally is file:///svn_repos. You should see the repository listed in the view, though it will be pretty dull as the repository is currently empty.

Save your Project to the Repository

You are all set up to actually store your Force.com Project in the repository.

1. Return to the Force.com perspective.
2. Right-click to bring up the context menu for the project and select **Team ➤ Share Project**. Select SVN as the Repository Type, if given a choice, and click **Next**.
3. In the dialog that opens, make sure that the Use existing repository location is selected, as well as the repository you just created. Click **Next**.
4. Select the Use project name as the folder name choice and click **Next**.
5. Enter a Check-in Comment and click **Finish**. You will be prompted for an author name, with your username as the default.,
6. You will then given a summary page, which you should close by clicking **OK**.

Adding a Second Developer

Now that your project is in the repository, multiple developers can access the project. In your single user environment, you will simulate a second developer by checking the project out to a second project within the Force.com IDE.

1. Change to the SVN Repository Exploring perspective in the Force.com IDE.
2. Right-click on the repository to bring up the context menu and click **Refresh**.
3. Using the context menu on the repository again, click **Checkout**.
4. Checkout the project into your workspace, entering a project name, accepting the default location, and clicking **Finish**. Since you are checking out the entire project, you will get a warning message from the IDE, which you can simply acknowledge by clicking **OK**.

This series of actions loads the code for the project into your IDE workspace. Normally, you then connect this project with a Force.com organization, so that this second developer has their own Force.com environment to use for testing the project. For this example, you can simply leave the project unconnected, since you are focusing on the use of the repository itself.

Making and Saving Changes

The second copy of the project in your workspace will simulate changes made by another developer.

1. Switch to the `Force.com perspective` in the IDE.
2. Navigate to **src ➤ objects** in the second project you just checked out and open the file for the `Location__c.object` by double-clicking on the object name.
3. Change the description for the object in the fourth line, replacing a word or two.
4. Click **Ctrl-S** to save. Since you haven't connected this project to an organization, the save is only to the local files.
5. Close the editor window by clicking **X** in the tab.

   You have made changes in your version of the project, and you can compare this version with the version currently in the repository.

    Caution: Remember, in this scenario, the repository version has remained static, but in the real world, other developers might have checked in changes to the stored project.

6. Using the context menu for the project, select **Compare with ➤ Latest from repository**. The Structure Compare view, as shown in the following figure, will open in the IDE.

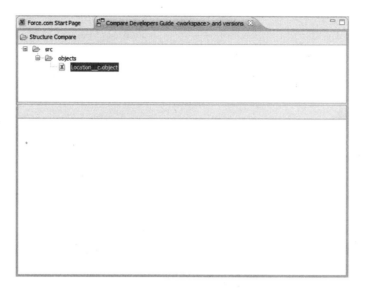

Figure 148: Structure Compare view in the Force.com IDE

7. In this view, you should see that a difference is detected in the
   `Location__c.object` file, as shown above. Double-click to open that file, and a
   Text Compare editor opens. Just as before, you can use this editor to look through
   the changes, and if there are any conflicting changes, you can resolve them.

8. For the purposes of this exercise, you can simply close the Compare editor.

   You can now commit the changes you have made to the repository.

9. Using the context menu, select **Team ➤ Commit** for the project you just edited.

   The Commit dialog only shows files that have been changed—in this case, the
   `Location__c.object` file.

10. Enter an appropriate `Check-in Comment`.

11. Click **OK** to complete the check-in process.

You have successfully checked in a new version of your project. The Subversion repository does
more than simply accept the new version, as you will see in the final step of your exploration.

Comparing Versions

The subversion repository also tracks changes made to stored projects.

1. Open the `SVN Repository Exploring` perspective.

2. Navigate to the `Locations__c.object` file, and use the context menu to select **Show History**.

3. The revisions will be shown in the History view, as shown below.

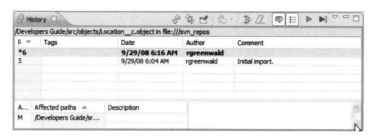

Figure 149: The History view of the subversion repository

4. In this window, revisions are shown as a multi-select list, so select the two revisions, select `Compare` from the context menu and click **OK**. A text Compare view opens to show you the differences between these versions, as shown below.

You, as the first developer, can clearly see the changes that have been made. Your final step is to bring these changes into your project, and then save them to your Force.com environment.

5. Return to the Force.com perspective and select your first project. Using the context menu, select **Team ➤ Update**. This will pick up the repository changes and merge them into this project.

At this point, you can open the `Location__c.object` file to make sure that the changes you wanted brought into your project have in fact shown up.

Your last step is to save the project to the Force.com server environment.

6. Using the context menu for the project, select **Force.com ➤ Save to Server**.

This final action will take the current project and save it to your Force Platform organization, where it will be used to generated and shape the runtime version of the project.

You have learned the basics of using the tools available in the Force Platform IDE environment to implement source code control. The SVC repository provides a selection of tools to control your source code, monitor the changes, and resolve conflicts between different versions of a file.

This extremely simple example showed you the basic functionality delivered by a source code repository. In an actual team development system, the source code control system is only a tool, which must be accompanied by clearly understood guidelines for usage. Using a source code control system provides a safer and more flexible multi-developer environment, but best practices for multi-developer efforts are equally, if not more, necessary for the successful coordination of these types of teams.

Summary

This chapter has provided an introduction to the basic functionality of the Force Platform IDE. You learned how to install and use the IDE to interact with the metadata that makes up the core of your Force Platform applications. You also learned how the Force Platform IDE exchanges metadata with your Force Platform server, and how you can find and resolve differences between the metadata in the two locations.

The chapter also gave you a quick introduction to the use of source code management systems, which can be crucial in coordinating the work of teams of developers.

In subsequent chapters, you will use the Force Platform IDE for creating and testing Apex code, as well as deploying your applications.

Chapter 9

Visualforce Pages

So far, you have learned a lot about the functionality of the Force Platform available to youby simply declaring attributes through the Setup menu, which in turn shapes the built-in capabilities of the platform through metadata. In this chapter, you will start to explore the ways you can extend those capabilities with procedural logic.

This chapter begins the exploration of one of the two main areas of the Force Platform that use procedural code, Visualforce. Visualforce gives you the ability to provide your users with virtually any interaction with your Force Platform data, both in terms of the user interface and the interface between their actions and the Force Platform data model.

 Important: If you have been following the examples in the previous chapter, your Force Platform organization should be ready for the exercises in this chapter. If you have not done the exercises, or want to start with a fresh version of the sample Recruiting application, please refer to the instructions in the Code Share project for this book. You can find information on how to access that project in *Chapter 1: Welcome to the Force Platform*. In addition, the project contains instructions on how to update your organization with changes required for this chapter.

Why Visualforce?

As you have seen, you can create powerful and flexible applications for the Force Platform with simply declarative methods. The Force Platform applications you create with these methods are fully functional and robust, although there are some limitations to the features of those applications. For instance, you can use a variety of different user interface styles, such as text fields, text boxes or picklists, to display fields in a standardized page, but you cannot create pages outside of that standardized look-and-feel. More importantly, the user interfaces you create implement standard functionality automatically, but you cannot necessarily change the ways that these user interfaces interact with Force Platform data, or implement a particular task. For instance, pages are automatically created for each object in the Force Platform database, but you cannot create a page that allows users to edit data from more than one object on a single page.

Visualforce technology provides a means for developers to create any type of browser-based user interface, interacting with any combination of data, in your on-demand Force Platform applications. You can create user interfaces with a simple tag-based syntax, similar to HTML, which accesses one or more Force Platform objects.

Visualforce gives you this flexibility while still using all the power embedded in the metadata you have defined for your Force Platform objects—truly the best of both worlds.

Visualforce Concepts

The Visualforce technology is an implementation of the model-view-controller architecture pattern, as shown in the figure below. This pattern separates the user interface layer, or view, from the underlying data layer, or model. The connection between the model and the view is the controller layer, which handles the interaction between the user interface and the data.

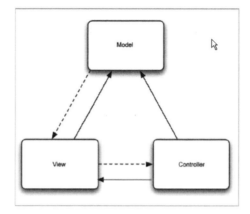

Figure 150: Model-View-Controller architecture

The model component of Visualforce is typically the data model, which you have been working with throughout the previous portion of this book. The view component of Visualforce are Visualforce pages, the subject of the rest of this chapter, and the controller component is handled by Visualforce components, discussed in this chapter and *Chapter 12: Extended Visualforce Components and Controllers*

 Tip: You can also use Apex classes as the model component for Visualforce, which you will learn about in *Chapter 10: Apex*.

Visualforce Pages

The user interface layer of Visualforce, representing the view of the model-view-controller architecture, is implemented with Visualforce pages, which are the focus of this chapter. You create Visualforce pages with both standard HTML and a set of special tags that tap into the power of the Force Platform model.

Visualforce tags cover two basic areas of functionality. One group of tags creates user interface objects that are automatically associated with Force Platform objects or that interact with functions implemented on the Force Platform. Another group of tags handles interactions between the page and the Force Platform server without refetching the page, similar to the way that AJAX (asynchronous Java script and XML) operates.

You can combine a Visualforce page with standard Force Platform tabs in your applications. You can integrate a Visualforce page into your application from a number of different points in your application:

- From a custom tab
- As an override for a standard tab, replacing a normal display for an object
- As an override for standard or custom buttons or links
- Embedded in a detail page layout.

Visualforce Controllers

Visualforce technology can be used to implement both the view and the controller portion of the model-view-controller architecture. The controller portion of Visualforce comes in two varieties. The Force Platform automatically creates a standard controller for every object in your Force Platform database. These standard controllers provide the basic functionality embedded in a Force Platform tab page. The second type of controller is a custom controller, created with Apex code, which you will learn about in *Chapter 10: Apex* and *Chapter 11: Apex and Data.*

You can create extensions to a standard controller to deliver additional functionality to your Visualforce pages with Apex code. You can also create custom controllers with Apex code, which handle all the interaction between a Visualforce page and one or more Force Platform objects. Both controller extensions and custom controllers are covered in *Chapter 12: Extended Visualforce Components and Controllers*, after you have learned about Apex code.

Visualforce controllers run on the Force Platform servers, maintaining the Platform-as-a-Service architecture while expanding the functionality of your Force Platform applications. The actual Visualforce pages are rendered in straight HTML, which means you do not have to write extensive amounts of client-side code to implement any type of interaction you need for your applications.

Visualforce and s-controls

If you have been using the Force Platform for a while, you are probably familiar with a technology known as s-controls. S-controls use client-side browser technologies, like Javascript and Flex, to replace or augment standard Force Platform interfaces. These technologies use the Force Platform API to interact with data in Force Platform objects. An s-control uses the Force Platform API to interact with Force Platform data. S-controls can be placed on detail pages, be used to replace tabs, or the destination of standard or custom buttons or links.

Developers use s-controls to implement functionality that is beyond the scope of the standard Force Platform components, but there are a few problems:

- An s-control runs on the client. The code for an s-control is included in the HTML page requested as part of a Force Platform application. This architecture can lead to potentially large pieces of client-side code that can impact performance, as well as being problematic to maintain.
- An s-control lives outside of the Force Platform environment. This simple fact means that you must re-implement a lot of the standard look, feel, and functionality that is part of the standard Force Platform environment as soon as you move to an s-control.
- This disconnected nature also means that code in the s-control is fragile and subject to failure when administrators change fields or accessibility rules for Force Platform data, or that the s-control needs to dynamically confirm data attributes and session status with lots of additional other API calls.
- And whenever an s-control has to modify data, that data is retrieved to the client, changed and then sent back to the Force Platform servers, which could have a significant performance impact.

Visualforce is intended to completely eliminate the need for s-controls, without any of these issues. Visualforce pages automatically use the look and feel of standard Force Platform tabs, as you will see in this chapter, while still giving you the option of extending or modifying this look and feel. Visualforce pages can access standard Force Platform functionality with a simple set of tags. And Visualforce custom controllers allow you to extend the functionality of the standard environment with the productivity of Apex code, while still running on the Force Platform servers. So if you do know s-controls, you should look to Visualforce as the way to implement the same functionality. If you don't know s-controls, you don't really have to learn them.

Developing Visualforce Pages

Now that you understand the basic architecture of Visualforce, you can jump right into creating Visualforce pages. This section covers creating and modifying pages, and displaying related records.

Creating Your First Page

Visualforce includes a new development method that allows you to immediately see the implementation of your Visualforce pages. This method, referred to as developer mode, is not turned on for all developers by default. To take advantage of this mode, check to make sure that your user profile includes this permission.

1. Go to **Setup ➤ Manage Users ➤ Users** and select your user. Click **Edit** and make sure the `Development Mode` permission is selected, then click **Save**.

   Development mode gives you the ability to work on your Visualforce pages (as well as controllers) dynamically. Visualforce also includes the ability to create a page on the fly by simply attempting to navigate to the URL for the page. This capability is referred to as a *quick fix*.

2. Go to the navigation tool bar of your browser. Edit the URL so that the Force Platform instance is followed by `/apex/VisualforcePosition`. For example, if the URL of your Force Platform instance is `http://na1.salesforce.com`, the URL is `http://c.na1.visual.force.com/apex/VisualforcePosition`. This URL brings up the page shown below.

Figure 151: Prompting to create a new Visualforce Page

3. The quick fix functionality of Visualforce development mode recognizes that no Visualforce page exists with the name VisualforcePosition, so, because you have Development Mode enabled, you are given the opportunity to create the page.

   Click the **Create Page** link to create the VisualforcePosition Visualforce page and bring up the page shown below.

   And yes, congratulations are in order, as you have just created a Visualforce page. The content of the page is less than thrilling, a situation you will change in a matter of minutes.

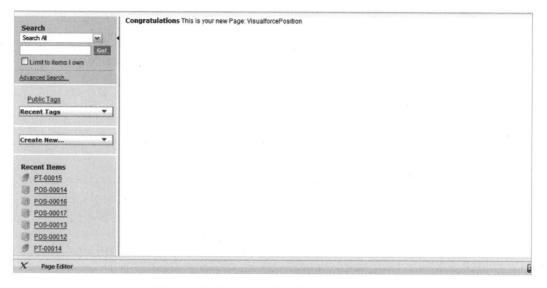

Figure 152: Your first Visualforce Page

2. Click on the `Page Editor` link in the footer of the page to change the appearance of the page to the page shown next.

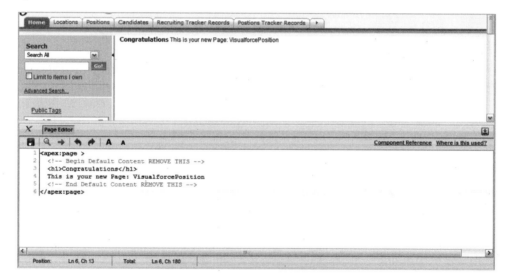

Figure 153: Visualforce Page Editor

There are quite a few things to notice in this new page. First of all, you are in development mode, which means that the Visualforce page code is visible in the lower window, with the actual Visualforce page taking up the upper half of the page. The Visualforce code editor includes some standard tools, such as the ability to search for values, including values that satisfy regular expressions, go to a certain line, and undo and redo changes.

Whenever you save your Visualforce code, the save action checks your code to make sure it is valid, flagging the first error it encounters. If the code is valid, the new version is saved and the upper page is refreshed with the new version of the page.

You can also see your first example of Visualforce tags, with the `<apex:page>` start and end tags. Any Visualforce page must be surrounded by these page tags.

The `apex:` portion of a Visualforce tag is actually the namespace for the component referenced by the tag. A namespace is a way to qualify the name of a component, insuring that the Visualforce components you will be using in this chapter are all from this standard namespace. Later in this book, you will both create your own component and use Visualforce messaging components, which each have their own namepace.

Finally, you can see that this page includes standard HTML, including the `<h1>` heading tag. Visualforce pages let you seamlessly use HTML tags with the extended functionality of Visualforce specific tags.

Tip: You can also create or edit Visualforce pages through the **Setup ➤ Develop ➤ Pages** menu or through the Force Platform IDE. Accessing Visualforce pages through the Setup menu presents the code as a text file that you can edit in place and save, but without receiving the immediate feedback of development mode.

There are three additional features available in these Setup menu Visualforce listing pages that you might find helpful: the ability to clone a page to make a quick copy, access to reports that list where the Visualforce page (or custom component) is used, and what other components the page depends on.

You use Visualforce tags to both specify various components of your page, as well as bind components to matching data fields, data attributes, and functionality available on the Force Platform. As usual, the best way to see exactly what this means is to create a Visualforce page.

3. Start your editing process by deleting all the code between the `<apex:page>` tags.
4. Modify the initial page tag to include the `standardController` tag, as shown below:

```
<apex:page standardController="Position__c">
```

This simple attribute connects this Visualforce page with the Position custom object, referenced by the API name of the object, Position__c.

This binding also exposes all the actions present in standard controllers, such as save. You will learn about how to override these actions in *Chapter 12: Extended Visualforce Components and Controllers.*

This attribute produces a number of effects in the page. First of all, by default, you can automatically use the same look and feel for the Visualforce page as a standard tab for the object in a regular Force Platform application uses. You do not have to use any extended styling to match this page with your environment, making it easy to integrate Visualforce pages into your standard apps.

Secondly, this attribute binds the page to this custom object. You can make easy references to that object, its fields, and the objects that are related to the Position__c object. You can see the power of this binding by adding one component to your Visualforce page.

5. Position the cursor below the initial page tag. Type in `<apex:d`

As you type in your apex tag, a helper window appears with the tags that match the initial letter, in this example, d, as shown below.

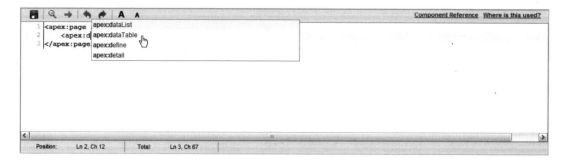

Figure 154: Visualforce Page helper

6. Select the `<apex:detail>` choice from the helper window to insert the beginning and ending tags into the Visualforce page.

Believe it or not, you have just added the only tag you need to completely reproduce the detail page for the Position object.

7. Click **Save** to check your code, save the new version and display the page in the window above. The completed code for this version of your Visualforce page is as follows:

```
<apex:page>
<apex:detail></apex:detail>
</apex:page>
```

That went well, except there is nothing showing in the page above. Well, almost nothing. You can see that the Positions tab is highlighted, which is appropriate behavior for a page bound to the Position object.

There is a simple reason why there is no content for the page. You can only show the details for a particular record, and this Visualforce page does not have a particular Position record specified.

You can address this by adding a record ID to the URL for the page, but it is easier to just connect this Visualforce page to a button on the detail page for the Position object. This connection automatically passes the unique record ID for the Position record to the Visualforce page.

8. Go to **Setup ➤ Create ➤ Objects** and select the Position object.
9. Go to the Standard Buttons and Links section, and click the **Override link** for the View entry, which brings up the Edit page shown in its completed form shown below.

The View option executes whenever a user clicks a link to this position, such as the list view shown when the Positions tab is selected, or a link in a related list. By replacing the standard destination with your Visualforce page, you are simply substituting your new page for the default page across your application.

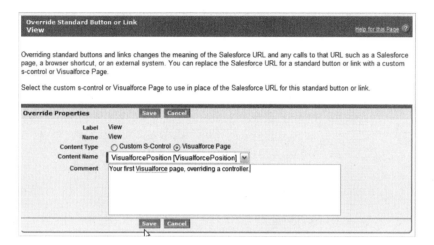

Figure 155: Overriding a standard link

10. Select `Visualforce page` as the `Content Type` and the Visualforce Position page you just created from the Content Name picklist. Click **Save**.

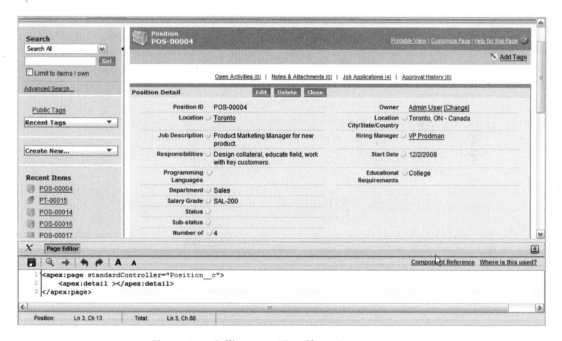

Figure 156: Calling your Visualforce Page

11. Click on the Positions tab and select any position from the list view to bring up the page shown above.

This page looks exactly like the default detail page for the selected position, with the exception being that the page comes up in development mode with the Page Editor visible at the bottom of the page. Since you used a simple Visualforce tag that is designed to pick up all the default properties of the page, this outcome is expected.

Note: When you call a Visualforce page from a standard Force Platform page, the ID for the context record automatically passes to the target page. You can simulate this behavior by adding on the ID for the record to the URL constructed for the page which uses your Force Platform instance. If the record ID for a Position record is `a07D0000001Kt7L`, your Force Platform instance is `na1.salesforce.com`, then the URL for the VisualforcePosition page would add `/?id=a07D0000001Kt7L` to the URL for your instance.

You can modify the default behavior by just adding a couple of attributes to the apex:detail tag. The Page Editor has built-in help to guide you to the right attributes for the job.

12. Enter the Page Editor and click **Component Reference** on the right.

Note: You can see a lot of components in this reference. You will be using some of them in this and subsequent chapters, but you should review all the available components to understand the scope and specific capabilities of these components.

Select the **apex:detail** link to bring up a list of attributes for the tag. This help page can also include code samples for the selected component on the Usage tab.

13. Change the starting `apex:detail` tag to the following code to eliminate the display of related lists and the title.

```
<apex:detail relatedList="false" title="false">
```

14. Save the page to change the display to the page shown below.

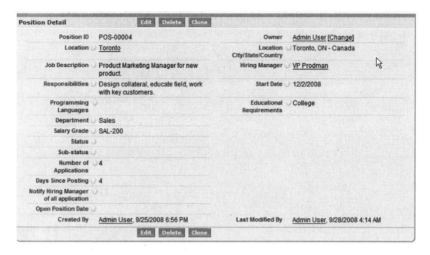

Figure 157: Your Visualforce page, modified

Visualforce development mode once again brings home one of the key virtues of development as a service. As soon as you save your modified Visualforce code, the results of those changes are immediately visible.

Your first Visualforce page is designed to show you the power of the combination of Visualforce pages and the default functionality provided by the Force Platform. In the next two sections, you modify this initial page to provide a more customized view of the record while still being able to leverage the power provided by the Force Platform.

Modifying Your First Page

It was nice to see how easy it is to create a Visualforce page, but, in the real world, you probably do not want to simply replicate the default page for an object. The `apex:detail` tag brings in a lot of functionality, but other Visualforce tags give you a finer level of control.

In this section, you create a Visualforce page that still uses the metadata attributes of Force Platform fields, but only displays a small number of fields to present a cleaner interface to your users.

1. Delete the `<apex:detail>` tags from your Visualforce page.

   You will be adding fields to the new version of the page that accept inputs from your users, so the fields will be part of a form. You have to add tags to let the Force Platform environment know that you intend to write data through the page.

2. Give the initial `apex:page` an `id` attribute of "thePage", so that the initial pageBlock tag looks like this:

```
<apex:page standardController="Position__c" id="thePage">
```

Although you will not be referencing this page directly, you will use the `id` to help locate a portion of the page you will be adding shortly.

3. Add `<apex:form>` tags to the page the same way you added `<apex:detail>` tags before to begin the redesign process. These tags allow your Visualforce page to send values back to the Force Platform.

4. Add `<apex:pageBlock>` tags between the form tags to create an area on the page that inherits the look and feel of standard Force Platform applications from the object identified for the page.

5. Between the two pageBlock tags, add `<apex:pageBlockSection>` tags to indicate a section of the larger block. You are now ready to add some individual items to the section.

6. Using the Apex tag helper, add `<apex:inputField>` tags within the page block section. Open the Component Reference to see the attribute possibilities for this component.

   You can see that this component has many more potential attributes than the detail component you used earlier. A lot of these components are used for AJAX-like interaction. The one attribute that does the most initial work for you is the value element. This element is used to identify the particular data field to which the inputField is bound.

   You use an expression field to form a bidirectional connection between a Force Platform field to a Visualforce page component. The format for this expression is similar to merge field syntax:

```
{!object_name.field_name}
```

   It uses the API name for both object and field names.

7. Change the first inputField by adding the value attribute so that the tag now reads like this:

```
<apex:inputField value="{!Position__c.Department__c}">"
```

8. Add another input field to the page block section, with a value of `Position__c.Job_Description__c`.

9. Save the new version of the page, changing the displayed Visualforce page to look like the figure which follows below.

The code for this version of your Visualforce page is

```
<apex:page standardController="Position__c" id="thePage">
    <apex:form>
        <apex:pageBlock>
        <apex:pageBlockSection>
            <apex:inputField
                value="{!Position__c.Department__c}">
                </apex:inputField>
            <apex:inputField
                value="{!Position__c.Job_Description__c}">
                </apex:inputField>
        </apex:pageBlockSection>
        </apex:pageBlock>
    </apex:form>
</apex:page>
```

These few lines of tags have changed the page significantly. You can see that the new page does have input elements, and that the specific types of input elements were derived from the meta-data for the fields: the Department field is shown as a picklist, and the Job Description field is shown as a text area. Both of these fields have the labels and online help that are associated with the fields in the field definition. And these fields are bound to the data in the specified record—the fields contain the current data for this particular record.

Since there are only two lonely fields on this page, you might want to stack them in a single column, which can be accomplished with an attribute on the section.

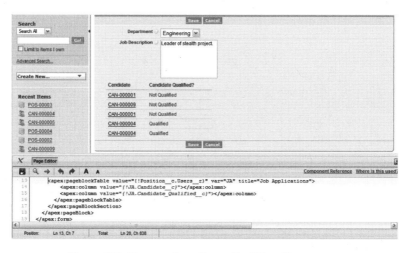

Figure 158: New version of your first Visualforce page

10. Add the attribute `columns="1"` to the initial pageBlockSection tag.

You have no doubt already noticed that all the attribute values are expressed as text values. This requirement makes sense when you realize that this is HTML, which only supports text, not numbers.

You have input fields, but no way to interact with the database record that produced the current values. With a couple more tags, you can provide users with a way to summon up standard actions on the record.

11. Add `<apex:pageBlockButton>` tags to the page below the initial pageBlock tag, and add the attribute `location="bottom"` to the initial tag. These tags create an area that holds the buttons you use on your page, with the standard formatting used for Force Platform applications. The location attribute can be `top`, `bottom` or `both`, the default.

12. Add a set of `<apex:commandButton>` tags between the pageBlockButton tags. Change the initial tag to:

```
<apex:commandButton action="{!save}" value="Save">
```

These two attributes call the default save action for the standard controller and assign text to display on the button, respectively. Both actions use the same marker (`{! }`) to bind the action with an action in the controller for the object. The save action is one of the actions available in all standard controllers. The simple name belies some fairly detailed functionality, which includes running all validations on the saved data, performing either an insert or update action as appropriate, and handling any errors. The cancel action is also standard across standard controllers, simply sending the user back to the previous page without taking any actions on the data submitted with the button click.

13. Add another command button just below the Save button, with an action and name of `Cancel`. You should give your users a way to back out of their changes.

Whenever your Visualforce page makes a change in Force Platform data, there is a possibility of an error occurring during the save. You should always add a section on your Visualforce page to display any messages produced by errors.

Fortunately, Visualforce has a simple component to handle this requirement

14. Using the helper, add the following tags to your Visualforce page, just below the initial pageBlock tag:

```
<apex:pageMessages></apex:pageMessages>
```

This single component will only appear on the page if messages, such as error messages, are returned to the page. All the remaining Visualforce pages that write data will include a pageMessage component—a good programming practice for you to follow in all your Visualforce pages as well.

15. Save the page, changing the displayed page to look like the figure below.

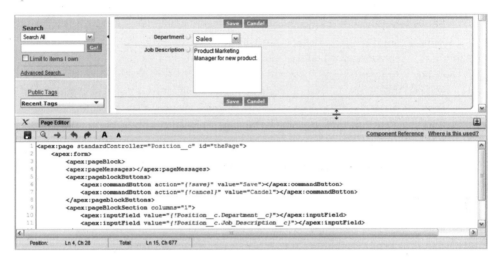

Figure 159: Adding command buttons

16. Change the value of the Job Description field and click the new **Save** button.
17. Click the Positions tab to return to the list view and see that the value for the field has been changed.

In this section, you have quickly seen the flexibility you can get with Visualforce pages while still using the functionality provided by the data definitions on the Force Platform.

Your next step is to expand the information shown on your page to include related records.

Displaying Related Records

The Force Platform automatically includes lists of related records on the default tabs produced for an object. You can add `apex:relatedList` tags to include a related list as part of this page.

You still want to show related records on this page, but you would like to control what is shown, other than the default related list display.

1. Add a new page block section below the current one, and add:
   `<apex:pageBlockTable>` tags within the section.

The pageBlockTable is one of several tags you can use to iterate over a collection of records. Other built-in tags that will deliver this result are dataTable, which will not pick up the styling of the pageBlock, dataList, which uses the display format of a list, and repeat, which allows you to repeat a group of components. You will learn more about some of these components in this chapter and *Chapter 12: Extended Visualforce Components and Controllers*.

2. Edit the initial tag for the page block table to read like this:

```
<apex:pageBlockTable value="{!Position__c.Job_Application__r}"
 var="JA" title="Job Applications" >
```

The value attribute points to the API name of the relationship that connects the parent Position object with the child Job_Application object. Notice that the relationship has __r (two underscores and the letter "r"), rather than __c. The var attribute assigns a label that the columns of the table use to reference the related object.

3. Add `<apex:column>` tags within the page block table.
4. Modify the initial column tag to:

```
<apex:column value="{!JA.Candidate__c}">
```

Use the string defined as the var for the page block table to identify the object, and use dot notation to indicate the field in the record.

5. Add another column to the table, this time with a value of:
   `Candidate_Qualified__c`.
6. Save the Visualforce page code to produce the page shown in below.

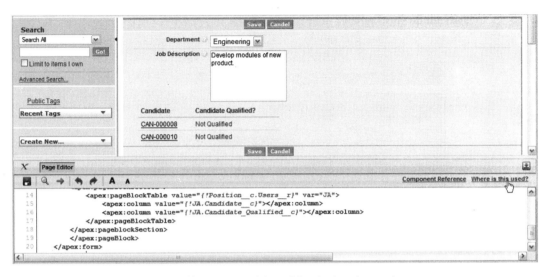

Figure 160: Visualforce Page with a table of related records

The page shown is highly functional, with the Candidate field automatically providing a link to the detail page for the candidate, just as it would in a standard Force Platform page.

But you might as well take advantage of the flexibility provided by Visualforce pages to offer information that is a little more user friendly, such as providing the first and last names of the candidate, rather than the somewhat cryptic identifier.

7. Change the `value` attribute for the first column to: "`{!JA.Candidate__r.First_Name__c}`".

   Once again, you are using the name of the relationship from the Job Application object to the Candidate object, so the API name ends with __r.

8. Add another column to the table to display the last name of the candidate with a `value` attribute of "`{!JA.Candidate__r.Last_Name__c}`".

9. Save the page to produce the new version of the page shown below.

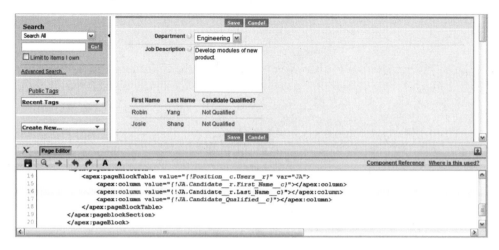

Figure 161: Visualforce Page with pageBlockTable

The code for this version of your Visualforce page is as follows:

```
<apex:page standardController="Position__c" id="thePage">
    <apex:form >
        <apex:pageBlock>
        <apex:pageMessages></apex:pageMessages>
        <apex:pageBlockButtons location="bottom">
            <apex:commandButton
                action="{!save}" value="Save">
                </apex:commandButton>
            <apex:commandButton
                action="{!cancel}" value="Cancel">
                </apex:commandButton>
        </apex:pageBlockButtons>
        <apex:pageBlockSection columns="1">
            <apex:inputField
                value="{!Position__c.Department__c}">
                </apex:inputField>
            <apex:inputField
                value="{!Position__c.Job_Description__c}">
                </apex:inputField>
        </apex:pageBlockSection>
        </apex:pageBlock>
        <apex:pageBlock>
        <apex:pageblockTable
          value="{!Position__c.Job_Application__r}" var="JA">
            <apex:column value="{!JA.Candidate__r.First_Name__c}">
                </apex:column>
            <apex:column value="{!JA.Candidate__r.Last_Name__c}">
                </apex:column>
            <apex:column value="{!JA.Candidate_Qualified__c}">
                </apex:column>
        </apex:pageblockTable>
        </apex:pageBlock>
```

```
      </apex:form>
</apex:page>
```

With only a few more tags, you have gone beyond the capabilities of a standard Force Platform page. You can display fields from a record that is two relationships away from your Position record.

The possibilities of Visualforce pages are hopefully starting to open up before you. But there is more to come in the remaining sections of this chapter.

Using Links to Standard Force Platform Pages

You have already seen the use of a command button to call the standard Force Platform save function for the Position record. You can do even more with buttons and links on your Visualforce page.

In an earlier version of this Visualforce page, the Name field for the Job Application was displayed as a link to the detail page for the record. In this section, you learn how to implement the same functionality through the more user-friendly combination of first and last name and another Visualforce component, without having to use the Name field.

1. Return to the Page Editor. Delete the first two columns for the pageBlocktable.
2. Add `<apex:column>` tags to the table. Add the attribute `headerValue="Candidate"` to place the proper title over the column which will act as a link to the candidate. Add `<apex:outputLink>` tags between the initial and final column tags.

   The outputLink is a Visualforce component that generates a link in the Visualforce page.

3. Add the following code between the two outputLink tags to display the first and last names of all related candidates in the table:

   ```
   {!JA.Candidate__r.First_Name__c} {!JA.Candidate__r.Last_Name__c}
   ```

   Notice that you can use these expressions within the standard display areas of a Visualforce page.

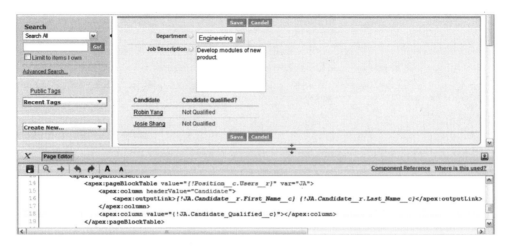

Figure 162: outputLinks in place

4. Save your page to see the new display, as shown in the figure above.

   Now add an action for the link. You want to use this link to call the standard Force Platform page for viewing information about the candidate. To accomplish this task, you need to use the URLFOR() function and a global Force Platform variable to point to the page.

   The URLFOR() function has two required parameters—an identifier for the target page and a value for the ID used for the page. You can already guess how to represent the ID value in this table: with the JA.Candidate__r.ID, which contains to the ID of the related Candidate record.

   You can reference the destination page with the global $Action variable. To represent the page used to view the Candidate__C object, the syntax is: $Action.Candidate__c.View. Other actions available include New and Edit.

   The last step is to add this formula as the value attribute of the outputLink, whose initial tag now looks like this:

   ```
   <apex:outputLink value="{!URLFOR($Action.Candidate__c.View,
   JA.Candidate__r.ID)}">
   ```

5. Edit the initial outputLink tag to include the value attribute code and save your code.

   The code for this version of your Visualforce page is:

   ```
   <apex:page standardController="Position__c" id="thePage">
       <apex:form >
           <apex:pageBlock>
   ```

```
                <apex:pageMessages></apex:pageMessages>
                <apex:pageBlockButtons location="bottom">
                    <apex:commandButton
                      action="{!save}" value="Save">
                      </apex:commandButton>
                    <apex:commandButton
                      action="{!cancel}" value="Cancel">
                      </apex:commandButton>
                </apex:pageBlockButtons>
                <apex:pageBlockSection columns="1">
                    <apex:inputField
                      value="{!Position__c.Department__c}">
                      </apex:inputField>
                    <apex:inputField
                      value="{!Position__c.Job_Description__c}">
                      </apex:inputField>
                </apex:pageBlockSection>
            </apex:pageBlock>
            <apex:pageBlock >
            <apex:pageblockTable
               value="{!Position__c.Job_Application__r}" var="JA">
                <apex:column headerValue="Candidate">
                <apex:outputLink
                  value="{!URLFOR($Action.Candidate__c.View,
                  JA.Candidate__r.ID)}">
                  {!JA.Candidate__r.First_Name__c}
                  {!JA.Candidate__r.Last_Name__c}
                  </apex:outputLink>
                </apex:column >
                <apex:column
                  value="{!JA.Candidate_Qualified__c}">
                  </apex:column>
            </apex:pageblockTable>
          </apex:pageBlock>
      </apex:form>
  </apex:page>
```

6. Click the link for any of the candidates to take you directly to the detail page.

With these slight modifications, you can integrate all the standard functionality of your Force Platform pages into your Visualforce page. This ability means that you can use Visualforce to supplement your standard applications, rather than replace every page with a new alternative Visualforce page.

The functionality works just fine, but your users will still find themselves navigating to a completely different page to view detailed information for a related candidate. Isn't there some way to show that information on the same Visualforce page? You bet.

Adding a Related Detail View to a Visualforce Page

You can modify your Visualforce page to display the detail information on the same page. You already know that you can use a single detail tag to bring up detail information, so you only have to learn how to summon that information to your current Visualforce page.

The outputLink component you used in the previous section simply created a link in your page that directed the user to another page. In order to get additional information to display on the same page, you must change the page specification a little bit.

The `apex:command` components, when activated by a user, submits the current page to the Force Platform server, and returns a new version of the page to the user.

 Note: Submitting a page also submits, by default, any changes the user has made to data presented by the page.

You already used this functionality with the Save button for the main Position portion of the page. The commandButton submitted the page to the Force Platform standard controller that executed the standard Save action for the record and returned an updated version of the page to the browser.

For this task, you use a commandLink without asking for a specific action on the Force Platform server.

You start by adding a detail component to your page.

1. Add `<apex:detail>` tags between the closing form tag (`</apex:form>`) and the closing page tag (`</apex:page>`). Add the `title="false"` attribute to suppress the title and heading for the detail. You will add an attribute to this component to point to the right detail later in this section.
2. Remove the contents of the first column in the pageBlockTable. Add `<apex:comandLink>` tags within the column tags.
3. Add a `value` attribute to make the link show the first and last name of the candidate, which will change the initial commandLink tag to the following:

```
<apex:commandLink  value="{!JA.Candidate__r.First_Name__c}
{!JA.Candidate__r.Last_Name__c}">
```

4. To complete the display of your new column, add `headervalue="Candidates"` to the initial column tag for the first column.

You have your command link in place, but you still have to find a way to point the detail component to the proper Candidate record. You know the expression syntax for the appropriate ID field, but how do you pass it over to the detail component?

Several different Visualforce components, including outputLink, outputText and the different action components, allow you to attach a parameter to the page. A parameter is available to other components on the page, so the apex:param is a perfect way to hand over the Candidate ID to the detail component.

5. Add <apex:param> tags within the commandLink tags. Set the name attribute of the initial tag to "candidate" and the value attribute to the expression for the Candidate ID, resulting in the following markup:

```
<apex:param name="candidate" value="{!JA.Candidate__r.ID}">
```

Now you can return to the detail component and use this value to associate the proper record with the component.

6. Add a subject attribute to the initial detail tag. The value for the subject uses another global Visualforce variable to access parameters by name, as in this markup:

```
<apex:detail subject="{!$CurrentPage.parameters.candidate}"
title="false">
```

 Tip: What happens if this parameter does not have a value, as when a user first enters the page? The display of the detail component is automatically suppressed if the subject value for the component is null. You can use this capability to hide the detail component by simply using a link or action function to set the value of the candidate param to null.

7. Your work is done. Save your Visualforce page and then click a candidate link to produce the page shown below.

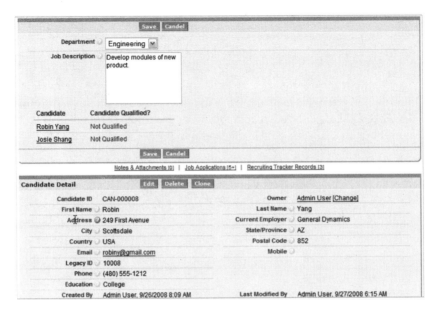

Figure 163: Your Visualforce Page displaying an added detail view

The code for this version of your Visualforce page is:

```
<apex:page standardController="Position__c" id="thePage">
    <apex:form >
        <apex:pageBlock>
        <apex:pageMessages></apex:pageMessages>
        <apex:pageBlockButtons location="bottom">
            <apex:commandButton
                action="{!save}" value="Save">
                </apex:commandButton>
            <apex:commandButton
                action="{!cancel}" value="Cancel">
                </apex:commandButton>
        </apex:pageBlockButtons>
        <apex:pageBlockSection columns="1">
            <apex:inputField
                value="{!Position__c.Department__c}">
                </apex:inputField>
            <apex:inputField
                value="{!Position__c.Job_Description__c}">
                </apex:inputField>
        </apex:pageBlockSection>
        </apex:pageBlock>
        <apex:pageBlock >
        <apex:pageblockSection>
        <apex:pageblockTable
            value="{!Position__c.Job_Application__r}" var="JA">
            <apex:column headerValue="Candidate">
                <apex:commandLink
                    value="{!JA.Candidate__r.First_Name__c}
```

```
                     {!JA.Candidate__r.Last_Name__c}">
                <apex:param name="candidate"
                     value="{!JA.Candidate__r.ID}"></apex:param>
         </apex:commandLink>
            </apex:column >
            <apex:column
              value="{!JA.Candidate_Qualified__c}">
                </apex:column>
         </apex:pageblockTable>
         </apex:pageblockSection>
         </apex:pageBlock>
     </apex:form>
         <apex:detail
           subject="{!$CurrentPage.parameters.candidate}"
           title="false" id="candidateDetail">
         </apex:detail>
</apex:page>
```

Your Visualforce page is getting more and more robust. Your next task is to bring this page into the world of Web 2.0, with its wondrous AJAX capabilities.

Partial Page Refreshes

Asynchrounous JavaScript and XML, or AJAX, is a technology that underlies a lot of the Web 2.0 world. HTML-based browser pages were originally meant to be treated as one large atomic object. If you wanted any part of the page to change, you had to re-fetch the entire page. This process can be cumbersome, both in terms of implementing functionality and reduced performance, due to retrieving static portions of a page.

One of the features of AJAX is the ability to use partial page refreshes. As the term implies, this feature makes it possible to replace part of a Web page without having to request and receive the entire page.

Visualforce pages give you this same capability through the use of a single attribute. You can use this attribute to give your users a richer interface with the higher performance they want, without increasing your development workload.

For this task, you start by marking out the portion of the page that will be refreshed.

1. Add `<apex:outputPanel>` tags before and after the beginning and ending tags for the detail component of the Candidate object, to nest the detail component within the outputPanel tags. If you use the code helper, you must move the closing tag after the closing detail tag.
2. Edit the initial outputPanel tag by adding an `id="candidateDetail"` attribute.

The outputPanel marks off a section of the page that can be refreshed independently, and the ID attribute gives the panel a name that is referenced from other parts of the page.

You are almost to the promised land of partial page refreshes.

3. Add an attribute to the initial commandLink tag that reads:

`rerender="thePage:candidateDetail"`

This simple attribute lists the panels that are refreshed as part of the partial page refresh. The `candidateDetail` outputPanel is within `thePage` page, so you use both to qualify the reference, separated by a colon. You can have more than one identifier, separated by commas, for this attribute.

The code for this version of your Visualforce page is as follows:

```
<apex:page standardController="Position__c" id="thePage">
    <apex:form >
        <apex:pageMessages></apex:pageMessages>
        <apex:pageBlock>
        <apex:pageMessages></apex:pageMessages>
        <apex:pageBlockButtons location="bottom">
            <apex:commandButton
              action="{!save}" value="Save">
              </apex:commandButton>
            <apex:commandButton
              action="{!cancel}" value="Cancel">
              </apex:commandButton>
        </apex:pageBlockButtons>
        <apex:pageBlockSection columns="1">
            <apex:inputField
              value="{!Position__c.Department__c}">
              </apex:inputField>
            <apex:inputField
              value="{!Position__c.Job_Description__c}">
              </apex:inputField>
        </apex:pageBlockSection>
        </apex:pageBlock>
        <apex:pageBlock >
        <apex:pageblockSection >
        <apex:pageblockTable
          value="{!Position__c.Job_Application__r}" var="JA">
            <apex:facet name="header">Job Applicants
              </apex:facet>
            <apex:column headerValue="Candidate" >
                <apex:commandLink
                  rerender="thePage:candidateDetail">
                    {!JA.Candidate__r.First_Name__c}
                    {!JA.Candidate__r.Last_Name__c}
                  <apex:param name="candidate"
                    value="{!JA.Candidate__c}"></apex:param>
            </apex:commandLink>
```

```
            </apex:column >
            <apex:column
              value="{!JA.Candidate_Qualified__c}">
              </apex:column>
          </apex:pageblockTable>
          </apex:pageblockSection>
          </apex:pageBlock>
      </apex:form>
      <apex:outputPanel id="candidateDetail"
        styleclass="candidate">
          <apex:detail
            subject="{!$CurrentPage.parameters.candidate}"
            title="false">
          </apex:detail>
          </apex:outputPanel>
</apex:page>
```

Re-rendering part of your page causes your page to be submitted to the Force Platform server, and parts of your page are returned from the server. These events can occur very rapidly, or take some time. In order to keep your users appraised of what is going on, you can use the `actionStatus` component.

Some Visualforce components, such as the `actionStatus` component, have the ability to include a facet. A facet acts as a placeholder that allows you to add text or other components.

The `actionStatus` component comes with two facets – `start` and `stop`. The components you put within these facets are displayed when the initial AJAX request is made (`start`), and when the AJAX request is complete (`stop`).

You have to give the `actionStatus` component an `ID` attribute, which you then reference as the status attribute for the `commandLink` whose status will be tracked, as in the following:

```
<apex:commandLink rerender="thePage:candidateDetail"
status="status">
```

4. Add the highlighted code to your Visualforce page to include the status of the AJAX request.

```
<apex:page standardController="Position__c" id="thePage">
    <apex:form >
        <apex:pageMessages></apex:pageMessages>
        <apex:pageBlock>
        <apex:pageMessages></apex:pageMessages>
        <apex:pageBlockButtons location="bottom">
            <apex:commandButton
              action="{!save}" value="Save">
            </apex:commandButton>
            <apex:commandButton
```

```
                        action="{!cancel}" value="Cancel">
                    </apex:commandButton>
            </apex:pageBlockButtons>
            <apex:pageBlockSection columns="1">
                <apex:inputField
                    value="{!Position__c.Department__c}">
                    </apex:inputField>
                <apex:inputField
                    value="{!Position__c.Job_Description__c}">
                    </apex:inputField>
            </apex:pageBlockSection>
        </apex:pageBlock>
        <apex:pageBlock >
        <apex:pageblockSection >
        <apex:pageblockTable
            value="{!Position__c.Job_Application__r}" var="JA">
                <apex:facet name="header">Job Applicants
                    </apex:facet>
                <apex:column headerValue="Candidate" >
                    <apex:commandLink
                        rerender="thePage:candidateDetail"
                        status="status">
                            {!JA.Candidate__r.First_Name__c}
                            {!JA.Candidate__r.Last_Name__c}
                        <apex:param name="candidate"
                        value="{!JA.Candidate__c}"></apex:param>
                </apex:commandLink>
                    </apex:column >
                <apex:column
                    value="{!JA.Candidate_Qualified__c}">
                    </apex:column>
            </apex:pageblockTable>
            <apex:actionStatus startText="Fetching candidate..."
                stopText="" id="status"/>
            </apex:pageblockSection>
        </apex:pageBlock>
    </apex:form>
    <apex:outputPanel id="candidateDetail"
        styleclass="candidate">
        <apex:detail
            subject="{!$CurrentPage.parameters.candidate}"
            title="false">
        </apex:detail>
        </apex:outputPanel>
</apex:page>
```

5. Save your Visualforce page and click the output link.

Voila! With these few keystrokes, you have added a much more pleasing (and efficient) way to display the detail section.

Important: Command buttons and links are integrated into the security scheme you have created for your Force Platform environment. If the current user does not have permission to execute the command called by a button or link for the current record, the user interface object is not even displayed on the page.

Get Some Action

Visualforce pages can perform partial page refreshes in response to almost any Javascript event. You can trigger an AJAX partial page refresh in response to more than just mouse clicks. Action support in Visualforce pages adds new dimensions of possibilities for your user interface–without any AJAX code.

Some minor modifications of your Visualforce page adds this type of service to your Force Platform application.

1. Remove the `commandLink` tags from the column in your `pageBlockTable`.
2. Add two expressions to show the name of the candidate after the initial column tags, the `{!JA.Candidate__r.First_Name__C}` and `{!JA.Candidate__r.Last_Name__C}` expressions.
3. Add `<apex:actionSupport>` tags immediately after the expressions you just added. Add two attributes to the initial actionSupport tag: an `event` tag that indicates the type of mouse event that triggers the action, and a `rerender` tag that points to the sections of the page that are rerendered in response to the action. This initial tag looks like this:

```
<apex:actionSupport event="onmouseover"
rerender="thePage:candidateDetail" status="status">
```

4. Move the closing actionSupport tag after the apex:param tags.
5. You are finished adding mouse over support for the page. Save your code to run the page and then move your mouse over one of the candidate names.

The code for this version of your Visualforce page is as follows:

```
<apex:page standardController="Position__c" id="thePage">
    <apex:form >
        <apex:pageBlock>
        <apex:pageMessages></apex:pageMessages>
        <apex:pageBlockButtons location="bottom">
            <apex:commandButton
                action="{!save}" value="Save">
                </apex:commandButton>
            <apex:commandButton
                action="{!cancel}" value="Cancel">
```

```
                      </apex:commandButton>
            </apex:pageBlockButtons>
            <apex:pageBlockSection columns="1">
                <apex:inputField
                  value="{!Position__c.Department__c}">
                  </apex:inputField>
                <apex:inputField
                  value="{!Position__c.Job_Description__c}">
                  </apex:inputField>
            </apex:pageBlockSection>
            </apex:pageBlock>
            <apex:pageBlock >
            <apex:pageblockSection >
            <apex:pageblockTable
              value="{!Position__c.Job_Application__r}" var="JA">
                <apex:column headerValue="Candidate" >
                  {!JA.Candidate__r.First_Name__c}
                  {!JA.Candidate__r.Last_Name__c}
                  <apex:param name="candidate"
                    value="{!JA.Candidate__c}"></apex:param>
                  <apex:actionSupport event="onmouseover"
                    rerender="thePage:candidateDetail">
                  <apex:actionStatus startText="Fetching
candidate..."
                    stopText=""></apex:actionStatus>
                </apex:column >
                <apex:column
                 value="{!JA.Candidate_Qualified__c}">
                  </apex:column>
            </apex:pageblockTable>
            </apex:pageblockSection>
            </apex:pageBlock>
        </apex:form>
        <apex:outputPanel id="candidateDetail"
          styleclass="candidate">
            <apex:detail
              subject="{!$CurrentPage.parameters.candidate}"
              title="false">
            </apex:detail>
            </apex:outputPanel>
</apex:page>
```

Pretty slick. The first time you roll your mouse over one of the candidates, it may take a moment to initially fetch the detail section, but subsequent refreshes happen very quickly.

The page you created is not a complete replacement for the standard Position detail page, so you would either want to enhance your Visualforce page or, for the purposes of this book, simply reset the View button to call up the original detail page for Position.

6. Go to Objects Position, scroll to the Standard Buttons and Links section, and click **Reset** to connect this link to the default detail page for the Position record.

In the next section, you return to the province of HTML to see how you can give virtually any appearance to your Visualforce pages.

Changing the Look and Feel

The last few sections have discussed the extended AJAX capabilities of Visualforce pages. Remember, though, that Visualforce pages combine the capabilities of both HTML and AJAX in a highly productive way.

Standard HTML uses the concept of style sheets to shape the look and feel of a page. A style sheet contains style classes that are collections of visual attributes you can assign to a particular HTML element.

Modern HTML uses the cascading style sheets, or CSS, that let developers supplement or replace the styles in an existing style sheet. The look and feel of standard Force Platform pages is governed by a set of cascading style sheets.

You have the ability to supplement or replace these standard style sheets and use their styles in Visualforce pages. With this feature, you can change virtually every aspect of the appearance of your Visualforce pages while still using the functionality of the Force Platform. For instance, the following figure shows an online discussion blog built with Visualforce pages that looks nothing like a standard Force Platform application.

Paying to be Perplexed

Buyers of "IT security" products report that they don't feel much more secure, but that they now perceive the complexity of their security solutions as their single biggest security challenge -- even more so than breach prevention, policy enforcement, user education or risk assessment. From the story linked above: So-called "defense-in-depth" is just another way of saying "you've got a bunch of technologies that overlap and that don't handle security in a straightforward manner," says Alastair MacWillson, global managing director of Accenture's security practice. "It's like putting 20 locks on your door because you're not comfortable that any of them works." Yet a case can be made that respondents aren't worried enough." MacWillson is further quoted as warning that the complexity of security products is perhaps just the problem but the volume of that data makes it like the man who lost his keys up the street, it's possible that those operators are only looking where the streetlight is shining. Leakage of data through theft and carelessness may be much greater risks. The story I first cited above narrates incidents of trade secrets downloaded from a company's PDF servers and shopped to competitors, as well as familiar tales of backup devices and laptops being stolen from employees' cars. It's all part of a perfect storm of exploding data volumes colliding with escalating standards of governance. Quoting that same report once more: Over the past 12 months, the change at Eisenhower Medical Center in Rancho Mirage, Calif., that's had the greatest impact on security is the health care organization's move from a paper-based to an electronic patient records system. "This put more responsibility on us to make sure the patient's data is secure," says CIO David Perez. "And it's not just the movement of the data online but the volume of that data makes it more challenging. A CAT scan a few years ago would provide 250 to 500 images, but our new system can produce up to 5,000 images." As more and more physicians and medical staff log on to Eisenhower's intranet portal to do their work, Perez and his team must increase their monitoring for security problems and ensure that only the appropriate physicians and staff are accessing different medical records, as required by the Health Insurance Portability and Accountability Act. This isn't the kind of problem that's solved by throwing more money into on-premise security technology and questionably effective training. When you're in a hole, the thing to do is to stop digging. Issues of information security are perhaps among the strongest arguments for moving key systems into an on-demand space -- instead of clinging to the illusion that data are more secure on-premise, merely because the storage devices are where you can see them.

Posted by Andrew Waite on Thu Aug 16 06:43:57 GMT 2007

Salesforce.com Development in the Social Good Sector

My name is Steve Wright. I'm the Director of Innovation for the Salesforce.com Foundation. We have been

Figure 164: Visualforce Pages as an online blog

You can use your own style sheet instead of the standard Force Platform cascading style sheet, or you can add your own styles to the standard cascading style sheet. Using cascading style sheets is fairly easy, but in order to completely change the look and feel of a Visualforce page, you must first understand the details of the standard style sheets that you are replacing. Since cascading style sheets act in concert with existing styles, which are in turn applied to different parts of a Visualforce page, a simple replacement might not have such a simple effect. That level of understanding is beyond the scope of this section, which will concentrate on the tasks you need to accomplish to use any type of style that is not part of the standard cascading style sheets.

You will first go through the steps required to add style classes to your Visualforce page. The cascading style sheet you use for this series of steps is fairly rudimentary, but the implementation will be the same for more complex style sheets. The directions stored in the Code Share project for this book, will point you to this style sheet.

Since a Visualforce page can use HTML code, you could include an entire style sheet for your page with an HTML link element. For this exercise, you will first add your cascading style sheet into the Force Platform environment as a static resource. As you will see, you can access a static resource using global variables.

1. Go to the Code Share project for this book to find an example style sheet for this exercise and save it to your machine.

2. Go to **Setup** ➤ **Develop** ➤ **Static Resources** and click **New** to bring up the page shown below

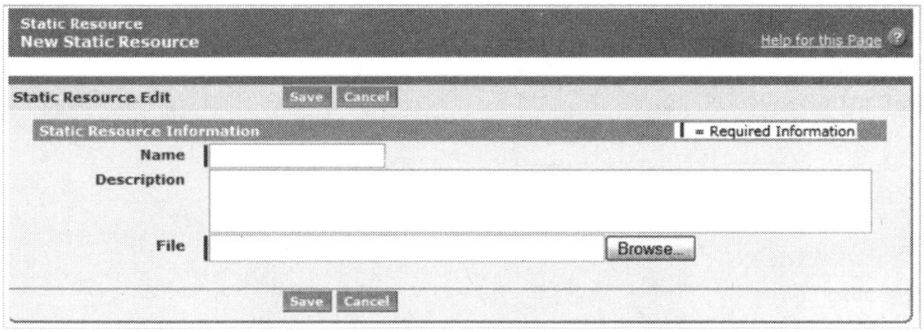

Figure 165: Adding a static resource

3. Give the style sheet a name of `CandidateStyleSheet` and description, and then browse to find and select the style sheet.

   Be aware that the Force Platform environment classifies the file based on its extension, so your style sheet should use the standard .css extension.

4. Save the static resource.

5. Go to edit your Visualforce page in development mode. Add `<apex:stylesheet>` tags to the page just below the initial page tag, and then add a value attribute so that the tag reads like this:

   ```
   <apex:stylesheet value="{!$Resource.CandidateStyleSheet}">
   ```

   The value attribute accepts a URL to reference any external style sheets and the `$Resource` variable links in the static resource you just loaded.

6. Add the following line of code just above the initial pageBlockSection tag that contains the job applications:

   ```
   <apex:outputText value="These are the candidates for the
   position." styleclass="candidate"/>
   ```

   There are two things to notice about this new tag. The first is that you are including the attribute styleclass to indicate that the value of this outputText should use the candidate style that was added to your page.

   You can also see that you have a single forward slash at the end of this tag, which replaces the closing tag. You can use this syntax to reduce your overall code whenever you do not need to enclose other elements within the body of the tag. Although the tag helper automatically gives you a separate closing tag, you can use this closing slash instead where appropriate.

Code listings from this point on will use this abbreviated syntax where appropriate.

7. Save your modified Visualforce page to display the page shown below.

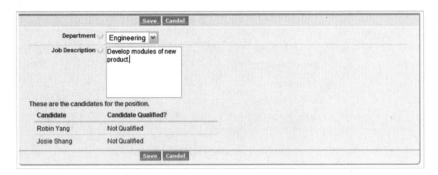

Figure 166: Using styles in a Visualforce Page

As mentioned above, this particular use of a new style is fairly simple, but cascading style sheets give you enormous flexibility in adjusting the look and feel of your Force Platform page without sacrificing any of the functionality used by the page.

Tip: You can combine multiple static resources together in a single ZIP file.

Visualforce Pages and Data Sets

Up until this point, your Visualforce pages have been accessing data through the single starting point of a Position record. Visualforce pages can also be used for retrieving sets of data, with a lot of built-in functionality that already exists on the Force Platform. You can retrieve sets of data from any object using a standard controller, leading to the name of the feature, standard set controllers.

In this final section of this introductory chapter on Visualforce, you will see how you can extend the default list functionality of the Force Platform with standard set controllers. With this capability, you can create pages that display multiple records from a single object, as well as use some of the built-in functionality that comes with Force Platform list views.

The end result of your efforts will be a page that can be used to replace the standard list view for Job Applications, shown by default whenever a user clicks the Job Applications tab. This new page will give your users everything they expect from a list view—and more.

Standard Set Controller Basics

Standard set controllers join the best of two worlds—the flexibility of Visualforce pages and the built-in power of views and searches on the Force Platform.

You already know almost everything you need to create a Visualforce page that displays multiple records from a standard controller. The one new aspect for your page is an attribute for the page tag itself. The attribute is `recordSetVar`, and it takes a string value. This string is the variable name for the set of records that the standard set controller makes available to the page, which will be used as the value of an iterative data component, such as a data table.

1. Create a new Visualforce page with a quick fix to a new page called `JobApplications`.
2. Modify the default code for the page to the following:

```
<apex:page standardController="Job_Application__c"
    recordSetVar="JobApps" tabstyle="Job_Application__c">
</apex:page>
```

With the `recordSetVar` attribute, you have supplied a reference to the set of records that the standard controller supplies for the Job Application object. This new page also includes the tabstyle attribute, which associates the page with the tab and styling for a particular object—in this case, the Job Application object.

Your next step is to add a page block and a page block table.

3. Change the code for your Visualforce page to the following:

```
<apex:page standardController="Job_Application__c"
    recordSetVar="JobApps" tabstyle="Job_Application__c">
  <apex:pageblock id="thePage">
     <apex:pageblocktable value="{!JobApps}" var="JA"
       id="candidateTable">
        <apex:column value="{!JA.Name}"/>
        <apex:column value="{!JA.Candidate__c}"/>
        <apex:column
          value="{!JA.Candidate__r.First_Name__c}"/>
        <apex:column
          value="{!JA.Candidate__r.Last_Name__c}"/>
    <apex:column value="{!JA.Position__c}"/>
    <apex:column
      value="{!JA.Position__r.Job_Description__c}"/>
     </apex:pageblocktable>
  </apex:pageblock>
</apex:page>
```

Nothing new here—these tags define a pageBlockTable the same way you did for your earlier Visualforce page, with an id attribute so you can identify (and refresh) the table a little later in this chapter. But, of course, this page is displaying a set of records from your Job Applications object, not related records to a Position, so the value attribute is set to the var defined for the standard set controller.

Job Application ID	Candidate	First Name	Last Name	Position	Job Description
JA-00002	CAN-000001	Robert	Smith	POS-00008	Administrative assistant to VP of Finance.
JA-00003	CAN-000001	Robert	Smith	POS-00004	Product Marketing Manager for new product.
JA-00004	CAN-000001	Robert	Smith	POS-00012	Mid-level accountant
JA-00005	CAN-000001	Robert	Smith	POS-00016	Field rep.
JA-00006	CAN-000001	Robert	Smith	POS-00005	Vice President of channel sales.
JA-00007	CAN-000001	Robert	Smith	POS-00007	QA assistant.
JA-00008	CAN-000001	Robert	Smith	POS-00003	Leader of stealth project.
JA-00009	CAN-000001	Robert	Smith	POS-00009	HA specialist.
JA-00010	CAN-000002	Chuck	Grey	POS-00016	Field rep.
JA-00011	CAN-000003	Luann	Huff	POS-00017	Accounts receivables clerk.
JA-00012	CAN-000004	Rick	Ostenberg	POS-00008	Administrative assistant to VP of Finance.
JA-00013	CAN-000005	Donald	Daily	POS-00008	Administrative assistant to VP of Finance.
JA-00014	CAN-000005	Donald	Daily	POS-00016	Field rep.
JA-00015	CAN-000005	Donald	Daily	POS-00002	Second tier technical support.
JA-00016	CAN-000006	Paul	Revere	POS-00004	Product Marketing Manager for new product.
JA-00017	CAN-000006	Paul	Revere	POS-00005	Vice President of channel sales.
JA-00018	CAN-000006	Paul	Revere	POS-00013	Director of Auditing
JA-00019	CAN-000006	Paul	Revere	POS-00011	Support representative.
JA-00020	CAN-000007	Elinor	Vera	POS-00006	Quality Assurance engineer for new product.
JA-00021	CAN-000007	Elinor	Vera	POS-00016	Field rep.

Figure 167: Using a standard set controller

4. Save your code to see your new page in action, as shown in the figure above.

Your new page does look like a list view, having adopted the formatting associated with the Job Application object; however, you have combined fields from the related Candidate and Position objects. This would not have been possible in a list view, as well as including links to the related records in those objects by displaying the values for those lookup fields. This list displays more information and acts as a switchboard that can take you directly to related records.

Already you are ahead of the game, but you still do not want to sacrifice any of the functionality delivered by a list view. One favorite feature of a list view is the built-in pagination. Users are only presented with a page of records at a time, along with buttons or links to navigate through the extended list.

A standard Visualforce dataTable does not behave so nicely. These tables simply display all the records for the associated object. This downside has not affected your pages yet since you have merely been showing small numbers of related records. But with something like job applications across your entire company, you can end up with hundreds.

By default, a standard set controller Visualforce page only shows a page full of records, but the standard controllers that power these pages offer some built-in navigation actions.

5. Modify your Visualforce page to add the following highlighted code:

```
<apex:page standardController="Job_Application__c"
  recordSetVar="JobApps" tabstyle="JobApps__tab">
    <apex:form >
        <apex:pageblock id="thePageBlock">
            <apex:pageblocktable value="{!JobApps}" var="JA"
              id="candidateTable">
                <apex:column value="{!JA.Name}"/>
                <apex:column value="{!JA.Candidate__c}"/>
                <apex:column
                  value="{!JA.Candidate__r.First_Name__c}"/>
                <apex:column
                  value="{!JA.Candidate__r.Last_Name__c}"/>
                <apex:column value="{!JA.Position__c}"/>
                <apex:column
                  value="{!JA.Position__r.Job_Description__c}">

                </column>
            </apex:pageblocktable>
        </apex:pageblock>
        <apex:panelGrid columns="2">
            <apex:commandLink
              action="{!previous}">
              Previous</apex:commandLink>
            <apex:commandLink
              action="{!next}">
              Next</apex:commandLink>
        </apex:panelGrid>
    </apex:form>
</apex:page>
```

You have to add `<apex:form>` tags to your page, since commandLinks can only be used within a form. The two commandLinks call two new functions offered by standard set controllers, `previous` and `next`.

Note: Standard set controllers also support first and last actions.

The new version of your page is ready to roll.

6. Save your Visualforce page to change the page displayed to the one shown below.

Job Application ID	Candidate	First Name	Last Name	Position	Job Description
JA-00002	CAN-000001	Robert	Smith	POS-00008	Administrative assistant to VP of Finance.
JA-00003	CAN-000001	Robert	Smith	POS-00004	Product Marketing Manager for new product.
JA-00004	CAN-000001	Robert	Smith	POS-00012	Mid-level accountant
JA-00005	CAN-000001	Robert	Smith	POS-00016	Field rep.
JA-00006	CAN-000001	Robert	Smith	POS-00005	Vice President of channel sales.
JA-00007	CAN-000001	Robert	Smith	POS-00007	QA assistant.
JA-00008	CAN-000001	Robert	Smith	POS-00003	Leader of stealth project.
JA-00009	CAN-000001	Robert	Smith	POS-00009	HA specialist.
JA-00010	CAN-000002	Chuck	Grey	POS-00016	Field rep.
JA-00011	CAN-000003	Luann	Huff	POS-00017	Accounts receivables clerk.
JA-00012	CAN-000004	Rick	Ostenberg	POS-00008	Administrative assistant to VP of Finance.
JA-00013	CAN-000005	Donald	Daily	POS-00008	Administrative assistant to VP of Finance.
JA-00014	CAN-000005	Donald	Daily	POS-00016	Field rep.
JA-00015	CAN-000005	Donald	Daily	POS-00002	Second tier technical support.
JA-00016	CAN-000006	Paul	Revere	POS-00004	Product Marketing Manager for new product.
JA-00017	CAN-000006	Paul	Revere	POS-00005	Vice President of channel sales.
JA-00018	CAN-000006	Paul	Revere	POS-00013	Director of Auditing
JA-00019	CAN-000006	Paul	Revere	POS-00011	Support representative.
JA-00020	CAN-000007	Elinor	Vera	POS-00006	Quality Assurance engineer for new product.
JA-00021	CAN-000007	Elinor	Vera	POS-00016	Field rep.

Previous Next

Figure 168: Standard set-based Visualforce page with navigation

The set-based Visualforce page is working as you hoped, but you could make the navigation portion of the page a little more friendly. For instance, when you are on the first page of records, there is no need to have the Next link visible.

You can address this situation with another attribute of most Visualforce components—rendered. As the name implies, this attribute takes a Boolean value that will determine if the component is shown on the page. Standard set controllers includes values that you can use for exactly this purpose — the hasNext and hasPrevious values.

Add these attributes to the command links you previously defined. In addition, you give the outputPanel that contains these links an id attribute of "navigation", since you will want to rerender these links when the page changes. The code in the next section accomplishes this.

7. For now, add the highlighted code to your Visualforce page:

```
<apex:page standardController="Job_Application__c"
    recordSetVar="JobApps" tabstyle="JobApps__tab">
    <apex:form >
        <apex:pageblock id="thePageBlock">
            <apex:pageblocktable value="{!JobApps}" var="JA"
                id="candidateTable">
                <apex:column value="{!JA.Name}"/>
                <apex:column value="{!JA.Candidate__c}"/>
                <apex:column
                    value="{!JA.Candidate__r.First_Name__c}"/>
```

```
                <apex:column
                  value="{!JA.Candidate__r.Last_Name__c}"/>
                <apex:column value="{!JA.Position__c}"/>
                <apex:column
                  value="{!JA.Position__r.Job_Description__c}">

                  </column>
              </apex:pageblocktable>
          </apex:pageblock>
          <apex:panelGrid columns="2">
              <apex:commandLink
                action="{!previous}"
                rendered="{!hasPrevious}">
                Previous</apex:commandLink>
              <apex:commandLink
                action="{!next}"
                rendered="{!hasNext}">
                Next</apex:commandLink>
          </apex:panelGrid>
      </apex:form>
</apex:page>
```

Your new page can display many records, nicely displayed a page at a time. But how many records are displayed on a page? Right now, your Visualforce page is using the default number of records, as defined for your org. But you can change this quite easily.

Records Per Page

Any table based on a standard set controller contains a global variable size. You can set this variable through Apex code, which you will learn about in the next two chapters. You can also provide a Visualforce component, bound to the global variable, that allows your users to select the number of records they want to see displayed on a page.

1. Modify your Visualforce page to include the following new code:

```
<apex:page standardController="Job_Application__c"
  recordSetVar="JobApps" tabstyle="JobApps__tab">
    <apex:form >
        <apex:pageblock id="thePageBlock">
          <apex:actionRegion >
            <apex:outputText value="Records per page:  ">
              </apex:outputText>
            <apex:selectList value="{!pagesize}" size="1">
              <apex:selectOption itemLabel="10"
                itemValue="10"></apex:selectOption>
              <apex:selectOption itemLabel="15"
                itemValue="15"></apex:selectOption>
              <apex:selectOption itemLabel="20"
                itemValue="20"></apex:selectOption>
```

```
            <apex:selectOption itemLabel="20"
                itemValue="25"></apex:selectOption>
            </apex:selectList>
        </apex:actionRegion>
        <apex:pageblocktable value="{!JobApps}" var="JA"
            id="candidateTable">
            <apex:column value="{!JA.Name}"/>
            <apex:column value="{!JA.Candidate__c}"/>
            <apex:column
                value="{!JA.Candidate__r.First_Name__c}"/>
            <apex:column
                value="{!JA.Candidate__r.Last_Name__c}"/>
            <apex:column value="{!JA.Position__c}"/>
            <apex:column
            value="{!JA.Position__r.Job_Description__c}">

            </column>
        </apex:pageblocktable>
    </apex:pageblock>
    <apex:panelGrid columns="2" id="navigation">
        <apex:commandLink
            action="{!previous}"
            rendered="{!hasPrevious}">
            Previous</apex:commandLink>
        <apex:commandLink
            action="{!next}"
            rendered="{!hasNext}">
            Next</apex:commandLink>
    </apex:panelGrid>
  </apex:form>
</apex:page>
```

The newly added tags do a few things. First of all, you created an `actionRegion`
on the form. This area designates the portion of the page that is affected by AJAX
actions. Only those components within the `actionRegion` can send or receive
information from the Force Platform servers in response to an AJAX request. This
limitation means that only those components within the region will respond to user
actions and, even more importantly, only data from components within the region
will be sent to the server. You may have to use an `actionRegion` to limit data
interaction with the controller in this way. For instance, if you want to refresh part
of your page when the user has not completed entering all the data for the page, the
submission of the entire page of data can end up causing a required field to receive
a null value—which would result in an error. By leaving the component that is bound
to the required field out of the `actionRegion`, the data for the field will not be sent
to the server, avoiding the error.

The `selectList` component itself is bound to the `pagesize` attribute of the
Job_Application__c object that controls how many records are shown. You add
values to the `selectList` component with multiple `selectOption` components
within the `selectList` tags.

All these changes combine together to produce the desired effect–when the user changes the value in the picklist for the number of records, the `pageBlockTable` is redrawn with that number of records.

Your user now has a way to select the number of records they would like displayed on a page. Your last task is to automatically redraw the table of candidates and the navigation links after the user selects a different `pagesize` by adding `actionSupport` for the `selectList`.

2. Add the highlighted code to your Visualforce page:

```
<apex:page standardController="Job_Application__c"
  recordSetVar="JobApps" tabstyle="JobApps__tab">
    <apex:form >
        <apex:pageblock id="thePageBlock">
        <apex:actionRegion >
            <apex:outputText value="Records per page:  ">
            </apex:outputText>
            <apex:selectList value="{!pagesize}" size="1">
                <apex:selectOption itemLabel="10"
                   itemValue="10"></apex:selectOption>
                <apex:selectOption itemLabel="15"
                   itemValue="15"></apex:selectOption>
                <apex:selectOption itemLabel="20"
                   itemValue="20"></apex:selectOption>
                <apex:selectOption itemLabel="20"
                   itemValue="25"></apex:selectOption>
                <apex:actionSupport event="onchange"
                   rerender="thePage, navigation"/>
            </apex:selectList>
        </apex:actionRegion>
            <apex:pageblocktable value="{!JobApps}" var="JA"
                id="candidateTable">
                <apex:column value="{!JA.Name}"/>
                <apex:column value="{!JA.Candidate__c}"/>
                <apex:column
                   value="{!JA.Candidate__r.First_Name__c}"/>
                <apex:column
                   value="{!JA.Candidate__r.Last_Name__c}"/>
                <apex:column value="{!JA.Position__c}"/>
                <apex:column
                value="{!JA.Position__r.Job_Description__c}">

                </column>
            </apex:pageblocktable>
        </apex:pageblock>
        <apex:panelGrid columns="2" id="navigation">
            <apex:commandLink
                action="{!previous}"
                rendered="{!hasPrevious}">
                Previous</apex:commandLink>
            <apex:commandLink
                action="{!next}"
```

```
                rendered="{!hasNext}">
                Next</apex:commandLink>
            </apex:panelGrid>
        </apex:form>
    </apex:page>
```

3. Save your page. Change the value of the picklist and watch your page refresh.

Notice that the `rerender` attribute for the actionSupport designates two regions for refreshing—`thePage` and the navigation `panelGrid`.

Once a user sets the value for the `pagesize` attribute of an object, the value remains in effect until it is explicitly changed. So once a user sets that value, all subsequent list retrievals retrieve the same number of records, if available.

However, the ability to add pagination for the page can introduce some confusion for the user. What if the user ends up on this page when the number of records to display is less than the number of records allocated for the page size? The navigation links at the bottom of the page will not appear on the page—properly, since there will not be previous nor next records. But the user may just get confused and think something is amiss.

To address this potential usability issue, you can use the now familiar `actionStatus` component. When the user initially changes the page size for the page, the actionStatus should display a message indicating that a page refresh has started. When the page refresh completes, you can set the actionStatus to display the total number of records in this set of results. The effect of this status display will be to let the user easily understand if there are more records to display or not.

4. Add in the highlighted code for your Visualforce page:

```
<apex:page standardController="Job_Application__c"
   recordSetVar="JobApps" tabstyle="JobApps__tab">
    <apex:form >
        <apex:pageblock id="thePageBlock">
         <apex:actionRegion >
           <apex:outputText value="Records per page:   ">
            </apex:outputText>
           <apex:selectList value="{!pagesize}" size="1">
             <apex:selectOption itemLabel="10"
                itemValue="10"></apex:selectOption>
             <apex:selectOption itemLabel="15"
                itemValue="15"></apex:selectOption>
             <apex:selectOption itemLabel="20"
                itemValue="20"></apex:selectOption>
             <apex:selectOption itemLabel="20"
                itemValue="25"></apex:selectOption>
             <apex:actionSupport event="onchange"
                rerender="thePage, navigation"
```

```
            status="theStatus"/>
        </apex:selectList>
    <apex:actionStatus id="theStatus"
        startText="updating list..."
        stopText="  Total Result Size: {!resultSize}"/>
        </apex:actionRegion>
        <apex:pageblocktable value="{!JobApps}" var="JA"
            id="candidateTable">
            <apex:column value="{!JA.Name}"/>
            <apex:column value="{!JA.Candidate__c}"/>
            <apex:column
                value="{!JA.Candidate__r.First_Name__c}"/>
            <apex:column
                value="{!JA.Candidate__r.Last_Name__c}"/>
            <apex:column value="{!JA.Position__c}"/>
            <apex:column
            value="{!JA.Position__r.Job_Description__c}">

            </column>
        </apex:pageblocktable>
    </apex:pageblock>
    <apex:panelGrid columns="2" id="navigation">
        <apex:commandLink
            action="{!previous}"
            rendered="{!hasPrevious}">
            Previous</apex:commandLink>
        <apex:commandLink
            action="{!next}"
            rendered="{!hasNext}">
            Next</apex:commandLink>
    </apex:panelGrid>
    </apex:form>
</apex:page>
```

Voice of the Developer:

The ability to set the number of records returned for a standard list is one of the features of enhanced lists. You have to explicitly turn on the use of enhanced lists for your org through the **Setup ➤ Customize ➤ User Interface** page. Other enhanced list features include the ability to navigate directly to a particular page of results, changing the width of column in a list or the order of columns in a list by a drag-and-drop interaction, and allowing users to edit values in a list directly with inline editing. Please refer to the online documentation on enhanced lists for more information.

View Selection

Your latest Visualforce page is performing well, with most of the functionality currently available for standard Force Platform list views. In a standard Force Platform list view, users have the option of defining other list views with different columns from the source object and filter criteria.

With a standard set controller page, you could have already defined the columns you want to show in a table. By adding one more picklist to your page, you can give your users access to the filter conditions defined for any existing views.

1. Modify your Visualforce page to include the following new code:

```
<apex:page standardController="Job_Application__c"
  recordSetVar="JobApps" tabstyle="JobApps__tab">
    <apex:form >
        <apex:pageblock id="thePageBlock">
         <apex:actionRegion >
            <apex:outputText value="Records per page:  ">
            </apex:outputText>
            <apex:selectList value="{!pagesize}" size="1">
               <apex:selectOption itemLabel="10"
                  itemValue="10"></apex:selectOption>
               <apex:selectOption itemLabel="15"
                  itemValue="15"></apex:selectOption>
               <apex:selectOption itemLabel="20"
                  itemValue="20"></apex:selectOption>
               <apex:selectOption itemLabel="20"
                  itemValue="25"></apex:selectOption>
               <apex:actionSupport event="onchange"
                rerender="thePage, navigation"
                status="theStatus"/>
            </apex:selectList>
            <apex:outputLabel value="View: "
              for="viewList"></apex:outputLabel>
            <apex:selectList id="viewList" size="1"
              value="{!filterId}">
                <apex:actionSupport event="onchange"
                  rerender="thePage, navigation"/>
                <apex:selectOptions
                  value="{!listviewoptions}"/>
            </apex:selectList>
         <apex:actionStatus id="theStatus" startText="updating
list..."
            stopText="  Total Result Size: {!resultSize}"/>
         </apex:actionRegion>
            <apex:pageblocktable value="{!JobApps}" var="JA"
              id="candidateTable">
                <apex:column value="{!JA.Name}"/>
                <apex:column value="{!JA.Candidate__c}"/>
                <apex:column
                  value="{!JA.Candidate__r.First_Name__c}"/>
                <apex:column
                  value="{!JA.Candidate__r.Last_Name__c}"/>
                <apex:column value="{!JA.Position__c}"/>
                <apex:column
                  value="{!JA.Position__r.Job_Description__c}">
```

```
            </column>
        </apex:pageblocktable>
    </apex:pageblock>
    <apex:panelGrid columns="2" id="navigation">
        <apex:commandLink
          action="{!previous}"
          rendered="{!hasPrevious}">
          Previous</apex:commandLink>
        <apex:commandLink
          action="{!next}"
          rendered="{!hasNext}">
          Next</apex:commandLink>
    </apex:panelGrid>
  </apex:form>
</apex:page>
```

Some of this new code looks familiar. You used a `selectList` component before, but you filled it in your code with individual `selectOption` components. This time, you used the `selectOptions` component to populate the `selectList` component from the `listviewoptions` variable. This variable contains a list of all currently defined list views for an object.

Finally, you bound the `selectList` to the `filterID` global variable, used to identify a particular list view. By setting this variable, you impose the filters defined for the view on the result set returned from the standard set controller.

You also added `actionSupport` for this `selectList`, since any change in the filter should cause the relevant parts of the page to be refreshed. This `actionSupport` component is the same as the `actionSupport` component you used for the page size. You also should probably add an `actionStatus` component to keep your users informed as to the progress of their page refreshes.

It is time to see your new functionality in action.

2. Select a view from the picklist and see how the results in the table change. The initialization procedures described at the beginning of this chapter created some views for the Job Application object.

You easily blend the existing filters for views with your new standard set controller page. Although this example uses only existing filters that are defined by users, you can define your own filters with Apex code, which you will learn about in the next chapter.

Overriding Views with Visualforce Pages

You like your new Visualforce list view a lot – so much that you'd like to use it instead of that standard view that your user community sees when they click on the Job Applications tab. Since you have added the ability to use predefined user filters, your users will like the new version too. You can accomplish this task easily.

1. Go to **Setup ➤ Create ➤ Tabs**.
2. Click **New** in the Visualforce Tabs section, which will bring up the page shown in the figure below.

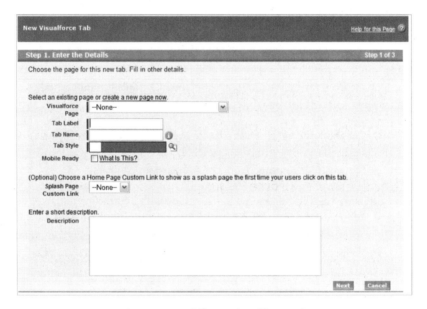

Figure 169: Adding a Visualforce tab

3. Select the Visualforce page you have been working on, `JobApplications`, as the Visualforce Page.
4. Give the tab the label of `New Job Applications`.
5. Change the name of the tab to `NewJobApps`, since you will want your new Visualforce page to highlight this new tab, as you will see shortly.
6. Select the same Hands icon you used for the original Job Applications tab.
7. Click on **Next** to accept the default security on the tab, and deselect all of the applications except for Recruiting, and click **Save**.

   When you see your application, you can see the tab you just created.

8. Click on the tab to bring up your Visualforce page.

It works—almost perfectly. The one problem is that when you bring up the Visualforce page, the original Job Applications tab gets the highlight. This result is because of the tabstyle attribute in your page—one you can easily change.

9. Change the value for the tabstyle in your page to `NewJobApps__tab`. A tab is identified by the tab name, followed by two underscores and the word `tab`.

10. Click on the second Job Applications tab again and see how well it works now.

11. At this point, you would probably want to at least remove the original Job Applications tab from the Recruiting applications, to avoid confusion.

You were able to use standard set controllers to implement most of the functionality of a list view, with quite a bit more flexibility. Your users will be able to use the list in the Job Application to see the job applications with extended information about each application, as well as giving them simple one-click access to the application or the position and candidate the application pulls together.

So far, you have seen how standard set controllers can be used to extend the reach of read-only lists. But, as you will see in the next section, Visualforce pages based on these controllers can also implement functionality that will transparently act on a group of selected records.

Mass Actions with Visualforce Pages

You have seen how a Visualforce page can display groups of records through a standard set controller, but these same pages can be used to perform mass actions.

A mass action is an action that is executed on a group of records. The standard Salesforce application already supports custom list buttons. A custom list button adds a selection box to a list and then performs an action on all the selected records.

You can use a standard Visualforce page to implement a mass action on a group of records. In this example, you create a simple Visualforce page allowing your users to update the status of one or more job applications for a particular position. This handy functionality lets a user quickly mark a number of candidates for a position as rejected, or select more than one candidate to interview, with just a few clicks.

Start by creating your Visualforce page.

1. Use the quickfix capability of Visualforce Developer mode to create a new Visualforce page with the name of `UpdateJobApps`.

2. Change the code for the page to the following code. You can get a text version of this code by following the instructions in the Code Share project for this book, described in *Chapter 1: Welcome to the Force Platform*.

```
<apex:page standardController="Job_Application__c"
  recordSetVar="jobApplications">
    <apex:form >
    <apex:sectionHeader
      title="Change status for Job Applicants"/>
        <apex:pageBlock mode="edit">
            <apex:pageMessages />
            <apex:pageblockSection title="Change">
                <apex:inputField
                  value="{!Job_Application__c.Status__c}"/>
            </apex:pageBlockSection>
            <apex:pageBlockSection
              title="Selected Job Applicants">
                <apex:pageBlockTable
                  value="{!selected}" var="j">
                    <apex:column
                      value="{!j.Candidate__r.First_Name__c}">

                    </column>
                    <apex:column
                      value="{!j.Candidate__r.Last_Name__c}">

                    </column>
                    <apex:column value="{!j.Status__c}"/>
                </apex:pageBlockTable>
            </apex:pageblockSection>
            <apex:pageBlockButtons location="bottom">
                <apex:commandButton
                  value="Save" action="{!save}"/>
                <apex:commandButton
                  value="Cancel" action="{!cancel}"/>
            </apex:pageBlockButtons>
        </apex:pageBlock>
    </apex:form>
</apex:page>
```

This code should look pretty familiar to you by now. The page is connected with the standard set controller for the Job Applications object. The upper portion of the page has some standard text, followed by a `dataList` component, and more text.

The first new portion of the code comes when you see the `value` for the pageBlockTable, which references `selected`. This variable points to the records in the standard set controller that have been selected by the user. You will see how the user selects these records in the following section, but be aware that this collection of records can contain any number of records the user selects. The fields displayed in the `pageBlockTable` provide feedback to the user on which records were selected.

The next section of code displays a standard `inputField`, bound to the Status field in the Job Applications object. This field will accept the status that will be used to set the Status values—for all of the selected records.

The page also includes a `pageMessages` element. As described earlier in this chapter, this component will display any messages returned from the Force Platform. If for any reason your save action should fail, that reason would appear in the `pageMessages` area.

The final portion of the code provides standard save and cancel buttons. The Force Platform understands that this save action is now a mass action—the save should set the value of the Status field to the value selected in the `inputField` for all the records in the selected collection.

Nice power, delivered automatically.

3. Save the code, which will show you the page shown in the figure below.

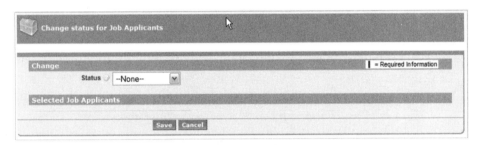

Figure 170: Visualforce Page for mass update

Your new Visualforce page is ready. Now all you need to do is to tie it into a way to allow your users to create that collection of selected records.

Adding a List Button

Now that you have your Visualforce page ready to receive and process a set of records, you just have to add a way for the user to select those records. Once again, the native functionality of the Force Platform makes this easy.

1. Go to **Setup ➤ Create ➤ Objects ➤ Job Application**, since your user will be selecting records from this object.
2. Go to the Custom Buttons and Links section and click **New** to bring up the page shown in the figure below.

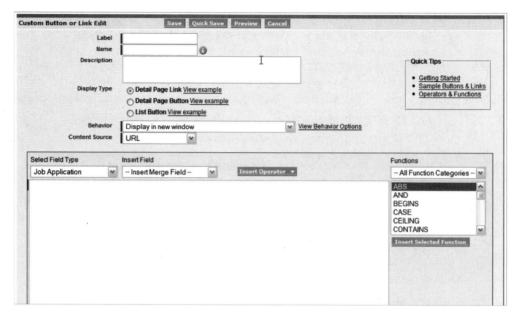

Figure 171: Defining a custom button

3. Give the new component a `Label` of `Update Status` and an appropriate description.

4. Select `List Button` as the display type, which will indicate that this button will act on a set of records. Leave the `Display Checkboxes` checkbox checked, which will allow users to select individual records in the list.

5. Choose `Display in existing window without sidebar or header` as the `Behavior`, since you will want your Visualforce page to appear in the standard application page space.

6. Select `Visualforce Page` as the `Content Source`, which will make the formula entry box disappear and a list of Visualforce pages appear in the Content picklist. Notice that the only Visualforce pages that are listed are those that access a standard set controller.

7. Select the `UpdateJobApps` page and click **Save**. You will be warned that you will have to add this button to a page layout, which you will do next.

8. Click **Objects ➤ Position** to bring up the detail page for that object, and scroll to the page layouts.

    Remember that you have two layouts for the two record types; however, since you designated the Non-technical Position Layout as inheriting the style of the Position Layout, you can simply edit this last layout to affect both.

9. Click **Edit** for the Position Layout, and then double-click the Job Applications related list to bring up the page shown completed in the following figure.

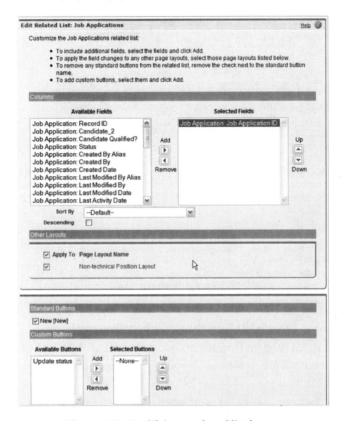

Figure 172: Modifying a related list layout

This page allows you to add fields to the related list layout, to apply the changes made to this layout to ripple down to the Non-technical Position Layout, to hide standard buttons on the layout and, to the point, to add any custom list buttons to the layout.

10. Move the Update status button from the Available Buttons picklist to the Selected Buttons picklist. Click **OK** to save this change and **OK** again to acknowledge that you have one more step, and then click **Save** in the page layout.

That's it—you are done.

Watch It Work

It seemed easy to add this somewhat sophisticated functionality to your application—maybe even too easy. As always with the Force Platform, you can verify the new functionality of your application by running it.

1. Click the Positions tab and select a position.
2. Scroll to the Job Applications related list, as shown below.

    You can see that your custom button is part of this section of the page.

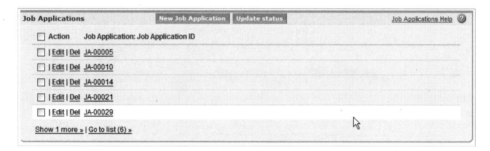

Figure 173: The new Job Applications related list

3. Select one or more Job Applications and click **Update Status** to bring up the populated page, as shown in the figure below.

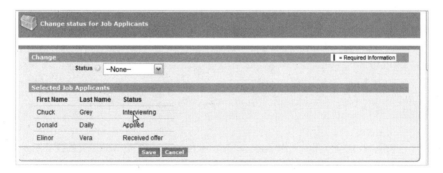

Figure 174: Your Visualforce Page in (mass) action

4. Choose a status for the selected records and click **Save**. You will be sent back to the Position page, where you can see that your Visualforce page did take the appropriate action.

This last feat concludes the exploration of standard set controllers and Visualforce pages.

Summary

This chapter has quickly introduced you to some of the capabilities of Visualforce pages. You have seen how you can change the look and feel of pages in a Force Platform application, as well as add AJAX-like functionality to increase the range of your pages, while providing advanced interface capabilities.

You also learned about the power of standard set controllers that make it possible for you to easily create pages that allow users to view multiple records in a handy, paginated format, and even perform actions on groups of selected records, all without any procedural code.

Visualforce pages give you all of this, but there is more to Visualforce technology than pages. At the start of this chapter, you learned about the full scope of this technology, which included the ability to create controllers that extend or replace the standard interactions between a Visualforce page and Force Platform data.

Visualforce custom controllers are implemented with Apex code, so before you can move into the creation of controllers and controller extensions, you need to learn Apex. Over the next two chapters, you will.

Chapter 10

Apex

Up until this point in the book, your development efforts on the Force Platform have used the highly productive, mainly declarative features of the platform. From relationships, through workflow, through tag-driven Visualforce pages, you have not had to write any code in creating the current version of the Recruiting application.

The creators of the Force Platform believe in providing robust access to the capabilities of the platform in the most efficient manner, both for development and execution. As a best practice, you should always use the declarative features to implement the functionality you require in your application, since there is no need to re-implement capabilities already provided for you.

But there are times when you have to go beyond even the broad capabilities of the declarative portion of the Force Platform. For these particular situations, the Force Platform offers Apex.

Important: If you have been following the examples in the previous chapter, your Force Platform organization should be ready for the exercises in this chapter. If you have not done the exercises, or want to start with a fresh version of the sample Recruiting application, please refer to the instructions in the Code Share project for this book. You can find information on how to access that project in *Chapter 1: Welcome to the Force Platform*. In addition, the project contains instructions on how to update your organization with changes required for this chapter.

Introducing Apex

Before you can begin to learn about the syntax and capabilities of Apex, you need to learn the basics—the whats, hows, and whys of Apex.

What is Apex?

Apex is a strongly-typed, object-based programming language that allows developers to execute logic, flow and transaction control statements on the Force Platform. As you would expect, Apex is intimately connected with Force Platform data, offering powerful data interactions through both a query language and a search language.

You will learn most of the basic syntax in this chapter, with the next chapter devoted specifically to Apex data access and manipulation.

How Can You Use Apex?

Apex logic can be used in two different ways:

- In a database trigger - A trigger is executed in response to a particular type of database interaction, on a particular Force Platform data object. For instance, you can have a trigger that is fired whenever a new Job Application record is inserted into the object.
- In a class - You also have the option of creating Apex classes. You can call a class from a trigger.

Apex triggers are called implicitly in response to a database action, but you can call an Apex class explicitly from several different places on the Force Platform. Apex classes can be used to implement email-to-Apex services, described in *Chapter 13: Email Services with the Force Platform*, Visualforce controllers, and web services, described later in this chapter. You can also call methods in a Apex class from the Force Platform IDE's interactive code window, or with the executeAnonymous method, described later in this chapter.

You can create Apex code in a Developer Edition organization or a Force Platform Sandbox, which is a copy of a production organization. Once you have completed your development effort and created test methods for the code, you can begin the process of deploying your code to a production environment, described in *Chapter 15: Deployment*.

As part of this deployment process, your test methods must successfully execute and provide over 75% code coverage. Once you have achieved this coverage, you can then deploy from either of these environments to your production organization.

The overall process is shown in the figure below.

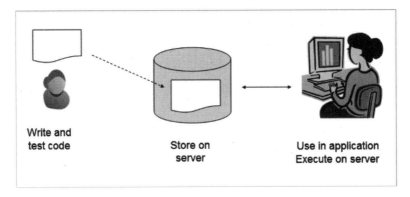

Write and
test code

Store on
server

Use in application
Execute on server

Figure 175: Developing with Apex

You will learn about creating test methods later in this chapter. As mentioned above, *Chapter 15: Deployment* is devoted to deploying Force Platform applications.

Why Required Testing?

As you may have noticed in the previous description, all Apex code deployed to production environments must include test methods. When you deploy Apex triggers and classes, the Force Platform checks the test methods to make sure that these methods exercise at least 75% of the code in your trigger or class—greater coverage insures greater benefits.

For those of you who are used to working in a structured development environment, this requirement does not seem unusual, since you are no doubt already including test methods in your code. For others, this condition can seem overly strict, but there are two very good reasons behind the requirement: general best practices for development and best practices for maintaining your application over time.

You have already experienced, repeatedly, the enormous productivity of the Force Platform, from creation of sophisticated functionality to instant deployment. This instant deployment might tempt you to rapidly implement functionality on the fly without proper testing—a practice which is always rife with danger. By requiring test methods, the Force Platform insures that you follow best practices for development on any platform. The Force Platform includes the ability to run all of your Apex test methods with a single button push or menu selection, giving you a productive way to carry out the best programming practices.

The most important aspect of test methods relates to the certainty they give to all developers. As you may know, the Force Platform delivers an ongoing stream of enhancements, typically three major releases a year. The good news is that all of this innovation comes directly to you, without any effort on your part. New releases are streamed into the Force Platform—no installation chores for you.

But those of you who are experienced developers may see this rapid improvement of the platform as a potential threat to the stability of your own applications. If you have been developing applications for very long, you have probably already experienced a situation where a new platform or product upgrade broke your beautiful application.

You never have to worry about an upgrade accidentally disrupting your Apex code, since the Force Platform supports multiple versions of the Apex runtime environment. When a new release comes out, your application will automatically run with the version of Apex with which it was initially compiled.

But what happens when you want to move your application to a new release, to take advantage of new functionality or other features? By using test methods, you can protect against this possibility. Your test methods should be designed to exercise all the crucial logic in your Apex code. When you move your application to a newer release, you can simply run your test methods against the new release. If your test methods work properly, you don't have to worry about new Force Platform releases affecting your own code, which greatly reduces the impediments to adoption of a new release.

How Is Apex Different?

Apex is a robust procedural language – but not the only robust procedural language which can access Force Platform data and platform functionality. Other languages, from .NET to Java, to JavaScript, can also access much of the functionality of the Force Platform, from procedural language and the use of the Force Platform Web Services API.

In fact, if you have been around the Force Platform for a while, you might have already implemented s-controls, which use Javascript to access the platform from the browser. How is using Apex different from using s-controls or these other languages?

The primary difference is where Apex executes. Apex logic runs on the Force Platform, eliminating the need for network traffic between a client and the Force Platform via the API. This different architecture can have a very large effect when doing data manipulation, since you will not have to bring data down to the client in order to make changes.

Apex code is tightly integrated with the rest of the Force Platform environment, leveraging the same metadata-driven productivity offered by the rest of the platform. This integration also gives a seamless interface to the rest of the functionality of the platform, an integration that continues to grow as the platform continues to expand.

Finally, the tight integration of Apex and the Force Platform means that Apex code works in concert with the rest of the platform. You can see the dependencies for any Apex class with the click of a button. Apex code is also automatically aware of changes in Force Platform metadata, so that a change in that metadata leads to automatic recompilation of Apex triggers and classes the next time those components are executed.

Over the course of the next two chapters, you will learn about Apex code, as well as how to best utilize these advantages in your own Force Platform applications.

Working With Apex

As with the other components of the Force Platform, you need to learn some of the basics about how to interact with Apex code.

How Do You Create Apex Code?

Apex code can be created with any tool that edits text files, but the standard methods of creating and editing Apex code are the Setup menu and the Force Platform IDE.

You can interact with Apex Classes through the **Setup ➤ Develop ➤ Apex Classes** choices to get to the page shown below.

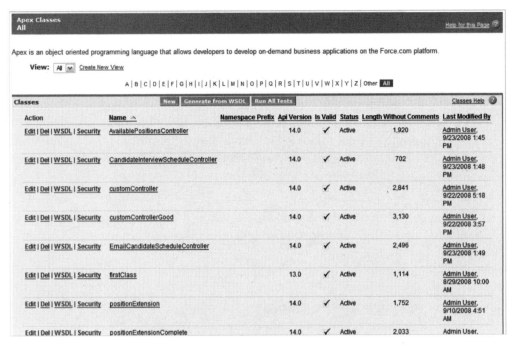

Figure 176: Accessing Apex Classes through Setup

This page lists the classes currently available and gives you the opportunity to create new ones. You can edit, delete and assign security, described below, through this interface.

When you edit a class, you are placed into a code editing window, as shown below. This edit window uses color to highlight different attributes in the code, such as variables and keywords. This window is similar to the window used to edit Visualforce pages in Developer Mode.

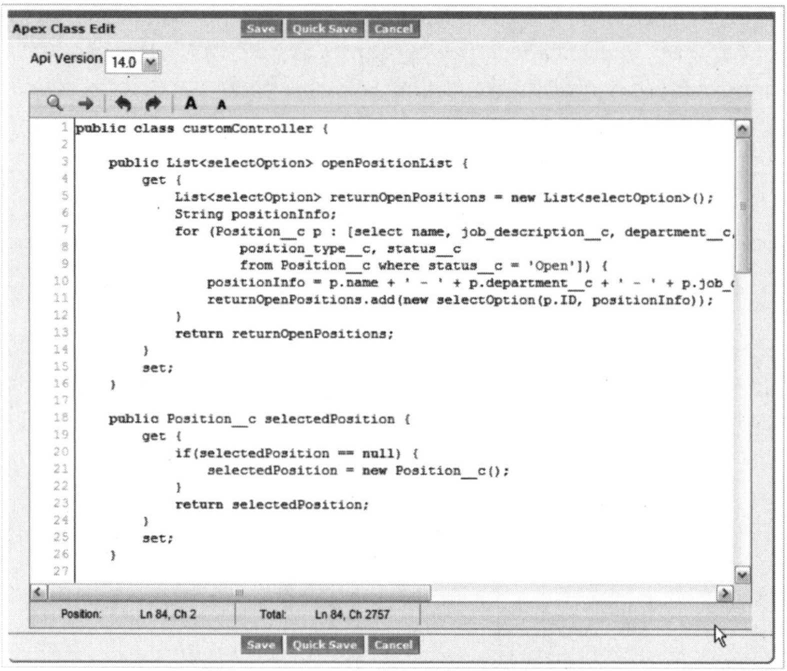

Figure 177: Editing an Apex class in Setup

If you are developing a trigger with Apex, you start from the detail page for the object that triggers the code. The Triggers section of the page lists existing triggers, along with a New button to create new triggers. Both creating a new trigger and editing an existing trigger or creating a new trigger puts you into the edit window shown above.

The Force Platform IDE is a plug-in to the industry standard Eclipse framework. Many developers are already familiar with the Eclipse, and the Force Platform IDE, as you saw in *Chapter 8: The Force Platform IDE*, is a highly productive environment for developing and testing Apex code. You can create and edit both Apex classes and triggers in the Force Platform IDE. The examples in the remainder of this chapter and the next use the Force Platform IDE as the development environment for hands-on examples.

Apex Code and Security

Apex code exists on the Force Platform. As such, no one can run your Apex code, whether implicitly, with triggers, or explicitly without first being authenticated users for your organization.

As you learned in *Chapter 7: Protecting Your Data*, the Force Platform has a rich security framework, consisting of component-based security, implemented through profiles, and record-based security, implemented through record ownership and sharing. All Apex code executes as system user, with all access to all data and other components, with one exception, which you will learn about later. A system user is not limited by any profiles, so component-based security limitations expressed through profiles are, by default, ignored.

Because of this, a user must have the powerful Modify All Data permission before they can be granted the Author Apex permission, required to develop Apex code.

However, you can limit the ability to use a class to one or more security profiles, so you can prevent groups of users from using the functionality of those classes in this manner. Although triggers use Apex code implicitly, a user cannot cause a trigger to fire if they do not have access to the operations that would cause the trigger to fire.

You can also add the keywords with sharing in your definition of an Apex class. These keywords indicate that the sharing rules for the user who has called the Apex class should be respected.

Apex Code and Web Services

Apex communicates with the outside world through the mechanism of web services. You can expose any method in an Apex class as a web service through the addition of the keyword `webservice` at the beginning of the method declaration. You can also expose variables within the class with the same keyword.

Once you have created methods designated as web services, you can generate Web Service Definition Language (WSDL) for them. The WSDL can be consumed by applications to access the Force Platform methods.

 Caution: Apex methods are run as a system user, so you should take great care to avoid potentially exposing your data through a web service call to an Apex method. However, a web service call to the Force Platform can only be executed by an authenticated user, as described above.

You can also create a Apex class stub from a WSDL specification for an external web service, and then call the methods in that class. Please be aware that there are some limitations in the use of this feature, such as a built-in timeout of 10 seconds for a response.

For more information on Apex code and web services, consult the *Apex Language Reference* manual.

Apex Code in the Runtime Environment

Apex code is stored and executed on the Force Platform. All Apex code is checked for errors before the code can be saved, insuring that the syntax for the code is correct. When Apex code is stored, the code is compiled into a set of instructions that are then executed by the Force Platform at runtime.

The Force Platform environment has built-in governors limiting the amount of work that can be performed by Apex classes and triggers. These governors are in place to protect the multi-tenant environment from runaway processes. Refer to the *Force Platform Apex* documentation for the specific resource limits placed on Apex code in different environments.

You can use various methods on the built-in Limits class to determine where a particular piece of Apex code is in comparison to resource limits. You can also configure your organization to send an email to a designated contact if any Apex code consumes more than 50% of an allowable resource.

Apex Basics

Like all languages, the power of Apex is contained within a syntactical framework. In this section, you will learn the basics about writing Apex code. If you are familiar with other strongly-typed, object-based language, especially Java, you might be able to simply skim this section to learn the key portions of Apex grammar.

Please note that this section is not intended to replace the depth of the Force Platform documentation, but rather to provide you with the essentials you need to create Force Platform code in this and subsequent chapters.

Apex Statements

Apex statements have several standard syntax conventions:

- Individual statements are ended by a semi-colon (;).
- Parentheses are used to group values, such as the variables for a method call, or the evaluated expression in a conditional statement.
- Braces, or curly brackets ({ }), are used to indicate a block of code.

You will become familiar with these conventions as you develop code in the course of this and the next few chapters.

You can indicate comments with your code in one of two ways. A single line comment must start with two forward slashes (//), while a multi-line comment begins with /* and ends with */. All text within comments is ignored.

Apex Variables

Apex code frequently requires variables to hold data values within a class or trigger. To make a variable available within a method, you declare the variable with the following basic syntax

```
Type([]) variable_name (= initialization);
```

You must declare a variable in the code before you can reference it. Variable names are case insensitive within your code.

The data type for a variable can be one of several options:

- A primitive data type - includes a variety of number and date data types, an ID that represents the internal Force Platform ID for a record, a string, an object, or Boolean, which can only contain values of true, false or null
- An sObject - a data object that references a standard or custom object defined in your Force Platform organization.
- A collection - covered later in this section.
- Another object type - frequently used with Visualforce object types, such as selectOptions.

You can declare an array by including square brackets ([])after the Type declaration. A variable declaration can initialize the variable, using the equals (=) sign and a value, as in:

```
String myString = 'Sample';
```

If a variable does not have an initial value assigned, the variable has a value of null.

Variable declarations can also use an access modifier at the start of the declaration. The access modifier identifies the visibility of the variable. There are three options for this modifier:

- private – the variable is only visible locally. This setting is the default if no access modifier is specified. You can have a class nested within a class. By default, these nested classes are private, meaning they are only visible within the outer class.
- public – the variable is visible within your application
- global – the variable is visible to all Apex scripts

A variable can also use the keyword final as part of the declaration, between the access modifier and the data type. The final keyword indicates that the variable can only have a value assigned once.

You can create constants with the same syntax as declaring variables by preceding the declaration with the keywords static and final. You must assign a value to a constant when the constant is declared.

Be aware that the only implicit data type conversions in Apex are between different numeric types.

Apex Expressions and Operators

Apex has a rich variety of operators that can be used in expressions. Apex uses the double equals sign (==)as a comparison operator. Please refer to the *Force Platform Apex* documentation for a complete listing and explanation of comparison operators.

String comparisons use case insensitive values for characters, so that 'a' and 'A' are equal in those comparisons. Null values are thought of as the lowest string value, in terms of string comparisons.

 Voice of the Developer: String comparisons with the comparison operator (==) are case insensitive. This quality means that the following clause returns true:

```
'a' == 'A'
```

If you want to compare string values with case sensitivity, you can use the equals method for the string. To perform a case sensitive equality test, you use code like the following to return false:

```
String xx = 'a';
xx.equals('A');
```

Apex Data Objects

IApex variables that hold recods from data objects are referred to as *sObjects*. sObjects take on the structure of the Force Platform standard or custom object that is declared as their data type. You initialize an sObject with the following syntax:

```
sObject name = new sObject();
```

You can also create a variable with the generic sObject type that is assigned a specific sObject type when the variable is initialized.

You typically assign values to any of the fields in an sObject in one of two ways. You can use a list of field names and values in the parens following the sObject assignment. For instance, creating a new Location__c record in a variable, with a value of `Toledo` for the name looks like the following:

```
Location__c homeOffice = new Location__c(Name = 'Toledo');
```

You can also initialize an sObject through an SOQL statement, such as

```
Location__c offices = [select Name, Address__c, City__c,
 State_Province__c from Location__c ];
```

Take care to properly initialize any sObject variables you use in your code. If your code attempts to access a value in an uninitialized sObject, you get a run-time exception.

Fields within an sObject are accessed through dot notation, as in the following:

```
Location.Name = 'Toledo';
```

Dot notation is also used to access related objects and their fields, described in more depth in the discussion of SOQL (Salesforce Object Query Language) in the next chapter.

Be aware that every record in an sObject includes a read-only ID field. The ID field is the unique identifier for the individual record–unique across all records in your Force Platform organization. The value for this field is automatically assigned when a record is created through an insert. You will learn much more about working with Apex code and data in the next chapter.

Apex Collections

In addition to sObjects, Apex supports three different types of collections: lists, sets and maps.

You use declaration syntax for any of these collections, such as:

```
List<dataType> name = new List<dataType>;
```

All collections share the following characteristics:

- Contain multiple data values
- Support a variety of methods

- Allow access to individual items within a collection with a value within brackets, such as:

```
sampleList[1] = "Second';
```

- No single collection can contain more than 1,000 items. If any collection exceeds this limit, the Force Platform will generate a run-time error.

You can have collections of collections, with each individual collection containing 1,000 records.

The three types of collections. lists, sets and maps, also have slightly different characteristics, as detailed in the following sections.

Apex Lists

A list is an unordered collection of values. Lists are declared with the initial number of items in the list, indicated by an integer within square brackets. The brackets are required when declaring a list, but the integer is not. A list declared without a size integer contains no elements.

An array can be used to represent a one-dimensional list. You can assign values to a list as part of its declaration by using curly brackets, as in the following:

```
String[] myTowns = new List<String>{'Toledo', 'Maumee', 'Perrysburg'};
```

which is the equivalent of

```
List<String> myTowns = new List<String>{'Toledo', 'Maumee',
'Perrysburg'};
```

Apex Sets

A set is also an unordered collection of values, with an important difference. A set cannot contain duplicate values. If you attempt to insert a value into a set that already exists, the add method returns false. You can use this feature to achieve some of your logical requirements, as you will later in this chapter.

You declare a set with syntax similar to declaring a list, as in

```
Set<String> myTowns = new List<String>{'Toledo', 'Maumee',
'Perrysburg'};
```

Apex Maps

Maps are collections of key-value pairs. The key for a map entry must be a primitive data type, while the value can be a primitive sObject, Apex object, or collection. You can have up to five levels of collections within a map.

You can assign key-value pairs to a map when you declare the map, with a syntax of the following:

```
Map<String, String> cityState = new Map<String, String>
 {'Toledo' => 'Ohio', 'Chicago' => 'Illinois',
 'Ann Arbor' => 'Michigan'}
```

Maps require the use of methods to retrieve values, and map methods are slightly different from the common methods used by lists and sets. For more details, please refer to the *Force Platform Apex* documentation.

Apex Conditional Logic

Of course, like all programming languages, Apex includes syntax to implement conditional logic, otherwise known as IF - THEN - ELSE logic.

The basic format for this type of code is the following:

```
if (Boolean_expression)
 Statement;
 else
 Statement;
```

Note that the Boolean must be within parentheses, even if it is a simple expression, and you need to have semi-colons to indicate the end of each statement in the conditional logic.

The form shown above includes a single statement for each condition. Normally, you create multiple statements for a condition, requiring the use of curly braces to group the statements, as in the following:

```
if (Boolean_expression){
 statement;
 statement;
 statement;
 statement;}
else {
 statement;
 statement;}
```

You can nest `if` statements, giving syntax similar to the following:

```
if (Location.Name == 'Toronto'){
 Location.country__c = 'Canada';
       }
else if {(Location.Name == 'London'){
 Location.country__c = 'United Kingdom';
       }
else {
 Location.country__c = 'United States';
 }
```

Apex Loops

Apex supports the three standard types of loops for implementing repeated actions: `Do-while`, `While`, and `For` loops.

Do-while Loops

A `Do-while` loop repeatedly executes a set of code statements. The syntax for the loop is as follows:

```
do {
 code_block;
       }
       while (Boolean_condition);
```

The code within the curly braces executes and then the condition is evaluated. A `Do-while` loop always executes at least once.

While Loops

A `While` loop is like a do-while loop, except that the while condition is evaluated before any of the statements in the code are executed. Because of this, the code in a `While` loop might not be executed at all. The syntax for the `While` loop is as follows:

```
while (Boolean_condition) {
 code_block;
       };
```

For Loops

Apex support three types of For loops: traditional, list/set iteration, and SOQL.

The traditional For loop uses the following syntax:

```
for (init_statement; exit_condition; increment_statement) {
 code_block;
 }
```

The init_statement executes when the loop is first entered and can initialize more than one variable. The exit_condition is evaluated every time the loop executes. If the condition evaluates to false, the loop ends. If the condition evaluates to true, the code_block executes, followed by the increment statement.

A typical For loop of this variety is as follows:

```
for (Integer I = 0; I < 10 ; I++) {
 System.debug('Iteration ' + I);
 }
```

This loop prints a list to the debug console consisting of the word Iteration followed by the values of I, from 0 to 9.

Apex also supports For loops that are based on the entries in a set or a list. The syntax is as follows:

```
for (variable : list_or_set) {
 code_block;
 }
```

This For loop executes once for each entry in the initial list or set variable. This variable must be the same data type as the list or set. You can use this syntax to get the same results as the previous For loop with the following code:

```
Integer[] listInts = new Integer[]{0,1,2,3,4,5,6,7,8,9};

for (Integer i : listInts) {
 System.debug('Iteration ' + i);
 }
```

Apex code also supports a very powerful For loop that is used in association with SOQL statements to iterate through a set of results. This loop syntax is especially powerful since you can use it to circumvent limitations on the number of entries in a collection. You will learn all about this type of For loop in the next chapter, which focuses on using Apex with data sets.

Future

Apex code supports annotations that influence the way code runs. An annotation is preceded by the '@' sign and is added right before the method that is affected by the annotation.

One particularly significant annotation is `future`. When you use this annotation, the following method is executed asynchronously. Asynchronous execution means that the method executes when the Force Platform has available resources. Control is immediately returned to the module calling the future method.

Methods with the future annotation have to be declared as static and must not return a value. For instance, the following is a valid declaration:

```
@future
Static void futureMethod() {
 code_block;
 }
```

The `future` annotation is ideal for use with web service callouts from Apex. You must add the `(callout=true)` modifier to the `future` annotation to use `future` methods for this purpose.

Another reason to use this annotation has to do with governor limits on data access, which you will learn about in the next chapter. Each method called with the `future` annotation is subject to its own governor limits. For instance, if you had a `For` loop that called a `future` method 10 times, each one of those invocations could retrieve the maximum number of records. If the method did not have a `future` annotation, all ten invocations would be subject to a single governor limit.

Apex Exception Handling

Of course, we all write perfect code, first time through. At least, that's what we wake up every morning hoping to accomplish—a hope that is normally dashed within the first 15 minutes of coding.

Any of the Apex development environments parse your code before allowing the code to be saved. This enforcement means that your code is syntactically correct, but there is no guarantee that the code will not encounter error conditions at run-time.

When an Apex trigger or class encounters an error at runtime, the Force Platform environment throws an exception and terminates the execution of the code immediately. You can include code that allows you to handle exceptions more gracefully with `try/catch` syntax.

The form for `try/catch` syntax is as follows:

```
try {
 code_block;
 }
catch (exception_type){
  code_block;
  }
finally {
  code_block;
  }
```

Whenever an exception is thrown in the `code_block` immediately following the keyword `try`, the execution drops out of that block.

There are different types of Force Platform exceptions so you can have more than one `catch` block, with no more than one `catch` block for a particular type of exception. You can also define your own exception types.

The `code_block` for a particular exception type is executed when an exception of that type is thrown. You can also specify the general exception type of `Exception`, catching any exceptions not intercepted by previous `catch` statements—because of this, a `catch` statement that uses the general `Exception` must be the last `catch` statement in the block.

Once the code for the appropriate `catch` block runs, the `code_block` listed for the `finally` statement is run. The `finally` statement is not required.

The following example shows the outline of `try/catch` syntax for a code block involves some type of data interaction that throws a `DmlException`:

```
try {
 code_block;
 }
catch (DmlException de){
  System.debug('Data exception:'+ de.getMessage());
  }
catch (Exception e) {
  System.debug('General exception:'+ e.getMessage());
  }
```

You can also throw exceptions explicitly in your code. You can learn more about the methods available for exception objects in the *Force Platform Apex* documentation.

Proper error handling can make the difference between a good application and a great application. At minimum, enclose data access statements in a `try/catch` block to account for any data access problems or limit problems. The Apex classes and triggers supplied from Code Share include `try/catch` blocks around all the code in order to gracefully handle any unanticipated problems at run-time.

Important: You do not have to worry about errors occurring because of changes in the structure of Force Platform objects in your Apex code. Once an object is used in a piece of Apex code, no one can change attributes of that object.

If an error occurs in the execution of your code, and that error is not intercepted through the use of a try/catch block, the error message is shown to the user on the page and an email is sent to the person who is identified in the LastModifiedBy field for the class.

Apex Classes

Apex, an object-based language, allows you to define classes. Classes contain both states, in the form of variables, and behaviors, in the form of methods.

Voice of the Developer: An Apex class can also define an interface. An interface specifies methods, but does not implement the functionality of the methods with code. Another Apex class can implement the interface, which means that the implementing class provides functionality for all the methods described in the interface.

Defining a Class

To define a Force Platform class, you need to use the following syntax:

```
access_modifier class class_name {
  //the body of the class
}
```

The access modifier identifies the visibility of the class. Classes can use the same modifiers as a variable: `private`, `public`, and `global`. A class can be nested within another class. In this scenario, the inner class is, by default, private, meaning that the class is only visible within the outer class.

Caution: Apex classes with methods defined as `webservices` must use the `global` access modifier.

The access modifier must be followed by the keyword `class`, and then the name of the class.

The keyword `this` refers to the current instance of a class. You use `this` to reference variables or methods within the class, such as the following:

```
this.Name = 'Elvis';
```

Additional keywords can specify that a class implements an already defined interface, or extend an already defined class. A class can implement multiple interfaces, but only extend one class. You use both of these options in code examples in later chapters. For more information on these classes, refer to the *Force Platform Apex* documentation.

Variables

Apex allows two different types of variables, instance variables and class variables. An instance variable is instantiated when the class is instantiated.

By default, the variables and methods used in a class are instantiated when the class is instantiated. The exception to this default are those variables that are defined with the keyword `static`.

Static variables and methods are instantiated outside of the instantiation of any individual class, and these variables and methods are available to all instances of the class. Because of this, you can use static variables and methods to share information across multiple versions of a class. For example, you might define a variable as follows:

```
Public static Boolean firstrun = true;
```

The first time this class runs, the value of `firstrun` is true. Code in the class would include an `if` construct to test to see if the variable is true and take some actions, setting the value to false once the actions are complete. Subsequent instances of this class see the value of `firstrun` as false.

Class Methods

Apex classes can contain methods. Methods are declared with the following syntax:

```
Access_modifier data_type name (parameters) {
  code_block;
  }
```

The optional `access_modifier` choices for a method are the same as those for a variable. The `data_type` indicates the data type for the value returned for the method. If a method does not return a value, you can use the keyword `void` in this position. If you do define a return data type, your code must return a value of that data type in all situations. For instance, if you use an `if` construct as the final piece in your code, all portions of the construct must return a value of the designated data type.

Method parameters are defined by specifying their data type and then their name. You can have up to 32 input parameters. Although parameters are not required for a method, you always have to include the parentheses.

A constructor is used to create an instance of a class. You do not have to specifically define a constructor for a class—the Force Platform uses the class name, followed by parentheses, as the default constructor. You can define a constructor for the class that accepts arguments.

Properties

A property is similar to a variable, with one significant exception. A property allows you to specify a `get` accessor, used to retrieve the value of the property, and a `set` accessor, used to write a value to the property. The syntax for defining a property is as follows:

```
access_modifier return_type property_name {
  get {
    code_block;
      }
  set {
    code_block;
  }
      }
```

If you do not specify code for the accessors for a property, the default implementation simply returns the value for the property for the `get` accessor and writes the value to the property for the `set` accessor. The following code shows the use of default accessors:

```
public String company_name {
  get; set;
  }
```

If you do write a `get` accessor, the code must return a value with the same data type as the property. You will be using properties and their accessors when you write Visualforce controller extensions and custom controllers in *Chapter 12: Extended Visualforce Components and Controllers*.

Writing Apex code

Now that you have a feeling for the basics of Apex syntax, you can finally jump into creating some Apex code. This example uses the Force Platform IDE to create the code. You will learn about triggers in the next chapter, which focuses on Apex and its interactions with Force Platform data.

Using the Force Platform IDE

In *Chapter 8: The Force Platform IDE*, you learned about the Force Platform IDE. This development environment is based on the popular Eclipse framework.

You will be using the Force Platform IDE to create and save Apex classes and methods, culminating in a class that uses features of Apex to insure a particular type of data integrity.

But you should walk before you run, so the next few sections develop some very simple Apex code, just to get used to the process. You will use a specific feature of the Force Platform IDE that allows you to enter and run Apex code interactively.

This feature is found at the bottom of the development environment. You can see there is a window along the bottom of the main development area on the right, with four tabs showing by default. If you click on the tab labeled Execute Anonymous, you can expand the window to look similar to the figure below:

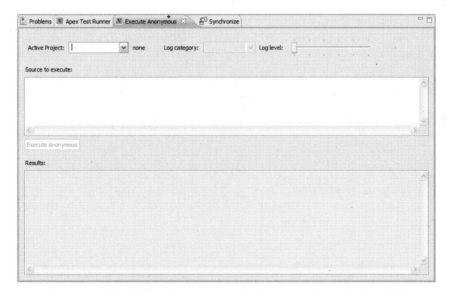

Figure 178: The ExecuteAnonymous window in the Force Platform IDE

 Caution: ExecuteAnonymous calls submit Apex code to run on the Force Platform server. The code runs with the security settings of the current user - this is the one exception to the rule that Apex always runs with system privileges.

The Execute Anonymous window uses the Force Platform API call of the same name to submit Apex code to the Force Platform server and receive the results of that code.

The same functionality is available through the Setup menu. If you click on the System Log link, you bring up the dialog window shown in the figure below. This dialog has a text area for entering Apex code at the bottom of the dialog, submitted with the **Execute Apex >>** button, and the results shown at the top of the window.

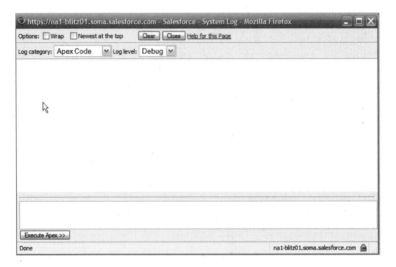

Figure 179: The System Log window

A Simple Script

Start your Apex work with one of the simplest statements—the Apex equivalent of 'Hello World'.

1. Start up the Force Platform IDE. If you did not start a project in *Chapter 8: The Force Platform IDE*, begin the development process by creating a Force Platform project. For more information about creating a Force Platform project in the Force Platform IDE, refer to that chapter to create one.

2. Enlarge the lower pane of the environment so that you have more room to enter your code and view the results. The configuration shown in the figure of the IDE above is appropriate for the tasks ahead.

3. Select the name of your current project as the `Active Project`.

4. Select `Apex_code` as the log category. You will be using a method of the System class to echo values back to the results area.

5. Enter the following code in the Source to execute window:

```
system.debug('Hello Apex!');
```

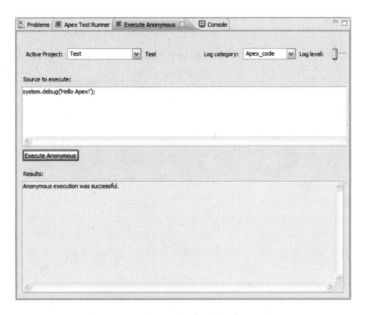

Figure 180: Results from Hello Apex

6. Click **Execute Anonymous** to produce the result shown in the figure above.

Well, at least you got back something. The message explains that the Apex code in the window executed successfully.

When you clicked Execute Anonymous, the Force Platform IDE sent the Apex code from the source window back to the Force Platform server where it was executed. The message was sent to the debug log, but you did not see it because your Results window is not set to display that level of detail.

7. Set the Log level slider on the right to `Fine`.

8. Click **Execute Anonymous** again. This time you get the desired message displayed to the right of a line that includes a timestamp marking the execution of the statement.

9. Set the Log level slider to `Finest` and execute the code again.

10. The final display of information is probably more than you need for these exercises so set the slider back to the `Fine` setting.

Now that you have conquered the task of entering and executing Apex code from the Force Platform IDE, you can modify the code to see a little more functionality at work.

Adding Repetition

You can expand this most basic line of Apex code by using a `For` loop to return multiple messages through the use of the system.debug method.

1. Change the code in the source window to the following:

```
for (Integer I = 0; I < 5; I++){
 System.debug('Execution ' + I);
 }
```

This code is an example of a standard `For` loop. The variable `I` controls the iteration through the code, the condition of `I < 5` determines when that iteration should stop, and the `I++` indicates that the value of the variable increases by 1 on each iteration. The loop executes 5 times and displays text with a count of the individual executions of the `system.debug` call numbered from 0 to 4.

2. Click **Execute Anonymous** to produce the display shown below.

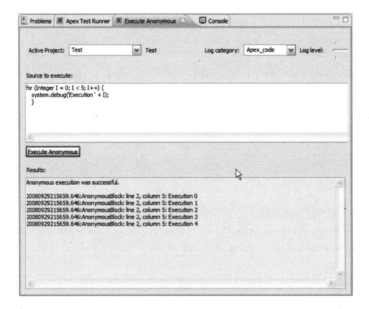

Figure 181: Iterated results

Success once again.

Creating a Method

Now that you have started to accomplish slightly more complex tasks with your interactive Apex code, you can move on to defining a method in the source window.

Creating a method in the Execute Anonymous window is not something you necessarily do normally, but going through the exercise helps you to get immediate feedback on the syntax and operation of your code.

1. Change the code in the source window to the following:

```
public void testRepeat() {
     for (Integer I = 0; I < 5; I++){
    system.debug('Execution ' + I);
  }
 }
```

The method does not return a value, as indicated by the `void` keyword.

2. Execute the code. All of a sudden, you are back to the same message you received on your first Apex coding attempt. But the reason this time is different. You defined your method, but there was nothing in your code to cause the method to actually execute.

3. 5. Add the following line to the end of the Apex code in the source window.

```
testRepeat();
```

4. Execute the code again.

Ah, that's more like it. The next step is to make this method more flexible by adding the ability to control the number of times the debug method executes.

Passing Values

For the next step in implementing your first sample method, you can add a way to pass a variable to the method. The method itself can use the variable to control the number of iterations that the code block executes.

1. Change the code in the source window to the following:

```
public void testRepeat(Integer inbound) {
     for (Integer I = 0; I < inbound; I++){
    system.debug('Execution ' + I);
  }
 }
```

2. Modify the last statement to include that integer in the call, as follows:

```
testRepeat(5);
```

3. Execute the code again.

   This time, the string returns 5 times, with an additional line in the results.

   Your last step is to add a way to return values back to the calling statement. To accomplish this, change the return data type from void, and add a return statement at the end of the method.

4. Change the code in the source window to the following:

```
public String testRepeat(Integer inbound) {
      for (Integer I = 0; I < inbound; I++){
    system.debug('Execution ' + I);
 }
 return ('The code ran ' + inbound + 'times.';
 }
```

5. Change the line of code that calls the method to the following:

```
system.debug(testRepeat(6));
```

   You have to use the system.debug to call the method, since this call directs the return from the method to the debug log.

   You also have to have a return in the method code if you specify a returned data type, and you must make sure that your method will always return an appropriate value, regardless of the path taken through the method.

   Notice that you cannot return the I variable in this method. The I variable is declared within the For loop, and so the variable is local to the code within the loop.

6. Execute the code again.

With this final modification, you have practiced using the most common features of Apex methods. You are ready to add a class and method to your Apex project.

Adding A Class To Your Project

You know your method code works properly, so you can now try creating a class and adding that method to the class.

1. Right click the `src` entry in the Package Explorer in the left panel. Select **New**, and then **Apex Class** in the drop down menu, bringing up a dialog box as shown below.

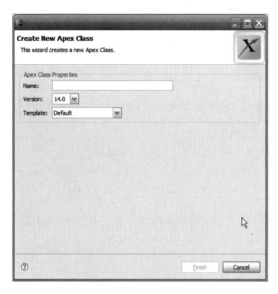

Figure 182: Adding a class

2. Enter `firstClass` as the `Name` for the class and then tab out of the field and click **Finish**. A window for your new class opens in the upper middle panel of the Force Platform IDE.

3. Copy the code for the method from the source window in the lower panel to the class, which will make the class code look as shown in the figure below.

```
Force.com Start Page    firstClass.ds
public class firstClass {

public string testRepeat(Integer inbound) {
    for (Integer I = 0; I < inbound; I++){
    system.debug('Execution ' + I);
    }
return ('The code ran '+ inbound + ' times.');
}

}
Source Metadata
```

Figure 183: Your code in your class

4. Click **Save**. The Save action checks your code for errors and saves the code to the server.

5. Clear out the source window in the lower panel and enter the following code:

```
firstClass xx = new firstClass();
system.debug(xx.testRepeat(7));
```

The first line of code creates an instance of your new class, while the second line of code runs the `testRepeat` method and directs the return from that method to the Results window.

 Tip: You could have reduced this code to a single line by creating an instance of the class as part of the method call, as follows:

```
system.debug(new firstClass()).testRepeat(7);
```

6. Run the code in the source window to produce the expected results.

All right, enough practice. It's time to add some useful functionality to your class.

Adding More Methods

You are now ready to create a method that provides some general functionality to use later in the book.

There are times when you want to be able to determine if a list of values contains any duplicate values. Remember that a set is a collection that does not allow duplicate values. If you try to insert a value into a set that already exists in the set, the `add()` method simply returns a value of false.

With this in mind, you can create a method that receives a list of values, checks the list for duplicates, and returns another list with the values that were duplicated.

This duplicate checking method accomplishes the simple task of identifying duplicates. The more difficult problem that organizations sometimes face is to determine which of the duplicate values should be preferred—a larger issue outside the scope of this book.

1. Enter the following code into your existing class.

```
public List<string> dupEntries(List<string> checkEntries) {
    List<string> dupValues = new List<string>();
    Set<string> dupID = new Set<string>();
    for(String s : checkEntries) {
        if (! dupID.add(s){
            dupValues.add(s);
            }
        }
```

```
        return dupValues;
}
```

This code should look pretty familiar. The declaration of the method indicates that the method requires a list as a parameter and returns a list upon completion.

Within the code, you start by declaring a list that holds any duplicate values found, and a set used to discover if any of the values in the submitted list are duplicates.

The `for` loop walks through the submitted list, `checkEntries`, and attempts to add each of the values into the set `dupID`. The code for the loop uses an `if` statement to check the return of the `add()` method for the `dupID` set. The Boolean condition for the If statement checks to see if the value returned from the add is false. You use the `'!'` character to reverse the value returned from the method—if the method returns true, this Boolean evaluates to false, and the code within the `if` construct executes.

If this method returns false, you know that the current value for the `checkEntries` list is a duplicate, so you use the `add()` method to insert that value into the `dupValues` list.

When the `for` loop is finished, the method returns the list of duplicate values, as collected by the `dupValues` list.

2. Click **Save**. When you save the class, the code is checked for syntax errors. If any errors occur, an error indicator, a small red circle with an x, appears to the left of the line, and the problem itself is listed in the Problems pane of the lowest window. If the code contains errors, the version of the code is only saved locally. If the code compiles successfully, the code is saved back to the Force Platform server.

 Tip: You can prevent your code from being automatically saved to the server by unchecking the `Build Automatically` choice under the `Project` menu for the Force Platform IDE. If you take this approach, you will have to explicitly save your code back to the server.

3. You are ready to test your new method. Since the method requires a list, start by creating and populating a list. Enter the following code in the source window of the Execute Anonymous page:

```
List<string> sampleTest = new list<string>();
     sampleTest.add('One');
     sampleTest.add('Two');
     sampleTest.add('Three');
     sampleTest.add('Four');
     sampleTest.add('Five');
```

These lines of code first create a list and then add the values. Notice that, right now, the list contains all unique values. You use this list to perform your initial test of the new method, although the method should not return any values if the method is working properly.

4. Add the following code to the code in the source window:

```
firstClass tester = new firstClass();
system.debug(tester.dupEntries(sampleTest));
```

5. Click **Execute Anonymous**.

The code you added in the last step creates an instance of the `firstClass` class, and then executes the `dupEntries` method from that instance. You should receive results that show the execution as successful, and then a simple pair of parentheses. When `system.debug` displays a list, the values of the list are shown in parentheses, so an empty set only contains that punctuation.

You know your method runs successfully, now to see if it actually works properly.

6. Change the value for one of the `add()` methods from `'Three'` to `'Two'` and run the method again.

This time, your result window contains the duplicate value of `'Two'` within the parentheses.

Your method works properly, as shown by your testing. You probably want to exercise a few more use cases, such as duplicating more than one value to show that the method can pick up multiple duplicates.

 Voice of the Developer: The way the method is currently written, you can get back multiple entries in the list returned. For instance, if the submitted list contains three entries for `'Two'`, the returned list gets two entries with that value since both of them duplicate an existing value. You can change this result by using a set instead of a list to collect and return the values.

You have created a class in your organization and added a couple of methods to the class. But you still have one more task to complete.

Test Methods

At this point, you might be feeling that you have completed your little programming task. The code has implemented the logic that you want, and you did some testing in the Force Platform IDE to prove it.

And if all you want is to simply run this code in your Developer Edition organization, or a sandbox, you are done. Remember, though, that you have to include test methods that exercise at least 75% of your code before you are allowed to deploy the code to a production environment.

As explained above, this testing provides some very real benefits, in both the quality of your applications, as well as the certainty the test methods provide. Although you might be allowed to deploy your code with only 75% coverage, you might as well get the benefits of testing for the entire class.

Your last step is to add test methods, also known as unit tests, that both satisfy the requirements of the Force Platform and provide you with the assurance that your code works as planned.

Test methods are declared with the following syntax:

```
static testMethod void test_name() {
  code_block;
  }
```

You must declare test methods as `static`, with the `testMethod` keyword, and with a void return. Test methods cannot accept any arguments, and no data changes performed in a test method are committed to the Force Platform database.

In a case where a method has multiple possible branches, due to logical conditions, create test methods to test all of these branches.

The key methods to use in your unit tests are the `system.assert()` methods:

- `System.assert(condition)` returns true if the condition argument is true
- `System.assertEquals(x, y)` compares the value of x and y and returns true if they are equal
- `System.assertNotEquals(x, y)` compares the value of x and y and returns true if they are not equal .

The following code is a test method to test the class you just created:

```
static testMethod void testDupEntries() {
    List<string> testDups = new List<string>();
    List<string> compareResult = new List<string>();
    firstClass testClass = new firstClass();
    testDups.add('One');
    testDups.add('Two');
    testDups.add('Three');
    testDups.add('Two');
    compareResult.add('Two');
    system.assertEquals(compareResult,
      testClass.dupEntries(testDups));
    }
```

1. Enter the code shown above into your `firstClass` class and save the class.

   The code for `testMethod` should look familiar. You create a list to use as the argument for the `dupEntries` method, and then create an instance of the `firstClass`. After this, you populate the list and call the method, using the `system.assertEquals()` method to insure that the expected result returns.

   Once you have one or more test classes, you can either run the tests for a single class or for all of your code.

2. Save the new version of your class to the Force Platform server by clicking on the **Save** icon in the toolbar.

3. Right click on the `classes` entry and select **Force Platform ➤ Run Tests** to run the tests for the classes. The results are shown below.

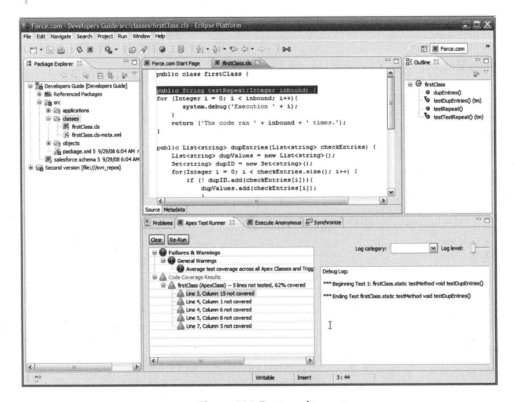

Figure 184: Test results

The Force Platform IDE offers some good information, calling out that the average test coverage has fallen below the required level. The Code Coverage results in the window list the lines of code not covered by tests, and you can go directly to those line of code by clicking on the entry. The deployment restriction that requires test methods requires that 75% of the code in your organization be covered by unit tests. But, as stated before, it is good practice to cover all of your code with test methods.

In this particular case, all of your code is not covered since you never included a test method to test the simple `testRepeat` method you initially created. In fact, since you wrote nicely compact code for the dupEntries method, you have not even achieved 75% coverage in this class.

Since this class is the only one in your development organization, you cannot deploy this application with the current code coverage. You can either delete or comment out the testRepeat method, or you can add the following code to also test that method:

```
static testMethod void testTestRepeat(){
    firstClass trTest = new firstClass();
    system.assertEquals('The code ran 4 many times',
      trTest.testRepeat(4));
    }
```

You can also run tests from the main Apex Classes page with the **Run Tests** button, as shown below.

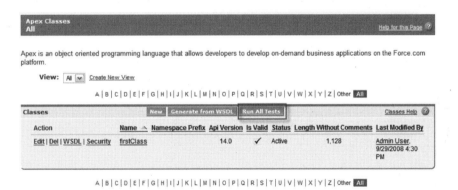

Figure 185: The Run Tests button in the Force Platform Setup menu

 Voice of the Developer: Test methods can be written alongside the code they test or in separate classes. For example you may want to consider structuring your test methods within dedicated classes based around your user stories. Prefixing test classes with Test or some other identifier allows developers to locate test more easily.

The Force Platform environment makes it easy for you to exercise your unit tests and see the results—reducing the overhead for performing this important task.

Summary

This chapter introduced you to the world of Apex—the syntax, constructs, and creation of Apex code. You learned how to work with the Force Platform IDE to interactively create and run Apex code, as well as adding Apex classes to your Force Platform projects.

You also learned why and how to add test methods to your code, insuring predictable results over time, even as the capabilities of the Force Platform grow with new releases.

Up to this point, you have been working with Apex classes since these classes do not need to interact with data in your Force Platform organization. The authors took this approach so you could rapidly learn the essentials of Apex in general. But in the real world, the great power and most frequent use of Apex is in conjunction with that Force Platform data. The next chapter covers the many facets of using of Apex with data.

Chapter 11

Apex and Data

In the previous chapter, you were introduced to Apex code. That introduction familiarized you with the basics of syntax and implementation, including using the Force Platform IDE and the use of test methods.

You developed Apex classes in that chapter, but Apex is frequently used in conjunction with data and data changes in your Force Platform application. This chapter focuses on using Apex with your data—in triggers, fired by changes in your data, in the use of SOQL and SOSL to retrieve data from your Force Platform organization, and using the Force Platform data manipulation language (DML) to write data back to your Force Platform objects.

You will also learn techniques for working with data in bulk, giving you complete flexibility in accessing large amounts of data in a way that delivers optimal performance.

Important: If you have been following the examples in the previous chapter, your Force Platform organization should be ready for the exercises in this chapter. If you have not done the exercises, or want to start with a fresh version of the sample Recruiting application, please refer to the instructions in the Code Share project for this book. You can find information on how to access that project in *Chapter 1: Welcome to the Force Platform.* In addition, the project contains instructions on how to update your organization with changes required for this chapter.

Triggers

As you learned in the last chapter, Apex code can be used in classes or in triggers. A trigger is a block of Apex code that executes in response to a particular type of change in a record's data.

Triggers are directly linked to the records in an object so that a trigger fires whenever a record is affected—whether that record is accessed by a standard Force Platform page, a Visualforce page, or through the Web Services API. Once you define logic in a trigger, you can be sure that logic is always executed in response to the appropriate type of change in the records for its object.

 Voice of the Developer: Triggers can be deactivated, this can be useful if you want to manage data (loading test or sample data via Data Loader for example) and don't want the trigger validation to get in the way.

Trigger options

When you define a trigger, you specify that the trigger comes either before or after a particular database event. These database events are inserting a record, updating a record, or deleting a record. In addition, you define a trigger that fires after a user undeletes a particular record.

The trigger options are defined as part of the trigger specification, as follows:

```
trigger <trigger_name> on <object_name> (<trigger_events>) {
  code_block;
  }
```

A trigger executes once for each database action that causes the trigger events for the trigger, such as an insert, update, or delete. The trigger operates on the set of records sent with a data manipulation command, discussed later in this chapter. You can define multiple triggers for each object, or you can specify more than one trigger event, such as in the following code fragment:

```
trigger beforeWrite on Position (before insert, before update) {
  code_block;
  }
```

Normally, you only combine multiple trigger events in the same trigger if all these events require all or some of the same logic.

You use trigger context variables to determine which action has spawned the execution of the trigger.

Tip: Remember that the standard `save()` operation executes all appropriate database actions, which could include insert, update, or delete. In addition, you can call an upsert operation, which will be discussed later in this chapter.

Trigger Context Variables

Every trigger supports a set of variables that reflect the current context of the trigger. These variables fall into three main areas:

- Execution context variables – These variables represent a Boolean value that describes whether the current execution of the trigger is fired by a particular event. The execution context variables include `isInsert`, `isUpdate`, `isDelete`, `isBefore`, `isAfter` and `isUndelete`.
- Record context variables – These variables give you access to the actual records affected by the trigger. The four record context variables are `new`, `old`, `newMap` and `oldMap`. Each of these variables is an array since all data manipulation in Apex is done in bulk. The `new` and `old` variables represent an array of records, while the `newMap` and `oldMap` represent maps with the key being the ID of the record and the value being the record itself.

All of these record context variables are not available in all triggers, as shown in the table that follows:

Table 9: Trigger context variables

Action	Timing	New	Old
Insert	Before	Can be modified (`newMap` not available)	Not available
	After	Can be read	Not available
Update	Before	Can be read	Can be read
	After	Can be read	Can be read
Delete	Before	Not available	Can be read
	After	Not available	Can be read

For instance, for an insert operation, you can add records to the `trigger.new[]` array in a `before` trigger, and read the records that are inserted in the same array in an `after` trigger. For an update trigger, the `old` and `new` arrays show the before and after values for the record, respectively. The `trigger.old[]` array for a delete action shows the records that will be or have been deleted, depending on whether the variable is accessed in a before or after trigger.

- Other trigger context variables – Triggers also give access to the `size` variable for all trigger events, which represents the number of records in the trigger invocation.

Order of execution

Programming is an exacting science, one where small differences can produce different logical effects. If you have been reading this book from the beginning, you have come across a number of places where the Force Platform imposes some type of logic on data, including data type specification, validation rules, workflow, and triggers. The following list explains the order in which these logical operations are executed once a record is saved.

1. The original record loads from the database or initializes for an insert operation.
2. The new values load from the incoming request and overwrite the old values in the record buffer. The old values are saved in the old context variable for update triggers.
3. Before triggers run.
4. All system validation rules run, including required field checking and user-defined validation rules.
5. The record is saved to the database, but the record is not committed.
6. After triggers run.
7. Assignment rules and auto-response rules run, which are typically created as part of extensions to the SalesForce Platform application
8. Workflow rules execute. If field updates are specified, the record updates again, and before and after triggers for the update fire.
9. Escalation rules execute, which are typically created as part of extensions to SalesForce Platform applications
10. All data manipulation operations are committed to the database.

Exceptions in Triggers

Triggers can be used to take actions when records are inserted, modified or deleted. There may be times when you want to use a trigger to stop a particular data operation from taking place.

You can implement this by using database exceptions. The `addError()` method adds an exception to the current record, or a field within the current record, in a before trigger. When the Force Platform platform goes to perform the data manipulation action, the action does not proceed if any of the records to be manipulated are marked with an `addError()` method. The `addError()` result causes a `DmlException` and the DML operation to be rolled back.

The feedback supplied in the event of a trigger exception depends on whether the `DmlException` is caught by the Apex code in the trigger. If the exception is caught, the trigger continues any processing to see if there are any other exceptions in the group of records affected by the trigger. If the exception is not caught, a single exception causes all processing to stop and for all records to be marked with an error.

Creating a Trigger

You have acquired the basic knowledge you need to use triggers, so it is time to define one for yourself. Since you have not yet explored the Salesforce Object Query Language (SOQL), which is used to retrieve records from objects in the Force Platform database, you can implement a simple trigger that throws a trigger exception in response to an invalid Job Application.

Different positions throughout Universal Containers have different levels of strictness about education requirements. Although reaching a certain level of educational attainment is always seen as a good thing, some positions absolutely require a specific level of education from any applicant.

The scripts mentioned at the start of this chapter added a new field to the Position record, a checkbox, Reject_Undereducated__c, that indicates whether Job Applications are rejected if the Candidate does not have the required level of education.

Your first trigger checks to see if that requirement is specified, and then checks to see if the Candidate has the required level of education.

1. Go to **Setup ➤ Create ➤ Objects ➤ Job Application**.
2. Click on **New** in the Triggers section to bring up the page shown below.

Figure 186: Creating a trigger

3. The template for the trigger gives you the basic syntactical structure of your trigger. With your knowledge of Apex, add in the following specification:

```
trigger rejectUndereducatedTrigger on Job_Application__c (
    before insert, before update) {
}
```

The new code gives the trigger a name and specifies that the trigger runs before a Job Application record is either inserted or changed.

4. The next step is to add the following `for` loop to iterate through the array of new records:

```
trigger rejectUndereducatedTrigger on Job_Application__c (
    before insert, before update) {
    for (Job_Application__c JA : trigger.new){
            }
    }
}
```

This loop is a SOQL `for` loop that was mentioned in the last chapter. The loop iterates through the collection of records in the `trigger.new` array, which will contain any records either inserted or updated.

5. The next step is to retrieve the value of the Reject_Undereducated__c checkbox into the trigger, which you do with the highlighted line of code, which uses a simple SOQL statement. You will be formally introduced to SOQL in the following section.

```
trigger rejectUndereducatedTrigger on Job_Application__c (
before insert, before update) {
    for (Job_Application__c JA : trigger.new){
        Position__C getBack = [select
            reject_undereducated__c from
            position__c where ID = :JA.position__c];
    }
}
```

Why do you have to explicitly retrieve the Position record that is related to the Job Application record that fired the trigger? The values of related records are not available in triggers, for good reason. A record can be related to many other records in many other objects, and retrieving all of them whenever a trigger is fired might result in excessive overhead.

Optimizing trigger code

The code shown in this trigger is used as an example, to help you to understand how to write a trigger. However, this code has one potential performance issue built into its structure. Remember, trigger code is fired implicitly on a set of records that are submitted. In the code example above, you are properly iterating through the set of records in the `trigger.new` collection. However, you are making an individual SOQL call to retrieve the value of the Reject_Undereducated__c field for each record. If the trigger.new collection contained 100 records, you would call the SOQL statement 100 times.

Another way to implement this trigger is to select all the relevant Position__c records into a set at the start of the trigger, and then use the objects in the map to locally retrieve the value for the Reject_Undereducated__c field, as with the following code:

```
trigger rejectUndereducatedTrigger on Job_Application__c (
before insert, before update) {
    List<String> positions = new List<String>;
    for (Job_Application__c JA : trigger.new){
        positions.add(JA.Position__c);
    }
    List<Position__c> rejections = [select
```

```
                    reject_undereducated__c from
                    position__c where ID in :positions];
                    }
    }
```

The in operator checks to see if the value is contained in a list of values, as you will see in the next section. You would then use the same index to examine the value of reject_undereducated__c and the value of the candidate_qualified__c field on the Job Application record.

The net result of this code will be to execute a single SOQL statement, regardless of the number of Job Applications passed to the trigger.

6. The next step for this trigger is to add the logic that checks to see if the Position record requires a certain level of education, and if the Candidate possesses the level of education required for the position. Add the highlighted code shown below to your trigger.

```
trigger rejectUndereducatedTrigger on Job_Application__c (
before insert, before update) {
    for (Job_Application__c JA : trigger.new){
        Position__C getBack = [select
          reject_undereducated__c from
          position__c where ID = :JA.position__c];
        if ( getBack.reject_undereducated__c &&
        (JA.candidate_qualified__c == 'Not qualified'))  {
            }
    }
}
```

The double ampersand sign (&&) represents an AND condition. The column reference uses a relationship to identify fields on the Position and Candidate records that are parents of this Job Application record, syntax you will learn more about in the next section on SOQL.

7. The final step is when you actually add an error to a Job Application record that qualifies to be rejected, with the last highlighted line of code.

```
trigger rejectUndereducatedTrigger on Job_Application__c (
before insert, before update) {
    for (Job_Application__c JA : trigger.new){
        Position__C getBack = [select
          reject_undereducated__c from
          position__c where ID = :JA.position__c];
        if ( getBack.reject_undereducated__c &&
        (JA.candidate_qualified__c == 'Not qualified'))  {
            JA.addError('You are not allowed to apply
```

```
                   without proper educational requirements.');
               }
          }
      }
```

If a Job Application record is about to be inserted or updated with values that fail this logical test, the `addError()` method flags the record and associates the text message argument with that error.

8. Click **Save** to save the new trigger and return to the detail page for the trigger.

   By default, triggers are active when saved. You can make a trigger inactive with a checkbox in the edit page for the trigger or by editing the metadata for the trigger in the Force Platform IDE.

You can easily see the results of this trigger in your application.

1. Go to the Positions tab and select a position.
2. Make sure that the checkbox labeled 'Reject undereducated' is checked and note the educational level.
3. Click **New Job Application** to add a job application.
4. Click the lookup icon to select a candidate for the job.

   The lookup results page layout has had the educational attainment of the candidate added to it in the script file you ran at the start of this chapter to make it easier for you to select a candidate.

5. Select a candidate who does not have the proper education.
6. Click **Save**, which should bring up the page shown below.

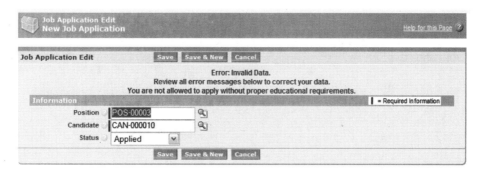

Figure 187: Your trigger at work

The figure above shows that the save action has been rejected, with the error message displayed at the top of the page.

With this trigger, you have guaranteed that no candidate whose educational achievement does not meet the requirements for a particular position is allowed to apply for that position. This trigger implements this logic whenever a Job Application record is written to the Force Platform object.

Now that you understand the basics of triggers, you can move on to learning about the languages used to access data in your Force Platform application.

Force Platform Query Languages

Data goes in, and data comes out. Apex is closely connected with data access on the Force Platform platform. There are two languages used to access data in your objects–Salesforce Object Query Language (SOQL) and Salesforce Object Search Language (SOSL). Both of these languages are used to retrieve a set of data from the Force Platform platform.

SOQL

As a developer, you are no doubt already familiar with some query languages. The most common query language is SQL, or Standard Query Language, the universal standard for interacting with relational databases.

Just as the Force Platform data repository is similar to a relational database, SOQL is similar to SQL. In most places where there is overlapping functionality, the syntax for SOQL is identical to SQL. But there are a few important differences between the two data access languages.

- SOQL is a query-only language – SQL has syntax for both reading and writing data, while SOQL is only used to retrieve records from your Force Platform objects. Later in this chapter, you will learn about how to write data using Apex data manipulation language.
- SOQL uses relationships, not joins – In SQL, you implement relationships between tables using join syntax in the `where` clause of the query. SOQL syntax recognizes relationship fields to identify the connections between objects, but does not support join syntax. You will see how to use relationships in your SOQL statements in the next section.
- SOQL does not support all SQL keywords – SOQL syntax is described in brief in the following section, and in more detail in the `Force Platform API` documentation. You should assume that SQL syntax not covered in the documentation is not accepted in SOQL.

SOQL syntax

At a high level, SOQL syntax follows this pattern:

```
select <fieldnames> from <object>
       [where <conditions>] [<order_by> field_name] [<limit> integer]
```

Each of the areas of the SOQL statement is explained in more detail below.

fieldnames

A list of fields returned from the SOQL statement. You can return any fields in any of the objects named in the statement, as well as the expression `count()`, which returns the number of records selected by the statement. All SOQL statements also return the IDs for the returned records.

Voice of the Developer: Note that the * qualifier in the `select` clause is not used in SOQL—you must explicitly state the fields you require. If your code attempts to read a field that has not been selected by the SOQL statement, an exception is thrown.

object

A SOQL query is aimed at an individual object, although you can also access data in related objects, as discussed below. You can specify an alias after the object name, as in the following:

```
select p.Name, p.Department from position__c p
```

where *<condition>*

The optional `where` clause can contain one or more conditions that limit the records returned from the SOQL query. Each `where` condition consists of a field name in the target object, a comparison operation, and a value. Comparison operators include all the standard comparisons, such as =, !=, <, >, <= and >=, as well as `LIKE`, `IN` and `NOT IN`. `LIKE` performs a case-insensitive comparison between the value of the field and the specified value. The values for the `LIKE` operator frequently use the wildcards '`_`' (to indicate a single character) or '`%`' (to indicate any number of characters, including no characters at all). The `IN` operator points at a set of values and returns true if the value for the field is one of the values listed, while `NOT IN` returns true if the field value is not in the list of values. Both of these operators can use a collection object as the value.

You can use the `AND` and `OR` keywords to combine multiple conditions. Best practices recommend that you use parentheses to insure clarity between multiple `where` conditions, as in the following:

```
where (p.Name like 'a') OR (p.Name like 'B%' and
p.Department = 'IT')
```

A `where` clause can use a bind variable for a value. A bind variable is a variable defined in your Apex code whose value is substituted into the SOQL statement at runtime. A bind variable is indicated by a colon preceding the variable name, as in the following:

```
String[] validNames =
    new string[]('Jones', 'Smith', 'Katz');
select Name from Candidate__c c
    where c.Last_Name__c IN :validNames;
```

order by *<field>*

The optional `order by` clause specifies an order for the records returned from a SOQL query. You can sort on one or more columns, and use the keywords ASC or DESC to indicate the sorting order. As with comparisons, all sorting is done in a case-insensitive manner.

You can also specify NULLS FIRST, the default, or NULLS LAST to indicate where null values are placed in the sorting order.

limit *integer*

The optional limit clause places a limit on the number of records returned from a SOQL query.

Relationship Queries

As mentioned above, SOQL statements target a single Force Platform object. But you can easily access related objects to the target object with simple syntax.

To access a parent object from a child object, you simply use dot notation, as in the following:

```
Select JA.Name, JA.postion__r.Job_Description__c
    from Job_Application__c JA
```

Your SOQL statement travels up the relationship chain from the base object, but notice that you use the syntax of __r (two underscores and an 'r') to indicate the relationship, rather than the __c to indicate the field.

The lookup field contains the ID of the related record.

You can traverse up to 5 levels of child to parent relationships, so the following SOQL statement is valid:

```
select Int.Name,
    Int.Job_Application__r.Position__r.Job_Description__c
    from Interview__c Int
```

You can also use SOQL to retrieve data from child objects of the target object. Among the objects you are using in this book, a Position record can be the parent of one or more Job Application records. To access the Position record and values from its related child Job Application records, you use syntax similar to a sub-query, as in the following:

```
Select p.Name, (select JA.Name from Job_Applications__c JA)
    from Position__c
```

You can only include one level of child records in a single SOQL statement.

Relationships and outer joins

With SOQL, the default behavior is to perform an outer join, which includes results that do not have a matching value on the other side of the relationship. This behavior has several repercussions involving lookup relationships.

If you use a lookup relationship field in a `where` clause, and there is no parent record, the condition is ignored. In the following query, an Interview record that does not have a parent Job Application is returned, along with any Interview records whose associated Job Application meet the selection criteria:

```
select Int.job_application__r.Name from Interview__c Int
       where Int.job_application__r.Status = 'Open';
```

SOQL in Action

Now that you understand the basics of SOQL, you can get some practice in using SOQL statements in your Apex code.

You begin by creating a trigger to assign interviewers for a particular Job Application. This trigger starts in this section and finishes when you learn about how to write data back to a Force Platform object in a later section.

This trigger automatically assigns interviewers for a candidate once the Status of their job application changes to Interview.

Create a trigger using the Force Platform Setup menu in the following manner.

1. Go to **Setup ➤ Objects ➤ Job Application** and click **New** in the Trigger section.
2. Set the name of the trigger to `assignInterviewers` and the events that will fire the trigger to `after insert` and `after update`. Your initial code should look like the following:

```
trigger assignInterviewers on Job_Application__c (after insert,
  after update) {
  }
```

3. Since all triggers work on bulk records, you should begin your trigger with a loop that will iterate through the members of the trigger.new array by adding the highlighted code:

```
trigger assignInterviewers on Job_Application__c (after insert,
  after update) {
  for (Job_Application__c JA : trigger.new){
    }
  }
```

4. You only want this trigger to run if the Status field on the Job Application object changes to `Interviewing`. Add a conditional statement to pick up this condition with the new code you see highlighted below:

```
trigger assignInterviewers on Job_Application__c (after insert,
  after update) {
for (Job_Application__c JA : trigger.new){
    if (JA.status__c == 'Interviewing') {
      }
    }
  }
```

 Caution:

This trigger automatically adds Interviewers to a Job Application record when the Status is changed to `Interviewing`, but does not handle other potential situations. In the current scenario, a user can change the Status from `Interviewing` to another Status. Prevent this from occurring with either a validation rule, which only allows the Status to be changed to certain values when the previous value was `Interviewing`, or another trigger to delete the existing Interview records associated with the Job Application in the appropriate situations.

5. Your first use of SOQL comes next, when you define a new variable to hold the User records for potential interviewers in the highlighted line of code below:

```
trigger assignInterviewers on Job_Application__c (after insert,
  after update) {
User selectedInterviewers = [select ID from user
    order by last_interview_assigned__c limit 2];
for (Job_Application__c JA : trigger.new){
    if (JA.status__c == 'Interviewing') {
      }
    }
  }
```

This SOQL statement returns records from the User object. The sorting of the records is on the last_interview_assigned__c field, which was added to the User record with the initialization scripts at the start of this chapter. insures that the three returned will be those users whose last interview was the most distant, since Universal Containers assigns interviews in a round robin fashion. Of course, you could have a different selection or sort criteria to retrieve different interviewers.

At this point, you are ready to assign interviewers to a particular job application, once the status of that application is changed to `Interviewing`. But before moving to the final stage of adding interview records to the job application record, you should learn about another way to retrieve records from your Force Platform data store—a method that allows you to retrieve records from different objects with a single query.

SOSL

One of the things you learned about SOQL is that all queries are based around a single Force Platform object. The Force Platform also offers another language that queries all objects in your organization, Salesforce Object Search Language, or SOSL

SOSL Syntax

The basic syntax for SOQL is as follows:

```
FIND {<search_term>} IN <search_group> RETURNING <field_spec>
```

The `search_term` is the string that is searched for. You can specify one or more strings or variables for this value. You join multiple strings together with an `AND`, a `NOT` or an `AND NOT`. All searches are case-insensitive, unless you use double quotes around the `search_term` to represent an exact string. You can also use double quotes to search for exact strings with spaces or punctuation marks. You can also use wildcards at the end or in the middle of a `search_term`: `*` for any number of characters, or `?` for a single character.

The `search_group` allows you to specify the fields you want to search. You can search `ALL FIELDS`, the default, `EMAIL FIELDS`, `PHONE FIELDS`, or `NAME FIELDS`.

Finally, the `RETURNING field_spec` lists the objects that are returned from a SOSL query. You can list one or more objects in this clause, and each object can have a list of fields following the object name in parentheses.

If you want to return a list of users who have the same area code as a job applicant, the basic SOSL query you use looks like the following:

```
FIND :areaCode IN PHONE FIELDS RETURNING User(ID)
```

Since you cannot call SOSL from a trigger, you will not implement this functionality in your current trigger. For more information on SOSL, please refer to the *Force Platform API Reference* manual.

Dynamic SOQL and SOSL

As repeatedly emphasized in this book, good Force Platform applications are data-driven. These applications naturally interact with data, even to the point of sometimes changing the user interface based on data values, such as with record types, dependent picklists, or the Visualforce example you will be creating in the next chapter.

All these examples use different data, but rely on a fixed set of data structures. What about those times when you want to go beyond the data structure of a single known object? What if you want to create some functionality that can operate on different objects, depending on application context?

To address this issue, Apex code includes the ability to create SOQL and SOSL statements dynamically, where the actual query statements are not determined until run-time. You can also use dynamic DML statements to use put and get methods, followed by the field name and a value, to write values to variable fields in an object.

For dynamic SOQL, use the `query()` method on the Database object to specify a SOQL query at runtime. For dynamic SOSL, use the `query()` method on the Search object. For both of these approaches, use Apex describe calls to retrieve information about the objects and fields in your Force Platform data store, insuring that the query strings submitted are valid at run-time.

Using dynamic queries in your applications opens up a whole new world of opportunities, but this capability must include checks to insure that the results fall within acceptable bounds. Because of this need, use standard, data-driven Apex scripts when possible, and move into the area of dynamic SOQL or SOSL only when this feature can uniquely solve your application challenges.

 Voice of the Developer: Take care not to jump to dynamic SOQL too quickly. You may believe that you need absolute flexibility in using fields and objects, but frequently this belief masks a reality that calls for loads of flexibility in selection criteria and a manageable flexibility in the sources of data.

For more information about using dynamic SOQL and SOSL, please refer to the *Apex Language Reference* documentation.

Data Manipulation with Apex

At this point, you have used SOQL to retrieve a set of User records. The last piece of the data manipulation puzzle is the ability to write data through Data Manipulation Language (DML) syntax. Apex has a set of commands that make this final step very simple.

Apex DML Syntax

There are two ways to perform data manipulation requests with Apex. The simplest uses a simple DML statement for each different data manipulation action, including the following:

- Insert - adds records to a Force Platform database object. The Force Platform automatically creates a unique ID for any record inserted.
- Update - updates values in an existing record in a Force Platform database object, based on the ID of the record.
- Delete - deletes records in a Force Platform object, based on the ID of the record. Deleting a master record in a master-detail relationship deletes all child records for that relationship.
- Upsert - performs either an insert or update, based on the presence of an ID for the record.
- Undelete - removes records from the Recycle bin and places them back into their original Force Platform object

Apex also supports the merge statement and convertLead statements, which are used for specific use cases and are detailed in the *Apex Language Reference* documentation.

As you will see in the example in the next section, all of these commands operate on a set of records.

As mentioned above, you can use methods on an instance of the Database class to perform the same data manipulation actions. These methods return a result object, with information about the execution of the operation. One key difference between using a simple DML statement and using a Database method is how you can handle errors with them. A simple DML statement either succeeds or fails. If any of the operations in a simple DML call fail, the entire call fails. With Database methods, you can specify that the overall operation continues if an individual operation on a specific record fails. With this flexibility, you can create database interactions that never throw an exception—you handle the exception circumstances yourself by analyzing the result object. Note that the merge action does not have a matching Database method.

For more information on Database methods, please refer to the *Apex Language Reference* documentation.

Data integrity

Data integrity is one of the highest virtues of any IT system. You must be able to count on your data reliably reflecting proper values in all scenarios. The Force Platform provides a lot of built-in robustness that protects your data, but whenever anyone is going to write data, you always have the possibility of conflicting user actions causing a loss of data integrity.

The basic unit used to protect data integrity is the transaction. A transaction is an all-or-nothing unit of work. Transactions on the Force Platform, by default, begin when your Apex code issues a DML statement and end when the Apex script that contains them completes. If the script ends without errors, the transaction's changes to the data commit. If the script does not complete successfully, the changes made by the transaction roll back.

Apex includes the ability to define *savepoints*. A savepoint is a place within a transaction. You can rollback a transaction to the beginning of the transaction, the default, or to a previously defined savepoint.

You define a savepoint with a method on the Database object, as follows:

```
Savepoint <name> = Database.setSavepoint();
```

To roll back to the beginning of a transaction, use the `Database.rollback()` method. If you include the name of a savepoint as an argument to the method, the transaction rolls back to the specified savepoint.

While a transaction is in progress, the records being used by the transaction are locked. These locks are released when the transaction completes, successfully or unsuccessfully. There might be situations where you want to lock values in a set of records when you initially query the records. For instance, if you are going to transfer values from one financial account to another, you want to lock the values in the original account until they are completely moved to the target account.

You can specifically lock a set of records in a result set by adding the keywords `for update` to a SOQL query. This approach protects the integrity of your data, but can also cause other processes to wait until the locking transaction completes, so carefully consider the use of these options.

Writing data

As you will now see, actually writing data to your Force Platform objects is a fairly simple matter.

1. Return to the trigger you created in the previous section.

2. Your first task is to create a variable in your trigger to hold the Interview records you want to insert into the Interview__c object. Add the highlighted code below.

```
trigger assignInterviewers on Job_Application__c (after insert,

  after update) {
    List<Interview__c> addInterviews =
      new List<Interview__c>();
    for (Job_Application__c JA : trigger.new){
        List<User> selectedInterviewers = [select ID
          from user
          order by last_interview_scheduled__c, name
          limit 2];
        if (JA.status__c == 'Interviewing') {
          }
      }
  }
```

The Interview object has two fields you want to include in the new record—the lookup relationships to the Job Application record, which represents the candidate and position, and the User record, which identifies the interviewer. You already have an array of IDs for those users – now you have to get the ID for the Job Application record.

3. Add the following highlighted code to the existing trigger code:

```
trigger assignInterviewers on Job_Application__c (after insert,

  after update) {
    List<Interview__c> addInterviews =
      new List<Interview__c>();
    for (Job_Application__c JA : trigger.new){
        List<User> selectedInterviewers = [select ID
          from user
          order by last_interview_scheduled__c, name
          limit 2];
        if (JA.status__c == 'Interviewing') {
          ID jobID = JA.ID;
          }
      }
  }
```

4. You are now ready to iterate through the array of User records, adding each as an interviewer for this Job Application. Add the following highlighted code to the existing trigger code:

```
trigger assignInterviewers on Job_Application__c (after insert,

  after update) {
    List<Interview__c> addInterviews = new List<Interview__c>();
```

```
for (Job_Application__c JA : trigger.new){
    List<User> selectedInterviewers = [select ID
    from user order by last_interview_scheduled__c, name

    limit 2];
    if (JA.status__c == 'Interviewing') {
        ID jobID = JA.ID;
        For ( User u : selectedInterviewers) {
            addInterviews.add(new Interview__c
                (Job_Application__c = jobID,
                interviewer__c = u.ID)));
        }
    }
    }
}
```

The code you have developed at this point will add Interview records that are associated with the Job Application records with a value of Interviewing for their Status field. You also have to collect the IDs for the User records being assigned for the interviews, since you will want to update those records to reflect when the interviews were assigned in the last_interview_assigned__c field.

5. Add the following highlighted code to your trigger:

```
trigger assignInterviewers on Job_Application__c (after insert,

after update) {
List<Interview__c> addInterviews = new List<Interview__c>();

List<ID> interviewersAssigned = new List<ID>();
for (Job_Application__c JA : trigger.new){
    List<User> selectedInterviewers = [select ID
    from user order by last_interview_scheduled__c, name

    limit 2];
    if (JA.status__c == 'Interviewing') {
        ID jobID = JA.ID;
        For ( User u : selectedInterviewers) {
            addInterviews.add(new Interview__c
                (Job_Application__c = jobID,
                interviewer__c = u.ID));
            interviewersAssigned.add(u.id);
        }
    }
    }
}
```

At this point, you have a variable with the structure of the Interview__c object, full of records you want to insert into the database. A single statement takes care of the action, surrounded, of course, by a try/catch block to guard against unforeseen errors.

6. Add the following highlighted code to your trigger:

```
trigger assignInterviewers on Job_Application__c (after insert,

  after update) {
  List<Interview__c> addInterviews = new List<Interview__c>();

  List<ID> interviewersAssigned = new List<ID>();
  for (Job_Application__c JA : trigger.new){
      List<User> selectedInterviewers = [select ID
        from user order by last_interview_scheduled__c, name

          limit 2];
      if (JA.status__c == 'Interviewing') {
          ID jobID = JA.ID;
          For ( User u : selectedInterviewers) {
              addInterviews.add(new Interview__c
              (Job_Application__c = jobID,
                interviewer__c = u.ID));
              interviewersAssigned.add(u.id);
              }
          try{
              insert addInterviews;
              }
          catch (DmlException de) {
            for (Integer i = 0; I < de.getNumDml(); i++) {
            JA.addError(de.getDmlMessage(i));
              }
          }
        }
      }
  }
```

The last requirement of this trigger is to update the User records with the time of this interview scheduling, which is used to implement the round robin scheduling. The User record is one of the standard Salesforce objects known as a setup object, since the values for the record are assembled from several different sources. This structure imposes a limitation on these objects, in that they cannot be modified in the same Apex code as non-setup objects, including all custom objects.

Because of this limitation, you will have to have the update statement in a method of a separate class, and that method will be marked with the `future` annotation, detailed in *Chapter 10: Apex*, which will place the method execution in a queue for future execution.

That class was loaded into your organization with the startup procedure detailed at the beginning of this chapter. The code for that class is:

```
public class updateUsers {

@future
```

```
public static void doUpdate(List<ID> targetUserIDs) {
   List<User> targetUsers = [select last_interview_scheduled__c

      from user where id in :targetUserIDs];
   for (User u : targetUsers) {
      u.Last_Interview_Scheduled__c = system.NOW();}
      try{
       update targetUsers;
       }
      catch (DmlException de) {
         for (Integer i = 0; I < de.getNumDml(); i++) {
            JA.addError(de2.getDmlMessage(i));
               }
            }
      }

}
```

You only have to call it from your current trigger.

7. Add the following highlighted code to your trigger:

```
trigger assignInterviewers on Job_Application__c (after insert,

  after update) {
   List<Interview__c> addInterviews = new List<Interview__c>();

   List<ID> interviewersAssigned = new List<ID>();
   for (Job_Application__c JA : trigger.new){
       List<User> selectedInterviewers = [select ID
         from user order by last_interview_scheduled__c, name

         limit 2];
       if (JA.status__c == 'Interviewing') {
          ID jobID = JA.ID;
          For ( User u : selectedInterviewers) {
             addInterviews.add(new Interview__c
               (Job_Application__c = jobID,
                interviewer__c = u.ID));
             interviewersAssigned.add(u.id);
          }
          try{
             insert addInterviews;
          }
          catch (DmlException de) {
             for (Integer i = 0; I < de.getNumDml();
                i++) {
                JA.addError(de.getDmlMessage(i));
             }
          }
          updateUsers.doUpdate(interviewersAssigned);
       }
   }
}
```

Since you are placing the updates to the User object into a future execution queue, the updates will be executed immediately, but the execution is typically fairly rapid.

8. Save your work.
9. To test your trigger, select the Position tab and then go to a Job Application for the position from the related list. Change the status of the record to `Interviewing` and save the record. You should see a set of interviews in the related list for the Job Application.

You could change the status for other Job Applications to see that the interviewers are being assigned with round robin scheduling.

When you save the updated Job Application record, the change, which began the transaction, caused the trigger to fire. The DML operations of the trigger are part of the same transaction as the save that caused them, so the new Interview records are present when you are returned to the detail page for the Job Application record.

The triggers you have created in this chapter are missing an essential component—test methods. There are complete versions of these triggers, including test methods, in the Code Share project for this chapter. One important factor to remember when creating test methods for data interaction is that none of the data changes you make in your test methods are ever committed to the database, so you can add, modify, and delete data in your tests without having to worry about the effect that these operations will have on your persistent data.

 Voice of the Developer: Inevitably your test code will require test data. Test methods are able to read data within the organisation they execute within. However, it is a bad idea to depend on the availability of this data, since it is unlikely to be present in the organizations your application is deployed into. Note that the Force Platform runs test methods during installation of your application into an end users' organization, when there may not be any data yet available. You should consider creating a class or number of classes that focus on setting up test data for your tests. Developers can then reuse these test data setup methods in the tests they write. Data created within test methods is automatically rolled back when the test completes.

Data manipulation is at the core of many of your Apex code chores. You have learned how to read and write data in your Force Platform objects with Apex. But you have to understand one more thing about interacting with your Force Platform data.

Bulk data operations with Apex

The basic flow of data manipulation operations for Apex is illustrated in the figure below.

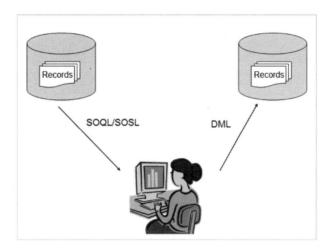

Figure 188: Data manipulation flow

Data is retrieved from an object in the Force Platform database with a query statement. The array of records is modified through the action of your Apex code, and then the array is sent back to the object through a data manipulation command.

These actions are performed in bulk on the Force Platform; however, there are limits to how many records can be affected by each stage of this operation. Since records are normally retrieved into a Force Platform collection, the number of records that can be retrieved is limited by the maximum size of a collection, which is 1,000 items. This limit means that queries retrieving records into a collection cannot retrieve more than 1,000 rows.

There is an easy way around this limitation. Instead of retrieving records into a collection, you can use a FOR SOQL loop, which was discussed in the previous chapter. The FOR SOQL loop iterates through the results of a query without holding those results in a declared object, so the 1,000-item limitation is removed.

There are other limits on Force Platform data interactions that are imposed by the platform itself. The Force Platform has limits on the number of records that can be read or written, in order to prevent any application or organization using too many resources and jeopardizing the overall performance of the platform.

The specific governor limits for different actions are detailed in the *Apex Language Reference* documentation, but there a few limits that you should be conscious of when creating Apex triggers. The first limit is on the number of data interactions in a trigger. You cannot have more than 20 queries or 20 DML statements in one trigger. Because of this limitation, you should not normally use either of these statements within a loop, since a larger number of loop iterations, which can occur naturally, depending on application context, can result in an error.

There is also a limit on both the number of records that can be retrieved in a query and the number of records that can be affected by a DML statement; however, these limits are based on the number of records on which the trigger is operating. The limits are 1,000 records retrieved and 100 records written per record received.

If a trigger is called when only one record is being affected, the trigger can only retrieve 1,000 records or write 100 records. If the same trigger is called when 10 records are being affected, the limits rise to 10,000 records read and 1,000 records written.

Regardless of the number of records passed to the trigger, there is a maximum of 10,000 rows read by the trigger. These limits are not onerous for the large majority of triggers, but being aware of these potential limitations will help you design your triggers to avoid potential runtime issues.

Summary

In this chapter, you learned about interacting with Force Platform data through Apex. Triggers use implicitly called Apex code to automatically execute logical operations.

The Force Platform includes data access through SOQL, which retrieves fields from a base object and its related objects, and SOSL, which queries across all objects.

Once you have a collection of records, you use Apex statements to write data back to Force Platform objects. You should be aware of bulk limits on data operations and write your Apex code using best practices for working with those limits.

Chapter 12

Extended Visualforce Components and Controllers

Back in *Chapter 9: Visualforce Pages*, you were introduced to Visualforce technology in the form of Visualforce pages that used standard controllers. You can expand the reach of your Force Platform applications even further by using Visualforce components, and both extensions to standard controllers and custom controllers, which require the use of Apex code.

In this chapter, you explore each of these areas and how they can increase your developer productivity and the productivity of your user community.

 Important: If you have been following the examples in the previous chapter, your Force Platform organization should be ready for the exercises in this chapter. If you have not done the exercises, or want to start with a fresh version of the sample Recruiting application, please refer to the instructions in the Code Share project for this book. You can find information on how to access that project in *Chapter 1: Welcome to the Force Platform*. In addition, the project contains instructions on how to update your organization with changes required for this chapter.

Visualforce Components

You have already learned about Visualforce components—you used many standard components in your Visualforce pages in *Chapter 9: Visualforce Pages*. You can also create your own Visualforce components to use in the same way as standard components in a Visualforce page.

Visualforce components do not require the use of any Apex code, but you use a slightly different path to create these components, as well as some syntax that is only relevant for reusable components.

For our example, the particular Visualforce component you create addresses a particular need at Universal Containers. Universal Containers is fortunate in having extremely creative employees, but they are perhaps a bit too fortunate in this area. The company, as a whole, has had trouble deciding on a single slogan for their enterprise, so they have reached a compromise solution. All slogans displayed in their Force Platform applications have the same form, with the Universal Containers logo, and one of many mottos underneath the logo.

Further, the executives at Universal Containers like emphatic slogans, with a normal statement followed by one of increased emphasis. To account for this scenario, you will be creating a Visualforce component with this form, but with the option of assigning different slogans for each use. This section introduces you to creating and using components.

Creating a Visualforce Component

Visualforce components use all the same syntax as a standard Visualforce page, with several added tags and attributes to provide component-specific capabilities. The starting place for component creation is the Setup environment.

1. Go to **Setup ➤ Develop ➤ Components ➤ New**, which will take you to the page shown in below.

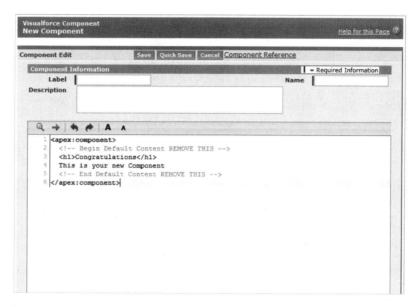

Figure 189: Creating a Visualforce component

2. Give the component the name of `slogo`, a combination of slogan and logo, and an appropriate description.

3. Modify the code for the page, eliminating the default code and adding an image component and an HTML page break, as shown in the code below:

```
<apex:component>
 <apex:image value="{!$Resource.Logo}"> </apex:image>
</apex:component>
```

You have just created your first component, The next step is to give this component more flexible capabilities.

Adding Attributes to a Component

You have created a basic component, with the Universal Containers logo. You now want to add a way for an instance of this component to receive words for the slogan.

You can create attributes to receive values passed from the Visualforce page that includes the component. An attribute, in a Visualforce component, is a way to pass values to the component. All attributes need a name, a description, and a data type, which is a primitive data type, such as string, number, or date. An attribute can also be specified as required or not.

1. Modify the code for the component by adding two attribute tag sets, as shown in the following code:

```
<apex:component>
<apex:attribute name="firstText"
        description="The first text string
          that is not italic"
        type="String" required="false"/>
<apex:attribute name="firstItalicText"
        description="The first italic text string."
        type="String"
        required="false"/>
<apex:image value="{!$Resource.Logo}"> </apex:image>
</apex:component>
```

Now that your component includes attributes, you can use them in the display of the component.

2. Modify your component code to use the attributes within the component, as shown in the following code:

```
<apex:component>
  <apex:attribute name="firstText"
        description="The first text string
          that is not italic"
        type="String" required="false"/>
    <apex:attribute name="firstItalicText"
        description="The first italic text string."
        type="String"
        required="false"/>
    <apex:image value="{!$Resource.Logo}"> </apex:image>
    <p/>
    {!firstText} <i> {!firstItalicText}</i>
</apex:component>
```

As you can see, an attribute within a component is accessed just like any other field, through bind syntax.

Your component is now complete and ready to use.

Using a Visualforce Component

Now that your Visualforce component has been created, you can use it in any of your Visualforce pages.

1. Call up the Visualforce page you created in *Chapter 9: Visualforce Pages* through the URL of

   `http://c.instance_name.visual.force.com/apex/VisualforcePositions`

2. Add the component to the page, just below the opening page tag, with the following code:

```
<c:slogo firstText="Reaching the top - "
 firstItalicText="together"/>
```

The tag used to insert the component does not start with `apex:`, but with `c:`. The initial portion of any Visualforce tag indicates the namespace for that tag. A namespace is simply a way of separating Force Platform components to insure unique naming for the components.

 Tip: Namespaces become important when you learn about packaging, discussed in *Chapter 15: Deployment.*

The `c:` namespace refers to any component in your org that has not been assigned to a specific namespace, such as the slogo component.

3. Save your page code to refresh your page and to display your new slogo component, as shown in the figure below.

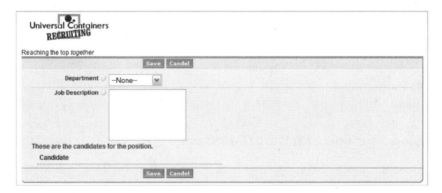

Figure 190: Your Visualforce component at work

Although you have only used your new Visualforce component in a single page, you can easily see how this flexible entity is used across your entire application.

Visualforce components can also be linked to their own custom controllers, which you will learn about later in this chapter.

Controller Extensions

In *Chapter 9: Visualforce Pages*, you experienced the different granularity of various Visualforce components. For instance, a single set of tags can create an entire detail page. But if you want to change the way a detail page looks beyond the scope of page layouts, you must build the entire Visualforce page using more discrete components.

Visualforce controllers give you similar options, but with a difference. You can build a custom controller with Apex code that replaces all the functionality of a standard controller, and there are times when this approach may be desirable; however, Visualforce also gives you another option, in the form of controller extensions.

A controller extension uses all the functionality in a standard controller. The controller extension expands or modifies that functionality by adding new capabilities or replacing standard capabilities with modified versions of the same actions. With this approach, you do not have to recreate everything that a standard controller does to simply tweak or extend its operation.

In this section, you create a controller extension to handle dynamically populating a picklist based on the value of another picklist. You are, in effect, duplicating the operation of a standard dependent picklist, but in a way that allows you to extend that functionality in the next section.

The dependent picklist adds a value for a position type to each Position record. The values available for this field are dependent on the particular department. For instance, you might have a Developer position in the Engineering department, but not in the Finance department. Time to begin.

Modifying Your Force Platform Database

Your first step is to add an object to your Force Platform database. The Position Type object will contain two fields: the Position Type field, which is the name of a position, and the Department field, which associates the particular Position Type with that Department.

In addition, you need to create a lookup relationship between the Product object and the new Position Type object.

The initialization task described at the start of this chapter created both of these components for you.

Creating a Controller Extension

Your next step is to create a controller extension to provide the new functionality for the Visualforce page.

The controller extension is an Apex class, which you learned about in the previous two chapters.

1. Create a new Apex class through clicking on the **Setup ➤ Develop ➤ Apex Classes ➤ New** button.
2. Add the following code to begin the creation of your controller extension:

```
public class positionExtension {

}
```

The initial code for this class should be familiar to you from the previous two chapters. You simply begin the class by identifying it and creating the pair of brackets that enclose the code.

3. Add the following line of code to the class:

```
public class positionExtension {

private final Position__c position;
}
```

This line of code is one of the two ways that you will tie your controller extension to the standard controller. The code creates an sObject with the structure of the Position__c object, and gives that object the name of position. This object will only be accessible to methods inside this class, so it is defined as `private`

4. Add the highlighted code to the class:

```
public class positionExtension {

private final Position__c position;

public positionExtension(ApexPages.StandardController
        positionController) {
    this.position =
        (Position__c)positionController.getRecord();
    }
}
```

This second step creates a controller extension object and then loads the position record with the current record used by the standard controller for the Position__c controller. The position variable is now tied to the same record as the standard controller, allowing the controller extension to operate in synch with the standard controller.

You have successfully created the shell of a controller extension. Your next step is to add the functionality you need to offer to your Visualforce page.

Populating a List of Options

The real work of your first controller extension is to provide a method to populate the picklist for the new Position_Type__c field.

1. Add the highlighted code to your controller extension:

```
public class positionExtension {

private final Position__c position;

public positionExtension(ApexPages.StandardController
     PositionController) {
   this.position =
     (Position__c)PositionController.getRecord();
   }

public List<selectOption> positionTypeOptions {get; {}
 private set;}


}
```

This property is declared with get and set accessors. When the variable is requested from a Visualforce page, the get accessor returns a value. Normally, when a page returns a value for the variable, the set accessor assigns that value. The `private` keyword before the set designates that only the code in this class can set the value of the property. If you do not define code for these properties, the Force Platform will take the default action.

The `positionTypeOptions` variable returns a list of values with a data type of `selectOption`. This data type contains a label that is displayed to the user and a value that can be bound to a column in a Force Platform object. The body of the `get` method populates this list.

2. Add the highlighted code to your controller extension:

```
public class positionExtension {

private final Position__c position;

public positionExtension(ApexPages.StandardController
```

```
    PositionController) {
    this.position =
        (Postion__c)postionController.getRecord();
    }

public List<selectOption> PositionTypeOptions {get {
    List<selectOption> positionTypes =
        new List<selectOption>();
    return positionTypes;
    }
    private set;}
}
```

These two lines of code create a list of selectOption fields, and then returns this
list in response to a request from the Visualforce page.

3. Add the highlighted lines of code to your controller extension:

```
public class positionExtension {

private final Position__c position;

public positionExtension(ApexPages.StandardController
        postionController) {
    this.position =
        (Position__c)postionController.getRecord();
    }
public List<selectOption> PositionTypeOptions {get {
    List<selectOption> positionTypes =
        new List<selectOption>();
    for (Position_Type__c ptr :
        [select name
            from Position_Type__c pt
            where pt.Department__c =
            :position.Department__c order by Name ])
        positionTypes.add(new selectOption(ptr.id, ptr.name));
    return positionTypes;
    }
    private set;}

}
```

This simple for loop should be familiar to you from the previous chapters on Apex
code. The for loop iterates through the result set returned from the SOQL
statement. This statement selects a label for the selectList entry, the name of the
record, that displays to the user. As with all SOQL statements, the unique Force
Platform ID is also returned with the result set.

The SOQL code introduces a new data object, which was added to your organization
with the initialization procedure at the start of this chapter. The Position_Type__c
object contains a set of records which associate a particular type of position with the

department which offers that position. The Position object also contains a lookup field to this object. The net effect of this interaction is to create a list of position types which are appropriate for the department which is offering a position - similar to the work of a dependent picklist, but with the ability to extend those capabilities, as ou will see.

The add() method for selectOptions adds two values to the object: the value for the entry and a label that presents to the user in the selectList. You use the ID as the value for the entry since the Position_Type__c is defined as a lookup relationship, which always points to the ID of the parent field. The name of the Position_Type__c record is the label for the entry in the select list.

You have one more task to accomplish before you can save this first version of your controller extension code.

4. Add the highlighted code to your class to declare another property:

```
public class positionExtension {

private final Postion__c position;

public string positionTypeID {get ; set ;}

public positionExtension(ApexPages.StandardController
     postionController) {
   this.position =
     (Position__c)postionController.getRecord();
   }
public List<selectOption> PositionTypeOptions {get {
   List<selectOption> positionTypes =
     new List<selectOption>();
   for (Position_Type__c ptr :
       [select name
           from Position_Type__c pt
           where pt.Department__c =
           :position.Department__c order by Name ])
     positionTypes.add(new selectOption(ptr.id, ptr.name));
   return positionTypes;
   }
   private set;}

}
```

The selectList that you will have in your Visualforce page will bind to this positionTypeID property. Why can't you simply bind the component to the Position_Type__c lookup field in the Position__c object? You will understand the full reason for this in the functionality you will add to your controller extension later in this chapter. You will be giving your users a chance to add new dependent values for the Position Type dynamically, so you will have to connect the selectList to an intermediate location—the positionTypeID property.

5. Save your code.

There you have it—the first version of your controller extension is complete. You can now create a Visualforce page to use your new functionality.

Your Visuaforce Page with Controller Extension

You need to use a Visualforce selectList component to implement the dynamic picklist operation for the new field, so you must have a Visualforce page to enter Position information. The load that you performed at the start of this chapter also added the basic Visualforce page with a name of `VisualforceExtension`. The code for this page is shown below.

```
<apex:page standardController="Position__c"
extensions="positionExtension" >
    <apex:form >
        <apex:sectionHeader title="Add New Position"/>
        <apex:pageBlock mode="edit" id="thePageBlock">
            <apex:pageBlocksection title="Information">
                <apex:inputField
                    value="{!Position__c.Location__c}"/>
                <apex:inputField
                    value="{!Position__c.Hiring_Manager__c}"/>
                <apex:inputField
                    value="{!Position__c.Status__c}"/>
                <apex:inputField
                    value="{!Position__c.Notification__c}"/>
                <apex:inputField
                    value="{!Position__c.Start_Date__c}"/>
            </apex:pageBlocksection>
                <apex:pageblocksection columns="1"
                    title="Department">
                    <apex:inputField
                        value="{!Position__c.Department__c}"/>
                </apex:pageblockSection>
            <apex:pageBlockSection title="Position Details">
                <apex:inputField
                    value="{!Position__c.Job_Description__c}"/>
                <apex:inputField
                    value="{!Position__c.Responsibilities__c}"/>
                <apex:inputField
                    value="{!Position__c.Programming_Languages__c}"/>
                <apex:inputField
                    value="{!Position__c.Educational_Requirements__c}"/>

            </apex:pageBlockSection>
        </apex:pageBlock>
    </apex:form>
</apex:page>
```

Although there is more code than in the Visualforce pages you worked with in Chapter 9, almost all of this code is familiar. You have `inputField` tags for each of the fields in the Position__c object that requires user input, and you have several different `pageBlockSection` tags, with appropriate titles, to break up the page for formatting purposes.

The most important change is the new `extensions` attribute in the initial page tag. With this tag, you have made the functionality implemented in your PositionExtension controller accessible to this page. As the name of the tag implies, you can have more than one controller extension for a page.

There is a new attribute in the initial `pageBlock` tag that designates the mode of the page as `edit`. This attribute simply sets up the appearance of the page to model that of a standard Force Platform edit page, without lines between the different input fields.

There is also a new tag just above the `pageBlock` tag for a `sectionHeader`. The tag itself gives this page a header just like a standard page, with the same colors and icon associated with the object (or defined as part of the `apex:page` component) and the text listed as the title tag. You can also have a `subtitle` tag with an additional line of text. This page, in its current state, is shown below.

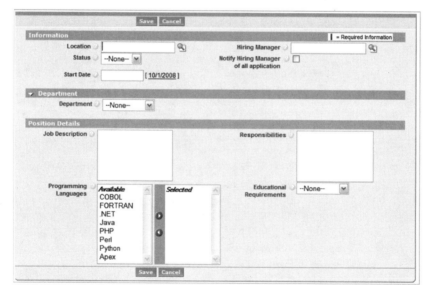

Figure 191: The initial version of your Visualforce controller extension page

Adding an apex:selectList

The page shown above presents an interface to most of the fields in the old version of the Position__c object. You need to add a new field to take care of the new Position_Type__c field in the object.

For all of the previous fields, you were able to simply use the `inputField` component within a `pageBlockSection`. This combination allowed your Visualforce page to simply use all the defaults associated with the field definition—yet another example of the metadata driven quality of the entire Force Platform environment.

This default will use a lookup field for the Position_Type__c object, but you want to add a little more functionality. As you saw in the definition of the Position_Type__c object, a user should not be able to see all position types for a position – just those associated with the department of the position. This functionality is very similar to that presented with a dependent picklist, but, as you will see later, can be expanded with additional capabilities.

The new field will be a `selectList` that is displayed as a picklist on the page, but the relationship to the Position_Type__c field is not as direct. Although you want to save the result of the user's selection into that lookup field, you populate the `selectList` with come of the code in the controller extension you created.

Because of this goal, you must use a slightly different set of tags for this field.

1. Bring up the new Visualforce page in your Force Platform environment, by adding `/apex/VisualforceExtension` to the base URL of your Force Platform org, explained above as `http://c.instance_name.visual.force.com`.
2. Open the Page Editor for your new page.
3. Add the highlighted code to your Visualforce page. The code is shown below, along with the code that precedes and follows it in the page.

```
<apex:pageblocksection columns="1" title="Department">
  <apex:inputField
    value="{!Position__c.Department__c}"/>
</apex:pageblockSection>
<apex:pageblockSection id="dependentPositionType"
  columns="1">
<apex:pageBlockSectionItem >
  <apex:outputLabel value="Position Type" for="pt"/>
  <apex:panelGrid columns="2">
    <apex:outputText
      value="{!Position__c.Position_Type__c}"
      rendered="false"/>
    <apex:selectList id="pt"
      value="{!positionTypeID}" size="1" >
        <apex:selectOptions
```

```
                    value="{!PositionTypeOptions}"/>
        </apex:selectList>
    </apex:panelGrid>
    </apex:pageBlockSectionItem>
</apex:pageBlockSection>
<apex:pageBlockSection title="Position Details">
```

You have added a new `pageBlockSection` to enclose the new `selectList` item, a requirement since you want to use a partial page refresh to refresh the values in this picklist when the value for the Department field changes.

The first new thing to see in the code for this new item is the use of the `pageBlockSectionItem` tags. Since your new picklist is not bound to a particular field in a Force Platform object, you need to use these tags to force the Visualforce page to use the same formatting for the field listed within the tags. The `pageBlockSectionItem` tags use the `outputLabel` as the label of the field and the next Visualforce component as the input field, in this case the `selectList` component. The `outputLabel` is further associated with the `selectList` by the use of the `id` tag on the `selectList` and the `for` tag that points to that ID in the `outputLabel` tag.

The `selectList` component presents to users as a picklist. The size attribute indicates the number of entries initially for the picklist. With a `size="1"` attribute, the picklist is displayed as an entry field with a drop down list, like a standard picklist.

You can see that the `selectList` is bound to the `positionTypeID` variable in the controller extension field through the familiar value attribute. As you saw inn the previous section, the variable is used to hold the value for the lookup field Position_Type__c, as well as a value that you will be using later in this chapter.

The `panelGrid` component is here for a specific purpose, but one that is not yet apparent. You can see that the component has a `columns="2"` attribute, which allows two components to be placed in a single column pageBlockSection. Right now there is only one component, but you will see the use of the grid later in this chapter.

Why the hidden column?

You may have noticed that there is an `outputText` column bound to the Position_Type__c field, but hidden. You need this column as having a column bound to a field in a Visualforce page is the only way to include the column in the SOQL query for a standard controller. Since you will want to insert a value into this column, having it referenced by field, but not shown, is the most efficient way to make sure the column is available to receive data.

You want to populate the values for this picklist with the values retrieved with the `get` method of the `postionTypeOptions` variable. The values in the list are populated with the `selectOptions` tag. The code behind that get method limits the values placed in the picklist through the selection condition in the SOQL statement.

4. Save the new version of your Visualforce page.

If you have modified the code properly, your new page should look like the figure below.

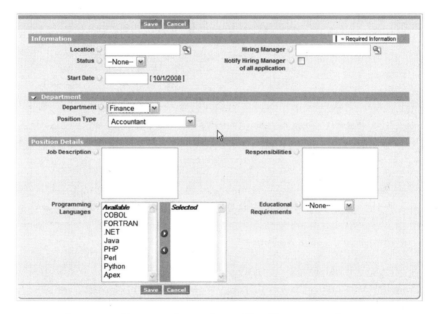

Figure 192: The next phase of your Visualforce extension page

Your new page does include a picklist for the Position Type field, but the values for that picklist are not being dynamically repopulated. Your next step is to add this key feature to your page.

Repopulating the selectList

In order to properly repopulate the Visualforce selectList, you can add AJAX functionality to your page, which is implemented automatically without having to write any Javascript code, whenever the user has changed the value in the Department list.

As you learned in Chapter 9, this interactive capability is easy to use with Visualforce.

1. Add the highlighted code to your Visualforce page.

```
</apex:pageBlocksection>
    <apex:actionRegion >
        <apex:pageblocksection columns="1"
            title="Department">
            <apex:inputField
                value="{!Position__c.Department__c}"/>
            <apex:actionSupport event="onchange"
                rerender="dependentPositionType"
                status="departmentStatus"/>
                <apex:actionStatus id="departmentStatus"
                    startText="Fetching position types..."/>
        </apex:pageblockSection>
        <apex:pageblockSection id="dependentPositionType"
```

Adding the `actionSupport` component to the `inputField` for the Department__c field enables this field to react to user actions—in this case, the `onchange` event that fires whenever the value for the field changes.

You have to include the `actionRegion` tags to insure that the only field values sent back to the controller are the Department and Position Type fields. If you send the entire page back, and the user does not enter a value for one of the required fields, the controller will return an error.

In response to this event, you want to re-render the `pageBlockSection` that contains the `selectList` for Position Type, which will cause the component to call the `get` method for the field again.

2. Save the code for your Visualforce page.
3. Change the value in the Department picklist to see the dynamic refresh of the Position Type picklist at work.

This single component brings it all together—the AJAX capability of the Visualforce page and the additional functionality implemented in your controller extension.

Housekeeping

So far, so good—in fact, almost completely good. Your selectList is repopulating as you want, but remember, getting your application to do what you want is only the first step. You also have to insure that the appropriate values in your controller are properly initialized, and that your controller does not allow users to do what they are not supposed to do.

First to the initialization.

1. Add the highlighted line of code to your positionExtension class.

```
public positionExtension(ApexPages.StandardController
        postionController) {
    this.position = (Position__c)
      postionController.getRecord();
  positionTypeID = position.position_type__c;
    }
```

Remember that the `positionTypeID` property is the intermediary between the Position_Type__c field and the input from the Visualforce page. This code initializes the value of that property to the initial value of the field in the current Position__c record.

The second housekeeping task can have a significant impact on data integrity. Remember that any enforcement of the relationship between the Position Type and the Department must be handled by your implementation.

When the value for the Department changes, the list of possible choices for Position Type changes. But the Position Type picklist is bound to the `positionTypeID` property and the value of this field does not change. You can have a scenario where the user selects a Department and then an appropriate Position Type. The user then changes the Department and saves the record. The value for the Position Type `selectList` can still be set to a position type for the previous department.

You can adjust for this problem by simply resetting the value for the positionTypeID field to null whenever the value for the Department field changes. To do this, you need to add a new method to the controller extension and call that method when the AJAX change event occurs.

2. Return to the development environment for the controller extension class by clicking **Setup ➤ Develop ➤ Apex Classes** and then clicking the **Edit** link for your controller extension.

3. Add the following code to the end of your existing controller code, just before the final right bracket:

```
public void resetPositionType() {
    positionTypeID = null;
    }
```

This function is very simple —it sets the value of the positionTypeID property to null.

Now call this function in your Visualforce page, which is done in an even simpler fashion.

4. Save the code for the new version of the controller extension and return to your Visualforce page code in the Page Editor by entering the base URL, followed by `/apex/VisualforceExtension`.

5. Modify the actionSupport tag to include the action attribute, as shown in the highlighted code below.

```
<apex:outputText value="{!Position__c.Position_Type__c}"
    rendered="false"/>
<apex:selectList id="pt" value="{!positionTypeID}"
    size="1">
<apex:selectOptions value="{!PositionTypeOptions}"/>
<apex:actionSupport event="onchange"
    action="{!resetPositionType}"
    rerender="dependentPositionType"
    status="typeStatus"/>
</apex:selectList>
```

6. Save your changes and change the value in the Department picklist to insure that your page works properly.

Although you modified the way your page works, you cannot really see the effects of the modification simply by the way the page acts. The value of the Position_Type__c field only becomes an issue once that value is stored, which you will address in the next section.

But before you get to that section, you have one other scenario to address. Remember how dependent picklists operate when there is no value selected for the parent picklist? The dependent picklist is disabled, which makes the picklist incapable of accepting user input.

You can accomplish the same result with a little more controller code and a single attribute on your Visualforce page.

7. Modify the selectList that receives the Position_Type__c values to add the highlighted new attribute:

```
<apex:outputText value="{!Position__c.Position_Type__c}"
    rendered="false"/>
<apex:selectList id="pt" value="{!positionTypeID}"
    size="1"
    disabled="{!ISNULL(Position__c.Department__c)}">
<apex:selectOptions value="{!PositionTypeOptions}"/>
<apex:actionSupport event="onchange"
    action="{!resetPositionType}"
    rerender="dependentPositionType"
    status="typeStatus"/>
</apex:selectList>
```

With this single attribute, you are disabling the component, based on whether the Department__c field is null. If the Department picklist is null, you want to disable the selectList that contains the Position Type.

Saving the Record

Your Visualforce page is now working just great. The dynamic repopulation of the Position Type picklist is swinging along splendidly, with data integrity enforced. But what do you do with this value once your user has selected it?

As mentioned at the beginning of this section, a controller extension can use all the functionality in a standard controller. In this case, that means you can use the standard Save and Cancel actions by simply adding buttons to your Visualforce page to call them.

8. Add the highlighted code to your Visualforce page:

```
<apex:pageBlock mode="edit" id="thePageBlock">
  <apex:pageBlockButtons >
    <apex:commandButton
      value="Save" action="{!save}"/>
    <apex:commandButton
      value="Cancel" action="{!cancel}"/>
  </apex:pageBlockButtons>
<apex:pageBlocksection title="Information">
```

The code shown here is added near the top of your page, but you could have added it in other places just as easily, as long as it is a direct descendent of a pageBlock. As you already have seen, Visualforce components that begin with pageBlock inherit their style and, in this case, functionality from the standard Force Platform controller. As described previously, the pageBlockButtons component indicates that the `commandButtons` within these tags display just like standard Force Platform buttons, at the top and bottom of the page.

Similarly, all you have to do to call the standard Save and Cancel methods is to use them as the action attribute of the `commandButtons`.

9. Save your Visualforce page. The refreshed page should look like the figure below.

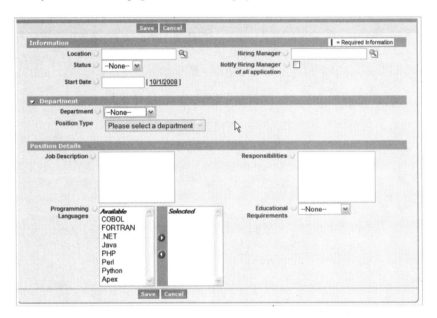

Figure 193: Your Visualforce controller extension page - with Position Type disabled

And there you have it—a new Visualforce page that delivers the functionality you added to your controller extension.

Integrating the page

Now that your Visualforce page is working properly, the final step is to integrate the page into your Force Platform application. You want your users to be able to use this page whenever they go to add a new Position or to edit an existing Position.

You achieve this result by overriding the default pages used for adding and editing a Position record.

1. Go to the **Setup ➤ Create ➤ Objects ➤ Position** page, and then to the Standard Buttons and Links area.

2. Click the **Override** link for the New action to bring up the page shown below.

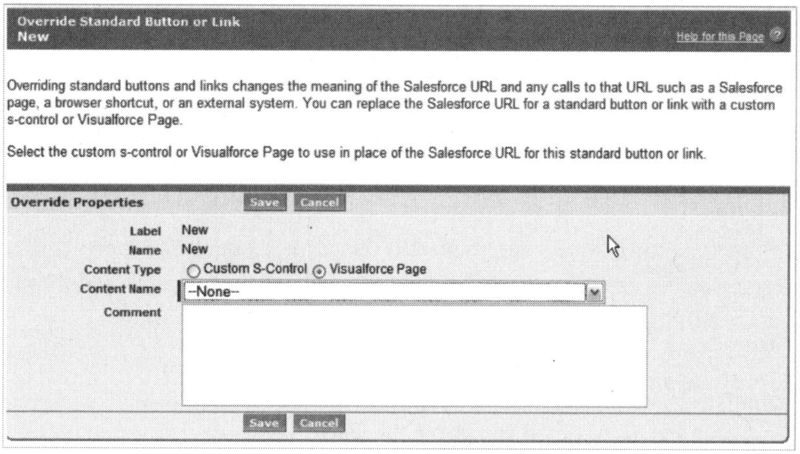

Figure 194: Overriding a standard action

3. Select the `Visualforce Page` for the `Content Type`, and then select the page you just created in the Content Type picklist. Notice that you are only presented with Visualforce pages tied to the controller for this object.

4. Save your work.

    When you return to the properties page for the Position__c object, you see that the New standard action now has an additional link, **Reset** that returns the destination of this action to the standard page.

5. Override the Edit action in the same manner.

6. Click the Positions tab in your Force Platform application and then **New**. You can see your new Visualforce page in action.

7. Click **Cancel** to return to the list page for Positions. Select a current position and then click **Edit** to again call up your Visualforce page.

This final integration was a snap. You can replace any of the standard pages in your Force Platform application with a Visualforce page while retaining the use of others. In this way, you can use the power of Visualforce technology without sacrificing any of the default power of the Force Platform.

The Next Step

Is there a question running through your mind right now? Are you asking "Wait—isn't this exactly what a dependent picklist can accomplish?" Well, yes, it is.

And, if you are on your way towards being a great Force Platform developer, the next question in your mind should be "Then why don't I just use that declarative feature?" Another good question.

You always use the built-in power of the Force Platform if you can, and if all you want is a dynamic display in a picklist, based on the value of another picklist, you certainly should use a dependent picklist. Those perceptive Force Platform developers already gave you this capability, nicely delivered through a declarative interface.

In the next section, you start to understand that the purpose of using your own implementation is to give your users a capability that dependent picklists do not possess, and to learn a little more about the things your Visualforce page can do for you and your users.

Conditional Display of Fields

The previous page worked well, dynamically displaying different values in a picklist based on the value of another picklist. Yes, this functionality is a recap of what is available in standard dependent picklists—so why reimplement it?

The reason to use this version of a dependent picklist is that you can expand the capabilities of this set of picklists to address a common user need. Normally, the position type for a particular position is available in its picklist. But what about those times when a user is posting a new type of position, one that is not currently available?

For a dependent picklist, this scenario is resolved by someone with developer privileges going in and modifying the values available on the dependent picklist.

With this new implementation, you can add a field to the page that allows a user to add a new position type. Of course, you do not want the user to add a new position type until they have at least looked at the currently available options.

In this section, you learn how to add a value to the Position Type list that triggers the display of an entry field for a new position type, and how to modify your controller code to save this new position type in a new record in the Position Type object.

Adding a Value to the selectList

The key to the capability you want to add to your Visualforce page is a value. This value is used to trigger the display of fields that allow a user to add a new position type for a particular department.

For the purposes of this exercise, you can use the value of Other to indicate this scenario.

1. Return to the controller extension you created earlier in this chapter through **Setup ➤ Develop ➤ Apex Classes** and then the **Edit** choice for the positionExtension class.

2. Modify the code that returns the selectOptions for the Position Type to include the highlighted lines of the following code:

```
public List<selectOption> PositionTypeOptions {get {
    List<selectOption> positionTypes =
      new List<selectOption>();
    for (Position_Type__c ptr :
        [select name from Position_Type__c pt
           where pt.Department__c =
             :position.Department__c order by Name ])
        positionTypes.add(new selectOption(ptr.id, ptr.name));
        if (position.Department__c != null) {
           positionTypes.add(new
               selectOption('other', 'Other'));}
    return positionTypes;
    }
    private set;}
```

This code adds another option to the list of position types, if a department has been selected. If a user selects this option, they have the opportunity to enter a new position type for the chosen department. You add the user interface for this new capability in the next section.

With this new code, you can see why you had to create the positionTypeID property to hold the ID of the Position Type. Up until this point, all the values for the positionTypeOptions have been valid ID values. You can bind the value of a selectList with only those ID values to the Position_Type__c lookup field, which only accepts an ID.

However, the value of 'other' is not a valid ID. As soon as your code attempts to associate that string with the Position_Type__c field, you will get an error. Consequently, you cannot bind the selectList to the Position_Type__c field, requiring the use of the postionTypeID property.

Before leaving this section of the code, you will add one option to the list returned to the page to help your users.

3. Add the highlighted code to your Apex class:

```
public List<selectOption> PositionTypeOptions {get {
    List<selectOption> positionTypes =
      new List<selectOption>();
    for (Position_Type__c ptr :
```

```
        [select name from Position_Type__c pt
          where pt.Department__c =
          :position.Department__c order by Name ])
     positionTypes.add(new
       selectOption(ptr.id, ptr.name));
     if (position.Department__c != null) {
        positionTypes.add(new
          selectOption('other', 'Other'));
        }
  Else {
        positionTypes.add(new
          selectOption('', '
          Please select a department', true));
      }
    return positionTypes;
    }
    private set;}
```

This condition adds a user-friendly message to the selectList for the Position Type if there is no value for the Department selectList. The message appears in the selectList and gently guides the user towards their next action. The constructor method for this selectOption includes a third optional parameter which, if true, indicates that this option is disabled in the selectList.

Note: Limiting the power

This modification of the controller extension allows everyone to have the ability to add a new position type, a power you might not want to grant so lightly. You can easily add an if condition for adding that last value to the selectListOptions so that only certain users, or users with a certain profile, have that value in the Position type picklist. Since the presence of this value controls the rest of the operations, eliminating the Other value prevents users from accessing the ability to add a new position.

Conditionally Displaying Fields

Now that you have added a data value that allows a user to add a new position type, you have to add a field to accept the Name for the new type. However, you do not want this field to show up all the time —only when a user has chosen the Other choice.

Visualforce components have an attribute that controls their display, just as another attribute controls whether the component is enabled. With this attribute, and another re-rendering of the page, you can provide this dynamic interface to your users.

1. Return to the Page Editor for your current Visualforce page. Since the page is now tied into the standard New action, you can get to the page by clicking on the Positions tab and then **New**.

2. Add the highlighted code to the Visualforce page:

```
<apex:pageblockSection id="dependentPositionType"
  columns="1">
    <apex:pageBlockSectionItem >
      <apex:outputLabel value="Position Type" for="pt"/>
      <apex:panelGrid columns="2">
       <apex:actionRegion >
        <apex:outputText
          value="{!Position__c.Position_Type__c}"
          rendered="false"/>
        <apex:selectList id="pt"
          value="{!positionTypeID}" size="1"
          disabled="{!ISNULL(Position__c.Department__c)}">
            <apex:selectOptions
              value="{!PositionTypeOptions}"/>
              <apex:actionSupport event="onchange"
                rerender="dependentPositionType"
                status="typeStatus"/>
        </apex:selectList>
       </apex:actionRegion>
          <apex:actionStatus id="typeStatus"
            startText="updating form...">
          <apex:facet name="stop">
          <apex:inputField
             rendered="{!positionTypeId == 'other'}"
             required="true"/>
          </apex:facet>
          </apex:actionStatus>
      </apex:panelGrid>
    </apex:pageBlockSectionItem>
</apex:pageBlockSection>
<apex:pageBlockSection title="Position Details">
```

There are three different places you have added code. The first is to define an actionRegion again, as you did previously. The second is to add the actionSupport, which rerenders the pageBlockSection that contains the Position Type information.

The third area is the actionStatus. As before, you use actionStatus to display text indicated that a refresh of the form is taking place. The next set of tags define a facet. A facet is an area in a page that can contain other text or, in this case, a component. The stop facet of an actionStatus component is displayed when the action has completed – in other words, once the dependentPositionType has been refreshed. This facet will contain an inputField to receive the name of a new Position Type. But you only want to show this field if the value selected for Position

Type is `Other`. The `rendered` attribute checks to see if the `positionTypeId`, which is the variable bound to the `selectList` for Position Type, contains `Other`. The `inputField` will display only if this condition is true.

Note that you have not bound your new `inputField` to a value in the controller yet. You will define the destination for a new Position Type in the next section, and then come back and bind the field with the `value` attribute.

Your Visualforce page will save without an error, but if you run it now, you will get a runtime error if you picked `Other` to try and show the `inputField` for the new Position Type. The error comes because the inputField is not yet bound to a field in the controller, which cannot be done until you add an instance of the Position_Type__c object in the controller. The next section will address this issue.

Holding the New Value

You may think of your Visualforce controller as simply a way to interact with data objects, but your controller performs an equally important role as a place where values are maintained on the Force Platform. When a user adds a value for a new position type into the dynamically displayed input field you just defined, your Visualforce controller receives that value and keeps it until your user decides to save the value to persistent storage in a Force Platform data object.

The eventual destination for this new position type is the Name field of the Position_Type__c object, so you first modify your controller extension to create a record that can be used to hold the new value.

1. Go to edit your controller code through **Setup ➤ Develop ➤ Apex Classes** and select the **Edit** choice for your custom controller.

   Voice of the Developer:

   While actively working on Visualforce pages and controllers, you can increase your productivity by having two tabs open, with one displaying the Page Editor for the Visualforce page and another in the Setup menu for the platform to make it easy to switch between the two environments.

2. Add the following property declaration to the existing code:

```
public Position_Type__c newPositionType{
  get{
    if (newPositionType == null) {
      newPositionType = new Position_Type__c();}
    return newPositionType;
```

```
    }
    private set;
}
```

This property will be used to insert a new Position_Type__c record, if the user create a new position type. The `get` accessor checks to see if the property has been initialized with a new record instance—if not, the method creates the new instance.

3. Save the new version of your controller code.

   With this step, you have created an object to hold the name for a new Postion Type. To open the channel between the user interface of the Visualforce page and your Visualforce controller extension, you will have to go back to your Visualforce page and add the `value` attribute to the last inputField.

4. Return to edit your Visualforce page. Add `value="{!newPositionType.Name}"` to the `inputField` you added in the previous section.

5. Save your Visualforce code. Try changing the value of the Position Type `Other` and back to see the new fields appear and disappear from the page. The page, with the new components visible, should look like the figure below.

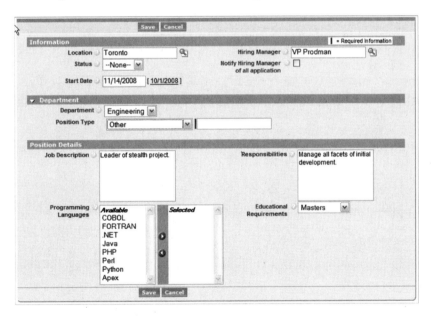

Figure 195: New field appearing on your Visualforce page

Your newly dynamic page is pretty nice, but you need to save the results of this pretty interface in your controller since you want to save the user's input into Force Platform objects.

Your last task to complete this implementation is to save this new value in the Force Platform database.

Saving the New Value

The last change you make to your controller extension is probably the biggest, in terms of its impact. A standard controller, by definition, is linked to a single Force Platform object. The functionality you have added to your Visualforce page calls for more than this. Once a user adds a new Position Type, you must add a record for this new value to the Position_Type__c table and then use the ID for this new record as the value for the Position_Type__c field in the Position__c table.

From the page point of view, you do this by replacing the Save method for the standard Position__c controller. This section covers the five basic logical steps for creating a successful save operation:

- Check for a new position type
- Add a new position type
- Set the new position type lookup
- Saves the Position record
- Catch errors

Checking For a New Position Type

If your user has created a new position type, you must add a record to the Position_Type__c object to represent the new type, but you only want to take this action if a new position type is indicated.

First, create a save method in your controller extension that makes this logical test.

1. Return to edit your controller extension class. Add the following code to the end of the existing code, just before the closing right brace:

```
public PageReference save() {

    }
```

This code defines the save method. This save procedure in your controller extension replaces the save procedure in the standard controller for the Position__c object, although your new save procedure will end up calling the default save for the object once you finish adding the specialized logic.

The save procedure returns a `PageReference`. The `PageReference` creates a URL that identifies the page sent back to the browser when the procedure completes. The default save procedure will take care of assigning a value to this return, but you will set `PageReference` variables explicitly later in the chapter.

2. Modify the save method to add the logical test shown highlighted below:

```
public PageReference save() {
      if (PositionTypeID == 'other') {
      }
      }
```

Why did you check for the other value in the PositionTypeID property instead of looking for a value in the newPositionType.Name field? Your user might have selected the `Other` choice for the position type, added a value in the `inputField` for the Name, and then changed the position type back to an existing position. The `inputField` would not be visible, but it would still have the previous value. Since the presence or absence of `other` value in the PositionTypeID property is the marker for this logical state, you should test that condition.

3. Click `Quick Save` to check your code for errors.

The `Quick Save` button parses and saves the Apex code in the edit window without sending you back to the list of Apex classes. Since you are still in the midst of developing your code, take this route to insure that you have entered the proper syntax.

Adding a New Position Type

If the user is adding a new Position Type, set the values for both fields in the record and save the record.

4. Add the highlighted code to the new `save` method in your Apex class:

```
public PageReference save() {
      if (PositionTypeID == 'other') {
         newPositionType.Department__c =
            position.Department__c;
         insert newPositionType;}
      }
```

The first line of code sets the Department__c field in the newPositionType record to the value of the Department__c field in the position record. You need to add the appropriate value for department, since this value populates the `selectList` used in your Visualforce page.

The second line of code inserts the values in the newPositionType record into their permanent home in the Position_Type__c object.

Setting the New Position Type Lookup Value

But simply storing the new position type is not enough to satisfy the needs of your Position__c record. Remember that the Position_Type__c field in the Position__c object is defined as a lookup relationship field. A lookup relationship field takes the unique ID of the related record, not the value of the Name of that record.

This unique ID is assigned when a record is created, as you are doing with the new Position_Type__c record now. Whenever you insert a record into a Force Platform data object, the in-memory representation of that object is updated to include the new ID.

5. Modify the code in your new save method add the highlighted line below:

```
public PageReference save() {
        if (PositionTypeID == 'other') {
        newPositionType.Department__c =
          position.Department__c;
        insert newPositionType;
        position.Position_Type__c = newPostionType.ID;
        }
    }
```

The code you currently have in your save method works for those cases when a user has added a new Position Type. What about those cases when a user has simply selected an existing Position Type?

6. Add the highlighted else code to your savemethod.

```
public PageReference save() {
        if (PositionTypeID == 'other') {
          newPositionType.Department__c =
            position.Department__c;
          insert newPositionType;
          position.Position_Type__c = newPostionType.ID;
        }
        else {
          Position.Position_Type__c = positionTypeID;
        }
    }
```

This condition simply transfers the value from the positionTypeID into the Position_Type__c field.

Saving the Position Record

Now, did you forget anything? Oh yes, you still have to save the Position__c record, the main focus of the page.

You don't want to do anything extraordinary with this record—simply take the standard actions to save the record. You can simply call the default `save` action for the standard controller to accomplish this task.

Except for one little problem. Remember, the `save` method in your extension overrides the `save` method for the standard controller. If you call the default `save` method, you find your code in an endless loop.

You can escape this problem by declaring another instance of the standard controller and then calling the `save` method on that instance.

7. Add the following code to the beginning of your class

```
private final ApexPages.standardController theController;
```

8. Add the highlighted line of code to your `save` method –

```
public PageReference save() {
   if (PositionTypeID == 'other') {
       newPositionType.Department__c =
        position.Department__c;
       insert newPositionType;
       position.Position_Type__c = newPostionType.ID;
       }
   else {
     Position.Position_Type__c = positionTypeID;
     }
   return theController.save();
}
```

This final line calls the save method on the new instance of the controller, which saves the current record and returns a `PageReference`, which is, in turn, returned to the calling page.

You have completed all of the proactive work for the new feature of your Force Platform application, but you still have to enable your application to react to any unexpected problems that might arise.

Catch Those Errors

Whenever your application attempts to write data to the Force Platform database, there is a chance that an error can occur during the process. For instance, even if you have created an exquisitely perfect data interaction, someone else's interaction with the underlying data might throw everything off.

For this reason, always include error handling code whenever your application writes to the database. This code gives you a way to handle the most difficult part of quality assurance for any application—the ability to fail (somewhat) gracefully.

9. Modify the code in your `save` method to match the code below by adding the highlighted code:

```
public PageReference save() {
        if (PositionTypeID == 'other') {
        try{
          newPositionType.Department__c =
               position.Department__c;
            insert newPositionType;
          position.Position_Type__c = newPostionType.ID;
          }
        catch (DmlException e) {
          ApexPages.addMessages(e)
          }
        }
  else {
    Position.Position_Type__c = positionTypeID;
    }
        return theController.save();
        }
```

The *try/catch method* on page 316 was described in the previous chapter on database interaction with Apex code. This syntax adds error handling to your Force Platform database interaction. If the database operation goes smoothly, no `DmlException` is thrown, so no message is received.

Without a **DmlException** handler, an error would cause a standard, generic error page to appear, which may be confusing to the user, and an email is sent to the owner of the trigger. With this exception handler, you will want to add the messages to the message collection, and then display that collection in an apex:messages component on the page.

The code above catches the errors and adds them to the `ApexPages.Message` variable. Your finishing step will be to add an `apex:message` component to your page to receive those messages.

10. Return to your VisualforceExtension page. Add the highlighted code near the top of the page:

```
<apex:pageBlock mode="edit" id="thePageBlock">
  <apex:pageMessages />
  <apex:pageBlockButtons >
```

As mentioned earlier, you should always include a `pageMessages` component in all your Visualforce pages, so hopefully this step is simply a reminder of something you have already done.

With this final important step, you have completed adding new functionality to your Force Platform application. You have explored using Visualforce pages with standard controllers and extending those controllers with some Apex code. For your last Visualforce task, you create your own custom controller that entirely replaces the functionality of a standard controller.

Visualforce Custom Controllers

You have accomplished a lot with Visualforce–shaping the look and feel of your Visualforce pages, using standard controllers to implement rich functionality, and extending those controllers when something a little extra is required. And your guiding philosophy for the Force Platform should be to always use as much default functionality as you can.

But Visualforce can take you even further. You can create your own custom controllers to back up your Visualforce pages. A controller extension extends or overrides standard controller functionality with a little bit of Apex code in a class. A custom controller completely replaces a standard controller with an Apex class.

In this final section on Visualforce, you create a custom controller to implement a wizard-like interface on the Force Platform. In this example, several different Visualforce pages access the same custom controller. Users navigate between pages, but the custom controller maintains the data over multiple Visualforce pages.

 Important: Saving state

Normally, when a controller redirects the user to another page, the state for the controller is flushed. The only way to avoid this is to use the same controller for multiple pages, with that controller handling the forwarding to different pages.

The wizard you will implement gives users a fast path to creating an interview schedule for a candidate for a position. The user selects from a list of positions, sees the candidates for that position, and then selects an interview schedule for that candidate, using three Visualforce pages and a custom controller.

Creating a Custom Controller

Your first step is to create the skeleton of the custom controller, which is an Apex class.

1. Go to **Setup ➤ Develop ➤ Apex Classes** and click **New**.
2. Enter the following code for the class, and do a **Quick Save** to valid your syntax and save the code:

```
public class customController {

}
```

This basic code simply creates the Apex class identified as the controller for the Visualforce pages.

3. To support the first page, which you create in the next part, add the following code, which is also available from the Code Share project for this book:

```
public class customController {

public List<selectOption> openPositionList {
  get {
    List<selectOption> returnOpenPositions =
     new List<selectOption>();
    String positionInfo;
    for (Position__c p : [select name, job_description__c,
      department__c, position_type__c, status__c
      from Position__c where status__c = 'Open']) {
        positionInfo = p.name + ' - ' + p.department__c
        + ' - ' + p.job_description__c;
        returnOpenPositions.add(new selectOption(p.ID,
          positionInfo));
      }
    return returnOpenPositions;
    }
    set;
  }

public Position__c selectedPosition {
  get {
    if(selectedPosition == null) {
      selectedPosition = new Position__c();
      }
    return selectedPosition;
    }
    set;
  }
```

```
public PageReference step2() {
  return null;
}

public PageReference step3() {
  return null;
}

}
```

The controller returns a list of `selectOptions`, with the value being the ID of the selected Position records and the label concatenated from several of the fields.. The SOQL query to populate this list has a `where` clause, limiting the positions displayed to those with a `Open` status, as the process flow at Universal Containers will only allow interviews to be set up for any open positions.

The final property defined in the current code, `selectedPostion` receives the position selected by the user in the first page of the wizard, which will be used to limit the selection in the second page of the wizard. The property uses an `if` statement to initialize itself, if this has not already been done, which is determined by checking for the property having a null value.

The class also contains two methods, `step2` and `step3`, used to navigate to the second and third pages of the wizard. These methods return a `PageReference`. When a `PageReference` is returned, the page referenced by the URL is returned to the browser from this function. The `PageReference` data type automatically uses the correct URL for the current Force Platform instance as the prefix for the URL, so returning null will return the user to the main page for the instance.

Right now, these methods cannot define the `PageReferences` to which the method navigates since these page references refer to Visualforce pages that are not yet created. You will modify these methods once you create the second and third pages of the wizard.

This small amount of code is all that you need to power the first page of the wizard. You are still be able to use all the default functionality in Visualforce page components, as you will see in the next section.

Displaying Positions

The first page of your wizard displays the Positions records retrieved by the SOQL statement you just created in your custom controller. Since you have had some experience defining Visualforce pages already, you will recognize almost everything in the code for this page:

```
<apex:page controller="customController">
    <apex:sectionHeader title="Interview Scheduler"
      subtitle="Step 1 of 3 - Select Position"/>
    <apex:form >
        <apex:pageBlock mode="edit">
            <apex:pageBlockSection columns="1">
                <apex:pageBlockSectionItem >
                    <apex:outputLabel
                       value="Select an open position: "
                       for="openPositionList"/>
                    <apex:selectList
                       value="{!selectedPosition.ID}"
                       id="openPositionList" size="1">
                        <apex:selectOptions
                            value="{!openPositionList}"/>
                    </apex:selectList>
                </apex:pageBlockSectionItem>
            </apex:pageBlockSection>
            <apex:pageBlockButtons location="bottom">
                <apex:commandButton
                    value="Get candidates" action="{!step2}"/>
            </apex:pageBlockButtons>
        </apex:pageBlock>
    </apex:form>
</apex:page>
```

You have already encountered the pageBlock, sectionheader and pageBlockTable in this chapter and *Chapter 9: Visualforce Pages*. The only new aspect of this page is in the initial page tag. Instead of having a standardController attribute, the page has a controller attribute that points to the name of the Apex class acting as the custom controller for the class.

This page has been loaded into your organization as part of the initialization procedure for this chapter, as described at the beginning of this chapter, under the name of wizard1.

Run this wizard1 page by appending /apex/wizard1 onto the base URL for your instance, which should be http://c.instance_name.visual.force.com, where *instance_name* is replaced with the name of your Force Platform instance. You should see the page shown below.

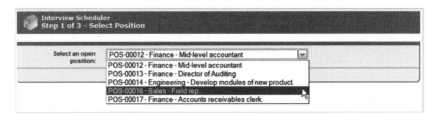

Figure 196: The first page of your wizard

Your Visualforce page looks just like other Visualforce pages—the only person who knows that there is a custom controller at work is you. This result is nothing but positive. You can supplement or replace standard controller functionality without changing anything in your Visualforce page, aside from pointing the page to a different controller.

Displaying Candidates

The first page of your wizard for scheduling interviews is complete. This page presented a list of open job applications, and gave your user a way to select one of them. Your next step is to first add code to your custom controller for delivering data to the second page of your wizard, and then creating that second Visualforce page.

1. Return to edit the custom controller through the **Setup ➤ Develop ➤ Apex Code**, and then click **Edit** for the custom controller class.
2. Add the following code to the controller class:

```
public List<selectOption> jobApplicationCandidates {
  get {
    List<selectOption> candidates = new List<selectOption>();
    for (Job_Application__c JA :
      [select Candidate__r.ID, Candidate__r.first_name__c,
        Candidate__r.last_name__c, status__c
        from Job_Application__c
        where (Position__r.ID = :selectedPosition.ID)
        and (Status__c = 'Interviewing')] ) {
          candidates.add(new
            selectoption(JA.ID,
              JA.Candidate__r.First_Name__c
            + ' ' + JA.Candidate__r.last_name__c));
      }
    return candidates;
    }
    set;
}
```

```
public ID selectedJobApplication {get; set;}
```

This code creates a `List` object that is returned to the second Visualforce page of your wizard. You can return an array of Candidate__c records, as you did in the previous page, and use the same `pageBlockTable` structure as you did in that page. This example uses this second option to illustrate a different possible approach.

As part of this approach, you also need to define an ID variable, `selectedJobApplication`. The `selectList` in the Visualforce page binds to this variable, whose value is used to limit the records retrieved for the next page.

3. Save the new version of the custom controller code.
4. The Visualforce page for the second step of the wizard was loaded into your organization with the initialization script at the start of this chapter under the name `wizard2`. The code for this page is shown below:

```
<apex:page controller="customController">
    <apex:sectionHeader title="Interview Scheduler"
        subtitle="Step 2 of 3 - Select Candidates"/>
    <apex:form >
        <apex:pageBlock >
            <apex:pageBlockSection columns="1">
                <apex:selectRadio
                    value="{!selectedJobApplication}"
                    layout="pageDirection">
                        <apex:selectOptions
                            value="{!jobApplicationCandidates}"/>
                        <apex:actionSupport event="onchange"
                            rerender="buttons"/>
                </apex:selectRadio>
            </apex:pageBlockSection>
            <apex:pageBlockSection id="buttons">
                <apex:commandButton
                    value="Schedule interviews"
                    action="{!step3}"
                    disabled="{!selectedJobApplication = NULL}"/>
            </apex:pageBlockSection>
        </apex:pageBlock>
    </apex:form>
</apex:page>
```

You can see a new Visualforce component at work in this page. The `radioList` component provides a group of values with a radio button, limiting the choice to a single selection. The `selectList` on the first page of the wizard also limited the selection to a single choice, but there were potentially too many values to be easily displayed on the page. For the candidates on this page, a group of radio buttons is more appropriate.

A `radioList` does not have to have a value selected, so this page uses the same technique used in your previous page for avoiding user errors. The third page of this wizard lists the interviewers for a particular candidate, so you do not want your user to be able to move to that page until they select a candidate. You can stop the user from trying to perform this invalid action by disabling the `commandButton` that navigates to the third page until the value for `selectedJobApplication`, the ID variable that holds the value for the selected candidate, is not null.

This simple attribute prevents an error, but you also have to add the `actionSupport` code to the radio group so that any change in value for that group rerenders the `pageBlockSection` that contains the `commandButtons`. The buttons are redrawn whenever the value for the group of radio buttons changes, and if a radio button is selected, the `commandButton` for navigation to the final page of the wizard is enabled.

5. Run the page now, with `/apex/wizard2` appended to the base URL to see that it looks like the figure below.

Figure 197: The second page of your Visualforce wizard

6. Return to edit your custom controller code. Change the method called `step2` to return the name of this second page, following the class name of `Page`. For instance, if your second page is called `wizard2`, the correct code for the `step2` method will be as follows:

```
public PageReference step2() {
       return Page.wizard2;
    }
```

7. Save your controller code.

You can now test the first two pages of your wizard by loading the first page, selecting a position, and then clicking **Select Candidate**.

You have provided your users with two Visualforce pages that lead them through the process of selecting a closed position and then a candidate for that position. The final page in your wizard provides a way to schedule interviews on a particular day with a time assigned for each interviewer.

Displaying Interviewers

Once again, create the final page of your wizard in the controller code.

This time, add two new elements to your controller code, and handle them slightly differently in your Visualforce page.

1. Return to edit the custom controller through the **Setup ➤ Develop ➤ Apex Code** choice, and then click **Edit** for the controller class.
2. Add the following code to the controller class:

```
public Interview__c intDate {
  get {
    if(intDate == null) {
      intDate = new Interview__c();
    }
    return intDate;
  }
  set;
}

public List<Interview__c> jobApplicationInterviewers {
  get {
    if(jobApplicationInterviewers == null) {
      jobApplicationInterviewers =
        [select Interview__c.ID, Interviewer__r.Name,
        Interview__c.Interview_Date__c,
        Interview__c.Interview_Time__c
        from Interview__c
        where Job_Application__r.ID =
        :selectedJobApplication];
      }
      return jobApplicationInterviewers;
  }
  set;
}
```

Once again, you add two new variables to the controller code. The first is an instance of the Interview__c object. You use this to hold a value for the date of the scheduled interviews. Since the value entered for this date is added to all the interview records, you do not want to bind the `inputField` on the Visualforce page to the collection of Interview__c records. As with the earlier property, this property performs an `if` test to determine if initialization is needed.

The second variable declares and populates that collection of Interview__c records that are related to the candidate for the position chosen on the previous page. The ID for the Job Application record is the value of the ID chosen in the selectList on the second page of the wizard, as it should be.

With these changes, you are ready to add the final Visualforce page for your wizard. The code for this page is shown below, and was loaded into your organization under the name of `wizard3` with the initialization script for this chapter:

```
<apex:page controller="customController">
    <apex:sectionHeader title="Interview Scheduler"
      subtitle="Step 3 of 3 - Schedule interview times"/>
    <apex:form >
        <apex:pageBlock >
            <apex:pageBlockSection columns="1">
                <apex:pageBlockTable
                  value="{!jobApplicationInterviewers}" var="int">
                    <apex:column headervalue="Interviewer"
                      value="{!int.Interviewer__r.Name}"/>
                    <apex:column headervalue="Interview Time">
                        <apex:inputField
                          value="{!int.Interview_Time__c}"/>
                    </apex:column>
                </apex:pageBlockTable>
            </apex:pageBlockSection>
            <apex:pageBlockSection >
                <apex:pageBlockSectionItem >
                    <apex:outputLabel
                      value="Date for interviews:"/>
                    <apex:inputField
                      value="{!intDate.Interview_Date__c}"/>
                </apex:pageBlockSectionItem>
            </apex:pageBlockSection>
            <apex:pageblockButtons location="bottom">
                <apex:commandButton action="{!Save}"
                  value="Save"/>
            </apex:pageblockButtons>
        </apex:pageBlock>
    </apex:form>
</apex:page>
```

This Visualforce page is slightly more complex than the previous pages. There are two `pageBlockSections`: one to hold the display of Interviewers in a `pageBlockTable` and another to specify the date for al the interviews. This paricular implementation assumes that all interviews will be conducted on the same day, so a user can specify a date once for all the interviews. The code you create for your save method adds this value to all of the interviews listed in this page.

3. Return to your controller code and edit the `step3` navigation method to point to this third page. Once you save the third page as `wizard3`, the completed method looks like this:

```
public PageReference step3() {
       return Page.wizard3;
    }
```

4. Run your wizard from the first page to the last to see how it flows. The third page, with data, should look like the figure below.

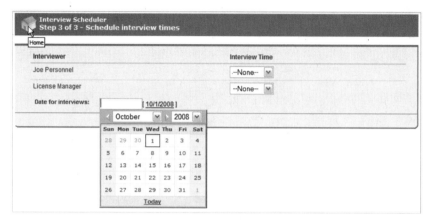

Figure 198: The third page of your Visualforce wizard

You have now implemented the user interface portion of your wizard, along with the custom controller code to make them work nicely together. Your last task is to complete the work that your user specified with the wizard by saving the interviews with their date and time.

Saving the Data

The last piece of functionality for your custom controller is the most important. The save method for a standard controller saves the changed records back to the Force Platform database object. The save method for this custom controller must first set the date selected on the third page as the value for the Interview_Date__c field for all appropriate interview records, and then save those records.

The code for this save method is shown below:

```
public PageReference save() {
  for (Interview__c i : jobApplicationInterviewers) {
    i.Interview_Date__c = intDate.Interview_Date__c;
  }
  update jobApplicationInterviewers;
  return new ApexPages.StandardController(new
    Job_Application__c(id = selectedJobApplication)).view();
}
```

The code first walks through the array of Interviewer records to add the date from the Interview Date inputField at the top of the page to any records that contain a value for the Interview_Time__c field. If an Interview record does not have a time specified, there is no reason to add a value for the Interview_Date__c field. Once you have properly set this value in the array, you can simply update the array.

Once the update is performed, the `return` sends back a page reference derived from the `ApexPages` class. The page returned is a view page for a standard controller for a Job Application record. The Job Application record displayed in the page is identified with the ID of the `selectJobApplication`, which was the focus of the update operation.

As usual, bracket your write operation with `try/catch` code, in the event that there is a problem with the update.

1. Open the Apex class for the custom controller.
2. Add the code for the save method to your custom controller.

The complete code for your custom controller class is included as a document in the Code Share project for this book and chapter under the name CustomController.txt, and is shown below:

```
public class customController {

public List<selectOption> openPositionList {
  get {
    List<selectOption> returnOpenPositions =
      new List<selectOption>();
    String positionInfo;
    for (Position__c p : [select name, job_description__c,
      department__c, position_type__c, status__c
      from Position__c where status__c = 'Open']) {
        positionInfo = p.name + ' - ' + p.department__c +
        ' - ' + p.job_description__c;
        returnOpenPositions.add(new
          selectOption(p.ID, positionInfo));
    }
    return returnOpenPositions;
    }
    set;
}

public Position__c selectedPosition {
  get {
    if(selectedPosition == null) {
    selectedPosition = new Position__c();
    }
    return selectedPosition;
    }
    set;
}

public List<selectOption> jobApplicationCandidates {
  get {
    List<selectOption> candidates =
```

```
            new List<selectOption>();
        for (Job_Application__c JA : [select Candidate__r.ID,
            Candidate__r.first_name__c, Candidate__r.last_name__c,
            status__c
            from Job_Application__c
            where (Position__r.ID = :selectedPosition.ID) and
            (Status__c = 'Interviewing')] ) {
                candidates.add(new selectoption(JA.ID,
                    JA.Candidate__r.First_Name__c + ' ' +
                    JA.Candidate__r.last_name__c));
        }
        return candidates;
        }
        set;
}

public ID selectedJobApplication {get; set;}

public Interview__c intDate {
    get {
        if(intDate == null) {
            intDate = new Interview__c();
        }
        return intDate;
        }
        set;
}

public List<Interview__c> jobApplicationInterviewers {
    get {
        if(jobApplicationInterviewers == null) {
            jobApplicationInterviewers = [select Interview__c.ID,
                Interviewer__r.Name, Interview__c.Interview_Date__c,
                Interview__c.Interview_Time__c
                from Interview__c
                where Job_Application__r.ID = :selectedJobApplication];
            }
        return jobApplicationInterviewers;
    }
    set;
}

public PageReference step2() {
    return Page.wizard2;
}

public PageReference step3() {
    return Page.wizard3;
}


public PageReference save() {
    for (Interview__c i : jobApplicationInterviewers) {
        i.Interview_Date__c = intDate.Interview_Date__c;
        }
    update jobApplicationInterviewers;
```

```
    return new ApexPages.StandardController(new
      Job_Application__c(id = selectedJobApplication)).view();
}

}
```

Of course, you might want to implement even more logic in your custom controller. For instance, you might want to add code to check and make sure that none of the interviews occurred at the same time, or that every interview had a time scheduled.

 Tip: An enhanced version of the custom controller code with this functionlaity is available in the Code Share project for this book.

This type of logic is simply more Apex code, which, as a developer, you should be able to implement to match your particular use cases.

Integrating Your Wizard

Your wizard should now be working properly. The custom controller maintains data values across multiple pages and handles the logic needed to properly apply the simplified user interface to the appropriate records. In this particular use case, your users want to be able to access this interview scheduling capability directly from a tab.

1. Go to **Setup ➤ Create ➤ Tabs**.
2. Click **Create** in the Visualforce Tabs section.
3. On the next page, specify a tab label and tab name. Give your tab a `Label` of `Interview Wizard` and accept the default tab name. Select a tab style and give the new tab a brief description. Click **Next**.
4. Accept the default security settings and click **Next**.
5. Uncheck the `Include Tab` checkbox for all applications except your Recruiting application and click **Save**.

The new tab appears as part of the tab set in your application. Clicking the tab brings you to the first page of your interview wizard, just the way your users wanted.

Summary

Over the course of *Chapter 9: Visualforce Pages* and this chapter, you have had a quick tour of the capabilities of Visualforce technology. You learned how you can implement flexible and robust user interface pages with standard controllers, and how you can expand your options even more with extensions to standard controllers and custom controllers. You also had a brief look at creating your own Visualforce components, which can improve your productivity by eliminating multiple implementations of the same interface.

You can go even further with Visualforce and Apex, as you will learn in the next chapter, which covers how you can allow people to use email to communicate to your Force Platform data objects, and how to use Visualforce pages to create email templates and Adobe PDF documents.

Chapter 13

Email Services with the Force Platform

So far, this book has focused on areas of the Force Platform that allow you to build solutions for your community of Force Platform users. This chapter introduces four features that allow you to extend your application out into the broader population of users through the use of email and the popular PDF (Portable Document Format) format from Adobe.

The examples in this chapter add functionality to the existing recruiting application. You will learn how to build an email handler that receives an applicant email for a given position and automatically creates a Candidate record, associates that candidate with the appropriate position, and creates a Job Application record. email attachments, such as resumes, will be associated with the Job Application record. Those candidates chosen for interviews will be sent an email with interview schedule information attached in PDF form. You will also see how you and your users are able to customize emails through email templates created as Visualforce pages.

 Note: If you have been following the examples in the previous chapter, your Force Platform organization should be ready for the exercises in this chapter. If you have not done the exercises, or want to start with a fresh version of the sample Recruiting application, please refer to the instructions in the Code Share project for this book. You can find information on how to access that project in *Chapter 1: Welcome to the Force Platform*. In addition, the project contains instructions on how to update your organization with changes required for this chapter.

Handling Inbound Emails

Email has become one of the most common communication methods in the electronic world. The Force Platform has done a lot of the heavy lifting for receiving inbound email, in terms of security, authenticity, and parsing of messages.

In order to handle incoming emails, you need to perform two tasks. The first is to create an Apex class that implements a specific Apex interface for the incoming emails. The second is to perform some setup tasks to enable this interface through the Email Services page.

Once you have completed these tasks, the Force Platform automatically generates an email address that receives incoming messages. The receipt of a message triggers the execution of this functionality, implemented in the same Apex class.

Implementing the InboundEmailHandler Interface

The role of interfaces in Apex is to describe a set of methods in terms of their names, parameters and the type of data they return. These three aspects are known as a methods signature. An interface does not define the actual code within the methods, just the signature for the methods.

In this section you will implement methods for a Force Platform-supplied interface, enabling the platform to call your code when an inbound email message arrives.

The first step to handling inbound emails is to create an Apex class. The class, which was loaded into your organization with the initialization procedure called out at the beginning of the chapter, uses the `implements` Apex language keyword to create a class that implements the Force Platform Messaging.InboundMailHandler interface. This class includes a method that matches the signature defined in the interface.

The following code sample shows a basic implementation of this interface:

```
global class ProcessApplicants implements
  Messaging.InboundEmailHandler
{
  global Messaging.InboundEmailResult handleInboundEmail
        (Messaging.InboundEmail email,
         Messaging.InboundEnvelope env)
  {
    Messaging.InboundEmailResult result = new
      Messaging.InboundEmailresult();
    return result;
  }
}
```

The class and the interface methods use the global access modifier, covered in *Chapter 10: Apex*. The `handleInboundEmail` method uses two parameters that are passed to your code by the Force Platform. These parameters contain information taken from the inbound message, relieving you of the need to parse the raw SMTP message.

The code samples in this section are taken from the full implementation of the `ProcessApplicants` Apex class, which handles the incoming emails. This class was loaded into your organization as part of the setup process for this chapter, described above. You can view the code in this class in full from either your Eclipse environment or through **Setup ➤ Develop ➤ Apex Classes**.

The `email` parameter represents the email itself, and gives you access to various header information, such as from, to, and cc, as well as the body of the email and potentially any attachments, covered later in this chapter. The envelope parameter provides additional information relating specifically to the actual email addresses used for sending and receiving the email. The `InboundEmailResult` object and result is used to return any errors handling the message to the calling Apex class.

Access to additional email information

The headers field on the InboundEmail class also provides access to information not explicitly exposed as fields, such as RFC 2822 headers like Message-ID, Date, and also any custom headers as defined by the sending server.

Only text-based attachments with a MIME type of either text or application/octet-stream are supported, in the later case only file names ending with .vcf or .vcs extension specifically. Binary attachments are available through the bindaryAttachments field and text through the textAttachments field on the InboundEmail class. Attachments within the email, such as inline graphics, are not supported.

You have a variety of options to specify how your Apex message handler handles the information in the incoming email message. The example in this chapter makes some basic assumptions about the email content in terms of the subject and body contents. The subject of the email is always the Name of the record for the position in the Position__c object, which was defined as an auto-number field that produces values like POS-00004. Any attachments on an incoming email is automatically attached to the resulting Job Application record.

The figure below shows an example of the type of email the code in this chapter is expecting.

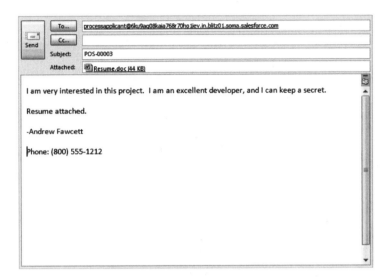

Figure 199: Sample incoming email

These emails are generated from hyperlinks on a Visualforce page in the Universal Containers recruiting application.

 Note: In *Chapter 14: Taking Your Application Public with Force Platform Sites*, you will learn how to use Force Platform Sites to expose a Visualforce page to the outside world.

The links automatically add the Position name as the subject and direct the email to the correct Force Platform email address.

Your application will use a Visualforce page to create incoming email applications. This Visualforce page, `availablePositions`, and the custom controller it uses, the `AvailablePositionsController`, were also loaded into your organization with the initialization scripts described at the start of this chapter.

Parsing the Inbound Message

The following code fragment from the `processApplicant` class shows how the Position name in the subject line, and the candidates' first and second names are read from the `email` parameter via the `fromName` and `subject` fields.

```
String firstName =
  email.fromName.substring(0,email.fromName.indexOf(' '));
String lastName =
```

```
email.fromName.substring(email.fromName.indexOf(' '));
String positionName = email.subject;
```

The code shown in the next fragment is used to obtain the phone number, parsed from the `plainTextBody` field.

```
integer phoneMatchIdx = email.indexOf( PHONE_MATCH );
if(phoneMatchIdx==-1)
  throw new ProcessApplicantException(
    'Please state your phone number following
      Phone: in your message.');
String phoneNumber =
  email.plainTextBody.substring( phoneMatchIdx +
    PHONE_MATCH.length() );
```

The text string `Phone:` is placed in a static String variable `PHONE_MATCH` at the top of the `ProcessApplicants` class for reuse purposes. The `indexOf` method searches the `plainTextBody` field for the first occurrence of 'Phone:', with the assumption that the next characters are the phone number. The search either returns an index for the initial position of the text for the phone number or -1 if no match is found. If no match is found, the `indexOf` function returns -1, which causes an exception to be thrown and feedback is sent the user.

Catching errors

In the code sample below, you can see that the class throws its own exception in the event of a logical error. The message field on the `Messaging.InboundEmailResult` class is then used to catch potential problems in the incoming emails, such as missing required information. The code sample used in this chapter uses an Apex exception class and a `try/catch` block to manage error handling in the handler as shown below.

```
Messaging.InboundEmailResult result = new
Messaging.InboundEmailresult();
  try
  {
    // Obtain the applicants Phone number from the message body
    integer phoneMatchIdx =
      email.plainTextBody.indexOf( PHONE_MATCH );
    if(phoneMatchIdx==-1)
      throw new ProcessApplicantException(
        'Please state your phone number following Phone:
          in your message.');
    String phoneNumber =
      email.plainTextBody.substring( phoneMatchIdx +
        PHONE_MATCH.length() );

    // ...
```

```
    result.success = true;
  }
  catch (Exception e)
  {
    // Return an email message to the user
    result.success = false;
    result.message =
      'An error occurred processing your message.' +
        e.getMessage();
  }
  return result;
```

Loading the Position

Once the required information is extracted from the incoming email, additional Apex code handles the next task of reading the Position record for the job application being processed. The SOQL query for the record retrieval is wrapped within a `try/catch` block to handle the circumstance where the Position record is not found. If the Position record is not located, the resulting `DmlException` is caught and a new exception is thrown with text explaining the issue to the user.

```
// Resolve the Id of the Position they are applying for
Id positionId;
try
{
  // Lookup the Position they are applying for by name
  Position__c position =
    [select Id from Position__c where name = :positionName limit 1];
  positionId = position.Id;
}
catch (Exception e)
{
  // Record not found
  throw new ProcessApplicantException(
    'Sorry the position ' + positionName +
      ' does not currently exist.');
}
```

Checking for the Candidate

Once your Apex code extracts the required information from the email and determines what Position is being applied for, the code checks to see if a Candidate record exists for the person who sent in the email. The logical test used is a comparison of the sender's email address with the email addresses in Candidate records. If a Candidate is not found, the code creates a new Candidate record.

Once again, the code uses a `try/catch` block around the SOQL that used the Candidate's email address to try and find the matching record. If the record is not found, the code catches the `DmlException` and then creates a new Candidate record.

```
// Candidate record for the applicant sending this email
Candidate__c candidate;
try
{
  // Attempt to read an existing Candidate by email address
  Candidate__c[] candidates =
    [select Id from Candidate__c where email__c = :emailFrom];
  candidate = candidates[0];
}
catch (Exception e)
{
  // Record not found, create a new Candidate record for this applicant

  candidate = new Candidate__c();
  candidate.email__c = :emailFrom;
  candidate.first_name__c = firstName;
  candidate.last_name__c = lastName;
  candidate.phone__c = phoneNumber;
  insert candidate;
}
```

Creating the Job Application

A Job Application record is created as a junction object between an individual candidate and an individual position. Once you know the Position and the Candidate, your code can create a Job Application record, as shown below.

```
// Create the Job Application record
Job_Application__c jobApplication = new Job_Application__c();
jobApplication.Position__c = positionId;
jobApplication.Candidate__c = candidate.id;
insert jobApplication;
```

Handling Attachments

Once the Job Application record exists, your code can add attachments to the record. You use the `binaryAttachments` field to discover any attachments to the email and then create an Attachment record for each one. This logic, attaches any resume the candidate might have attached to the email with the following code:

```
if (binaryAttachments!=null && binaryAttachments.size() > 0)
  {
```

```
for (integer i = 0 ; i < binaryAttachments.size() ; i++)
{
  Attachment attachment = new Attachment();
  attachment.ParentId = jobApplication[0].Id;
  attachment.Name = binaryAttachments[i].Filename;
  attachment.Body = binaryAttachments[i].Body;
  insert attachment;
  }
}
```

Note the `Body` field on the `BinaryAttachment` class can be directly assigned to the `Body` field on the Attachment object record since this field is defined by a Force Platform email class as being a BLOB (Binary Large Object) field.

Later in this chapter, you will see how to add code to this handler to send a notification email back to the applicant to confirm successful receipt of their email.

The previous sections covered the Apex class that does the main work of handling the interface to Force Platform email services. But before you can use them, you have to set up email services.

Setting up Email Services

Now that you have created an Apex class to handle incoming emails, you need to setup and configure Email Services in your organization. You can accomplish this through the **Email Services** page in the **Develop** section of the App Setup area.

On this page, you can create any number of named Email Services and associate them with the Apex classes you have written to handle incoming emails received by these services.

The figure below illustrates the flow of messages into your organization.

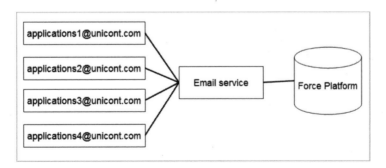

Figure 200: Flow of email messages into an organization

Each Email Service can be associated with one or more email addresses, defined in part by you and in part automatically by the Force Platform. You can designate an Email Service as active or inactive. You can define how the Force Platform responds to inactive email addresses when you setup the Email Service.

Create an Email Service with the following steps and the `ProcessApplicant` Apex class, described above and already loaded into your organization.

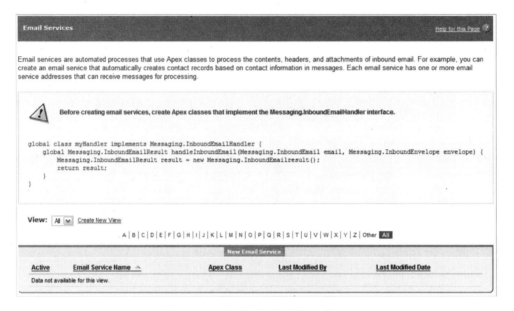

Figure 201: Defining Email services

1. Go to **Setup ➤ Develop ➤ Email Services**, to display the page shown above.
2. Click **New Email Services**.
3. Name the service `ProcessApplicant`.
4. Use the lookup button to search for applicable Apex classes. Select the `AvailablePositionsController`
5. For `Accept Attachments`, select `Binary Attachments only`, as the code in this chapter only supports these.
6. Leave `Advanced Email Security` unchecked. When enabled, this option provides greater authenticity against the sending email server. Checking this option requires the sending server to support at least one of the following security protocols: `SPF`, `SenderID` or `DomainKeys`.

   For more information on this feature and these protocols, click the Help link for this page.

7. The `Accept From` field allows you to explicitly state email addresses or domains from which this service accepts inbound email, in a comma-separated list. For the purposes of this exercise, leave this field blank.

8. Select the `Active` checkbox.

9. You can configure how Force Platform responds to various conditions, such as deactivated email addresses or services, or, as described above, servers that are unable to authenticate themselves. Leave the defaults as they are for now.

10. Click **Save and New Email Address** to move to the Email Services Address page, shown below.

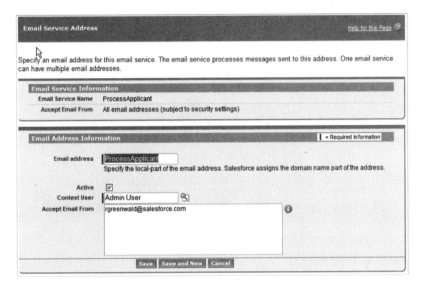

Figure 202: Email Services Address page

11. Accept the default values on this page and click **Save** to create an email address for this service. The resulting email address is a combination of the address field on this page plus a system-generated domain part.

Email Address Page

The email address associated with a service can be set to activate or inactive.

The Context User field allows you to define the user the Force Platform uses to run your Apex message handler. If you change the default for this field, make sure this user has the correct permissions to execute the Apex class.

If your Apex code or code it calls uses any of the methods from the `UserInfo` system class, provided as a part of Apex, be aware that these methods return the user defined on the email address as the Context user and not the user sending the email message.

The **Accept Email From** field must contain a subset of the emails and domains listed in the **Accept From** field on the previous Email Service definition page.

Testing Inbound Emails from Applicants

Now that you have written your Apex handler and created an Email Service to receive the emails, you are ready to test your new functionality.

As part of the setup for this chapter, a Visualforce page and controller was added to your organization to render a list of available positions with appropriate email hyperlinks for applicants to click on. To navigate to the page as shown below, enter `/apex/availablepositions` after the instance part of the URL in your browser, for example `http://c.emea.visualforce.com/apex/availablepositions`.

Available Positions
The following positions are currently available

Action	Job Description	Salary Grade
Apply	Second tier technical support.	SUP-200
Apply	Leader of stealth project.	ENG-400
Apply	Product Marketing Manager for new product.	SAL-200
Apply	Vice President of channel sales.	SAL-400
Apply	Quality Assurance engineer for new product.	ENG-200
Apply	QA assistant.	ENG-100
Apply	Administrative assistant to VP of Finance.	FIN-100
Apply	HA specialist.	IT-400
Apply	Technical marketing manager.	ENG-200
Apply	Support representative.	SUP-100
Apply	Mid-level accountant	FIN-200
Apply	Director of Auditing	FIN-300
Apply	Develop modules of new product.	ENG-300
Apply	Field rep.	SAL-100
Apply	Accounts receivables clerk.	FIN-100

Figure 203: Visualforce page to send an email

1. Bring up the Visualforce page shown above in your browser.
2. Click the **Apply** link for a given Job Description to open your email client. Note that the hyperlinks have pre-filled the email recipient and subject line for the user, as well as the phone number of the current user.

3. Complete the rest of the email with an appropriate message, such as the one shown earlier in this chapter..

4. Attach a file to the message and send it.

If your Apex class works properly, the email address you used to send the message receives an automated confirmation email that your job application has been received and processed. This response email is sent using the Apex Outbound Email API, covered in the next section.

 Caution: Was the incoming application accepted, or was an error reported? If the position that was receiving the application had the requirement to reject undereducated applicants, indicated with a checkbox, the incoming application may have been rejected for this reason. This rejection is good news, since it indicates that the validations are still enforced, even for applications made through the email handling service.

5. Use the Candidates and Job Applications tabs to look for the new records.

 Caution: The code in the `AvailablePositionsController` Apex class used as the controller for this page has automatically read the first email address from the Email Service, named `ProcessApplicant`. For this page to work properly, you must have completed all the steps earlier in this chapter to setup this specific Email Service with the name of `ProcessApplicant`.

Sending Email

To help your applications send emails, the Force Platform provides a comprehensive set of built-in classes and methods that allow you to send either basic text-based messages or rich HTML messages with attachments through the use of Apex code.

Basics of Sending Email

You do not need to be an expert to get started sending emails from your Apex code. The `SendEmail` Apex class has been uploaded into your organization as part of the chapter setup; the methods within it are referenced throughout this section.

Before running the following code samples in this section, open your preferred Apex code editor and modify the value of the `EMAIL_ADDRESS` static variable in the `sendMail` class, as shown in the following code. Your email address will be used throughout the samples in the

SendEMail class using this variable. The method in this class, SendSimple, sends an email to you using only five lines of code.

```
public class SendEMail
{
  private static final String EMAIL_ADDRESS = 'fred.blogs@acme.com';

  public static void sendSimple()
  {
    Messaging.SingleEmailMessage mail = new
Messaging.SingleEmailMessage();
    mail.setToAddresses(new String[] { EMAIL_ADDRESS });
    mail.setSubject('Message from Apex!');
    mail.setPlainTextBody('This is the message body');
    Messaging.SendEmailResult result =
    Messaging.sendEmail(new Messaging.SingleEmailMessage[]
    { mail });
  }
}
```

You can see this code at work through the Force Platform IDE.

To execute the sendSimple method in this class, either enter the following line of Apex code into the Execute Anonymous tab within the Force Platform IDE, or, if you are using the Setup menu, click the System Log link (located in the top right of the page when logged into your organization). Enter the following code into the edit field above the Execute Apex >> button and click that button.

```
SendEmail.sendSimple();
```

You should see the following in the diagnostics output:

```
13:58:16 INFO  - 20080724125816.360:Class.SendEMail.simple: line 9,
column 9:    Single email queued for send (pending commit) :  subject:
 Message from Apex!, bccSender: false, saveAsActivity: true,
useSignature: true, toAddresses: [fred.blogs@acme.com], plainTextBody:
 This is the message body,
```

The platform has queued your email for sending. Be aware that email messages generated from the Apex are placed in a queue, rather than being sent immediately when the code is executed, although the messages are typically sent within a few seconds.

 Voice of the Developer:

You might have noticed that the Message.sendMail method takes an array of messages to send, so you can send multiple messages in one single call. This feature is important to avoid hitting limits on the email governor.

As with SOQL and DML statements executed in Apex code, the number of email invocations per request is governed by the platform. By default, the Messaging.sendEmail method can only be called a maximum of 10 times in a request before an exception is thrown. In addition to this limit, there is a daily limit for the sending organization. Once this is reached, an error status of MASS_MAIL_LIMIT_EXCEEDED is returned for all subsequent calls that day.

Error messages are retrieved via the Messaging.SendEmailResult object returned from the SendMail method. The getSendEmailError method on this object returns a list of SendEmailError objects (one for each email object passed in). If the isSuccess field on this object is false, then the getStatusCode method on each of the SendEmailError objects should be checked for more information.

In the simple example above, the email address is hard-coded in the class, which is rarely a good practice. Your Apex code can get email addresses dynamically by executing SOQL statements to read email addresses.

Since email clients can be configured to disallow HTML emails, make sure that you provide at least a text-based representation of your email via the setPlainTextBody method. Then, if you wish, call setHTMLBody.

There are other methods on the Messaging.SingleEmailMessage class that allow you to have further control over the email message sent, such as the sender display name, reply to address, CC, BCC addresses, and the use of email signatures. The class also supports attachments to email messages.

For a full list of the methods on the classes referenced in this chapter, refer to the *Force Platform Apex Language Reference* documentation.

Sending Email with Attachments

The Messaging.SingleEmailMessage class provides two options for you to add an attachment to the emails you generate from your Apex code: the setDocumentAttachments and the setFileAttachments methods.

The setDocumentAttachments method leverages the standard Document functionality available to users, allowing them to store documents and images within the organization database. Before running the sample code, use the Documents tab to upload a document entitled SampleEmailAttachment.doc, so that the code used to attach the document works properly.

This code resolves the ID for this document and uses the `setDocumentAttachments` method to attach it to the email.

```
public static void sendWithDocumentAttachment()
{
  Messaging.SingleEmailMessage mail =
   new Messaging.SingleEmailMessage();
  mail.setToAddresses( new String[] { EMAIL_ADDRESS });
  mail.setSubject('Message from Apex!');
  mail.setPlainTextBody('This is the message body');
  mail.setDocumentAttachments(new Id[] {
   [select Id from Document where Name =
    'SampleEmailAttachment.doc'][0].Id });
  Messaging.sendEmail(new Messaging.SingleEmailMessage[] { mail });
}
```

The `setFileAttachments` method requires a bit more work to use, but also provides more flexibility. This flexibility is vital to an example later in this chapter that uses dynamically generated documents. The following code illustrates attaching a dynamically generated text attachment.

```
public static void sendWithDynamicAttachment()
{
  Messaging.SingleEmailMessage mail =
   new Messaging.SingleEmailMessage();
  mail.setToAddresses( new String[] { EMAIL_ADDRESS });
  mail.setSubject('Message from Apex!');
  mail.setPlainTextBody('This is the message body');
  Messaging.EmailFileAttachment mailAttachment;
  mailAttachment = new Messaging.EmailFileAttachment();
  mailAttachment.setFileName('readme.txt');
  mailAttachment.setBody(Blob.valueOf('This is an
   Apex-generated attachment'));
  mail.setFileAttachments(new
   Messaging.EmailFileAttachment[]{mailAttachment});
  Messaging.sendEmail(new Messaging.SingleEmailMessage[] { mail });
}
```

As described earlier, you can execute the sample code in this section using the browser System Log link or the Force Platform IDE. Before executing the following sample, you need to add a file attachment to a given Candidate record and make an edit to the code.

1. Using the Candidate tab, attach a file of your choosing to a Candidate record, making note of the Candidate name, such as CAN-00001.

   The following code is used to attach the document related to this candidate to an email message. Note that the Body field value of Attachment record can be passed directly to the `setBody` method on the `Messaging.EmailFileAttachment` object.

```
public static void sendWithRecordAttachment(ID candidateID)
{
  Attachment candidateAttachment =
    [select Name, Body from Attachment where ParentId =
      :candidateId][0];

  Messaging.SingleEmailMessage mail =
    new Messaging.SingleEmailMessage();
  mail.setToAddresses( new String[] { EMAIL_ADDRESS });
  mail.setSubject('Message from Apex!');
  mail.setPlainTextBody('This is the message body');
  Messaging.EmailFileAttachment mailAttachment;
  mailAttachment = new Messaging.EmailFileAttachment();
  mailAttachment.setFileName(candidateAttachment.Name);
  mailAttachment.setBody(candidateAttachment.Body);
  mail.setFileAttachments(new
    Messaging.EmailFileAttachment[]{mailAttachment});
  Messaging.sendEmail(new Messaging.SingleEmailMessage[] { mail
  });
}
```

You can use this class to send an email with the document attached to the Candidate record attached to the message.

2. Execute the Apex call `SendEmail.sendWithRecordAttachment(string)`, where *string* is the name of the Candidate record with the attachment.

This slightly more complex method of sending a customized email message will be used again, in an expanded version, in the next section.

Sending an Automatic Email Response Back to the Applicant

Now that you understand how Apex code can be used to send emails, you can fully understand how the `ProcessApplicants` class is able to send an automated confirmation email back to the applicant. The code in this class used to achieve this is as follows:

```
// Confirm receipt of the applicants email
Messaging.SingleEmailMessage mail = new Messaging.SingleEmailMessage();
mail.setToAddresses( new String[] { emailFrom });
mail.setSubject('Your job application has been received');
mail.setPlainTextBody('Thank you for submitting your resume.
  We will contact you shortly to setup interviews');
Messaging.sendEmail(new Messaging.SingleEmailMessage[] { mail });
```

PDFs with Visualforce Pages

Over the past few chapters of this book, you have seen the power of Visualforce technology, with its ability to format virtually any style of HTML, and interact with almost any sources of data; however, the display of these Visualforce pages has always been within a browser, meaning that the results are eventually generated as HTML pages.

There are times when your users may want something more. In this section, you will see how an interview schedule can be produced in PDF form with the `candidateinterviewschedule` Visualforce page. This page was loaded into your organization as part of the chapter setup. This section will also show you how the PDF this page produces can be attached to an email sent out to candidates.

The samples in this section can be executed by two Custom Buttons: `View Schedule` and `Email Schedule`. As part of the setup for this chapter, these two buttons have been added to the Job Application layout, as shown below.

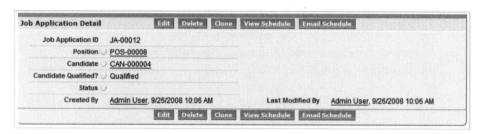

Figure 204: Custom buttons to interact with a Visualforce PDF

Creating a PDF with Visualforce

Instructing Visualforce pages to render as PDF documents is pretty straight forward, as the following boiler plate page shows. You accomplish this using the `renderAs` attribute on the `<apex:page>` root element of the page, with a value of `pdf`, as shown in the basic code which follows.

```
<apex:page controller="CandidateInterviewFormController" renderAs="pdf">
</apex:page>
```

Although you can apply the `renderAs` attribute retroactively to existing Visualforce pages, the results might vary depending on what other Visualforce elements have been used. Because of this, it is recommended that you design such Visualforce pages with printed output in mind from the outset, using only output elements, such as text and image. Any CSS or image files used on the page via `<apex:stylesheet>` or `<apex:image>` are automatically embedded within the resulting PDF document.

 Voice of the Developer: It might sometimes be desirable to develop a reusable page that can conditionally target both HTML output and PDF output since you may want to avoid a strict dependency on PDF rendering. You can achieve this result by adding a field to your controller class and referencing it from the renderAs attribute; for example: `renderAs="{!renderAs}"`, where the value of this variable determines the format of the output. For instance, this bind variable can be set based on a Page URL parameter. In this scenario, you can have two buttons for the user to choose from: `Print Interview Form (HTML)` and `Print Interview Form (PDF)`, each passing a URL parameter to indicate to the controller what to return in the `getRenderAs` method.

The Job Application and Interviewer records rendered within the PDF are retrieved by the associated page controller. The following Apex code uses SOQL to return a list of Interview object records that relate to a specific Job Application record ID.

```
public class CandidateInterviewScheduleController
{
  public Job_Application__c getJobApplication()
  {
    // Retrieve Job Application based on Id parameter of this page
    return [Select Id,
              Position__r.Job_Description__c,
              Position__r.Department__c,
              Candidate__r.First_Name__c,
              Candidate__r.Last_Name__c
            from Job_Application__c j
            where Id =
ApexPages.currentPage().getParameters().get('id')];
  }

  public List<Interview__c> getInterviewList()
  {
    // Full list of interview times
    return [select Name, Interviewer__r.Name, Interview_Date__c
            from Interview__c
            where Job_Application__c =
            ApexPages.currentPage().getParameters().get('id') ];
  }
}
```

The implementation of the `candidateinterviewschedule` page retrieves the data for the page in the same way that it does for an HTML Visualforce page. To style PDF output, use standard CSS styling. The PDF rendering in Visualforce responds to additional CSS described in the CSS3 Module: Paged Media W3C standard. Read more about this at `http://www.w3.org/TR/css3-page/`.

The following fragment from this page shows you how the box layout was achieved for the interview dates using standard Visualforce elements and some inline CSS styling.

```
<apex:dataTable value="{!interviewlist}" var="interview"
columnsWidth="30px,200px, 200px" rules="rows" cellpadding="2px">
        <apex:column style="border: 1px solid black">
            <apex:facet name="header">Interview ID</apex:facet>
            <apex:outputText value="{!interview.Name}"/>
        </apex:column>
        <apex:column style="border: 1px solid black">
            <apex:facet name="header">Interviewer</apex:facet>
            <apex:outputText
                value="{!interview.Interviewer__r.Name}"/>
        </apex:column>
        <apex:column style="border: 1px solid black">
            <apex:facet name="header">Date</apex:facet>
            <apex:outputText
                value="{!interview.Interview_Date__c}"/>
        </apex:column>
        <apex:column style="border: 1px solid black">
            <apex:facet name="header">Time</apex:facet>
            <apex:outputText
                value="{!interview.Interview_Time_2__c}"/>
        </apex:column>
    </apex:dataTable>
```

Adding a Button to the Job Application Page

The Visualforce page that will be rendered as a PDF is ready, along with the custom controller used to populate it. Your last step is to integrate the page into the standard Job Application detail page through a custom button.

1. 1. Go to **Setup ➤ Create ➤ Objects ➤ Job Application** and scroll to the Custom Buttons and Links section of the page to click **New**.
2. Select the `Detail Page Button` for the `Type`. Give the new button a `Label` of `View Schedule`, and an appropriate description. Leave the `Behavior` and the `Content Source` with the default values.
3. Add the following code to the formula window:

   ```
   /apex/candidateinterviewschedule?id={!Job_Application__c.Id}
   ```

   This code will append onto your instance to call the candidateinterviewschedule Visualforce page, passing the ID of the current Job Application as a parameter.

4. Click **Save**.
5. Scroll to the Page Layouts section of the Job Application object detail page and click **Edit** for the only page layout listed.

6. Double-click Detail Page Buttons in the Button Section and add the `View Schedule` button to the Selected Buttons list.

7. Click **Save** to include the button in the page layout.

8. Select the Job Application tab in your application and click on a Job Application record.

9. Click the **View Schedule** button.

The figure below shows the PDF Interview Schedule for the associated candidate summoned from the button.

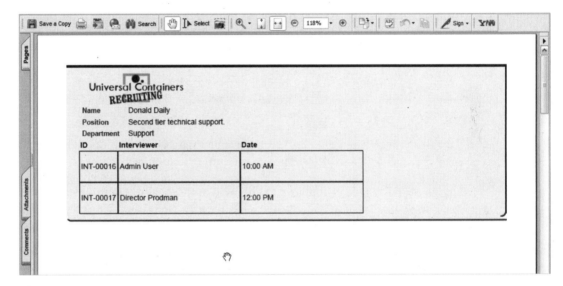

Figure 205: A Visualforce PDF

Attaching a Visualforce PDF to an Email

You can also use the `candidateinterviewschedule` Visualforce page from another Visualforce page. The initiating Visualforce page can be called from the button associated with the Job Applications object. You can create the button just as you did for the **View Schedule** button, except that this time you should have the button call the Visualforce page called `emailCandidateSchedule`, which was loaded, along with its custom controller, in the initialization process for this chapter.

Clicking on the button brings up the page shown below, which allows you to specify the recipient of the emailed schedule.

Figure 206: Using a Visualforce page to send an email

The controller code for the Visualforce page simply calls the method in the `sendMail` class that is used to send a message with an attachment.

Visualforce Email Templates

Earlier in this chapter, you created a simple email message by setting the value of the email body in your Apex code.

The Force Platform gives you the ability to create and use email templates that can be used to send email messages with a particular format, substituting relevant data where appropriate.

You can create email templates with text, HTML, or with Visualforce. In this section, you will learn how to use Visualforce to create an email template, and then use that template to send an email to a job applicant. In fact, the Visualforce template you use significantly reduces the amount of code needed to send out the email in the existing code, while also improving the flexibility of the emails sent.

Creating an Email Template

The first of your two steps is to create an email template for the message. You have to have Administrator rights in order to create a template, which you should have with your core developer account.

1. Go to **Setup ➤ Communications Templates ➤ Email Templates** and click **New Template** to bring up the page shown in the figure below.

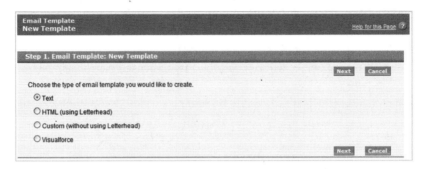

Figure 207: Defining an email template

2. Select `Visualforce` as the template type and click **Next**.

   The following page, shown completed in the figure below, prompts you, in the upper panel, for the basic information required to create this template:

   - Folder - specifies the folder in which to store the template
   - Available for use - makes the template available to users
   - Email Template Name, Developer Name and Description - labels the template, providing a unique identifier for use with the API, and provides a description for internal use

   The lower panel asks for information used to create the outline of the Visualforce page template:

   - Email Subject - the subject of the subsequent email
   - Recipient Type - the source of the email recipient; indicate that a recipient comes from the Salesforce standard objects of Contact or Lead, or the more general User, which contains all Force Platform users.
   - Related To Type - the base table used in the Visualforce controller

   You can use fields from either the Recipient Type object or the Related To Type object in your Visualforce template, as well as any fields you can access through related syntax, just as you can in a standard Visualforce Page.

   For this particular example, you will not need to use the Recipient Type object for Users, as you will see in the remainder of this section.

3. Click the **Available for Use** checkbox, enter `Interview Schedule` as the **Email Template Name** and give the template a description.

4. In the lower panel, enter `Interview Schedule` as the email subject, `User` for the **Recipient Type**, and `Job_Application__c` as the **Related To Type**, and click **Save**.

The following figure displays the lower portion of the newly-created template. The default template text is displayed in the Plain Text Preview, along with two related lists of Visualforce attachments and standard attachments. You can test your email template right now, but why not edit the Visualforce template a bit before getting to that step?

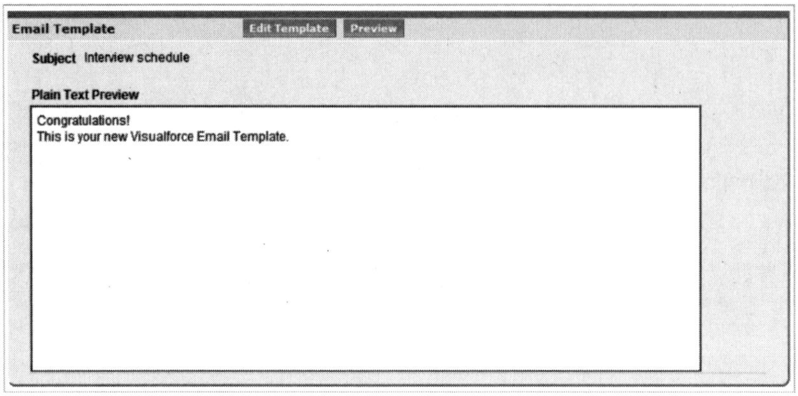

Figure 208: Part of a Visualforce email template

5. Click Edit Template, which will bring you into a standard Visualforce edit window with the generated template code.

   You can see that this template is using components prefaced by messaging: instead of apex:, since these components are from the messaging workspace.

   The template, as currently implemented, uses plainTextEmailBody tags to indicate standard text content. Although best practices call for implementing both a plain text and HTML version of every email, for the purposes of this exercise you can replace this body with an HTML body.

6. Replace the plainTextEmailBody with the new Visualforce code, as shown below.

```
<messaging:emailTemplate
        subject="Interview Schedule"
recipientType="User" relatedToType="Job_Application__c">
<messaging:htmlEmailBody >
Dear {!recipient.Name}, <p/>

You have been selected to interview for position
{!relatedTo.Position__r.Job_Description__c}.   <p/>

The interview schedule is attached.

</messaging:htmlEmailBody>
</messaging:emailTemplate>
```

This template seems to have all the basic information your email needs. You are ready to save the new version and try it out.

7. Save your Visualforce page to return to the detail page for the template.

8. Click **Preview** in the Email Template section of the page to bring up a dialog box, as shown below.

The Preview dialog prompts you for the two values you need to create an email from the template: a User record (or ID) and a Job Application record (or ID).

If you simply give those values, the generated email previews in the Preview area on the detail page for the template. You can also choose to have the email message sent to an email address for further verification that the email looks good.

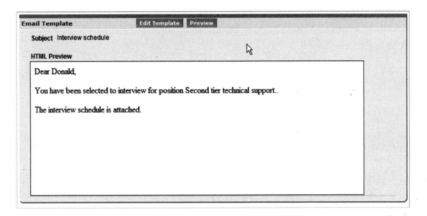

Figure 209: Previewing your Visualforce email template

9. Select a User and a Job Application record, click the `Send email preview` box, and **OK**.

The email appears in the preview box and you should receive an email message that looks very similar to the preview shown above.

The email looks fine, so you can return to the class code for the `sendCandidateSchedule` class to use this template, instead of simply setting the body of the email message. In order to change the code, you need to know the unique ID of the template you just created.

10. Look at the URL of the detail page for your template. Your instance name should be followed by a 15-character unique ID. Copy that ID, in preparation for changing your code.

11. Go to **Setup ➤ Develop ➤ Apex Classes ➤ sendEmail**, and go to the `sendCandidateSchedule` method.

12. Delete all the code in the 'Create the email' section after the first two lines, so that this section looks like the following code:

```
// Create the email to the candidate and attach schedule
  Messaging.SingleEmailMessage mail =
    new Messaging.SingleEmailMessage();
  mail.setToAddresses( new String[]
    { jobApplication.Candidate__r.Email__c });
```

13. Add in the following lines of code:

```
// Create the email to the candidate and attach schedule
Messaging.SingleEmailMessage mail =
    new Messaging.SingleEmailMessage();
mail.setToAddresses( new String[]
    { jobApplication.Candidate__r.Email__c });
mail.setTemplateId(your_template_id);
mail.setwhatId(JobApplicationId);
```

Replace *your_template_id* with the ID for your template. Save your modified code

These two lines of code supply everything your template needs to assemble the email message body. You have successfully integrated your new template into your code, improving the appearance of the outgoing email, as well as simplifying the code used to perform this task.

When you deleted the previous code for the email, you also got rid of the code that attached a Visualforce document to the message. How will you replace that?

As you may have noticed, the email template mentions that the interview schedule is attached to the message. Since the email template itself is a Visualforce page, you can create a Visualforce attachment as part of the template—and it's quite easy.

1. Return to the email template you just created and click **Edit Template**.

2. Place your cursor after the closing tag for the `htmlEmailBody` and before the end tag for the emailTemplate.

3. Enter `<mess` as the start of a new tag. Select the `<messaging:attachment>` tag for inclusion into the code. Save the code for the template.

With these tags, you have identified a portion of the Visualforce page that is created as an attachment. And you already have the Visualforce code for that attachment written.

4. Get the code for the Visualforce attachment from the Code Share project for this book. The code is very similar to the code for the `candidateinterviewschedule`

Visualforce page, with the main differences being that references in field expressions to `Job Application` object have been replaced with the keyword `relatedTo`, since te Job_Applicatoin__c object was identified as that entity in the template.

5. Return to your template and paste the code for the attachment between the `messaging:attachment` tags, removing the beginning and ending page tags.

6. Save the new version of the template.

Now that your Visualforce PDF has been properly added as an attachment, you can see it listed in the related list for your template. You should be able to run this new version of your email from the same button you used before.

1. Return to the detail page for a Job Application and click **Email Schedule**.

2. Enter an email address on the next page and click **Send**. The email sent should look like the figure below, with the attachment included in the email.

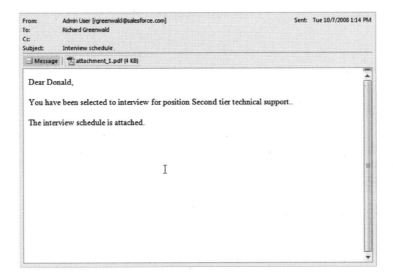

Figure 210: An email from a Visualforce email template

With this code, you have matched the functionality in the previous version of this Apex class. But you may have noticed that you did not use the recipient attribute of the Visualforce template since you used the `setToAddresses` to indicate the address for the email. You had to address the email this way since the recipient attribute was set to point to a record in the User object, and your Candidates, being outside the Force Platform organization, did not have a User record.

Using a Visualforce template for your outgoing emails allows you to include a Visualforce page, rendered as a PDF, with the template, and simplifies the code you need to send a message based on that template.

Summary

In this chapter, you have learned how to extend the reach of your Force Platform applications beyond the confines of your specific organization and its users. The Force Platform includes the ability to receive and send email messages, which you can use to interact with people who are not users of your Force Platform environment.

As you learned about these email services and their implementation, you also discovered how to create PDFs from Visualforce pages, which allowed you to translate information from your Force Platform environment into a portable format for sharing with a broader audience.

Finally, you learned how to use Visualforce to create email templates, which can be combined with those email services to deliver information to users outside your organization in a more attractive fashion.

In the next chapter, you will learn how to open up your Force Platform environment even further.

Chapter 14

Taking Your Application Public with Force Platform Sites

Force Platform organizations contain valuable information about partners, solutions, products, users, ideas, and other business data. Some of this information would be useful to people outside your organization, but only users with the right access and permissions can view and use it. In the past, to make this data available to the general public, you had to set up a Web server, create custom Web pages (JSP, PHP, or other), and perform API integration between your site and your organization. Additionally, if you wanted to collect information using a Web form, you had to program your pages to perform data validation.

With Force Platform Sites, you no longer have to do any of those things. Force Platform Sites enable you to create public websites and applications that are directly integrated with your Force Platform organization—without requiring users to log in with a username and password.

In this chapter, you will walk through an example of how you can use sites to create a public job posting site from the data in your Force Platform organization. The examples include information on developing the Visualforce pages you need, customizing the site's look and feel, configuring your site to accept online applications and resumes, allowing online registration and login to the Customer Portal, and testing your site.

What Are Force Platform Sites?

Use Force Platform Sites to publicly expose any information stored in your organization through pages that you can brand to match the look and feel for your company. Sites are hosted on the Force Platform servers, so there are no data integration issues. And because sites are built on native Visualforce pages, data validation on collected information is performed automatically. You can also enable users to register for or log in to an associated Customer Portal seamlessly from your public site.

The following examples illustrate a few ways that you can use Force Platform Sites:

- Create a Salesforce Ideas site—Use Force Platform Sites to host a public community forum for sharing and voting on ideas about your company, services, or products. Salesforce Ideas sites can be made public using Force Platform Sites.
- Publish a support FAQ—Provide helpful information on a public website where customers can search for solutions to their issues.
- Create a store locator tool—Add a public tool to your portal that helps customers find stores in their area.
- Publish an employee directory—Add an employee directory to your company's intranet by creating a site restricted by IP range.
- Create a recruiting website—Post job openings to a public site and allow visitors to submit applications and resumes online.
- Publish a catalog of products—List all of your company's products on a public website, with model numbers, current prices, and product images pulled dynamically from your organization.

 Important: To enable Force Platform Sites for your Developer Edition organization, go to `http://developer.force.com` and follow the instructions posted under "Featured Content."

If you have been following the examples in the previous chapter, your Force Platform organization should be ready for the exercises in this chapter. If you have not done the exercises, or want to start with a fresh version of the sample Recruiting application, please refer to the instructions in the Code Share project for this book. You can find information on how to access that project in *Chapter 1: Welcome to the Force Platform*.

In addition, the project contains instructions on how to update your organization with changes required for this chapter.

Registering for and Creating Your First Force Platform Site

Your unique Force Platform domain, which hosts your site, is constructed from the unique *domain prefix* that you register, plus `force.com`. For example, if you choose "mycompany" as your domain prefix, your domain name would be `http://www.mycompany.force.com`.

 Note: The construction of the secure URLs for your Force Platform sites depends on the type of organization they are built on. In the following examples, the domain prefix is "mycompany," the sandbox name is "mysandbox," the instance name is "na1," and the sandbox instance name is "cs1 ":

Organization Type	Secure URL
Developer Edition	https://mycompany-developer-edition.na1.force.com
Developer Sandbox	https://mysandbox.mycompany.cs1.force.com
Production	https://mycompany.secure.force.com

The domain prefix for Developer Edition must contain 22 characters or fewer. The secure URL is displayed on the Login Settings page.

To get started, register your company's Force Platform domain by doing the following:

1. Click **Setup ➤ Develop ➤ Sites**.
2. Enter a unique name for your Force Platform domain. The name is case-sensitive. Only alphanumeric characters are allowed. Salesforce.com recommends using your company's name or a variation, such as "mycompany."

    Caution: You cannot modify your Force Platform domain name after you have registered it.

3. Click **Check Availability** to confirm that the domain name you entered is unique. If it is not unique, you are prompted to change it.
4. Read and accept the Force Platform Sites Terms and Use by selecting the checkbox.
5. Click **Register My Force.com Domain**. After you accept the Terms and Use and register your Force Platform domain, the change is tracked in your organization's setup audit trail.

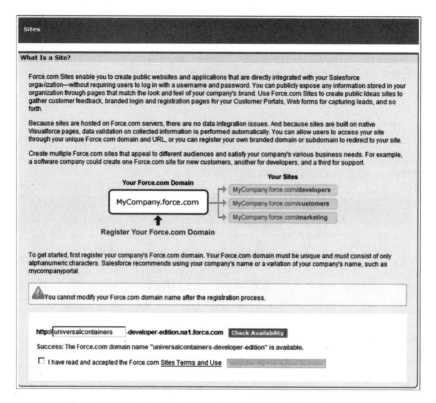

Figure 211: Registering Your Force Platform Domain Name

Congratulations! You are now ready to create your first Force Platform site. On the Sites page, do the following:

1. Click **New**.
2. On the Site Edit page, enter the `Site Label` and `Site Name` (the API name). Select the UnderConstruction page for the `Active Site Home Page` and the InMaintenance page for the `Inactive Site Home Page`. Leave your site inactive for now.

 Note: Custom Web addresses registered through a domain name registrar, such as `www.mycompany.com`, are not supported in Developer Edition.

3. Click **Save**.

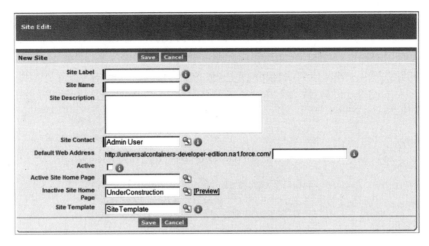

Figure 212: Creating Your First Site

Your site is inactive, so when you open your site URL in a browser, you will see the InMaintenance page, as expected. Now activate your site by clicking **Activate** on the Site Details page. Browse to your site again. You will see the UnderConstruction page, the home page you set for your site when it's active. If users go to your site, they will see the UnderConstruction page until you replace the Active Site Home Page with the actual pages for your site, which you are ready to create in Visualforce.

Overview: Creating the Public Recruiting Application

Universal Containers has a number of available positions that they want to advertise to the general public. Since the necessary information is already stored in their organization, the easiest way to make these Position records public is to post them on a Force Platform site. To accomplish this, you will build a custom job postings application using Apex and Visualforce.

The sites recruiting application example walks you through the following topics:

- *Creating the Public Job Postings Page*
- *Customizing the Look and Feel of Your Force Platform Site*
- *Creating the Job Detail Page*
- *Enabling Users to Submit Job Applications Online*
- *Configuring Registration and Login for Your Force Platform Site*
- *Testing Your Force Platform Site*

Creating the Public Job Postings Page

The heart of the public recruiting application is the job postings page. Here, Universal Containers can list all of their available positions, and visitors can search for positions. Later, you will add a job detail page where users can view more information, and a job application page, where users can submit applications—but first, create the job postings page.

This topic covers the following steps:

- *Creating the Custom Controller*
- *Creating and Enabling the Job Postings Page*
- *Granting Public Access Settings*
- *Setting Your Active Home Page*

 Note: You learned about Apex and Visualforce in earlier chapters; these examples will build on that knowledge.

Creating the Custom Controller

Before building the Visualforce page, create the custom Apex controller. This controller, named PublicJobSearchController, extends the standard Visualforce functionality by adding custom search capabilities on the Position custom object, allowing visitors to your Force Platform site to search by department, geographic location, and keyword. The controller also determines the content of the query results.

 Note: You can find the completed controllers and pages in the Recruiting Application by navigating to **Setup ➤ Develop ➤ Pages**.

Define the `Department` and `Location` fields as lists, and the `Keyword` field as a string. Display the `ID`, `Name`, `Department`, `City`, `State`, `Country`, `Job Description`, `Position Open Date`, and `Status` fields to the user.

Your Apex controller should look like this:

```
public class PublicJobSearchController {
  Position__c[] ccts;
  String searchPosition;
  String positionid;
  String DepartmentName = '%';
  String LocationName = '%';
  String likeStr = '%';
```

```
    private String viewDepartmentName = 'Department';
    private String viewLocationName = 'Locations';
// Department picklist for the search page
    private static final List<SelectOption>
        VIEW_DEPARTMENT = new SelectOption[] {
      new SelectOption('0','All Departments'),
      new SelectOption('Engineering','Engineering'),
      new SelectOption('Finance','Finance'),
      new SelectOption('IT','IT'),
      new SelectOption('Sales','Sales'),
      new SelectOption('Support','Support')
    };
// Location picklist for search page
    private static final List<SelectOption>
        VIEW_LOCATION = new SelectOption[] {
      new SelectOption('0','All Locations'),
      new SelectOption('San Francisco','San Francisco'),
      new SelectOption('New York','New York'),
      new SelectOption('Reston','Reston'),
      new SelectOption('Toronto','Toronto')
    };
    public List<SelectOption> getDepartmentViewNames() {
      return VIEW_DEPARTMENT;
    }
    public List<SelectOption> getLocationViewNames() {
      return VIEW_LOCATION;
    }
    public void setViewDepartmentName(String viewDepartmentName) {
      this.viewDepartmentName = viewDepartmentName;
    }
    public String getViewDepartmentName() {
      return viewDepartmentName;
    }
    public void setViewLocationName(String viewLocationName) {
      this.viewLocationName = viewLocationName;
    }
    public String getViewLocationName() {
      return viewLocationName;
    }
// Page onLoad action to auto-run the job postings query
    public void initList() {
      query();
    }
    public String getSearchPosition() {
      return this.searchPosition;
    }
    public void setSearchPosition(String search) {
      this.searchPosition = search;
    }
    public void populateQuery() {
      likeStr = '%' + searchPosition + '%';
      if (viewDepartmentName != '0') DepartmentName =
          viewDepartmentName;
      if (viewLocationName != '0') LocationName = viewLocationName;
      query();
    }
```

```
// Query to return the first 100 matching positions
public PageReference query() {
    ccts = [SELECT id, name, Department__c, Position_Type__r.Name,
               Location__r.City__c, Location_City_State_Country__c,
               Job_Description__c, Open_Position_Date__c, Status__c
            FROM Position__c
            WHERE Department__c like :DepartmentName
            AND Location__r.City__c like :LocationName
            AND name like :likeStr
            ORDER BY Name ASC
            LIMIT 100];
    return null;
}
public Position__c[] getPosition() {
    return ccts;
}
}
```

Creating and Enabling the Job Postings Page

Now create a new Visualforce page, named PublicJobs, that uses the PublicJobSearchController custom controller that you just created. This page displays all available positions and allows users to search for available jobs based on department, location, and keyword. Your Visualforce page should look like this:

```
<apex:page showheader="false" action="{!initList}"
    controller="PublicJobSearchController"
    standardStylesheets="true">
<apex:form>
<!-- Search by Department, Location, or Keyword -->
    <apex:pageBlock title="Search Job Postings">
      <apex:pageBlockSection columns="1">
        <apex:pageBlockSectionItem>
          <apex:outputText value="Department"/>
          <apex:selectList value="{!viewDepartmentName}"
              id="departmentViews" size="1" required="true">
            <apex:selectOptions value="{!DepartmentViewNames}"/>
          </apex:selectList>
        </apex:pageBlockSectionItem>
        <apex:pageBlockSectionItem>
          <apex:outputText value="Location"/>
          <apex:selectList value="{!viewLocationName}"
              id="locationViews" size="1" required="true">
            <apex:selectOptions value="{!LocationViewNames}"/>
          </apex:selectList>
        </apex:pageBlockSectionItem>
        <apex:pageBlockSectionItem >
          <apex:outputText value="Keyword"/>
          <apex:inputText value="{!searchPosition}"/>
        </apex:pageBlockSectionItem>
        <apex:pageBlockSectionItem >
          <apex:outputText value=""/>
```

```
              <apex:commandButton value="Search"
                  action="{!PopulateQuery}" reRender="JobList" />
          </apex:pageBlockSectionItem>
        </apex:pageBlockSection>
      </apex:pageBlock>
  </apex:form>
  <!-- Search results -->
    <apex:pageBlock title="Search Results">
      <apex:pageBlockTable id="JobList" value="{!Position}"
          var="Position__c" rendered="{!NOT(ISNULL(Position))}">
        <apex:column>
          <apex:facet name="header">
            <apex:outputText value="Position ID"/>
          </apex:facet>
          <!-- Position name field linked to job details page -->
          <apex:outputText value="{!Position__c.name}"/>
        </apex:column>
        <apex:column>
          <apex:facet name="header">
            <apex:outputText value="Title"/>
          </apex:facet>
          <apex:outputText value=
              "{! Position__c.Position_Type__r.Name}"/>
        </apex:column>
        <apex:column>
          <apex:facet name="header">
            <apex:outputText value="Department"/>
          </apex:facet>
          <apex:outputText value="{!Position__c.Department__c}"/>
        </apex:column>
        <apex:column>
          <apex:facet name="header">
            <apex:outputText value="Location"/>
          </apex:facet>
          <apex:outputText value=
              "{!Position__c.Location_City_State_Country__c}"/>
        </apex:column>
        <apex:column>
          <apex:facet name="header">
            <apex:outputText value="Job Description"/>
          </apex:facet>
         <apex:outputText value="{!Position__c.Job_Description__c}"/>

        </apex:column>
        <apex:column>
          <apex:facet name="header">
            <apex:outputText value="Position Open Date"/>
          </apex:facet>
          <apex:outputText value=
              "{!Position__c.Open_Position_Date__c}"/>
        </apex:column>
      </apex:pageBlockTable>
```

```
    </apex:pageBlock>
</apex:page>
```

Now that your Visualforce page is ready, go back to the application and enable the page for your site by doing the following:

1. Click **Setup ➤ Develop ➤ Sites**.
2. Click the site label link for your site. This takes you to the Site Details page.
3. Click **Edit** on the Site Pages related list.
4. Add the PublicJobs page to the Enabled Visualforce Pages list.
5. Click **Save**.

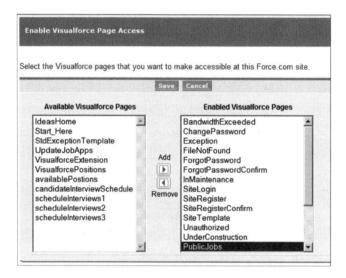

Figure 213: Enabling Your New Visualforce Page

Granting Public Access Settings

The job postings that website users see are object records, so you have to give your site's users permission to view the Position object by doing the following:

1. From the Site Details page, click **Public Access Settings**.
2. Click **Edit**.
3. Under Custom Object Permissions, enable "Read" permission on Positions. The custom object permissions for this example should match the following figure.
4. Click **Save**.

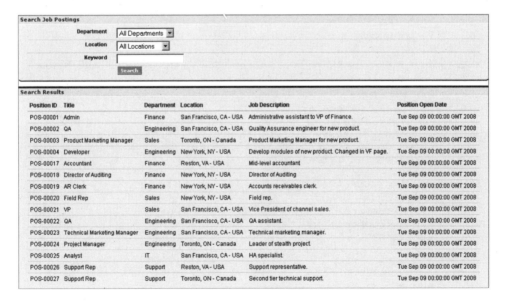

Figure 214: Setting Custom Object Permissions for Site Users

Setting Your Active Home Page

You have created the Apex controller and Visualforce pages, enabled the PublicJobs page, and granted public users permission to view Positions. Now all that's left to do is to make the PublicJobs page the home page for your active site:

1. Click **Setup ➤ Develop ➤ Sites**.
2. Click **Edit**.
3. Use the lookup field to find and select PublicJobs for the `Active Site Home Page` field.
4. Click **Save**.

Browse to your site's URL to see your new Visualforce page in action.

Figure 215: Viewing the Job Postings Page Through Your Site

Customizing the Look and Feel of Your Force Platform Site

Your site is up and running, but the pages don't have your company's look and feel. The public sees the standard Salesforce colors. By tweaking the site template and referencing it from your Visualforce pages, you can brand your site with your logo, colors, and layouts.

The *site template* is a powerful, yet simple component that enables you to control the look and feel for your entire site. Once you associate the site template with your site, you must code each Visualforce page to reference the template using the `{!$Site.Template}` expression shown below.

Upload static resource files and reference them from the site template, site header, or site footer to easily control the look and feel for your site pages. *Static resources* are files—including archives (such as .zip and .jar files), images, stylesheets, JavaScript, and other files—that you can reference from Visualforce pages.

To customize the look and feel of your site:

1. First, assign the template for your site by doing the following:

   a. Click **Setup ➤ Develop ➤ Sites**.
   b. Click **Edit**.
   c. Use the lookup field to find and select SiteTemplate for the `Site Template` field.
   d. Click **Save**.

2. Reference the site template by adding the following tags (shown in bold) to your existing PublicJobs Visualforce page:

```
<apex:page showheader="false" action="{!initList}"
    controller="PositionSearchController"
    standardStylesheets="true">
  <apex:composition template="{!$Site.Template}">
  <apex:define name="body">
    . . .
    . . .
    . . .
  </apex:define>
  </apex:composition>
</apex:page>
```

3. Next, upload your stylesheet and company logo as static resources by doing the following:

   a. Click **Setup ➤ Develop ➤ Static Resources**.
   b. For each static resource:

      a. Click **New**.

      b. Enter the name and description, and browse to the file to upload. In this example, the stylesheet is named SiteCSS and the logo is named Logo.

      c. Set the **Cache Control** setting to Public. Static resources with private cache control do not show up in sites.

      d. Click **Save**.

4. Now modify the site header component to display the Universal Containers logo and use the company's stylesheet by doing the following:

      a. Click **Setup ➤ Develop ➤ Components**.

      b. Click **Edit** next to the SiteHeader component.

      c. Replace the following line:

```
<apex:image url="{!$Site.Prefix}
  {!$Label.site.img_path}/force_logo.gif"
  style="align: left;" alt="Salesforce"
  width="233" height="55" title="Salesforce"/>
```

      with this new line:

```
<apex:image id="logo" value="{!$Resource.Logo}"/>
```

      d. Add the following line after `<apex:stylesheet value="{!$Resource.SiteCSS}"/>`:

```
<apex:stylesheet value="{!$Resource.SiteCSS}"/>
```

      e. Click **Save**.

5. Browse to your site's URL to see the Universal Containers company logo and the new color scheme.

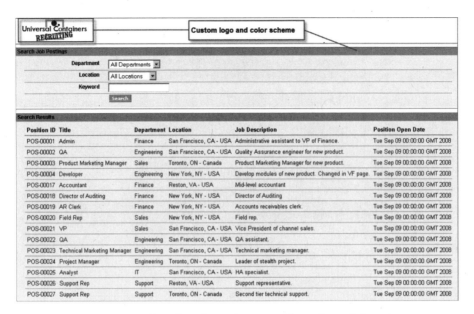

Figure 216: Branding the Job Postings Page for Universal Containers

Creating the Job Detail Page

Visitors to your Force Platform site can search for job postings and see them in a list, but you also want them to be able to drill-down to see the details for individual positions. To accomplish this, you need to provide links to positions on the PublicJobs page, as well as create a Job Details page. In this example, by leveraging the functionality built in to the standard controller—for basic operations, such as editing, deleting, cloning, etc.—you only have to code the Visualforce page.

First, create the PublicJobDetails page in Visualforce. Your Visualforce page should look like this:

```
<apex:page standardController="Position__c" title="Job Details"
    showHeader="false" standardStylesheets="true">
<!-- The site template provides the site layout and style -->
<apex:composition template="{!$Site.Template}">
<apex:define name="body">
  <apex:form>
   <apex:sectionHeader title="{!$ObjectType.Position__c.label}"
       subtitle="{!Position__c.name}"/>
    <!-- Breadcrumb link back to the search page -->
    <apex:outputLink value="<- Back to Search"
        onclick="top.history.go(-1);return false;" />
     <apex:pageBlock title="Job Detail">
```

```
            <apex:pageBlockButtons>
               <!-- The Apply button is linked to the job application
                    page in a later step -->
               <apex:commandButton value="Apply" onclick="#"/>
            </apex:pageBlockButtons>
            <!-- Job details -->
            <apex:pageBlockSection title="Information"
                collapsible="false" columns="1">
               <apex:outputField value="{!Position__c.name}"/>
               <apex:outputField value=
                   "{!Position__c.Location_City_State_Country__c}"/>
               <apex:outputField value="{!Position__c.Status__c}"/>
               <apex:outputField value=
                   "{!Position__c.Position_type__r.Name}"/>
               <apex:outputField value="{!Position__c.Department__c}"/>
               <apex:outputField value="{!Position__c.Start_Date__c}"/>
               <apex:outputField value=
                   "{!Position__c.Programming_Languages__c}"/>
               <apex:outputField value=
                   "{!Position__c.Job_Description__c}" />
               <apex:outputField value=
                   "{!Position__c.Responsibilities__c}" />
               <apex:outputField value=
                   "{!Position__c.Educational_Requirements__c}" />
            </apex:pageBlockSection>
         </apex:pageBlock>
      </apex:form>
   </apex:define>
</apex:composition>
</apex:page>
```

Make sure to enable the PublicJobDetails page for your site, as you did for the PublicJobs page you created earlier.

Now that you have the page, update the PublicJobs page to include Position ID links that take users to the PublicJobDetails page by doing the following:

1. Click **Setup ➤ Develop ➤ Sites**.
2. Click the site label link for your site. This takes you to the Site Details page.
3. On the Site Pages related list, click the **PublicJobs** link.
4. Click **Edit**.
5. Replace the following line:

```
<apex:outputText value="{!Position__c.name}"/>
```

with this new one:

```
<apex:outputLink value="PublicJobDetails?id={!Position__c.id}"

   id="theLink">{!Position__c.name}</apex:outputLink>
```

6. Click **Save**.

Browse to your site's URL to see that the Position IDs show up as hyperlinks.

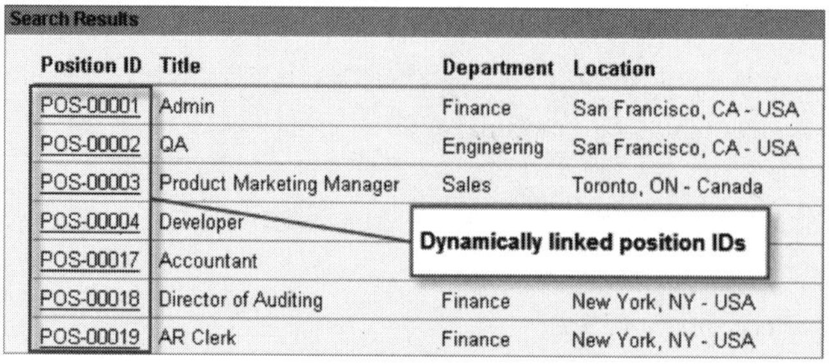

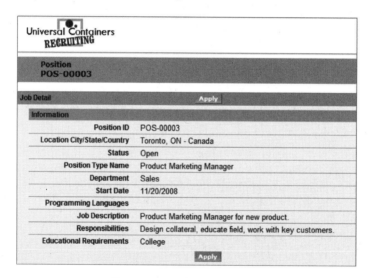

Figure 217: Job Postings Page with Linked Position IDs

Click a position link to drill down to that job's detail page. But what happens when a user clicks that **Apply** button? Right now, nothing. You tackle that in the next section.

Figure 218: Job Details Page

Enabling Users to Submit Job Applications Online

In *Chapter 13: Email Services with the Force Platform*, you learned how to use email to extend the recruiting application. In this section, you go one step further and create public Web pages to accomplish similar goals. If you want to let public users apply online for open positions, you need to create a new Visualforce page, named PublicJobApplication, to accept applications.

Use the standard controller for the Candidate object, and create a new extension controller, named myPublicJobApplicationExtension, to do the following:

- Create a new Candidate record
- Attach the uploaded resume file to the Candidate record
- Create a new Job Application record that's linked to the Position and Candidate records
- Redirect users to the confirmation page

This topic covers the following steps:

- *Extending the Standard Apex Controller*
- *Creating the Confirmation Page*
- *Creating the Application Page and Linking to Job Details*
- *Testing the Online Application Process and Verifying the Results*

Extending the Standard Apex Controller

By adding an extension to the standard controller, you can add powerful functionality without having to create an entire custom controller. The extension in this example allows users to apply online and upload files—functions not available in the standard controller. On application, the controller extension creates new candidate and job application records related to the position. You will see how this is used in *Creating the Application Page and Linking to Job Details* on page 453.

Your Apex extension should look like this:

```
public class PublicJobApplicationExtension {
// This controller extends the standard controller, overwrites
// the actions, creates a candidate record, creates an attachment
// on the candidate record based on the uploaded file, creates a
// job application record that links the candidate record and
// the related position.

  private final Candidate__c candidate;
  private ID positionid =
      ApexPages.currentPage().getParameters().get('jobid');
  private Job_Application__c jobapplication {get; private set;}
  public Blob resume {get; set;}
  public String contentType {get; set;}
  public String fileName {get; set;}

// Extends the standard controller for the candidate object
  public PublicJobApplicationExtension
      (ApexPages.StandardController stdController) {
    candidate = (Candidate__c)stdController.getRecord();
  }
```

```
    public Position__c getPosition() {
      return [SELECT id, name, Position_type__r.Name,
          Job_Description__c FROM Position__c
            WHERE id = :positionid];
    }

    public PageReference saveApplication() {
// Creates the candidate record
      try {
          insert(candidate);
      } catch(System.DMLException e) {
          ApexPages.addMessages(e);
          return null;
      }
      jobapplication = new Job_Application__c();
      jobapplication.Candidate__c = candidate.id;
      jobapplication.Position__c = positionid;

// Creates an attachment to the candidate record if a
      resume file is uploaded
      if (resume != null) {
        Attachment attach = new Attachment();
        attach.Body = resume;
        attach.Name = fileName;
        attach.ContentType = contentType;
        attach.ParentId = candidate.id;
        try {
            insert(attach);
        } catch(System.DMLException e) {
            ApexPages.addMessages(e);
            return null;
        }
      }

    }

// Creates the job application record to link the candidate
      and the related position
      try {
          insert(jobapplication);
      } catch(System.DMLException e) {
          ApexPages.addMessages(e);
          return null;
      }
      PageReference p = Page.PublicJobApplicationConfirmation;
      p.setRedirect(true);
      return p;
      }
```

```
}
```

Creating the Confirmation Page

Create a confirmation page in Visualforce, named PublicJobApplicationConfirmation, to inform users that their job application has been saved to the system. Your Visualforce page should look like this:

```
<apex:page title="Job Application Confirmation"
    showHeader="false" standardStylesheets="true">
<!-- The site template provides the site layout and style -->
  <apex:composition template="{!$Site.Template}">
  <apex:define name="body">
    <apex:form>
      <apex:commandLink value="<- Back to Job Search"
          onclick="window.top.location=
          '{!$Page.PublicJobs}';return false;"/>
      <br/>
      <br/>
      <center><apex:outputText value="Your application has been
          saved. Thank you for your interest!"/></center>
      <br/>
      <br/>
    </apex:form>
  </apex:define>
  </apex:composition>
</apex:page>
```

 Note: Notice that there is no Apex controller associated with this Visualforce page. This is because there is no dynamic data or behavior to control. Non-interactive pages don't require a controller.

Creating the Application Page and Linking to Job Details

Now that you have created your controller extension and confirmation page, create the PublicJobApplication page. This page allows users to enter information, as well as attach a resume file. Once an application is saved, new Candidate and Job Application records are created for the user. Resume files are stored as attachments to the Candidate record.

Your Visualforce page should look like this:

```
<!-- This page uses the standard controller and extends it to
    overwrite the action buttons and file upload -->
<apex:page standardController="Candidate__c" extensions=
    "PublicJobApplicationExtension" title="Job Application"
```

```
      showHeader="false" standardStylesheets="true">
<!-- The site template provides the site layout and style -->
  <apex:composition template="{!$Site.Template}">
  <apex:define name="body">
    <apex:form>
      <apex:sectionHeader title="" subtitle="{!Position.name}"/>
      <!-- Breadcrumb link back to the job details page -->
      <apex:commandLink value="<- Back to Job Details"
          onclick="top.history.go(-1);return false;" />
      <!-- Section to display the error mesages -->
      <apex:messages id="error" styleClass="errorMsg"
          layout="table" style="margin-top:1em;"/>
      <apex:pageBlock title="Job Application Form" mode="edit">
        <apex:pageBlockButtons >
          <apex:commandButton value="Save"
              action="{!saveApplication}"/>
          <apex:commandButton value="Cancel" onclick=
              "top.history.go(-1);return false;"/>
        </apex:pageBlockButtons>
        <!-- Job information in read only -->
        <apex:pageBlockSection title="Job Information"
            collapsible="false" columns="1">
          <apex:outputField value="{!Position.name}"/>
          <apex:outputField value=
              "{!Position.Position_type__r.Name}"/>
          <apex:outputField value=
              "{!Position.Job_Description__c}" />
        </apex:pageBlockSection>
        <!-- Candidate information editable-->
        <apex:pageBlockSection title="Candidate Information"
            collapsible="false" columns="1">
          <apex:inputField value="{!Candidate__c.First_Name__c}"/>
          <apex:inputField value="{!Candidate__c.Last_Name__c}"/>
          <apex:inputField value="{!Candidate__c.Gender__c}"/>
          <apex:inputField value="{!Candidate__c.Address__c}"/>
          <apex:inputField value="{!Candidate__c.City__c}"/>
          <apex:inputField value="{!Candidate__c.Postal_Code__c}"/>
          <apex:inputField value=
              "{!Candidate__c.State_Province__c}"/>
          <apex:inputField value="{!Candidate__c.Country__c}"/>
          <apex:inputField value="{!Candidate__c.Email__c}"/>
          <apex:inputField value="{!Candidate__c.Phone__c}"/>
          <apex:inputField value="{!Candidate__c.Mobile__c}"/>
          <apex:inputField value="{!Candidate__c.Education__c}"/>
          <apex:inputField value=
              "{!Candidate__c.Current_Employer__c}"/>
          <!-- Field to upload candiadte resume -->
          <apex:pageBlockSectionItem>
          Upload your resume
          <apex:inputFile accept="doc, txt, pdf" filename=
              "{!fileName}" contentType="{!contentType}"
              filesize="1000" size="50" value="{!resume}"/>
          </apex:pageBlockSectionItem>
        </apex:pageBlockSection>
      </apex:pageBlock>
    </apex:form>
```

```
    </apex:define>
    </apex:composition>
</apex:page>
```

Now you need to link the PublicJobApplication page to the **Apply** button on the PublicJob Details page. The Job Details page passes the Position ID as a parameter to the newly created Application record, creating a relationship between the candidate and position records.

1. Click **Setup ➤ Develop ➤ Sites**.
2. Click the site label link for your site. This takes you to the Site Details page.
3. On the Site Pages related list, click the **PublicJobs** link.
4. Click **Edit**.
5. Replace the following line:

    ```
    <apex:commandButton value="Apply" onclick="#"/>
    ```

    with this new one:

    ```
    <apex:commandButton value="Apply" onclick=
      "window.top.location='{!$Site.Prefix}/
      PublicJobApplication?jobid={!Position__c.Id}';
      return false;"/>
    ```

6. Click **Save**.

As with all Visualforce pages, make sure to *enable the PublicJobApplication and PublicJobApplicationConfirmation pages* on page 444 for your site.

Testing the Online Application Process and Verifying the Results

Browse to your site's URL and search for any open position. Click the **Position ID** link, then click **Apply**. Click the **New User?** link to register.to see your new Job Application page.

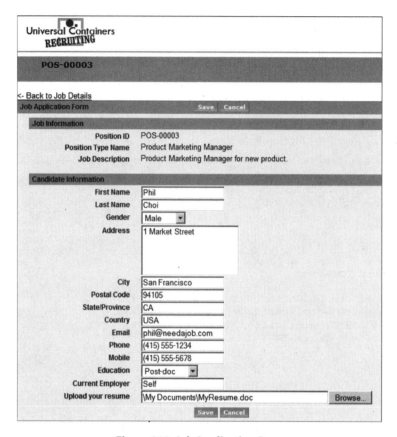

Figure 219: Job Application Page

To test that the online application process works, enter all required information, attach a file, and click **Save**. You should see the confirmation page:

Figure 220: Job Application Confirmation Page

Now, let's go into the application to see the results. Log in to your organization and click the Candidates tab. You should be see the new candidate record created by applying online from your Force Platform site. On the Candidate Detail page, notice the attached resume under Notes & Attachments. A new record will be automatically created for each online applicant.

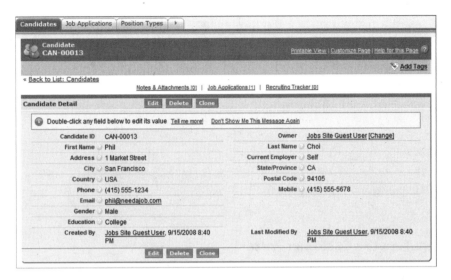

Figure 221: Candidate Detail Page

You should also see the related Job Application record connecting the Position and Candidate records. If you open the Job Application record, you will see links to the position being applied for, and the candidate applying for this position.

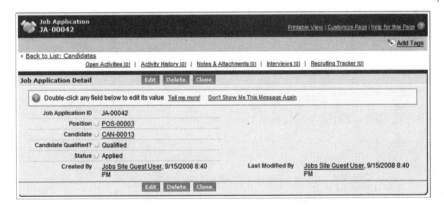

Figure 222: Job Application Detail Page

Configuring Registration and Login for Your Force Platform Site

An authenticated user is easier to track. By enabling your site for login and registration, you can capture data on prospective candidates, communicate with them, and allow them to update their own information. Having registered job applicants makes the application process easier. Force Platform Sites provides seamless integration with the Customer Portal product, as well as built-in login and registration logic, making it easy for public users become authenticated users.

This topic covers the following steps:

- *Configuring the Customer Portal*
- *Associating the Customer Portal with Your Site*
- *Creating an Account and Updating the Apex Class with the Account ID*
- *Associating a Role with the Account User Record*

Configuring the Customer Portal

Force Platform Sites leverages a lot of existing Customer Portal settings. To integrate your site with a Customer Portal, you first need to enable the Customer Portal by doing the following:

1. Click **Setup ➤ Customize ➤ Customer Portal ➤ Settings**.
2. Click **Edit**.
3. Select the `Enable Customer Portal` checkbox and click **Save**.
4. Clone the Customer Portal User profile. Because the standard Customer Portal User profile is not editable, you need to create a clone so that you can give newly registered users access to the custom objects in the recruiting application. After login, users can view positions and other custom objects.

   To clone the profile, do the following:

   a. Click **Setup ➤ Manage Users ➤ Profiles**.
   b. Click the **Customer Portal User** profile link.
   c. Click **Clone**.
   d. Name the profile "Custom: Customer Portal User" and click **Save**.
   e. Edit the profile you just created by clicking **Edit** on the User Profiles page.
   f. Under Custom Object Permissions, grant the profile Read access on all custom objects and Create access on Candidates.

5. Now that the Customer Portal is enabled for registration and login, you must remove the PublicJobApplication and PublicJobApplicationConfirmation pages from the Enabled Visualforce Page Access list for your site. (You enable them for the Customer Portal user in the next step.) If you don't, public site users will be able to see the application and confirmation pages without logging in!

   Set the page access for your site by doing the following:

    a. Click **Setup ➤ Develop ➤ Sites**.

    b. Click the site label link for your site. This takes you to the Site Details page.

    c. Click **Edit** on the Site Pages related list.

    d. Remove the PublicJobApplication and PublicJobApplicationConfirmation pages from the Enabled Visualforce Pages list.

    e. Click **Save**.

6. By disabling the PublicJobApplication and PublicJobApplicationConfirmation pages for your site and enabling them for the Custom:Customer Portal User profile, you allow only authenticated users to view these pages. By default, Customer Portal users can see all pages enabled for the associated public site, so you only have to enable these two pages for the profile.

   Set the page access for profile by doing the following:

    a. Click **Setup ➤ Manage Users ➤ Profiles**.

    b. Click the **Custom: Customer Portal User** profile link.

    c. Scroll down to the Enabled Visualforce Page Access section and click **Edit**.

    d. Add the PublicJobApplication and PublicJobApplicationConfirmation pages to the `Enabled Visualforce Pages` list. This allows the default Customer Portal User to view these pages.

7. Click **Edit** for the Customer Portal you just enabled.

8. Configure the Customer Portal as follows:

   • Select the `Login Enabled` checkbox.

   • Select the `Self-Registration Enabled` checkbox.

   • Select a user for the `Administrator` field.

   • Optionally, set the `Logout URL`. If this isn't set, users are taken to the site home page on logout.

   • Select Customer Portal User for the `Default New User License`.

   • Select the newly created Custom: Customer Portal User profile for the `Default New User Profile`.

   • Select User for the `Default New User Role` field.

9. Click **Save**.

Your Self-Registration Settings section of the Customer Portal Setup page should look like this:

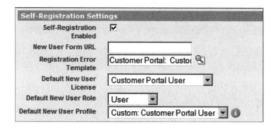

Figure 223: Customer Portal Self-Registration Settings

Associating the Customer Portal with Your Site

By associating your Force Platform site with a Customer Portal, you create a seamless bridge between your public website and the authenticated Customer Portal. Now that you have enabled and configured Customer Portal, you need to associate it with your site by doing the following:

1. Click **Setup ➤ Develop ➤ Sites**.
2. Click the site label link for your site. This takes you to the Site Details page.
3. Click **Login Settings**.
4. Click **Edit**.
5. From the Enable Login For list, select the Customer Portal that you just configured.
6. Select a **Change Password Page**. A default page is provided, but you can select your own page using the lookup field instead.
7. Select the `Require Non-Secure Connections (HTTP)` checkbox if you want to override your organization's security settings and exclusively use HTTP when logging in to the Customer Portal. If this checkbox is not selected, the `Require Secure Connections (HTTPS)` setting found at **Setup ➤ Security Controls ➤ Session Settings** is used to determine the security level.
8. Click **Save**.

Browse to your site's URL and notice that your site contains new login and registration links on the site header. The system automatically created the Visualforce pages and Apex classes necessary to integrate with the Customer Portal. The SiteHeader component automatically enabled the **Login**, **Forgot Your Password?**, and **New User?** links and associated them to the correct pages.

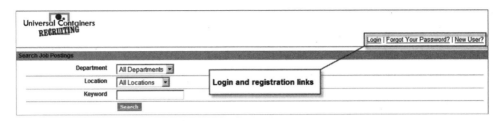

Figure 224: Job Posting Page with Registration and Login Links

Creating an Account and Updating the Apex Class with the Account ID

There are just a few more steps before your online recruiting flow is fully functional. Customer Portal users need to be associated with a contact under an account so that they can be tracked in the system. By creating an account that is associated with all of your job applicants, you can track applicant information as user records.

First, create a new Account, named Online Registration Account, and copy the 15-digit Account ID from the URL. The ID comes at the end of the URL. Update the SiteRegisterController with this ID. This ensures that all candidates registering through your public site are associated with the Online Registration Account.

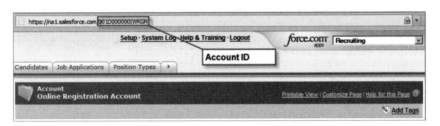

Figure 225: Online Registration Account ID

To update the Account ID in the SiteRegisterController, do the following:

1. Click **Setup ➤ Develop ➤ Apex Classes**.
2. Click **Edit** next to SiteRegisterController.
3. Find the `private static Id PORTAL_ACCOUNT_ID = '<Account_ID>';` line and insert the ID for the Online Registration Account that you just created. The line should look like this:

```
private static Id PORTAL_ACCOUNT_ID = '001D000000IVvTF';
```

4. Click **Save**.

461

Associating a Role with the Account User Record

The Customer Portal requires that the owner of the account you just created is associated with a role to control what new users can and can't see. In this example, since you created the account, your user record must be associated with a role. This is a required to create Customer Portal users.

To associate your user record with a role, do the following:

1. Click to **Setup ➤ My Personal Information ➤ Personal Information**.
2. Click **Edit**.
3. Select a role for your own user if one hasn't already been selected.

 Note: If you don't see any roles in the picklist, you need to create a role hierarchy for your organization. Click **Setup ➤ Manage Users ➤ Roles** and follow the instructions given. Once you've created a role hierarchy, go back and assign your user record that role.

Testing Your Force Platform Site

By following the simple steps outlined in this chapter, you have created a powerful, branded public recruiting application that serves up job information stored directly in your organization—without any additional overhead. Users can search on available positions, view position details, and register for the Customer Portal. Users can also submit job applications online, including attaching a resume. When a user applies online, the Apex controller that you used for the job application Visualforce page creates corresponding candidate and job application records that are associated with the respective position. With Force Platform sites, Universal Containers will fill their open positions in no time!

The coding and configuration are done. All that remains is to test your new online job postings site:

1. Browse to your site's URL.
2. Search for a job.
3. Click a Position ID to drill-down to the job details page.
4. Click **Apply**. You will see the Authentication Required page.
5. Click the **New User?** link and register as a new user.
6. After registration, you are redirected to the Job Application page. Enter application information, including a resume attachment.

7. Submit your job application and verify that new Candidate and Job Application records were created in your organization.

8. Log out of the site and move on to the next chapter!

 Note: Test methods for the Apex controllers are included with the controllers in the Code Share project.

Chapter 15

Deployment

In a traditional software development practice, applications are always developed offline. You write source code, assemble, compile, or link that code, and then deploy and run the executable in a test system to see if it does what you want. Then you come back to the code to make any changes, test again, and, in this way, iterate towards a working solution to your requirement.

The Force Platform differs somewhat from this traditional model, in that when you make changes to our application or organization, those changes are immediately available—'deployment' is automatic, at least so far as the environment within which you are working is concerned.

For many application and organization changes, for many businesses, that is enough. Either the application modifications aren't risky, or the application is not mission critical, so making changes directly within a production organization is the right practice.

For more complex changes, or companies whose business is more dependent on verifiably correct operation of their IT systems, making application changes directly within production isn't an option. Instead they require application development to follow more formal procedures where changes are implemented and tested in isolation from production code and data.

This chapter covers the options available to you to deploy your Force Platform applications and components from a development environment to a production environment.

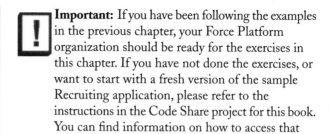

Important: If you have been following the examples in the previous chapter, your Force Platform organization should be ready for the exercises in this chapter. If you have not done the exercises, or want to start with a fresh version of the sample Recruiting application, please refer to the instructions in the Code Share project for this book. You can find information on how to access that project in *Chapter 1: Welcome to the Force Platform*.

Application Development Methodology and Architecture

Application development is typically achieved through some sort of process, which guides the activity from initial requirements collection through deployment of a completed system. As a developer, you are most interested in the particular span of the process that covers application creation and testing.

There are a variety of development methodologies currently in use, such as the waterfall model, Rational Unified Process (RUP), and Agile methodologies. You can use any of these methodologies to create Force Platform applications.

Development methodologies can be as simple or as complicated as you need them to be, given the complexity of your application, the size of your team, or how deliberate your release process is. In a typical large enterprise, developers have private environments within which to do initial development, after which the application is taken through integration, functional and regression testing, QA, user acceptance testing, and staging, before being finally deployed to production. Depending on the team size and release formalisms in place, there may be many different envionments for these different stages.

The Force Platform allows developers to create Force Platform organizations as isolated environments, for development, test and user acceptance activities, and to migrate changes between these environments. This isolation is at the core of implementing your application development methodology.

The simplest example of these separate environments uses the Force Platform IDE to move a copy of metadata from one organization to another, as you will see below. This chapter also covers the ability to publish an application, making it available to multiple organizations.

Simple Deployment with the Force Platform IDE

The Force Platform includes two basic interfaces to the metadata that defines your objects and applications—the Force Platform Setup menu and the Force Platform IDE. You have seen how some declarative aspects of the platform are best addressed through the Force Platform Setup menu, while developing Apex code and, to some extent, Visualforce pages is best handled through the IDE.

So far, the process of development has focused on a single organization. Deployment in the Force Platform, by its very definition, is not about one organization, it is about moving configuration from one organization to another. This deployment process requires a tool that can log into two Force Platform organizations at once, via the Metadata API.

The Metadata API was introduced in *Chapter 8: The Force Platform IDE* as a mechanism for accessing and transporting metadata components from the Force Platform server to the Force Platform IDE. The Metadata API is used in a similar way to deploy an application from one organization to another. While it is possible to write your own Metadata API client to deploy an application, most Force Platform developers will want to leverage existing tools built for this purpose, such as the Force Platform Migration Tool and the Force Platform IDE.

Preparing For Deployment

Before you can get some hands-on experience deploying an application, you will need another Force Platform environment to be the target of the deployment.

Go to `http://developer.force.com`, the home page for Force Platform developers, and obtain a free Developer Edition account.

In order to properly deploy to another organization, you will need to connect to that organization with user credentials having the Modify All Data permission. In fact, you must have that permission in both the originating organization and the target organization.

Finally, you need to have adequate test coverage for any Apex code you want to deploy to a production organization. As described in *Chapter 10: Apex*, you must include test methods that exercise at least 75% of all of your Apex code to allow this code to be deployed. Some of the examples in earlier chapters did not include test methods in the implementations as described in the text, but all the sample code from the Code Share project does include a complete set of test methods and classes. If you choose to initialize your organization from the Code Share project, as described at the start of this chapter, your Apex code will have adequate test coverage. Refer to the Code Share project for additional information about test methods and classes for your organization.

All test methods and classes are run again as part of the deployment process, so if, for any reason, they fail, then the Metadata API will not allow the deployment.

Using the Force Platform Deployment Wizard

Now that you have a target organization defined, along with a user with proper permissions, you can use the Force Platform IDE to deploy a project to another organization.

Your first step is to create a project in the Force Platform IDE. If you have been reading this book from the beginning, you already have a Force Platform IDE workspace with a project. You should create another project for the deployment exercises of this chapter. If you are not familiar with using the Force Platform IDE, read *Chapter 8: The Force Platform IDE*, which provides an introduction to this key development tool.

1. Open the Force Platform IDE.
2. Create a project from your organization. Include **all** components in the following categories in the new project:

   - Applications
   - Classes
   - Homepagelayouts
   - Layouts
   - Objects-custom
   - Pages
   - Tabs
   - Triggers

   as well as the User object from the `Objects - standard` category.

 Voice of the Developer: If you look at the list of entries under any component type, and don't see a component you know is present in the target org, you can click on the Refresh icon int this page to refresh the metadata which is used to generate these lists.

3. Click **OK** to add the selected components to the request list.
4. Click **Finish** to download the components to your new project.

   Now that your project is loaded into your Force Platform IDE workspace, you can deploy the project to another server.

5. In the Package Exporer, right click the `src` folder in your new project, and select the **Force Platform ➤ Deploy to Server** choice, which starts the deployment wizard.

   The Force Platform IDE first checks to insure that the contents of the project and the server metadata on which the project is based are still in agreement. Once this check passes, you are prompted for a username, password and environment for your deployment target, as shown in the figure below.

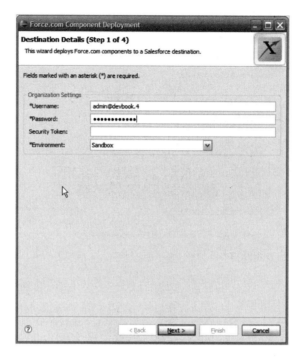

Figure 226: Preparing to save a project

6. Click **Next**. The IDE logs into the target organization and verifies your permissions.

   In the second step, you are prompted to archive the setup already present in the destination, and to archive the content being deployed. Archiving is a good idea so you can remember when you've made changes, but also because the archives will be needed if at any time in the future you might want to reverse one or more of the changes.

7. Select a directory for the destination archive and click **Next**.

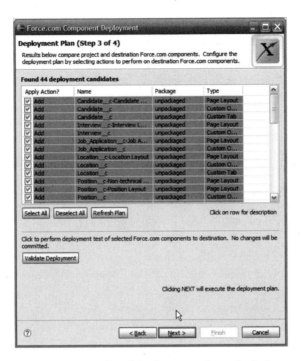

Figure 227: Results of deployment plan calculation

8. In the next panel, a deployment plan is calculated and displayed, as shown above.

The list in the dialog box covers all the deployment component candidates. Each component is shown in one of three colors, and each component has a check box to the left of the line, which indicates if the suggested action should be taken as part of this deployment.

If a candidate component is not present in the target organization, the entry is shown in green, indicating that the component will be added to the target organization. If the candidate component is present in the target organization, but the metadata for that component is identical to the metadata in the project, the entry is shown in grey, indicating that no action will be taken for this component. If the candidate component is present in the target organization with different metadata, the entry is shown in yellow, indicating that the component in the target organization will be overwritten with the new metadata. By default, all green and yellow entries are shown with the Action checkbox checked. You can uncheck that box for any candidate, as appropriate.

Before you deploy to a server, the Force Platform IDE checks to see if there are any components in the target organization which are not in the project you are deploying. You are given the option to delete these extra components, if you wish.

9. Once you have reviewed the deployment plan and are satisfied with the choices, you can optionally perform a trial deployment by clicking **Validate Deployment**. This performs all the steps of the deployment plan, but without actually committing the changes. This action is recommended to check for deployment errors or confirm code coverage requirements are met, in advance of your actual deployment schedule.

 Voice of the Developer: The **Valid Deployment** option performs the exact same set of actions that the deployment plan will, but without actually sending the project to the target server. The action is like a database update without a commit action. If the Validate Deployment reports any issues that can cause the deployment to fail, the deployment itself will not succeed, and deliver the same messages. Because of this, you will typically want to either do a Validate Deployment or an actual deployment—doing both is redundant.

If the validation of the deployment completes successfully, you are presented with another dialog that reports on the success. This report includes any statistics on the code coverage for Apex code included in the deployment. The dialog includes an option to view the log of the validation effort, which will have entries for the deployment of every individual component.

Remember that Apex cannot be saved into a production organization without a successful execution of test methods that achieve the required coverage level. The Validate Deployment option will check to make sure that the proper test coverage is in place, among other tests.

10. When you are certain you wish to deploy this plan, you can click **Next**. The deployment proceeds and, if it is successful, the changes are saved to your destination organization. You will receive messages as to the results of the deployment in the final page of the Deployment Wizard, shown below.

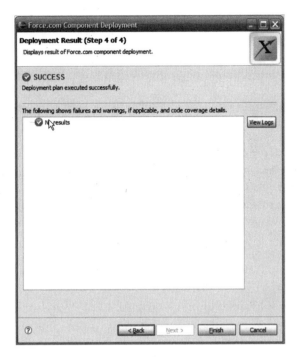

Figure 228: The final page of the Force Platform IDE Deployment Wizard

11. After this type of deployment, log into the target organization and check out the results of the deployment.

Keep in mind what has, and has not, happened. The deployment process from the Force Platform IDE moved the metadata for the components in the project to the new organization. This metadata controls the definition of the components in the package, in this case, most of the application you have been working on.

The deployment itself does not load any data into your organization. Use Data Loader to copy over any data required in the new organization.

Deployment Using the Force Platform Migration Tool

If you have been reading this book from the beginning, you have already used another deployment tool. The scripts you have used to update or refresh your development organization used the Force Platform Migration Tool.

The Force Platform Migration Tool is a library that is used in conjunction with Apache ANT. Apache ANT is a project that is used to run a series of scripts that define your deployment process. ANT is extensible, which means you can blend additional functionality into the basic scripting environment.

The Force Platform Migration Tool provides a higher level interface from ANT to the Metadata API, the same API used by the Force Platform IDE. You can use the scripts for this tool to both deploy components, as well as remove components in the target organization. Because the Migration Tool is used with ANT, you can include other scripts as part of your deployment.

The scripting capabilities of the Migration Tool mean that this option is well-suited to repeatedly perform the same tasks that you would perform with the Deploy to Server choice from within the IDE. This repeatability makes the use of this approach very appropriate when you are migrating Force Platform components to more than one internal target, since you will still have to have access to an appropriate user in the receiving organization.

You can find out more about the use of the Force Platform Migration Tool in additional documentation available through the Code Share project for this book.

Packages

The previous portion of this chapter introduced you to deploying with the Force Platform IDE, which is essentially creating a project from components in one organization to the Force Platform IDE, and then from the IDE to another target organization.

This approach to deployment works fine if you are moving your work from one organization to another. But what about the scenario where you want to deploy an application from one organization to many other organizations, which may be outside your company? Using the Force Platform IDE might work, but this approach requires you to have access to both the originating and target organization with a high level of permissions.

The Force Platform also supports a publish-and-subscribe method of deployment, where you can create a single deployment that can be downloaded and installed by many different organizations.

The vehicle for this type of deployment is the package. A package is a collection of Force Platform components gathered together into one entity. Your can create a package once and make the package available to a wider community. Individual members of this community can install the package into their organization.

What is a Package?

Packages provide you with a powerful way to distribute your application to many other organizations. Packages are like suitcases that can contain your components, code, or apps. You can use a package to bundle something as small as an individual component or as large as a set of related apps.

Packages come in two forms: managed and unmanaged. Unmanaged packages can be used for a one-time distribution, like a template. Managed packages are ideal when building an app with plans to upgrade. You can publish updates to a managed package after it has been deployed, and subscribers can install those updates over previous versions.

Packages can be distributed privately to a community of specific users, or listed publicly on the Force Platform AppExchange.

Creating a Package

As with most aspects of the Force Platform, the most efficient way to learn about packages is to create one.

1. Go to **Setup ➤ Create ➤ Packages**, which will bring up the page shown below. The page shown contains some information about the type of packages you can create in your organization. For now, the ability to create unmanaged packages is all you really need.

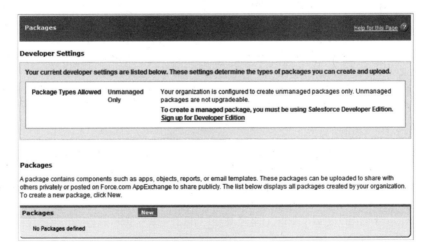

Figure 229: Creating a package - first page

2. Click **New** to begin creation of a new package, which brings up the page shown below.

You must give your package a name. You can optionally specify a configuration link, which is a custom link that points to a page with configuration information. The custom link is defined through the **Setup ➤ Customize ➤ Home Custom Links** page.

You can also specify a user who will receive notifications if an Apex exception occurs when any instance of the packaged components is run in any organization. This linkage allows you to be notified if the Apex code in any downloaded instance of the package throws an uncaught exception.

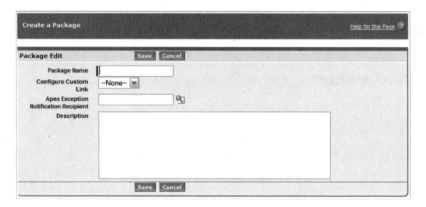

Figure 230: Creating a package - second page

3. Give the package the name of Test, an appropriate description, and click **Save**, which takes you to the page shown below.

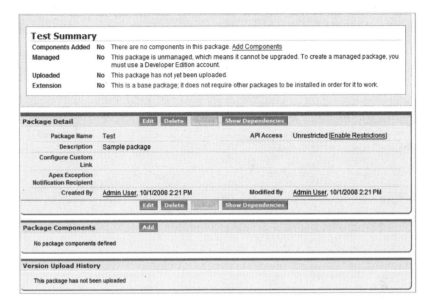

Figure 231: A successful package creation

You have successfully created your first package. The next step is to add components to the package.

Adding Components to a Package

Your newly created package is a container waiting for components to be added.

The interface for adding a component to a package is pretty simple. You simply choose a component type and then the specific component. But this simple selection generates some fairly sophisticated results.

1. Click **Add** in the Package Component section of the Package detail page to bring up the page shown below with the picklist of component types extended.

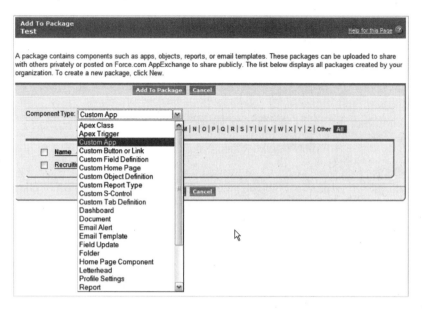

Figure 232: Adding components to a package

2. Select `Custom Object Definition` as the component type, and then select the Position object. Click **Add to Package**, which returns you to the Package detail page, now filled with many different components.

   When you add any component to a package, all components that are directly referenced by the selected component are also included. In this case, more than 60 other components are included when you select the Position object—custom fields in the object, other objects referenced by the Position object and their custom fields, and Apex Triggers used by the object, as well as the Apex classes called by those triggers.

   If you scroll down in the now lengthy list of included components, you will see that only one of them can be removed—the Position object that you selected. The other components are part of the package because they have to be included for the integrity of the Position object.

3. Add the custom tab for the Positions object, since you will want to be able to see the object in the new organization through this interface.

Your package is now ready for uploading, which will make the package available to others through a URL.

Uploading a package

To install your package in another organization, you must first upload the package, which makes the package available to others. An overview of the process is shown below.

Figure 233: Uploading a package

1. Click **Upload** in the Package detail page.

   Ooops, the upload attempt was unsuccessful for the reason shown below. If you read *Chapter 10: Apex*, you should be aware of the requirement to supply test methods for at least 75% of your code, along with other restrictions. There are triggers on the Job Application object, which is included in this package, so you will have to include the test class that exercises those triggers. The test class is called `testTriggers`.

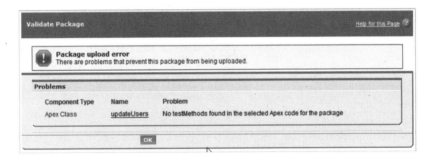

Figure 234: A failed attempt at uploading a package

2. Add the `testTriggers` class to the package.
3. Click **Upload** again, which takes you to the page shown below.

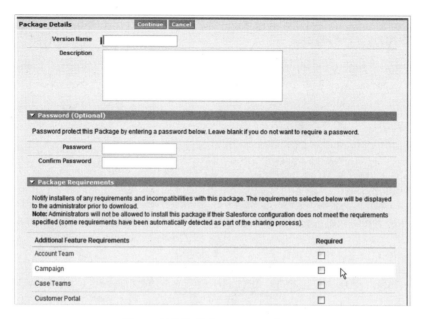

Figure 235: Defining your package

4. Enter `Position Package` as the name for the package and give the package a description.

5. Enter a password for the package.

6. You do not have to add any additional feature or object requirements to your package. You can see that there is a requirement for record types to exist for the Position__c object, a requirement that came with that object. Since this object requires record types, this package can only be installed in an organization with a license type that allows for this option. Click **Continue**.

The upload for your package begins. Once the upload completes, the email address associated with the organization will receive notification that the upload has been completed successfully. You can refresh the package page to the page shown partially in the following figure.

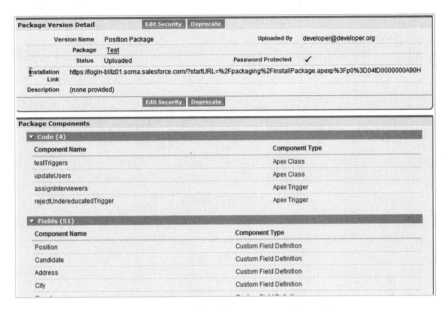

Figure 236: Recapping the contents of a package

This page gives a recap of the contents of the package. You also have the option to change the security on the package, such as altering, removing or adding a password. This page also allows you to deprecate the package. Once you take this action, no one will be allowed to download the package; however, users who have already downloaded the package will be allowed to install it.

In addition, when the package upload completes, an email is sent to the address of the organization. This email includes the URL that can be used to install the package in a new organization—which you will test right now.

Installing the Package

You have made the package available to others. The final step in the deployment process is for these others to download and install the package.

1. Copy the installation URL from the email received at the successful conclusion of the package upload.
2. Paste the URL into your browser. You will be prompted to log into a Force Platform organization.
3. Since you password-protected this package, the next page prompts for that password. Enter the password and click **Submit** to bring up the page shown below.

4. This page delivers a summary of the package contents and the version name, publisher and description of the package.

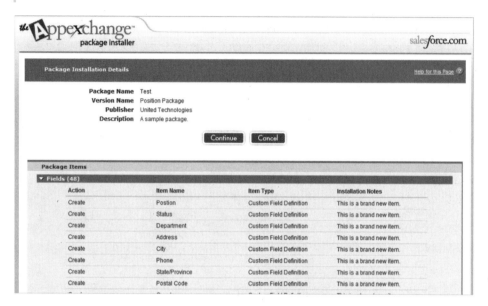

Figure 237: Summary of a package to be installed

4. Click **Continue**.

   The first step the Force Platform performs in the installation process is to check to make sure that components within the new package will not conflict with any components currently in the organization. If there are any existing components of the same type with the same name as components within the package, the package installation, by default, will immediately fail. You also have the option of automatically renaming some types of components in the installation process to avoid this problem.

5. Assuming that your package passes the validity check, the first page of the installation recaps the Force Platform API access that the components in this package will have. With this option, you can prevent the publisher of the package from gaining access to standard objects in your organization through the API. Click **Continue**.

6. The next page allows the installer to specify access to the components of the package. Just as with any component you create through standard methods, you can specify whether existing profiles have access to the components in this package. Change the `Select security settings` option to Select security settings.

7. Click **Set All for Full Access** for the existing profiles and click **Next**.

8. On the final page, leave the defaults and click **Install** to complete the installation.

If the installation completes successfully, you will receive a page that lists some follow up steps you should perform to properly configure the results of the installation, including setting up the organization-specific targets for workflow actions.

If you choose not to deploy the package immediately, the package will be shown in the **Packages** section under App Setup in the **Setup** menu. Going to this listing and clicking **Deploy** will have the same effect as clicking **Deploy Now**.

9. Click **Deploy Now**, which will take you to a page that summarizes the components that will be deployed.
10. Click **Deploy** on the final page, which will deploy the components in the package into your organization.

Once you deploy the package, the tab that you included for the package is available from the additional tabs page, accessed by clicking the arrow tab to the right of the existing tabs.

You can uninstall any package that has been installed by going to the selection of **View Installed Packages** at the bottom of the App Setup menu in **Setup** and clicking on the **Uninstall** button.

AppExchange

This section on packaging, and the section on managed packages that follow, discuss the technology involved in making and distributing packages. However, some readers may be interested in distributing packages more widely, becoming an independent software vendor (ISV) whose products run on the Force Platform. Salesforce.com has an entire infrastructure designed to support the distribution of applications to customers, including the collection of license fees, as well as License Management technology to manage and monitor the use of applications distributed as managed packages.

AppExchange is the name for the overall program for the promotion and sales of Force Platform-based applications. With AppExchange, you can list your application on the Salesforce.com web site, as well as offer trial versions of your products and collateral on the applications.

The Code Share project for this book includes documents and links to provide you with information about AppExchange and its related programs.

Managed Packages

You probably have already noticed the occasional qualification of 'unmanaged' used with packages. There are actually two types of packages: managed and unmanaged.

A managed package is designed to serve the needs of developers who are looking to sell their applications for use in other Force Platform organizations. Managed packages differ from unmanaged packages in the following ways:

- Managed packages are designed to be upgradeable. Unlike an unmanaged package, which will not install if any like-named components are in the target organization, a user can install a newer version of a managed package over an older one.
- Users cannot see your Apex code in a managed package, which protects your intellectual property.
- Managed packages can use the Force Platform License Management technology to monitor and manage licenses.
- The installing organization cannot make destructive changes to an application that is part of a managed package, although some components can be edited by subscribers.

Managed packages also have some restrictions on how they are created and deployed.

- A managed package must have a namespace prefix defined. A namespace, as discussed in *Chapter 12: Extended Visualforce Components and Controllers*, isolates components by making their names unique when combined with a component name.
- A managed package can only be developed in a Developer Edition organization, whereas all editions can create unmanaged packages.
- Each Developer Edition organization can only contain one managed package, while there is no limit to the number of unmanaged packages.

Managed packages have many other characteristics and capabilities. If you are a prospective independent software vendor (ISV) who is intending to distribute Force Platform applications, you should review the online documentation on managed packages, as well as the additional information described in the Code Share project for this chapter.

How to deploy?

The bottom line to this entire discussion of deployment centers on a simple question—which method should you use to deploy your applications?

You should generally go with the simplest method you can use that will completely address your needs. The core of the answer to this question revolves around whether you have access to users in both the originating organization and the target organization.

A Force Platform IDE deployment is quite simple, but the deployment is done by a single administrator who must have access to both the source and target organizations.

With the IDE, each individual deployment is a separate process. The Force Platform Migration Tool allows you to automate this process with scripts, so you can deploy to multiple organizations without having to do each one by hand.

If you have access to both sides of the deployment, and you are only deploying to a small number of targets, using the Force Platform IDE is probably the best method. If you have access to both organizations and are deploying to a larger number of servers, or if you are repeatedly deploying to a set of organizations, the Force Platform Migration Tool is probably your best choice.

Packaging separates the publishing of an application from the installation of the application in another organization, so you can perform a single publishing operation and have many other organizations install the result. The most crucial difference between this one-to-many deployment method and the use of the Force Platform IDE is the publish and subscribe model, which separates the task of making an application (or a set of components) available and the task of installing them in a target organization. The packaging method is required if you do not have access to the target organization—the typical scenario for an independent software vendor (ISV) who is selling a product to a wider audience.

The procedure for making a package is also built into the Force Platform Setup menu, so creating a package is a fairly easy task. Because of this, you might want to consider using packages to create one-off templates to act as a starting point for the development of other applications.

Unmanaged packages cannot tolerate any component name conflicts, so distribution through unmanaged packages will work for scenarios where the package is only being installed once. Although a target organization can uninstall an existing package and install a new version, this procedure is more resource intensive on the part of the target organization, since uninstalling a package will delete the objects and their data. Typically, you will export the data, uninstall an unmanaged package, install the new unmanaged package and reload the data..

Sandboxes

Up to this point, this chapter has been focusing on the mechanism for moving Force Platform components from a development environment to a production environment. Using two environments for development and deployment is not only a good practice, but a requirement for Apex code, which cannot be authored in a production environment.

You have probably been using a free Developer Edition organization for the examples in this book. For more details on the various license types, please refer to the salesforce.com company website `www.salesforce.com`.

The scenario also gets more complex if you are creating additional applications or customizations for existing organizations. A Developer Edition organization, such as the one you have been using, is great if you are developing a new application that doesn't depend on customizations you may already have made to your production organization.

If, however, your project is to extend or further customize your existing environment, or to build a new application that intersects your existing setup in significant ways, you'll probably want to develop and test in environments containing your current production configuration. You'll also want these environments to reflect the Salesforce edition and licenses you have purchased, any applications you have installed from Salesforce and AppExchange partners, and other features you may have enabled or disabled.

A Force Platform Sandbox is a copy of your production organization that may be used for development, test, and training purposes. You can create a sandbox with a push of a button—just like using Force Platform itself, there is no special hardware or software to purchase and configure.

There are three kinds of Sandboxes:

- A Full Sandbox is a copy of all configuration and data from your production organization.
- A Configuration-only Sandbox is a copy of the entire metadata configuration, but not the data. This sandbox will contain the definition of all custom fields, objects, workflows, Apex code, Visualforce, and so on, but won't contain any of the records your production users have entered. You can load data into a configuration only sandbox, but there is a limit as to the number of records which can be held in this type of sandbox.
- A Developer Sandbox is just like a Configuration-only Sandbox, except the data storage limit is smaller—about 5000 records.

All Sandboxes are a copy of a production organization, and are created simply with a push of a button. Different types of organization licenses come with different sandbox allowances. You should consult the license information area at `www.salesforce.com` for complete details on sandbox allowances. Since a Developer Edition organization is not a production environment, you cannot create a sandbox from this type of organization.

 Tip: All production usernames will be modified as they are copied to the sandbox, by appending the sandbox name. This is convenient, because if you want to log into your 'Dev' sandbox, your username is just your usual username with '.dev' appended. This makes it easy to remember your username for the separate organizations you may have access to.

A sandbox can be refreshed, erasing the sandbox configuration and contents and replacing it with a new copy, once 30 days have elapsed from the previous copy.

Sandbox Comparisons

The different types of Force Platform sandboxes are best suited for different purposes.

- **Developer Sandbox**

    The Developer Sandbox is usually the best environment for project development. Developer Sandboxes are intended to be readily available, so everyone on your team can have one or two to themselves.

    The storage limit of a Developer Sandbox should be ample for typical development tasks. Most of the time, while actually coding, a developer needs only a tiny amount of sample data to test their work, so the limit of 5,000 records for the Developer Sandbox is usually adequate. Small amounts of data can be loaded by hand through the web interface, but larger quantities of data can be loaded using the Force Platform Data Loader.

    The data limitation of a Developer Sandbox is, in some scenarios, an advantage. In some companies, development staff may have limited access, and possibly no access at all, to the production organization due to sensitivity of the data being stored. Development usually requires full admin rights, including Modify All Data and Modify Setup rights. In such cases, a production admin can provide a developer with full access to a Developer or Configuration-Only Sandbox without exposing sensitive data to an unauthorized individual.

- **Configuration-only Sandbox**

    Because the production data aren't copied to a Configuration-only Sandbox, this sandbox is created or refreshed much more quickly than a full-copy and can provide an empty slate appropriate for some uses. With room to load test data into the Configuration-only Sandbox, corresponding to approximately 250,000 records, you can do more accurate production-level testing than with the Developer Sandbox.

The Configuration-only Sandbox is very suitable for creating a test environment, in conjunction with a standard load of test data. You can use all the components from your production organization and simply reload the data with Data Loader when you want to begin a new round of testing. Although you can only refresh the sandbox itself every 30 days, you can reset the data as much as you need.

- **Full Sandbox**

A Full Sandbox is an exact copy of an organization, including all the data stored within. Based on the amount of data in your production organization, creating or refreshing a Full Sandbox can take some time.

But a Full Sandbox is sometimes required, based on company and compliance requirements. Some industries or customers have specific requirements for deployment processes to ensure consistent, accurate results in their applications. Sometimes this is the result of legislation, such as Sarbanes-Oxley or HIPPA. Sometimes they determine financial performance from reports in the application, and securities regulators monitor the accuracy of their published figures.

A Full Sandbox can address these issues and provide a staging platform for your applications that can also be used for user acceptance testing with a full production load. There is a 30-day refresh limit on full sandboxes, but this limitation can be easily integrated into a full testing cycle. You can simply refresh a Full Sandbox as part of your monthly or quarterly testing cycle.

 Caution: You cannot use a Sandbox as the originator of a managed package. Managed packages must have a specific originating organization. When a Full Sandbox is refreshed, the action essentially eliminates the previous version of the sandbox, which means the managed package will now be, in effect, orphaned.

Summary

This final chapter has completed the circle of Force Platform development, focusing on the distribution of your applications and components.

You learned about four methods of deployment:

- Using the Force Platform IDE to save components to another organization
- Using the Force Platform Migration Tool to move components to another organization using scripts
- Creating unmanaged packages, which can be published and installed by many organizations

- Creating managed packages, which allow for in-place upgrades and are ideally suited for Force Platform ISVs

You also learned about the various flavors of Force Platform Sandboxes, where you can replicate an environment for staging, testing, and development purposes.

With this last bit of information, you have now moved through the entire cycle of Force Platform development, from defining your first custom object, through adding workflow and analytic capabilities to your applications, through using Apex code to extend the logical functionality of your application, and Visualforce to shape the way your application looks, feels and interacts with data. You even learned how to open your Force Platform environment up to the larger community, through email interaction and Force Platform Sites.

With this foundation, you should be fully ready to begin your exciting efforts at creating your own applications for Force Platform. We hope the benefits provided by this platform help you to transform your own companies into enormously productive and efficient organizations.

Glossary

Apex

A procedural scripting language that allows developers to execute flow and transaction control statements in the Force Platform environment. Apex code runs on Force Platform servers and is closely integrated with the Force Platform environment.

App

A collection of components such as tabs, reports, dashboards, and custom s-controls that address a specific business need. Short for "application."

Analytic Snapshots

Used to capture and store data from a particular point in time.

Application programming interface (API)

The interface that a computer system, library, or application provides in order to allow other computer programs to request services from it and exchange data between them.

Apex-managed sharing

The ability to designate certain sharing entries as protected from deletion when sharing is recalculated.

Approval process

An automated process your organization can use to approve records on the platform. An approval process specifies the steps necessary for a record to be approved and who must approve it at each step. Approval processes also specify the actions to take when a record is approved, rejected, or first submitted for approval.

Auto number

A custom field type that automatically adds a unique sequential number to each record.

Cascading style sheets

Files that contain all of the information relevant to color, font, borders, and images that are displayed in a user interface.

Child relationship

A relationship that has been defined on an SObject that references a selected SObject as the "one" side of a one-to-many relationship. For example, if you expand the Child Relationships node under the Account object, contacts, opportunities, and tasks are included in this list.

Class, Apex

A template or blueprint from which Apex objects are created. Classes consist of other classes, user-defined methods, variables, exception types, and static initialization code. In most cases, Apex classes are modeled on their counterparts in Java and can be quickly understood by those who are familiar with them.

Cloud computing

A virtual development and deployment computing environment that eliminates the need for computing hardware and software infrastructure and components. Developers and users connect to this environment through a browser.

Component, Visualforce

An entity which can be added to a Visualforce page with a set of tags. You can create your own Visualforce components, which can contain multiple standard components.

Controller, Visualforce

An Apex class that provides a Visualforce page with the data and business logic it needs to run. Visualforce pages can use the standard controllers that come by default with every standard or custom object, or they can define custom controllers.

Custom field

Fields that can be added to customize an object for your organization's needs.

Custom link

A custom URL defined by an administrator to integrate your data with external websites and back-office systems.

Custom object

An entity that you build to store information, analogous to a table in a relational database.

Dashboard

A graphical representation of data from up to 20 summary or matrix reports arranged in a two- or three-column layout. Every user can select a favorite dashboard to display on his or her Home tab.

Data Loader

A Force Platform tool used to import and export data from your Force Platform organization.

Dependent field

Any custom picklist or multi-select picklist field that displays available values based on the value selected in its corresponding controlling field.

Delegated authentication

An security process where an external authority is used to authenticate Force Platform users.

Developer Edition

A free Salesforce edition that allows you to get hands-on experience with all aspects of the platform in an environment designed for development. Developer Edition accounts are available at developer.force.com.

Developer Force

The Developer Force website at developer.force.com provides a full range of resources for platform developers, including sample code, toolkits, an online developer community, and the ability to obtain limited Force Platform environments.

DML statement

An Apex statement that inserts, updates, or deletes records from the Force Platform database.

Email template

A built-in feature that enables you to create form emails that communicate a standard message, such as a welcome letter to new employees or an acknowledgement that a customer service request has been received.

Email service

A service set up for your Force Platform organization that can receive incoming emails and direct them to an Apex class for processing.

Enterprise Edition

A Salesforce edition designed to meet the needs of larger, more complex businesses. In addition to all of the functionality available in Professional Edition, Enterprise Edition organizations get advanced customization and administration tools that can support large-scale deployments.

Field

A part of an object that holds a specific piece of information, such as a text or currency value.

Field dependency

A filter that allows you to change the contents of a picklist based on the value of another field.

Field-level security

Settings that determine whether fields are hidden, visible, read only, or editable for users based on their profiles.

Force Platform

A platform for building cloud computing applications from salesforce.com. The Force Platform provides a full stack of default and extensible functionality which allows you to create cloud computing applications for your entire enterprise.

Force Platform API

A Web services-based application programming interface that provides access to your Salesforce organization's information.

Force Platform AppExchange

A Web directory where hundreds of AppExchange apps are available to Salesforce customers to review, demo, comment upon, and/or install. Developers can submit their apps for listing on AppExchange if they wish to share them with the community.

Force Platform IDE

An Eclipse plug-in that allows developers to manage, author, debug and deploy Force Platform applications classes and triggers in the Eclipse development environment.

Force Platform Migration Tool

A toolkit that allows you to write an Apache Ant build script for migrating Force Platform applications and components between two Salesforce organizations.

Force Platform Sites

A feature that allows access to Force Platform applications by users outside of a Force Platform organization.

Formula field

A type of custom field that automatically calculates its value based on the values of merge fields, expressions, or other values.

Group

A set of users that can contain individual users, other groups, or the users in a role. Groups can be used to help define sharing access to data.

Group Edition

A Salesforce edition designed for small businesses and workgroups with a limited number of users. Group Edition offers access to accounts, contacts, opportunities, leads, cases, dashboards, and reports.

Home tab

The starting page from which users can view a dashboard, choose sidebar shortcuts and options, view current tasks and activities, or select each of the major tabs.

ID

A unique 15- or 18-character alphanumeric string that identifies a single record in Salesforce.

Import Wizard

An tool for importing data into your Force Platform organization, accessible from the Setup menu.

Instance

A server that hosts an organization's Force Platform data and runs their applications. The platform runs on multiple instances, but data for any single organization is always consolidated on a single instance.

Junction object

A custom object that implements a many-to-many relationship between two other objects.

Lookup relationship

A relationship between two objects that allows you to associate records with each other. On one side of the relationship, a lookup field allows users to click a lookup icon and select another record from a list. On the associated record, you can then display a related list to show all of the records that have been linked to it.

Managed package

A collection of application components that are posted as a unit on Force Platform AppExchange, and that are associated with a namespace and a License

Management Organization. A package must be managed for it to be published publicly on AppExchange, and for it to support upgrades.

Many-to-many relationship

A relationship where each side of the relationship can have many children on the other side. Implemented through the use of junction objects.

Manual sharing

Record-level access rule that allows record owners to give read and edit permissions to other users who might not have access to the record any other way.

Matrix report

A report that presents data summarized in two dimensions, like a spreadsheet.

Metadata

The foundation of Force Platform applications. Metadata is used to shape the functionality and appearance of Force Platform applications. A developer modifies the metadata to create an application, and the Force Platform uses metadata to create application components as needed.

Merge field

A field you can place in an email template, custom link, or formula to incorporate values from a record. For example, `Dear {!Contact.FirstName}`, uses a contact merge field to obtain the value of a contact record's `First Name` field to address an email recipient by his or her first name.

Mini-Page Layout

A reduced display of information about a record that can be enabled to display when a user leaves their mouse on a link to the record.

Multitenancy

An application model where all users and apps share a single, common infrastructure and code base.

MVC (Model-View-Controller)

A design paradigm that deconstructs applications into components that represent data (the model), ways of displaying that data in a user interface (the view), and ways of manipulating that data with business logic (the controller).

Namespace

A one- to 15-character alphanumeric identifier that distinguishes your package and its contents from packages of other developers on Force PlatformAppExchange, similar to a domain name. Salesforce automatically prepends your namespace prefix, followed by two underscores ("__"), to all unique component names in your Salesforce organization.

Object

In Force Platform terms, an object is similar to a database table—a list of information, presented with rows and columns, about the person, thing, or concept you want to track. An object is the core component of the data-driven Force Platform environment, with automatically generated user interfaces, a security and sharing model, workflow processes, and much more.

Object-level security

Settings that allow an administrator to hide whole tabs and objects from a user, so that they don't even know that type of data exists. On the platform, you set object-level access rules with object permissions on user profiles.

One-to-many relationship

A relationship in which a single object is related to many other objects. For example, each Candidate may have one or more related Job Applications.

Organization, or org

The virtual space provided to an individual customer of salesforce.com. Your org includes all of your data and applications, and your org is separate from all other organizations.

Organization-wide defaults

Settings that allow you to specify the baseline level of data access that a user has in your organization. For example, you can make it so that any user can see any record of a particular object that's enabled in their user profile, but that they'll need extra permissions to actually edit one.

Outbound message

A SOAP message from Salesforce to an external Web service. You can send outbound messages from a workflow rule or Apex.

Package

A group of Force Platform components and applications that are made available to other organizations through a publish and subscribe architecture.

Page layout

The organization of fields, custom links, related lists, and other components on a record detail or edit page. Use page layouts primarily for organizing pages for your users, rather than for security.

Personal Edition

A free Salesforce edition designed for an individual sales representative or other single user. Personal Edition provides access to key contact management features such as accounts, contacts, and synchronization with Outlook. It also provides sales representatives with critical sales tools such as opportunities.

Picklist

A selection list of options available for specific fields, for example, the `Country` field for a Candidate object. Users can choose a single value from a list of options rather than make an entry directly in the field.

Picklist values

The selections displayed in drop-down lists for particular fields. Some values come predefined, and other values can be changed or defined by an administrator.

Platform Edition

A Salesforce edition based on either Enterprise Edition or Unlimited Edition that does not include any of the standard Salesforce CRM apps, such as Sales or Service & Support.

Production organization

A Salesforce organization that has live users accessing data.

Professional Edition

A Salesforce edition designed for businesses who need full-featured CRM functionality. Professional Edition includes straightforward and easy-to-use customization, integration, and administration tools to facilitate any small- to mid-sized deployment.

Profile

A component of the platform that defines a user's permission to perform different functions. The platform includes a set of standard profiles with every organization, and administrators can also define custom profiles to satisfy business needs.

Queue

A collection of records that don't have an owner. Users who have access to a queue can examine every record that's in it and claim ownership of the records they want.

Record

A single instance of an object. For example, Software Engineer is a single Position object record.

Record name

A standard field on all Force Platform objects. Whenever a record name is displayed in a Force Platform application, the value is represented as a link to a detail view of the record. A record name can be either free-form text or an autonumber field. The Record Name does not have to be a unique value.

Record-level security

A method of controlling data in which we can allow particular users to view and edit an object, but then restrict the individual object records that they're allowed to see.

Related list

A section of a record or other detail page that lists items related to that record.

Relationship

A connection between two objects in which matching values in a specified field in both objects are used to link related data. For example, if one object stores data about companies and another object stores data about people, a relationship allows you to find out which people work at the company.

Report types

The foundation of Force Platform reports. A report type specifies the objects and their fields that can be used as the basis of a report. Standard report types are created by the Force Platform, while you can create custom report types for more advanced or specific reporting requirements.

Role hierarchy

A record-level security setting that defines different levels of users such that users at higher levels can view and edit information owned by or shared with users beneath them in the role hierarchy, regardless of the organization-wide sharing model settings.

Roll-Up Summary Field

A field type that automatically provides aggregate values from child records in a master-detail relationship.

S-Control

A component that allows you to embed custom HTML and JavaScript into Salesforce detail pages, custom links, Web tabs, or custom buttons. For example, you can define a custom s-control containing JavaScript and address merge fields to display a map of a contact's address. The functionality provided by s-controls has been replaced by Visualforce.

Sandbox organization

A nearly identical copy of a Salesforce production organization. You can create multiple sandboxes in separate environments for a variety of purposes, such as testing and training, without compromising the data and applications in your production environment.

Search layout

The organization of fields included in search results, lookup dialogs, and the recent items lists on tab home pages.

Session ID

An authentication token that's returned when a user successfully logs in to Salesforce. The Session ID prevents a user from having to log in again every time he or she wants to perform another action in Salesforce.

Session timeout

The amount of time a single session ID remains valid before expiring. While a session is always valid for a user while he or she is working in the Web interface, sessions instantiated via the API expire after the duration of the session timeout, regardless of how many transactions are still taking place.

Setup menu

Interface to Force Platform metadata that allows you to create and shape Force Platform applications. You get access to the Setup menu through the Setup link in a standard Force Platform application.

Sharing model

A security model that defines the default organization-wide access levels that users have to each other's information.

Sharing rules

Rules that allow an administrator to specify that all information created by users within a given group or role is automatically shared to the members of another group or role. Sharing rules also allow administrators to make automatic exceptions to org-wide defaults for particular groups of users.

SOQL (Salesforce Object Query Language)

A query language that allows you to construct simple but powerful query strings and to specify the criteria that should be used to select the data from the database.

SOSL (Salesforce Object Search Language)

A query language that allows you to perform text-based searches using the API.

Standard object

A built-in object included with the Force Platform. You can also build custom objects to store information that's unique to your app.

Tab

An interface item that allows you to navigate around an app. A tab serves as the starting point for viewing, editing, and entering information for a particular object. When you click a tab at the top of the page, the corresponding tab home page for that object appears. A tab can be associated with a Force Platform object, a web page or a Visualforce page.

Tag

An identifier that can be attached by a user to an individual record. Force Platform tags can be public or private.

Test method

An Apex class method that verifies whether a particular piece of code is working properly. Test methods take no arguments, commit no data to the database, and can be executed by the `runTests()` system method either via the command line or in an Apex IDE, such as Eclipse with the Force Platform IDE.

Time-dependent workflow action

A workflow action that occurs before or after a certain amount of time has elapsed. Time-dependent workflow actions can fire tasks, field updates, outbound messages, and email alerts while the condition of a workflow rule remains true.

Trigger

A piece of Apex that executes before or after records of a particular type are inserted, updated, or deleted from the database. Every trigger runs with a set of context variables that provide access to the records that caused the trigger to fire, and all triggers run in bulk mode—that is, they process several records at once, rather than just one record at a time.

Trigger context variables

Default variables that provide access to information about the trigger and the records that caused it to fire.

Unlimited Edition

A Salesforce edition designed to extend customer success through the entire enterprise. Unlimited Edition includes all Enterprise Edition functionality, plus Apex, Force Platform Sandbox, Force Platform Mobile, premium support, and additional storage.

Unmanaged package

A Force Platform AppExchange package that cannot be upgraded or controlled by its developer. Unmanaged packages allow you to take any app components and move them "as is" to AppExchange without going through a lengthy publishing process.

URL (Uniform Resource Locator)

The global address of a website, document, or other resource on the Internet. For example, http://www.salesforce.com.

Validation rule

A rule that prevents a record from being saved if it does not meet the standards that are specified.

Visualforce

A simple, tag-based markup language that allows developers to easily define custom pages and components for apps built on the platform. Each tag corresponds to a coarse or fine-grained component, such as a section of a page, a related list, or a field. The components can either be controlled by the same logic that's used in standard Salesforce pages, or developers can associate their own logic with a controller written in Apex.

Web service

A mechanism by which two applications can easily exchange data over the Internet, even if they run on different platforms, are written in different languages, or are geographically remote from each other.

WebService method

An Apex class method or variable that can be used by external systems, such as an s-control or mash-up with a third-party application. Web service methods must be defined in a global class.

Web tab

A custom tab that allows your users to use external websites from within the application.

Wizard

A user interface that leads a user through a complex task in multiple steps.

Workflow action

An email alert, field update, outbound message, or task that fires when the conditions of a workflow rule are met.

Workflow email alert

A workflow action that sends an email when a workflow rule is triggered. Unlike workflow tasks, which can only be assigned to application users, workflow alerts can be sent to any user or contact, as long as they have a valid email address.

Workflow field update

A workflow action that changes the value of a particular field on a record when a workflow rule is triggered.

Workflow outbound message

A workflow action that sends data to an external Web service, such as another cloud computing application. Outbound messages are used primarily with composite apps.

Workflow queue

A list of workflow actions that are scheduled to fire based on workflow rules that have one or more time-dependent workflow actions.

Workflow rule

A "container" for a set of workflow instructions that includes the criteria for when the workflow should be activated, as well as the particular tasks, alerts, and field updates that should take place when the criteria for that rule are met.

Workflow task

A workflow action that assigns a task to an application user when a workflow rule is triggered.

Index

Advance Praise for Global Uprising

Global Uprising is an exciting piece of contemporary history.
It brings us the voices of some of the finest young people of this generation,
accompanied by the commentaries of veteran activists and scholars. There are inspiring
personal stories and thoughtful reflections on the tactics of direct action.
For anyone despairing of the rule of money and power over human life,
here is a testament to the spirit of resistance, a reason to hope.

— Howard Zinn, historian, activist, and author of
A People's History of the United States

These are the voices of the world ... of youth emerging into radical adulthood ... beautiful,
hopeful, youthful, even in the face of great and terrible repression.

— Mumia Abu-Jamal, political prisoner
and award-winning journalist

To hear these informed and insistent voices is to hear from people doing
the essential work of democracy. I revel in them! They are daring to
confront The Powers That Be with the most basic of political questions:
"Who the hell is going to be in charge — a handful of global greedheads,
or We the People?"

— Jim Hightower, Hightower Radio

This book of stories from a new generation of activists who are engaged in a
life-transforming endeavor to make the world what the Qur'an calls "an abode of peace"
is of historic significance. In Islam, justice is a pre-condition for peace.
The stories in this book represent a passionate quest for justice in a profoundly
unjust world. The book is enlightening, uplifting and inspiring.
It will be a blessing to those who read it.

— Dr. Riffat Hassan, professor of religious studies at the University of Louisville,
Kentucky and the founding director of the INRFVVP, a network of organizations
to combat violence against women in South Asia

Global Uprising goes deeper into what made headlines in the Battle of Seattle. It makes it clear that youth are not leaders of tomorrow – they are leaders of today. It not only puts a human face to the struggle, but it awakens us to the possibility of change lying within each one of us. A must-read.

— Anuradha Mittal, Co Director, Food First/Institute
for Food and Development Policy

Global Uprising is essential reading for anyone who cares not to live in a dying world of personal oppression, under the thumb of a rising neo-fascism called the corporate-political-military complex. Peaceful nonviolent resistance is our only way out, as most of the writers in this book understand.

— Doris "Granny D" Haddock, author of
Granny D: Walking Across America in my 90th Year

A powerful global kaleidoscope of people working for justice.

— Paul Loeb, author of *Soul of a Citizen*

Collections have many facets, to be explored differently by different people. For me, the special worth of this collection rests in the stories of people's action, of how individuals and groups arouse themselves, prod and inform themselves, organize themselves, reach out and get good things done. These stories should inform others, helping them travel their own unique, yet also so similar, roads.

— Michael Albert, co-founder of South End Press, *Z Magazine,* and ZNet

Inspiration is the fuel of movements and *Global Uprising* represents a diverse range of inspiring voices that bring hope to our relentless struggle against local and global injustice. This coming together of insights, motivations and strategies shines the light on the optimism and creativity fueling our many movements that are destined to create new models for governance and co-existence. Yet the light also exposes some of the human misery that also fuels these movements as we strive to work with humility, clarity and compassion. The more we learn about the struggles and successes of others, the greater our chances for linking up and mobilizing in unity. This book helps explain the parallel-path strategies of exposing the injustices and greed while we build new models that will someday allow us to ignore and move beyond our corrupt and out-dated systems. *Global Uprising* confirms that we are on the right path.

— Dan Merkle, a Seattle attorney who helped start the Independent Media Center for the WTO protests, currently working to reform the criminal justice system.